PRIMA SCRIPTURA

PRIMA SCRIPTURA

AN INTRODUCTION
to
NEW TESTAMENT
INTERPRETATION

N. CLAYTON CROY

Baker Academic
a division of Baker Publishing Group
Grand Rapids, Michigan

© 2011 by N. Clayton Croy

Published by Baker Academic
a division of Baker Publishing Group
P.O. Box 6287, Grand Rapids, MI 49516-6287
www.bakeracademic.com

Printed in the United States of America

Library of Congress Cataloging-in-Publication Data

Croy, N. Clayton.
    Prima Scriptura : an introduction to New Testament interpretation / N. Clayton Croy.
        p.   cm.
    Includes bibliographical references (p.   ) and indexes.
    ISBN 978-0-8010-3588-3 (pbk.)
    1. Bible. N. T.—Hermeneutics. I. Title.
BS2331.C76 2011
225.6′1—dc22   2010051136

11   12   13   14   15   16   17   7   6   5   4   3   2   1

In keeping with biblical principles of creation stewardship, Baker Publishing Group advocates the responsible use of our natural resources. As a member of the Green Press Initiative, our company uses recycled paper when possible. The text paper of this book is composed in part of post-consumer waste.

green press
INITIATIVE

To my parents, Otis and Helen Croy,
who were my first teachers of the Bible
and examples of Christian living

Contents

Preface

A Complex and Contested Enterprise

In January 2005 the Executive Council of the Society of Biblical Literature (SBL), the largest professional association of teachers and scholars of the Bible, faced a dilemma. The council had received a resolution from a group of members responding to the recent U.S. election in November 2004. The resolution observed that "values," sometimes specifically called "Christian values" or "biblical values," had emerged in the campaign as a key political issue. The group contended that the values "most commonly identified in public debates were the issues of gay marriage, abortion, and stem-cell research."

The resolution went on to argue that these values "are not major concerns in the Bible, and in fact are not even directly addressed in the Bible. Rather, they tend to reflect the underlying problems of homophobia, misogyny, control of reproductive rights, and restraint of expression (including scientific research) in U.S. society today." The proponents of the resolution asserted that "the moral issues dominating the biblical texts focus instead on concerns such as the well-being of individuals, the integrity of community, care for the powerless and the vulnerable, economic justice, the establishment of peace, and the stewardship of the environment." They concluded that the Society should work toward securing these goals and values.

The Executive Council had at least three alternatives:

1. to reject the resolution out of hand;
2. to endorse the resolution as an official statement of the Society; or
3. to refer the resolution to the membership for responses and comments.

The council wisely chose the third course. The resolution was sent electronically to 5,585 members, asking them to vote "agree" or "disagree" and inviting comments. The response was quantitatively strong (35 percent of those receiving the resolution) and qualitatively vigorous (thoughtful and spirited comments were given by 46 percent of the respondents). When the dust settled, the vote was 56 percent in agreement with the resolution, 44 percent in disagreement. The vote was unscientific since participation was voluntary, but the response was large enough to indicate a deep divide on the issues raised by the resolution.

There are several lessons in this controversy. The Society of Biblical Literature is a diverse group. The Bible is regarded as relevant, by one group or another, to a wide range of public policy issues, including social justice issues traditionally, and stereotypically, identified as "liberal" concerns, as well as "family values" similarly identified as "conservative." Finally, and perhaps most poignantly, the response to the resolution indicates that biblical interpretation is a complex and contested enterprise. The SBL is a professional organization of scholarly experts, most of whom hold doctorates or are student members in the process of earning them. When trained experts disagree so sharply, what hope of consensus can be entertained by laypersons (in either the ecclesial or academic sense)?

The status quo need not be wholly discouraging, however. As Brevard S. Childs observes about the general state of contemporary biblical scholarship, "The very intensity of the conflicting voices serves to confirm the impression that the problem of biblical interpretation does not arise from apathy. . . . Cannot one draw the implication that in spite of confusion and conflict in respect to biblical interpretation, there is an unexpressed consensus that the Bible still possesses a seriousness of content and an evocative power for raising basic questions which offers hope in a search for its renewed understanding in the twenty-first century?" (Childs, foreword to Bartholomew, 2000: xv). While Childs rightly observes that indifference to the Bible is seldom a problem, nevertheless, complex and sometimes contradictory visions emerge from its study.

Several factors complicate the interpretation of the Bible (Porter, 1997a: 11–15; Hayes and Holladay, 2007: 12–16). Some of them have to do with the Bible itself, its distance from us, and its foreignness. Other factors have to do with the interpreters, the modern readers of the text, their limitations, biases, skills, and perspectives. Both kinds deserve some elaboration.

1. *Our outsider status.* All modern readers are outsiders to the original communicative act of Scripture. In this sense, the Bible was not written for us. Our common humanity, the providence of God, and the illumination of the Holy Spirit enable the Bible to continue to speak to persons today, but they neither erase its foreign qualities nor provide a quick and easy bridge to a critical understanding of its message. Most of the writings of the Bible are more aptly described as having a timely message than a timeless one. Their assumptions, modes of thought, teachings, exhortations, laments, and

exultations are rooted in another era and are addressed to circumstances that prevailed in the two millennia prior to the birth of Jesus and in the first century CE, not the twenty-first century CE. Among the New Testament writings our outsider status is especially evident with respect to epistolary literature. The old quip has an element of truth: when we read Paul's Letters, we are reading someone else's mail (Hayes and Holladay, 2007: 12). The other side of this coin, however, is that Christian readers of Scripture often feel directly addressed by its words, sometimes to their comfort, sometimes to their dismay (Green, 2007b: 50–59).

2. *Language.* Modern English translations make most passages of Scripture fairly intelligible, and we should be grateful for the generations of scholars who have toiled over manuscripts, lexicons, and manuals of style to make the Scriptures available in the vernacular. But the ease of reading such works belies the fact that they are the product of countless hours of intense study, debate, and decision making. We have learned much over the centuries about Hebrew, Aramaic, and Greek lexicography, syntax, idiom, and style, but difficult decisions remain in which even highly trained experts are compelled to make their best guesses. Translations by necessity do not reveal the difficulty of those decisions. Neither is it a transparent fact to all readers that translation involves interpretation. Although the goal of translation is to convey the meaning of the original text into the target language and not to modify it, differences between the original language and the target language often require translators to choose among possible nuances of a word or alternative construals of grammatical phenomena. A person only needs to read a few English translations of the same passage to see how slight, and sometimes significant, differences emerge in the process of translation.

3. *History.* Almost two thousand years separate us from the writings of the New Testament. One need not read much of the biblical text for that distance to become apparent. Medicine was primitive, infant mortality was common, and physical ailments were sometimes attributed to evil spirits. Roman rule was sometimes brutal. Democracy at best was a Greek institution of centuries past, only traces of which existed during the Roman Republic, and human rights as a concept lay a millennium and a half in the future. The economy was chiefly agricultural, slavery was a given, and lifestyles were modest for the vast majority of people. Transportation was slow; mail service was limited to official correspondence. Religious traditions were often polytheistic, and deities were frequently conceived in anthropomorphic terms. Animal sacrifices were commonplace.

4. *Cultural assumptions.* The ancient Mediterranean world differed markedly from the modern Western world in its cultural assumptions (Achtemeier, Green, and Thompson, 2001: 284–88). Novelty was viewed with suspicion rather than favor, and old ways were assumed to be superior to innovation. Religion and politics were thoroughly intertwined rather than kept separate

from one another. Political decisions were seldom made without first seeking divine guidance by auspices and omens. Our modern practice of beginning sessions of Congress with prayer pales by comparison to the intermingling of religion and politics in the Roman Empire. In contrast to modern American misgivings, people in antiquity generally would have had scruples about *not* mixing the two. Finally, both households and society at large were hierarchically structured and patriarchal. The modern Western world, of course, has unfinished business in this regard, but in the first-century Mediterranean world this assumption was commonplace, and there were few voices of protest against it.

5. *Differences in readers' perspectives.* Interpretation is also complicated by the great disparity among interpreters. We come to the text from different places socially, economically, politically, religiously, and ethnically. We have different understandings about what is possible, what is reasonable, what is just, and what is useful. Even differences in personality type can influence how one hears the biblical text. Ben Meyer correctly points out that the foundational commitments held by various interpreters account for the most vexing controversies in biblical interpretation: "The root of our deepest divisions is not lack of evidence. It is the fact of opposed horizons and, above all, of irreducibly opposed horizons, as a moment's reflection on public controversies will suggest and as sustained reflection will confirm. Irreducibly opposed horizons are a massive human reality labyrinthine in its consequences, leading some sincerely to champion as true and good what others with equal sincerity repudiate as false and evil" (1989: 81). Such fundamental distinctions in personal "horizons" were evident in the disparate responses to the resolution proposed to the Society of Biblical Literature.

6. *Differences in readers' abilities.* Interpreters of Scripture have different levels of linguistic skill, historical awareness, spiritual insight, and common sense. As Georg Lichtenberg, the eighteenth-century aphorist, observed, "A book is a mirror: if an ape looks into it, an apostle is hardly likely to look out" (2000: 71). While we might prefer to refrain from likening readers to primates, whether of the simian or episcopal variety, Lichtenberg has a point: the quality of an interpretation is, in part, a function of the interpreter, and it will usually not be more erudite, creative, or faithful than the interpreter is. Other things being equal, a trained and sensitive interpreter has an advantage over an untrained and insensitive one. In short, the better the reader, the better the reading.

The good news, however, is that less-skilled readers can become more skilled through intellectual and spiritual discipline. On the one hand, the interpretation of the New Testament as a literary work from antiquity demands intellectual skills that can be acquired through study and practice. On the other hand, the New Testament as a religious text rewards readers who have spiritual sensitivities, and the best academic training does not necessarily confer them. Ben Meyer refers to this disposition as "being attuned to the text," and he correctly notes that our culture and our institutions do not necessarily facilitate it. "In view of the devastating alienations of our time, this being in tune cannot be presupposed as standard equipment among interpreters. Graduate schools do not pledge to confer or cultivate it and may never so much as mention it" (1989: 90). Faith and devotion that are nurtured by Christian community can, however, cultivate this disposition, and such qualities, combined with rigorous academic training, represent the ideal hermeneutical resources for grasping the theological meaning of the New Testament.

The perspectives and abilities of an interpreter are thus the product of many things: accidents of birth, physical and psychological characteristics, education, socialization, religious upbringing, theological commitments, life experiences, and so forth. Any of these factors may impede or enhance one's ability to interpret Scripture. Because of their critical importance, they will receive further attention in chapter 1.

Despite these complexities about how to interpret and apply the Bible, millions of people still look to this collection of writings for spiritual guidance in personal and public life. Indeed, it is the religious value of Scripture, more than its historical or literary qualities (without denigrating the latter), that accounts for its historical and cultural impact. As one introductory text on the New Testament asserts, "The most distinctive characteristic of the New Testament documents is surely their function as Scripture within the Christian church." "Most people who read the New Testament do so . . . because they share the conviction that this collection of documents, together with the Old Testament, comprise the Scriptures of the church, its normative witness to the work of God in the world through Jesus Christ" (Achtemeier, Green, and Thompson, 2001: 1, 9).

It is to this audience that this book is primarily directed, to persons who regard the Bible as an authoritative and revelatory text, or more precisely, a collection or canon of texts. I am primarily addressing confessional readers, those who belong to communities of faith that affirm the authority of Scripture and the faith of the classic creeds. This readership is intentionally broad and thus able to encompass Catholic, Protestant, and Orthodox expressions of Christianity. My hope is that the book will serve communities who regard the Bible as more than an edifying story but less than divine dictation. That describes a fairly wide swath of Christendom.

The book's subtitle indicates that it has an (almost) exclusive focus on the interpretation of the New Testament. This restriction does not imply a devaluation of the Old Testament or Hebrew Scriptures. The church rejected that option when it excommunicated Marcion, the second-century heretic who discarded the Old Testament as the product of a lesser deity. Contra Marcion, the Hebrew Scriptures are *Christian* Scriptures, no less essential, no less revelatory than the New Testament. The reasons for my focus on the New Testament are professional and practical. My professional expertise is in the New Testament, and so I am better able to address its interpretation than that of the Hebrew Bible. Practically, I suspect that most, but by no means all, college, university, and seminary courses that deal with biblical interpretation will focus on one Testament or the other. There is not an entirely different set of interpretive principles for the Old Testament, and much of what is put forward in this book is applicable to the interpretation of either Testament, but when one turns to contextual issues, literary forms, linguistic tools, and specific textual examples, as this book will do frequently, it becomes cumbersome to treat both the Hebrew Scriptures and the Greek New Testament.

So the aim of this book is to propose a way for leaders of Christian communities methodically to study and reflect on Scripture, particularly the New Testament, with a view to informing and shaping the life of faith. The latter is by no means limited to matters of public policy, as was the resolution of the Society of Biblical Literature. The Bible has a variety of functions in confessional contexts. It shapes Christian identity. It provides resources for the church's worship life. It supplies the raw material of our proclamation. It informs our theology. It guides personal piety and communal polity. And, yes, it also contains a vision for the larger society, with implications for both social justice issues and family values. In sum, the Bible shapes not only one's personal devotion and discipleship but also informs larger matters of culture, politics, philosophy, theology, and ethics (Wright, 2005: 5–18). But before we launch into a description and demonstration of interpretive method, it will be helpful to define some key terms, to discuss a few theoretical issues, and to sketch the journey ahead. Those are the goals of the introduction.

Acknowledgments

A comprehensive list of persons who have contributed to my understanding of biblical interpretation would be a short book in itself. Here I will limit myself to those individuals who made direct contributions to the shaping, editing, and evolution of this book. My two New Testament colleagues at Trinity Lutheran Seminary, Mark Allan Powell and Walter Taylor, have been sounding boards for my ideas over many years. They have influenced me in numerous and subtle ways, but they were especially helpful in critiquing and improving the "Sample Exegesis Paper" included in this volume. Two of our institution's bible division research assistants, Brad Ross and Jerry O'Neal, provided exceptional assistance by proofreading the manuscript, checking bibliographical references, and offering substantive suggestions. Three colleagues read significant portions of the manuscript, providing helpful critique from their professional and/or denominational perspectives: Donald Huber of Trinity Lutheran Seminary, William H. Petersen of Bexley Hall Seminary, and John Clabeaux of the Pontifical College Josephinum. Special thanks go to Joseph Dongell of Asbury Theological Seminary for the yeoman service of reading the entire manuscript and providing valuable feedback, especially on broad, hermeneutical issues. Richard Barrett, a layman in my church, also offered several helpful suggestions. Finally, James Ernest, my editor at Baker Academic, has been a model of support, encouragement, and gentle provocation through a process that has spanned a few years.

As is always the case when others critique one's writing, these persons saved me the embarrassment of many careless errors, improved my thinking and its expression at many points, alerted me to resources or lines of thought that I had overlooked, and generally provided the inestimable gift of the perspective of a charitable "other." Any infelicities of style or judgment that remain are necessarily my responsibility, but without question, the book's utility has been greatly enhanced by my many helpers. I am in their debt.

Introduction

Definitions, Theoretical Issues, and Preview of the Method

The most striking characteristic of biblical interpretation during the last several decades is an explosion of interpretive methods. Fifty years ago it would have been much easier to outline the steps in exegetical method or describe what hermeneutics entails. During the last half of the twentieth century, the landscape of biblical scholarship underwent as many shifts and divisions as the map of Eastern Europe.

The interpretive smorgasbord nowadays includes historical, literary, rhetorical, canonical, narrative, reader-response, social-scientific, anthropological, structuralist, and a host of ideological methods (liberationist, feminist, womanist, African, African-American, Latino/a, Asian, postcolonial, gay/queer, and so forth). Unlike a food smorgasbord, however, there is no consensus about basic food groups or what constitutes the ideal diet.

The effect of this methodological explosion is twofold. On the one hand, interpretation is potentially enriched by the wide variety of lenses through which texts may be read. The new interpretations or "readings" resulting from these methods can be complementary: different but not disparate. On the other hand, chaos and confusion may result from the proliferation of interpretive methods. This is particularly so for interpreters who do not have the luxury of leisurely, abstract musing in multiple modes. Those who interpret Scripture in confessional contexts for personal or congregational guidance often have more practical and pressing goals. When one studies Scripture with a view to proclamation, teaching, and shaping Christian discipleship, one can easily feel overwhelmed by a dozen options rather than enriched. In the smorgasbord image, these interpreters are looking for meat and potatoes that will nourish life more so than exotic foods that tantalize the eye and pique the palate.

Let me clarify my perspective, lest I appear dismissive of newer interpretive methods. *Both* enrichment *and* confusion have resulted. The new insights that have been gleaned from strategies such as rhetorical, sociological, narrative, and feminist criticism—just to name some of the most fruitful techniques—are to be received gratefully. But the welter of methods leaves some interpreters, especially beginners, confused. Sandra Schneiders rightly observes, "The new voices, until recently peripheral, are establishing themselves inside the camp. Increasingly the question of the coherence of the project of biblical interpretation, given the plurality of methods and the validity of multiple interpretations, is emerging as urgent" (1991: 24). In the chaos it is easy to lose sight of the fact that these methods are not necessarily mutually exclusive. They have common features that can be gleaned and incorporated into a basic eclectic method that will serve the practical needs of ministers, teachers, and students.

That is the aim of this book: to provide a starting point or foundation, not the final word. I do not, however, imagine that an eclectic approach can possibly incorporate all the benefits of the new methods that have arisen in the last few decades. Explicit and rigorous rhetorical, sociological, narrative, and feminist readings will open perspectives on texts that the method described in the succeeding chapters will only suggest indirectly. Nevertheless, a basic method of interpretation with a finite number of discrete steps still has much value. When Sunday is looming and a preaching text or a Bible study lesson plan is staring you down, a practical, methodical approach to biblical interpretation is needed. This is true for both newcomers and seasoned exegetes. A trusty cookbook with a step-by-step method serves both beginners who are learning the culinary arts as well as master chefs, whose skill derives from a well-honed habit of attention to details. Far from stifling creativity, mastering a basic methodology enables creativity by providing it with discipline and direction.

Several preliminary issues and matters of definition need attention. Some of these are ancient cruxes; others have arisen in the theoretical debates of the last several decades. Needless to say, volumes have been written about each of the following questions. The treatment here makes no pretense of being comprehensive, but rather seeks to orient beginners to the journey ahead. Before one embarks on a lengthy voyage, it is wise to learn something about the history of seafaring and the prevailing ocean currents.

What Is the Meaning of "Meaning"?

If the interpretation of Scripture has something to do with deriving its meaning, an appropriate starting point is to inquire as to what we mean by "meaning." The answer to this question is neither simple nor self-evident. Indeed, there are several meanings for the word "meaning," and the occasional conflation of these meanings has, according to some theorists, worked much mischief in the field of hermeneutics.

The basic meaning of "meaning" is referential. A word is a linguistic sign that "means" that thing to which it refers. Thus the meaning of "book" is that bound collection of printed pages that you have before you. The meaning of "eyes" is the pair of ocular organs you are using to read this sentence. Referential meaning applies most obviously to physical things. This kind of meaning can easily be grasped by the mind when the referent can be grasped by the hand. It is less apparent what the referential meaning of a highly abstract word would be, such as "abstraction." Referential meaning is also inadequate for complex sentences, metaphor, or interjections. For example, the referential meaning of "rats" may be a certain genus of rodent, but that meaning scarcely applies in the sentence "Rats! The library is closed."

An alternative theory that avoids these weaknesses is the ideational theory of meaning. According to this theory, meaning inheres in the ideas and concepts that lie behind language. For some philosophers this was a way to preserve meaning from the limitations of language. By this view, language is finite, able to convey thought only imperfectly. The inability to find words to express one's thoughts is a common experience, but one could argue that in such cases the thought itself is unformed. Does thought truly exist apart from language? Ideational theories have the opposite problem from referential theories; they are inadequate for physical things. The meaning of "elephant" as a mental concept is quite different from an actual elephant. If there is an elephant in your living room, most people would want it to be of the ideational variety.

A third theory of meaning connects it with human intention. The meaning of a word is that which the speaker or writer intends by it. This theory has certain advantages. It relates meanings to minds, human consciousness. Surely all expressions of meaning and construals of meanings involve human minds. This theory also accounts for the fact that the same linguistic symbols may not in all cases convey the same meaning. The meaning of "flat" in the utterance "I'm mad about my flat" has a very different meaning if uttered by an angry American motorist stranded on the roadside or an enthusiastic Londoner moving into a new apartment (Caird, 1980: 50). In either case, the meaning is that which the speaker intends. Critics of this theory point out that an author's intention is often accessible only through the words of the text. If the words are ambiguous, how does one get behind them to the author's intent? In addition, what does one do with ancient texts whose authors are unknown (e.g., Hebrews) or pseudonymous (e.g., 2 Peter)? Authorial intention is not to be dismissed, but in the case of ancient authors, usually the most one can hope for is a reasonable understanding of the author's *communicative intention*: *what* the author intended to say and succeeded in expressing in the text. *Why* an ancient author wrote a certain thing, that is, the author's *motive*, is often beyond our ability to ascertain (Fowl, 2000: 74).

A fourth theory equates meaning with significance. The meaning of an utterance or a text is the importance, relevance, and impact that it has. This definition of "meaning" is especially seen in the adjectival form "meaningful." Speech or writing is meaningful when it has consequences for the hearer or reader. It may arouse interest, inspire action, or evoke awe. Meaning as significance is the sense normally elicited when we add a short prepositional phrase to the question "What does this mean . . . *to you?*" Mark Allan Powell has conducted an informal experiment showing that professional interpreters in particular (in this case, Christian ministers), when presented with a biblical text, respond differently to the question "What does this mean?" as over against "What does this mean *to you?*" (2001: 28–56, esp. 51–53). This experiment highlights the difference between meaning as human intention and meaning as significance, for which Powell uses the roughly equivalent language "meaning as message" versus "meaning as effect" (2001: 22–27). By either set of terms, the latter sense of meaning clearly transcends the former. Readers frequently find meanings in texts (= significance or effect) that go beyond the author's meaning (= intention or message).

Finally, semantic theories of meaning stress the author's choice of certain words from a large stock of linguistic options and the author's placement of those words in certain syntactical relationships. The meaning of a word in an utterance and the meaning of the utterance itself are determined by those contextual relationships.

This brief discussion by no means exhausts the possibilities. Indeed, one standard work on the subject delineates sixteen different meanings of "meaning" (Ogden and Richards, 1989: 185–208). But the above remarks should be sufficient to give the reader a sense of the philosophical questions that lie behind the act of interpretation. The most important distinction among the meanings of "meaning" is the one between the intention of the writer and the significance of the writing to the readers. Clarity on this point will lessen the confusion when we come to consider and evaluate diverse interpretations.

What Is Meant by "Exegesis" and "Hermeneutics"?

Both of these terms come directly from Greek words. *Exēgēsis* first referred to a detailed narrative or description and then came to mean a detailed explanation or interpretation. The meaning of the English is similar: an explanation or exposition; especially, an interpretation of a literary text. Etymologically the Greek word derives from a verb meaning "to lead forth, to draw out." Although etymology does not determine meaning, a relationship can be seen in the idea that exegesis involves a "drawing out" of the text's meaning. (As we will see later in this chapter, some practitioners take issue with that implication.) *Hermēneia* referred first to an utterance or expression of thought, then to an interpretation, either in the sense of a translation from one language to another, or in the sense of an explanation of the meaning of a text or state-ment. (The Greek word is related to the god Hermes, who served as the bearer of messages between the gods and mortals.) In English, "hermeneutics" refers to the study of methods or principles of interpretation.

Clearly the semantic fields of both the Greek and English words are overlap-ping. The usage of the English words in biblical scholarship has been somewhat fluid, but attempts are often made to distinguish hermeneutics from exegesis. Sometimes a rather simple distinction is offered: exegesis pertains to what the text *meant*; hermeneutics pertains to what the text *means* (Stendahl, 1962: 419–20; R. Brown, 1981: 23–44). But this is not the most helpful way to frame the matter. The meaning of a text does not automatically change simply by the passage of time. This way of distinguishing the terms conflates meaning with significance. What an ancient text "means" in modern times is really a matter of the *relationship* between the historical meaning and the modern readers and their context. This "meaning *to someone*," especially someone far removed from the original act of communication, is more properly a matter of the text's significance.

A more helpful way to distinguish exegesis from hermeneutics is to see the latter as the broader, more theoretical term, concerned especially with philosophical notions of meaning, language, and understanding, and with the formulation of interpretive principles. Exegesis would then refer to the practical application of those principles in interpreting specific texts. In short, hermeneutics is theory; exegesis is practice.

Another way of saying this is that exegesis has as its object a text to be inter-preted, whereas hermeneutics takes a step back and reflects on the very process of interpretation. As Ben Meyer puts it, "If the object of interpretation [or exegesis] is to understand the text, the object of hermeneutics is to understand the understanding of texts" (1989: 88). Hermeneutics is, in effect, the philosophy of interpretation, and discussions of it by its leading theorists tend to be very theoretical. In contrast, discussions of exegesis often read like a how-to book.

This book is concerned with both hermeneutics and exegesis. The large cen-tral portion of the book (chapter 2) has a how-to section on exegetical method. Surrounding that center, chapters 1, 3, and 4 take up pre- and postexegetical matters, though that language is somewhat artificial since all the chapters ad-dress a unified interpretive process. There is a logical sequence to the exegetical steps in chapter 2 and to all the chapters in the plan of the book, but the real-life practice of interpretation may unfold differently or shift emphases according to the particulars of the interpreter, the text, and the hermeneutical context.

Where Is Meaning to Be Sought?

Northrop Frye, a prominent twentieth-century literary critic, once wrote: "It has been said of [the German religious mystic Jakob] Boehme that his books are like a picnic to which the author brings the words and the reader the meaning. The remark may have been intended as a sneer at Boehme, but it is an exact description of all works of literary art without exception" (1962: 427–28). Some scholars would take strong exception to such a sweeping statement, but it forcefully articulates a point of view that became popular in the latter half of the twentieth century. The question can be stated simply: Where is meaning to be sought? Or perhaps, who or what determines meaning? Ben Meyer calls this the most basic hermeneutical issue: "Do *texts* mediate meaning *to us*, or do *we* lend meaning to *texts*?" (1994: 2) When readers read, do they discover meaning or generate it? Do they construe it or construct it? Northrop Frye clearly thought that the reader was the primary supplier of meaning, but at least three different answers have been given to the question of the source of meaning. These three answers also outline the major phases in literary theory. It would not be exaggerating to call them paradigm shifts.

1. *Meaning as located in the author's intention.* The traditional view was that meaning was inextricably linked to the author. Obviously this view draws upon the understanding of meaning as authorial intention: the text means what the author intended it to mean. For most people this theory has the aura of common sense. Anyone who has ever said, written, or thought, "That's not what I meant!" is a believer in the importance of authorial intent. This view of the locus of meaning prevailed from the early eighteenth century up to the mid-twentieth century. It received its definitive statement, however, in the book *Validity in Interpretation*, by E. D. Hirsch (1967; see also Juhl, 1980; Knapp and Michaels, 1982; and F. Watson, 1997: 95–126). Hirsch argues that meaning is rooted in the author's consciousness, specifically in the desire to convey a certain understanding by means of a sequence of linguistic symbols. Hirsch distinguishes "meaning" from "significance," the latter being the importance, relevance, or value of a particular meaning.

> *Meaning* is that which is represented by a text; it is what the author meant by his use of a particular sign sequence; it is what the signs represent. *Significance*, on the other hand, names a relationship between that meaning and a person, or a conception, or a situation, or indeed anything imaginable. (Hirsch, 1967: 8)

If the author and the interpreter are competent, Hirsch insists, this meaning is accessible and repeatable: it can be conveyed from author to interpreter. Indeed, interpretation is "re-cognition," that is, rethinking the author's thought. Hirsch stresses the distinction between meaning and significance because he views meaning as stable and determinate. In other words, the meaning of a text does not change willy-nilly, from one year to the next, or from one context to the next. Suppose an older reader says, "This text means something completely different to me now from when I read it as a young adult." Hirsch would argue that the meaning of the text did not change but that its significance to the reader did.

Hirsch and his notion of authorial intention have come under criticism from various angles (Beardsley, 1968; Dowling, 1983; Eagleton, 1983: 67–71; Fowl, 2000; Iseminger, 1992; Meyer, 1989: 36–41; Vanhoozer, 1998: 225). In particular, critics have objected that the author's consciousness cannot serve as a guide to textual meaning since it is not publicly available, whereas the author's words are. In the case of living authors, an interpreter could presumably contact the writer and ask, "What exactly did you mean when you wrote such-and-such?" In the case of ancient authors, this strategy has little utility unless the interpreter is gifted at conducting séances. Moreover, there were other objections against the emphasis on authorial intention, and the first volley was fired approximately a quarter of a century before Hirsch.

2. *Meaning as located in the text.* By the middle of the twentieth century, some literary scholars began to challenge the idea that the author's intent was the key to meaning. In its place came a focus on the text itself. In an encyclopedia article in 1942 and then in a longer essay in 1954, W. K. Wimsatt and Monroe C. Beardsley coined the term "intentional fallacy." The author's intent, they argue, is *not* the key to textual meaning. It is a fallacy to think that the critic must delve into psychology (the author's consciousness) or biography (the author's life and times) in order to interpret literature. The author's intention "is neither available nor desirable as a standard for judging the success of a work of literary art" (1954: 3). The author's intention may be the *cause* of a poem, but it is not the *standard* by which interpretations of the poem are to be judged.

Wimsatt and Beardsley were reacting to a mode of interpretation that had shifted the focal point of literary study away from the texts to something external to them. The new school of thought that they represented came to be known, appropriately, as "New Criticism." This school stressed that a literary text, particularly a poem, is "a self-contained unit of meaning which does not have to be explained in terms of its author's personality or biography, or in terms of historical and social factors" (Macey, 2000: 268–69). The meaning of a poem is to be found solely in the work itself, by a careful analysis of its language, syntax, structure, style, and so forth.

For our purposes, we should note that New Criticism eventually had an impact on biblical interpretation. Various modes of biblical criticism that focused primarily on the world of the author, that is, the world *behind* the text, prevailed from the Enlightenment to the mid-twentieth century. In the latter half of the twentieth century, literary methods arose that focused primarily on the text. Rather than investigating sources, forms, redaction, and tradition history, scholars were more concerned about the final form of the text. One could now interpret the Bible by a careful analysis of the text alone.

We should note, however, that a subtle shift occurred when New Criticism sidled over from the English department to religious studies. The chief objection of Wimsatt, Beardsley, and others was the use of authorial intent as the standard for judging *poetry*. Whether this objection applies equally to the narrative prose and epistles of the New Testament is not clear. Indeed, in their classic essay, Wimsatt and Beardsley acknowledge that "poetry differs from practical messages, which are successful if and only if we correctly infer the intention" (1954: 5). New Criticism's critique of early twentieth-century poetic interpretation should be applied cautiously to the literary genres of the New Testament.

3. *Meaning as located in the reader(s).* As I indicated earlier, the history of modern literary theory can be divided into three periods: a preoccupation with the author (eighteenth through early twentieth century), a focus on the text itself (ca. 1930–80), finally giving way to a shift of attention to the reader during the last few decades (Eagleton, 1983: 74). Thus the current phase of literary criticism emphasizes the reader's role in the production of meaning. The school of thought most often associated with this development is reader-response theory, and it comes in both moderate and more radical versions (Vanhoozer, 1998: 151–52).

Proponents of more moderate versions ascribe roles to both the text and the reader in the production of meaning. Readers fill in "gaps" left by the author as they strive to make sense of the text (Iser, 1978). Moderate reader-response theorists usually acknowledge that there are some controls or limits on interpretation, although they would not likely appeal to authorial intent as the touchstone of a "normative reading." Augustine anticipated such controls on interpretation in arguing that, when the author's intent is unknown, interpretations must be congruent with the teaching of Scripture elsewhere. In particular, they should foster the love of God and neighbor (Vanhoozer, 1998: 117). Another limit, particularly for New Testament interpretation, might be general coherence with the ethos of the gospel.

The leading representative of the more radical variety of reader-response theory is Stanley Fish (1980). According to Fish, meaning is not inherent in the text, lying there inert, waiting to be discovered by the reader like a pottery shard in an archaeological dig. Meaning is rather created in the act of reading. Questions naturally arise: If this is so, how does one distinguish between valid and invalid interpretations? Could there not be as many meanings as there are readers? This is not quite the case for Fish, but very nearly so. Fish would locate interpretive authority in the community of readers:

> Indeed, it is interpretive communities, rather than either the text or the reader, that produce meanings and are responsible for the emergence of formal features. Interpretive communities are made up of those who share interpretive strategies not for reading but for writing texts, for constituting their properties. In other words these strategies exist prior to the act of reading and therefore determine

the shape of what is read rather than, as is usually assumed, the other way around. (1980: 14)

Carrying this theory to its logical conclusion, Fish argues that the variety of interpretations is limited only by the availability of interpretive communities: "The fact that it remains easy to think of a reading that most of us would dismiss out of hand does not mean that the text excludes it but that there is as yet no elaborated interpretive procedure for producing that text. . . . It follows, then, that no reading, however outlandish it might appear, is inherently an impossible one" (1980: 345, 347). Fish's brand of reader-response theory represents a seismic shift in the locus of meaning from the text to the reader. The text virtually becomes a Rorschach inkblot, whose meaning owes its genesis to the reader, not the author.

In its most extreme forms, reader-response criticism confuses reading with writing, activities that are best kept distinct from one another (Vanhoozer, 1998: 153). If your passion is to *construct your own meaning*, put your book down and take up paper and pen. If you want to *construe another's meaning*, then read. As Francis Watson says bluntly (and controversially), "Readers can only *receive* meaning, they cannot *create* it" (1997: 104, with original emphasis). This should not be taken to mean that reading is a passive activity; it demands active engagement with and construal of another's meaning. Moreover, Watson adds, "Once they have received meaning, readers may engage in various creative activities: they may draw implications from it, apply it to their own circumstances, formulate counter-arguments or questions, link it to what is said elsewhere, and so on" (1997: 125n5).

Augustine relates his conversion experience when he overheard a child's voice in a garden saying, "Tolle et lege! [Pick it up and read!]" (*Confessions* 8.12). Augustine immediately took up a book of Paul's Epistles, read the first passage on which his eyes fell, and experienced a religious transformation. Paul (and I would say, God) spoke to Augustine through the medium of the text. "Tolle et lege" are words to heed when you want to hear a voice *outside* your own head. When your chief concern is to give expression to the voice (hopefully singular) *inside* your head, then listen instead to the scribal muse: "Pone et scribe! [Put (the book) down and write!]"

Ultimately, the ground of textual meaning is authorial intention *as expressed in the author's communicative activity*, not the author's consciousness (Vanhoozer, 1998: 225). Meaning would not "be there" if the author had not intended it. The text did not come into being by accident; its meaning came "out of a head, not out of a hat" (Wimsatt and Beardsley, 1954: 4). But meaning is encountered *through the text*, not in mystical communion with the author. Thus Francis Watson rightly insists that authorial intent "is to be understood not as some subjective occurrence lying behind the text but as the principle of the text's intelligibility" (1997: 112).

It was not so much a fallacy for E. D. Hirsch to emphasize authorial intention as it was for him to emphasize it exclusively. For most ancient texts, the author's intention is accessible only through the text itself. (Partial exceptions would be when other writings by the same author might elucidate the text under consideration or when general knowledge of the historical circumstances makes a particular theory of authorial intent more or less likely.) The intended sense is intrinsic to the text. Ben Meyer notes that "Hirsch might have successfully fielded all objections if he had defined the object of interpretation as the sense that the author *both intended and managed to encode or express in the text*" (1989: 40, with added emphasis). The meaning that is sought in exegesis, then, is the meaning intended by the author and conveyed by the text (Dunn, 2003b: 122; R. Brown, 1994: 6–9).

Exegesis is only one stage in the entire process of interpretation that I propose in this book, and confessional interpreters will rightly insist on moving beyond strict exegetical meanings. But the earnest pursuit of the authorial/textual meaning is a necessary application of the Golden Rule (Matt. 7:12; Luke 6:31) to biblical interpretation: we respect the texts of others and represent them as fairly as possible, since this is what we want others to do with our texts (Vanhoozer in Adam et al., 2006: 59–60).

Is the Meaning of a Text Determinate?

The advent of reader-response theory and the possibility of unlimited readings acutely raise a question that has always bubbled beneath the surface of hermeneutics: is textual meaning determinate? A determinate meaning is one that has defined limits, not necessarily so precisely defined as to be singular and exclusive of all other meanings, but defined within a finite range. A determinate meaning may not be determinable with exactitude, but it is not infinitely elastic. Needless to say, even a determinate meaning can be expressed in a variety of ways.

Closely related to the question of determinate meaning is the issue of controls or criteria for meaning. If, as most writers assume, it is not the case that a text can mean anything the reader wants it to mean, then what controls meaning, or what criteria may be employed to distinguish valid interpretations from invalid ones? The control that Stanley Fish offers is minimal. If one is dissatisfied with the apparent meaning of a text, one need only find a new interpretive community. For Fish, the meaning that one's community constructs *is* the meaning of the text, at least for that community (1980: 14). As another scholar put it bluntly, "Texts, like dead men and women, have no rights, no aims, no interests. They can be used in whatever way readers or interpreters choose" (Morgan and Barton, 1988: 7).

The movement known as deconstruction is also characterized by an emphasis on the instability of textual meaning. Deconstruction is notoriously difficult to define. As one critic aptly puts it, deconstruction extends a greasy palm to the one who would grasp it (Moore, 1989: 132). It is a kind of undoing of meaning. Deconstruction expands on the observation of linguists that words have no intrinsic connection with their referents. In other words, it is a purely human convention that the word "book" refers to, and thus means, a collection of printed pages bound together as one volume. Nothing about the appearance or the sound of the word "book" connects it with its referent. If meaning depends on signifiers that are ultimately arbitrary, deconstructionists argue, then meaning is inherently unstable. One harsh critic of deconstruction describes it as "an approach characterized by doctrinaire skepticism and infatuation with the thought that language is always so compromised by metaphor and ulterior motives that a text never means what it appears to mean" (Kimball, 1998: 122).

But deconstruction is much more than simply a way to analyze literary texts.

> Deconstruction is a painstaking taking-apart, a peeling away of the various layers—historical, rhetorical, ideological—of distinctions, concepts, texts, and whole philosophies, whose aim is to expose the arbitrary linguistic nature of their original construction. Deconstruction is an intense analytical method, occasionally perversely so, that results in the collapse from within of all that it touches. (Vanhoozer, 1998: 52)

The authors of *The Postmodern Bible* articulate succinctly the deconstructionist view of textual meaning: "Deconstruction rejects all 'container' theories of meaning. Meaning is not in the text but is brought to it and imposed upon it. The understanding of the author or of the original audience is not decisive; it is merely one reading among many. Texts may lend themselves more to some readings than to others, but the results of any reading have more to do with the reader's interests than with the text itself" (Eichele et al., 1995: 130–31).

Many readers of Scripture will be understandably wary of such extreme indeterminacy of meaning. Whether one locates meaning in the author, the text, or some combination thereof, meaning must have some degree of determinacy; otherwise communication cannot occur.

> Language is in essence a medium of communication. If the hearer takes words in a sense not intended by the speaker, that is not an enlargement of meaning but a breakdown of communication. This claim applies to all uses of language, but it is especially apposite where a claim of revelation is involved. Certainly anyone, when reading a text of Scripture, may have a bright idea which is independent of the author's intention, but which comes upon the reader with all the force and persuasiveness of revealed truth. But when that happens it is the reader's idea, not the meaning of what he or she was reading; and any authority which we may attach to the text is irrelevant to the question of the truth or validity of the reader's idea. (Caird, 1994: 423)

Authors normally assume that their intended meaning is communicable, and they expect that readers will receive something close to the message that they, the authors, intend to convey. Even reader-response theorists and deconstructionists do not like their words to be misinterpreted (Powell, 2001: 4–5). Moreover, a text is not just a single signifier, but a sequence of signifiers with a semantic integrity that ought to be respected. As Michael Root notes,

> A text may be interpreted many ways, but most texts do have a specificity that excludes some interpretations. Many interpretations of an ambiguous text, such as *Moby Dick*, might fall within the limits of the credible, but *Moby Dick* is not about numerical patterns in the 1983 Columbia, South Carolina, phonebook. The text limits the bounds of acceptable interpretation. (1984: 155)

The examples of indeterminate meaning adduced by Fish involve terse or intentionally ambiguous texts (1980: 305–10, 322–29). It goes without saying that the meaning of a verbal snippet, ripped from its context, or of a list of words with no syntactical connection to one another will be hard to determine. Different kinds of discourse have meanings with different degrees of determinacy. For example, poetry is generally less determinate in meaning than prose since the former is more evocative, emotional, and imaginative. Hence, many of the literary theories developed in relation to poetry may not be fully or easily applicable to prose writings. Shorter utterances are less determinate than longer ones. A sequence of five signifiers ("I'm mad about my flat") will obviously be more ambiguous than a sequence of fifty signifiers ("I'm mad about my flat. I just purchased this tire last week, and I've driven very carefully," etc.). Careless writing is less determinate than precise writing. (The meaning of a text may be indeterminate because the author is a nincompoop. Generally speaking, the more skilled the author, the clearer the meaning of the text.) Finally, some authors may aim to be ambiguous, and so the meaning of their texts is intentionally indeterminate. Such authors seek to confound rather than communicate (Vanhoozer, 1998: 333).

Ultimately, deconstructionists deny the possibility of what countless readers do every time they pick up a book: they read, hoping to discover the meaning that the author intended to convey. These critics are a bit like the scientist who insists that the bumblebee's weight to wing-area ratio makes its flight impossible. Meanwhile, the bumblebee, untutored in aerodynamics, goes about the business of flying. Likewise, average readers who do not have the advantage of deconstructive insight continue flitting from one text to another, busily engaged in what is, from all appearances, interpretation of "what is there." Oblivious to the philosophers' objections, they continue to gather the nectar of textual meaning under the assumption that they are getting the message the author intended.

Deconstructionists tend to absolutize the problems of interpretation and indeterminacy. Kevin Vanhoozer notes that Jacques Derrida, whose name is virtually synonymous with deconstruction, made a mistake "to conclude that, because there are no certain foundations for determining the author's intention, there is neither knowledge nor meaning. In other words, Derrida asks us to choose between the alternatives of absolute certainty or utter skepticism" (Vanhoozer, 1998: 211). But Hirsch rightly observes that "it is a logical mistake to confuse the impossibility of certainty in understanding with the impossibility of understanding" (1967: 17). If the assurance of certainty were a prerequisite, human beings would be paralyzed in all sorts of investigations. When it comes to literary knowledge (meaning derived from texts), as well as scientific knowledge (meaning derived from experimentation), good data and sound methodology take us as far as probable conclusions, and we live with probability all the time.

Interpretation is like throwing hand grenades: close is often good enough. Our grasp of textual meaning is neither absolutely certain nor hopelessly inconclusive. It is usually sufficient, and with training and practice it can improve. Human knowledge, whether historical, scientific, or literary, is always provisional and subject to correction, but the very concept of correction presupposes a normative meaning toward which interpreters are tending. To seek to understand the meaning intended by the author and conveyed by the author's words is not a hopeless cause. The linguistic, historical, and cultural obstacles that were described in the introduction can be sufficiently overcome so as to gain an adequate understanding for forming and informing Christian faith and practice.

Interpretation, particularly communal acts of interpretation that are done by the church for the church, should not sever the link between biblical text and biblical author. To do so would undermine continuity between the church's life and the revelatory process that is rooted in, though not limited to, divine inspiration of the writers of Scripture. Ben Meyer does not exaggerate when he says that "the maintenance of authentic Christian identity is the ultimate theological rationale of insistence on the intended sense of scriptural texts" (1989: 33). Individual believers sometimes read the Bible in idiosyncratic ways and yet remain faithful in their discipleship, but this is an inadequate model for Christian communities. All interpretations of Scripture, whether individual or communal, should strive at a minimum to "do no harm." But formal interpretation that guides the faith and practice of Christian communities must go beyond this minimum and provide faithful and sound teaching that maintains continuity with sacred Scripture and the church through the ages.

Mark Allan Powell notes that Christianity is much more than doctrine, but for the sake of orthodox faith, "theological doctrine needs to be grounded in interpretation of scripture as understood in light of the historical intentions of the Bible's original authors. Christian dogma should be expressive of the message of scripture, and that message is best determined with exegetical methods derived from an author-oriented hermeneutic" (2001: 56).

When I was in grade school, tetherball was a popular playground activity. A long, slender rope connected a volleyball-sized sphere to the top of a pole, and two players tried to wrap the rope completely around the pole by striking the ball in opposite directions. Several techniques were involved in this simple sport: serving, bumping, striking, blocking, tipping, and so forth; so the game could vary considerably in duration, strategy, skill, and number of personal injuries. But despite this variety, a few basic, immutable rules governed the game. A tetherball could not be untied from its pole, taken elsewhere, and used to play kickball. That would fundamentally alter the game such that one would no longer be playing tetherball. Similarly, valid interpretation embraces diverse methods and diverse expressions of textual meaning, but if interpreters sever meaning from the author by disregarding authorial intent and its textual expression, then the players are no longer interpreting but only playing kickball with the text.

To use the metaphor of geometry, we should not conceive of meaning as an exact geometric point with an absolutely precise location, but rather as a circle with dimensions. (The size of the circle will vary with the genre of the text and the skill and purposes of the author.) The desideratum of an interpreter is not a single, correct interpretation that admits of no variation whatsoever. There is, however, a center at which the interpreter aims. Interpretations that do not hit the exact center may still have value, but their value decreases the further they deviate from it. As Paul Ricoeur suggests, "Perhaps we should say that a text is a finite space of interpretations: there is not just one interpretation, but, on the other hand, there is not an infinite number of them. A text is a space of variations that has its own constraints" (1991: 496).

Is It Possible to Be Objective?

In the nineteenth and early twentieth centuries, biblical research was usually conducted under the assumptions of the school of thought known as positivism. Associated with the French philosopher Auguste Comte (1798–1857), positivism viewed theology and metaphysics as early, primitive modes of human existence. Humankind evolved through these imperfect modes to reach positivism, a state in which human beings seek "to discover the immutable universal laws that govern the universe by using observation, experimentation and calculation" (Macey, 2000: 303). Positivism owed much to the scientific method and in turn provided it with a philosophical history. Positivism was also a theory of knowledge or an epistemology. One gained knowledge by the objective, methodical analysis of data. This analysis involved two poles:

> At one pole was the object to be known, which once posited, remained substantially identical with itself and epistemologically "stationary" through successive

acts of knowing to which it was subjected. At the other pole was the knowing subject, who, by scientific method, could operate cognitively upon the object without influencing it. In other words, through the rigorous use of method the knower could approach the free-standing object with a mind that was virtually [a] *tabula rasa* in regard to the object and could come to know it "as it is" without contaminating or distorting objective knowledge (the scientific ideal) with "subjectivity." (Schneiders, 1991: 159)

Positivism had a natural affinity to the physical sciences. The subject/object polarity seemed accurately to describe the scientist hunched over a specimen in a petri dish. But its inadequacy became evident in the latter half of the twentieth century as philosophers realized that absolute objectivity was a myth. Scientists cannot escape their subjectivity, and that subjectivity has the potential to affect the process and results of scientific research. This is seen not just in cases of fraudulent or flagrantly biased research but also in subtle ways that may go undetected.

What is true in the physical sciences is all the more true in the humanities. The object of study in biblical interpretation is not quite analogous to a specimen in a petri dish. True, the Bible is an object for study, but it is an object with which we have a long relationship. This text is ingrained in our consciousness, our culture, and our deepest commitments. History, society, and we ourselves are profoundly shaped by it. So we can no longer claim to occupy a neutral, purely objective position from which to interpret Scripture.

This fact was recognized by Rudolf Bultmann in his celebrated essay "Is Exegesis without Presuppositions Possible?" Bultmann asserted that this question was to be answered in the affirmative, if by "without presuppositions" one meant "without presupposing the results of exegesis." "No exegesis that is guided by dogmatic prejudices hears what the text says but lets it say only what the exegete wants to hear" (1984: 145–46). Interpreters must not prejudge the matter under investigation, whether motivated by religious dogma, cultural prejudice, or rationalistic bias. (Bultmann himself sometimes fell prey to the latter.) But if by "without presuppositions" one means that the exegete has no interests, concerns, or "preunderstandings," then such an approach is neither possible nor desirable.

Bultmann understood that biblical exegesis, which he saw as a form of historical criticism,

is possible only for one who does not stand over against it as a neutral, nonparticipating spectator but also stands within it and shares responsibility for it. . . . This existential relation to history is the basic presupposition for understanding it. This does not mean that understanding history is "subjective" in the sense that it depends on the personal preference of the historian and thereby loses all objective significance. On the contrary, it means that history can be understood precisely in its objective content only by a subject who is existentially concerned and alive. It means that the scheme of subject and object that has validity for natural science is not valid for historical understanding. (1984: 150)

The claim about the natural sciences in the last sentence was a common assumption in 1957, when Bultmann wrote the German original of this essay, but as I noted above, scientists as well as historians in the postmodern world recognize the problematic nature of claiming absolute objectivity.

So all researchers must contend with the fact of their subjectivity: their personalities, biases, prejudices, idiosyncrasies, commitments, and so forth. Subjectivity, in essence, refers to the fact that all of us must "process" reality through physical perception, emotions, and rational analysis. But perception, emotions, and reason involve individual variability. One person sees a situation as threatening; another does not. One person sees a text as oppressive; another thinks it is rather benign. One person finds a solution to a problem to be reasonable; another regards it as folly.

If our subjectivity is inescapable, what do we do with it? We have seen that an earlier generation of positivists simply denied the problem. That solution is no longer tenable. Should interpreters therefore revel in their subjectivity? Should we say, "Let your interpretive imagination run wild! Produce the reading that seems best to you. Just don't regard your interpretation as normative for anyone else, not even for yourself in a different time or place"? Should we take philosopher Friedrich Nietzsche's maxim "There are no facts, only interpretations" (1967: 267, §481; also 327, §§604–5) to be a declaration of independence rather than a counsel of despair? Alternatively, perhaps interpreters should suppress their subjectivity at all costs, stifling their individuality so as to become detached, scientist-like observers? This alternative assumes that objectivity is arrived at through the subtraction, or at least suppression, of subjectivity (Meyer, 1994: 109).

A mediate solution that acknowledges subjectivity without giving it carte blanche is found in the philosophical system known as critical realism (Meyer, 1989, 1994; Wright, 1992a: 32–37; Dunn, 2003b: 110–11). Critical realism is a theory of knowing. Like positivism, it affirms the independent existence of the object of study. There really is something there apart from our perception of it, whether a protozoan under a microscope or a text in the hands of a reader. The modern critical text of the Greek New Testament is an objective entity of study. But unlike positivism, critical realism acknowledges that our only access to that object is through our very human and individual perception, perception that must always be subject to critique. Interpreters must not only reflect on the text but also on the process of interpretation itself, acknowledging the potential for misperception and standing ready to engage in self-critique and to receive critique from other interpreters. The maxim of the critical realist is, "There really are facts to be interpreted, but interpretations are always provisional."

Critical realism on the one hand responds to the error of positivism by its self-critical faculty, and on the other hand, to the errors of postmodern pluralism and indeterminacy of meaning by its insistence on the otherness of the data. Ben Meyer rightly stresses that "objectivity is not achieved by the flight from subjectivity nor by any and every cultivation of subjectivity, but by an intense and persevering effort to exercise subjectivity attentively, intelligently, reasonably, and responsibly" (1994: 4). In this way, objectivity is not to be confused with neutrality or disinterest (Green, 2007b: 74–75). Through the responsible exercise of (admittedly subjective) perception and reason, Christian interpreters of Scripture can achieve understanding, not perfect or final understanding, but sufficient for informed judgments about faith and practice.

In a sense, "complete objectivity" is a straw man whose refutation hardly advances the debate. James Barr offers the following bon mot: "It is true that complete objectivity is not attainable, but a high degree of objectivity is attainable, and a high degree of it is very much better than a low degree" (1980: 24; see also Stylianopoulos, 1997: 81; Marshall, 2004: 25). This statement is an island of common sense in a sea of hermeneutical confusion. We should not set the bar of objectivity so high that no one can attain it. Neither should we set the bar on the ground so that anyone can step over it without exertion. Absolute objectivity has rightly been demythologized, but if perfection is unattainable, it does not necessarily follow that excellence is too. We should resist all-or-none thinking vis-à-vis objectivity. A chastened and self-aware subjectivity can be combined with a humble commitment to the highest degree of objectivity that one can attain.

Is a Confessional Context Inherently Biased?

The Bible has a unique status in Christian communities, although it might be hard to give a detailed description of that status in terms that would be acknowledged by all such communities. Stanley Porter and Kent Clarke offer the following faith assumptions held by most Christians:

1. In some shape or form, the Bible is thought to record the word(s) of God.
2. More so than other writings, the Bible is considered to embody a truer or better reflection and more accurate representation of reality.
3. The degree of authority attached to the Bible by individuals and communities supersedes that of any other literary text. . . .
4. The Bible is ascribed a central role in informing and guiding the faith and practice of these individuals and communities. (Porter, 1997a: 15–16)

What is the difference between biblical interpretation in nonconfessional contexts, such as a public university, and confessional contexts? Among other things, the two approaches can be distinguished on the basis of their aims: descriptive versus prescriptive, respectively. Nonconfessional interpretation aims at describing the historical meaning of the text. The concern is what Mark, Luke, or Paul meant, not what existential relevance it might have for modern readers. The confessional approach is prescriptive, in that it seeks to determine the normative force of the text: its continuing significance in shaping the life of persons who stand under its authority. This distinction is useful so long as one bears in mind that a confessional approach by no means excludes description. Indeed, responsible interpretation in confessional contexts will first engage in thorough description before moving to the prescriptive phase. One must *understand* the meaning of the text before one can *stand under* the authority of the text.

So Christians claim that the biblical text is in some sense normative for faith and life, that it concerns matters that are transcendent and claims to which we are beholden. Indeed, many Christian interpreters would go beyond the claim of transcendence to an assertion of finality or ultimacy. Ben Meyer insists that the gospel cannot be reduced to one among many stories or "paradigms of transcendence" because of the particulars of its story: "The gospel cannot be reduced to one among many paradigms unless it can be shown that the story is essentially illusory: that the protagonist is not who the story says he is, that he does not do what the story says he does, that he has not been 'raised from the dead,' as the story says he has, and that he will not bring the story to the end that, in the story itself, he says he will" (1994: x). Thus the confessional context for New Testament interpretation entails significant assumptions concerning the transcendence, relevance, and uniqueness of the text's message. Do such assumptions hopelessly bias the process of interpretation? Is the secular context superior by virtue of its freedom from or denial of such claims?

The possibility of prejudicial interpretation in confessional contexts cannot be denied. If we recall Bultmann's influential essay on exegesis without presuppositions (1984), we will be chastened not to let faith predetermine the meaning of a passage. The text must be allowed to speak with its own voice and without the censorship of dogmatic convictions. But bias is not a necessary result of theological commitments. James Barr rightly asserts this and warns of bias from other quarters:

> The idea . . . that objectivity in biblical study can be attained through the exclusion of theological interest should not be accepted; and, as theologians have often and rightly pointed out, where theological interest has been excluded it has often been only to make room for some secular or pseudo-theological ideology which is equally destructive of objectivity. (1980: 24–25)

As Barr goes on to say, the critical issue is the *quality* of one's theological attitude. If one's theology permits Scripture to be heard, and if the interpreter remains open to transformation, even of cherished theological commitments, then "strong theological conviction can coexist with and rejoice in a very high degree of objectivity" (1980: 24).

Faith then is by no means inherently inimical to rigorous and critical study of Scripture. Sandra Schneiders goes beyond this (rightly, I think) to claim that faith in some sense is necessary for the fullest understanding and appropriation of the biblical text. She does not mean that only Christians validly interpret the New Testament but rather that "openness to the transcendent" is necessary for the interpretation of classic, religious texts: "One who approaches [the Bible] with an a priori and nonnegotiable conviction that no such claims [bearing on religious reality] can be taken seriously because they are without exception false cannot validly interpret this text" (1991: 60; see also 89–90). Readers who bracket out existential and religious claims are missing the New Testament's raison d'être. "Without facing the inalienably transformative and self-involving demands that these ecclesial writings place on a serious reader, it is impossible to make significant sense of them—or to understand why they were written or how they survived" (Bockmuehl, 2006: 46).

The website of a major public university had the following statement concerning its program in religious studies: "The Program engages in the academic study of religion. Its fundamental premise is that everything we consider 'religious'—whether found in literature, history, or society—is entirely a human phenomenon." The description went on to speak of the interdisciplinary and interdepartmental nature of the program and the variety of analytical tools used nowadays in religious studies. None of this is controversial or unique. Nevertheless, the description of religion as "*entirely* a human phenomenon" strikes me as both unfortunate and unnecessary. Certainly all religious phenomena *can be approached* in human terms: texts written by human beings, institutions shaped by human beings, rituals and practices engaged in by human beings, and so forth. But the description goes beyond that to exclude any transcendent dimension: "entirely human" in the sense of having nothing to do with the divine in any real, ontological way. Obviously a public institution in the United States must, by law and by practical necessity, employ a secular approach to religious phenomena, but one can bracket out certain perspectives without denying their validity, and the statement seems to do the latter. If the New Testament is read in this way, one's study is constrained from the outset, for central to the truth claims of the New Testament (indeed, of most religious literature) is the assertion that its subject matter is *more than* a human phenomenon.

So again, far from being necessarily detrimental to responsible biblical interpretation, the confessional context is appropriate to it. The church is the body of those who have heard and responded to the Bible's message. In particular, the New Testament is "indigenous" to the church, having originated in its social contexts and, in turn, having shaped its identity. If Christian interpreters remember that their understandings are always subject to correction and reform, the risk of faith's distortion will be outweighed by the fruit of faith's enrichment. Raymond Brown reaches a similar conclusion in the *New Jerome Bible Commentary*:

> Since the biblical books were written by believers for believers, the believing community is a good (and not necessarily a prejudiced) context for interpretation, provided that this community enters into frank dialogue with its tradition. . . . One may acknowledge that at times, because of the weaknesses of those who constitute it, the church does not immediately or adequately respond to a meaning of Scripture that is patent to exegetes—whence the constant need of renewal and reform from within. But despite that, the church remains par excellence the place where Scripture is heard in its truest and fullest meaning. (R. Brown, Fitzmyer, and Murphy, 1990: 1161, 1164)

Samuel Sandmel, a Jewish rabbi and scholar of early Christianity, makes a similar, if somewhat more modest, claim on the matter: "Objectivity is an ideal. No one truly attains it. One strives toward it, buoyed by extravagant hopes and discouraged by a recognition of personal shortcomings. But religiously committed Jews and Christians are no less capable of dealing objectively with historical material than are secular scholars" (1978: vii–viii).

What Claims Should Be Made for Scripture and Its Authority?

Volumes have been written on the topics of biblical authority, inspiration, infallibility, inerrancy, and a host of other descriptions of the character and function of Scripture. I make no pretense to have mastered that literature or to offer a summary of it in this short space. My aim is simply to describe the position that I embrace and to commend it to the reader. I think it is important not to overstate the role of Scripture or to make excessive claims in its behalf. Doing so causes people to become bogged down in defending the Bible against a host of technical difficulties and, as a result, to be distracted from the primary tasks of interpreting and responding to Scripture as the Word of God. As John Stott urges, the most important thing in our relationship to the Bible is "not subscription but submission. That is, it is not whether we subscribe to an impeccable formula about the Bible but whether we live in practical submission to what the Bible teaches" (1999: 62).

In some Christian circles "inerrant" and "infallible" have become important words to describe the nature of Scripture. They are used almost interchangeably, but a slight distinction exists (Schneiders, 1991: 53–55). "Inerrant" means "free from error." In the fundamentalist/modernist debates of the early twentieth century, the inerrancy of Scripture was one of the key doctrines defining fundamentalism. "Infallible" is a bit more nuanced in its meanings. Though it can mean "incapable of error," it may have a slightly more modest meaning: "not liable to deceive or mislead." Moreover, in theological debates about Scripture, "infallible" may carry the implicit qualification "incapable of error *in matters of doctrine or morals.*"

In the comprehensive sense of "*wholly* incapable of error," both "inerrant" and "infallible" are problematic terms. First, there are many practical challenges to the idea that Scripture is free from all errors. There are historical problems, internal discrepancies between parallel accounts, incorrect literary references, as well as theological and moral problems in the Bible. Persons who affirm a thoroughgoing version of inerrancy either have to dismiss the challenges of biblical criticism out of hand or engage in an endless series of critical skirmishes. The defense of inerrancy requires that these battles consistently be won or at least fought to a draw such that judgment may be suspended. Although the Bible should be defended against sweeping and unjustified claims of its being untrustworthy, the defense of absolute inerrancy is not time well spent. Second, there is a theological problem with this view of inerrancy in that it attributes to the Bible a level of perfection and authority that belongs to God alone. The Bible's authority is a *derived* authority. As N. T. Wright says, "The phrase 'authority of scripture' can make Christian sense only if it is a shorthand for 'the authority of the triune God, exercised somehow *through* scripture'" (2005: 23). The Bible is a product of both divine and human activity and, as the latter, it partakes of the limitations of human discourse and thought. If the Bible were wholly inerrant and intrinsically and unqualifiedly authoritative, it could only have been produced by an eclipse of the human authors. In such a case, thoroughgoing inerrancy has the same effect as the old "dictation theory" of inspiration, a view that is generally rejected even by inerrantists.

A more modest and defensible claim is that the teaching of Scripture is trustworthy in matters of faith and practice. When I was in graduate school at a major university, I was a teaching assistant for a professor who was a respected critical scholar as well as a practicing Catholic. One day after a session of the New Testament intro course, the professor was talking to a student who was a bit disturbed by remarks in the lecture about the nature of Scripture, particularly concerning such categories as "inerrancy," "inspiration," and so forth. I happened to be nearby, and the professor turned to me unexpectedly and said, "Well, Clayton, you believe in the inerrancy of Scripture, don't you?" Suddenly I knew how Jesus felt when the Pharisees tried to trap him with a question to which there was no good answer. An unqualified "yes" would disregard my critical training. An unqualified "no" would further dismay a student who was already struggling. I'm not always mentally agile when put on the spot, but on that occasion I managed an answer that was both truthful and pastoral. I said, "I believe that Scripture unerringly teaches the way of salvation."

Indeed, I do believe that Scripture is inerrant in this respect, but because of the history and the ambiguity of the term, I prefer simply to speak of Scripture's authority. (For reasons why even some evangelical Christians are uncomfortable with the word "inerrancy," see Stott, 1999: 61–62.) Even 2 Timothy 3:16, the locus classicus for biblical inspiration, makes a relatively modest claim for "Scripture." (By this term, the biblical author must have meant the sacred writings of that day, approximating our Old Testament, but perhaps more or less inclusive. The writings of the New Testament can be subsumed under this claim only by extension, as an implication of their canonical status.) What are the implied results of inspiration according to 2 Timothy 3:16? In short, they are practical and functional. Divinely inspired Scripture is useful for teaching, reproof, correction, and training in righteousness.

This functional authority of Scripture is similar, therefore, to the doctrine of the sufficiency of Scripture (Vanhoozer, 2005: 730–31). This too is a modest and defensible claim. The sufficiency of Scripture asserts that what God reveals in and through Scripture is sufficient for salvation and for faithful Christian discipleship. Thus the doctrine implies that Scripture is sufficient in keeping with the purposes that God intended for it. It may not be God's intent that Scripture be an inerrant science text, a book of precise genealogical records, or a journalistic report of historical events. Moreover, the sufficiency of Scripture is an ancient and enduring claim, having basis in both the patristic and medieval eras (Congar, 1967: 107–18; Stylianopoulos, 1997: 226; Ward, 2002).

So I offer the following definition of the inspiration of Scripture. What it lacks in succinctness it will hopefully make up for in soundness. *Inspiration is that influence of the Holy Spirit upon the human authors of the Bible that makes their writings sufficient, when taken as a whole and interpreted through the guidance of the same Spirit who inspired them, to reveal the nature and will of God, to lead persons to Christ and salvation, and to guide them in essential matters of faith and practice.*

What Is the Proper Disposition of the Interpreter?

Nowadays there is much discussion about whether suspicion or trust is the proper disposition of the interpreter of Scripture. Despite the revelatory power and transcendent subject matter of Scripture, it is still unmistakably written in human and thus finite language and is limited by human perspectives, particularly the cultural assumptions of the ancient Near East and the Hellenistic world. Modern readers will naturally find passages of Scripture that are peculiar, embarrassing, oppressive, or downright offensive. Issues that quickly come to mind include the justification or tacit acceptance of slavery

(Exod. 21:20–21; 1 Pet. 2:18), capital punishment for minor offenses (Exod. 21:17), the restriction of women's roles (1 Cor. 14:33–35; 1 Tim. 2:11–15), and anti-Jewish sentiments (John 8:44; 1 Thess. 2:15–16). The reasons for approaching Scripture with suspicion are plentiful.

Problematic passages of Scripture, such as those just listed, are evidence of the fact that texts have ideologies, interests, and agendas, just as interpreters do. Neither texts nor readers are neutral. The ideologies of the text, along with the ideologies of the history of interpretation, point to the need for a critical and judicious approach to Scripture, one that is not naive about the potential that texts possess to distort and do harm. This approach is often dubbed the "hermeneutics of suspicion." The term may have been coined by German New Testament scholar Ernst Fuchs (J. Robertson, 1979: 373n25), and as early as 1970 it was used by Paul Ricoeur (1970: 32–26), but feminist scholars, notably Elisabeth Schüssler Fiorenza (1995: 1–22), have given it wide currency in the last three decades.

Although a certain suspicion about the text is useful in unmasking a potentially harmful ideology, any hermeneutical approach is itself subject to criticism. If by "hermeneutics of suspicion" one means a negative, defensive, or adversarial predisposition toward the text, then it is an unwise stance. Suspicion in this sense does not work well as a persistent worldview (Vanhoozer, 1998: 458; see also Bockmuehl, 2006: 55). It morphs too easily into cynicism, paranoia, or indifference. N. T. Wright warns that "suspicion is all very well; there is also such a thing as a hermeneutic of paranoia. Somebody says something; they must have motive; therefore they must have made it up. Just because we are rightly determined to avoid a hermeneutic of credulity, that does not mean there is no such thing as appropriate trust, or even readiness to suspend disbelief for a while, and see where it gets us" (Borg and Wright, 1999: 18).

A hermeneutics of suspicion may also exaggerate the problem that it addresses. The patriarchy of antiquity has tainted the Bible in varying degrees. Some texts are deeply imbued by its harmful ideology; in others patriarchy is a minor aspect of the cultural background; and in still others, thankfully, we see an argument contrary to the prevailing patriarchal assumption. If one regards the Scriptures as *pervasively* oppressive, there is a danger of magnifying the disease that one hopes to cure, as well as failing to recognize and avail oneself of benign texts. As Richard Hays queries, "If the Bible itself, the revelatory, identity-defining text of the Christian community, is portrayed as oppressive, on what basis do we know God or relate to God?" (Hays, 1997: 218)

By the hermeneutics of suspicion, then, I mean a sober assessment of (1) the historical context of Scripture's production: the world of antiquity in which, among other things, men dominated nearly all power structures and the status quo of slavery was rarely questioned; and (2) the human context of Scripture's interpretation: our fallen world, in which texts *may* be, but need not invariably be, composed and/or interpreted to establish or perpetuate systems of injustice.

As Ben Meyer writes, "Critical distance and 'the hermeneutic of suspicion' in the sense of attention to bias, to ideology, to rationalizing explanations, screening devices, etc., not only in the text but [also] in the [critics themselves], are indispensable to critique" (Meyer, 1989: 23).

As a counterpoint to the hermeneutics of suspicion, other scholars have emphasized the hermeneutics of trust, goodwill, or openness. Goodwill in hermeneutics "is neither sentimental affection nor guaranteed uncritical agreement." On the contrary, "it is the willingness to take the other seriously, to allow our conversation partner's questions to engage us personally as real questions, to let his or her concerns concern us. . . . Goodwill entertains the possibility that one's own achievements and one's own cultural assumptions may not be the highest point in human history" (J. Robertson, 1979: 376). Goodwill consists of openness and receptivity, but it need not entail reflexive capitulation to the text. Readers need not sell their souls, just open their minds.

A number of critics recommend openness or goodwill as the most appropriate disposition, not just when reading sacred Scripture, but also in reading literature generally. Genuine attention and sympathy are required because we are engaging and being engaged by another human being's discourse. "Good will is an antecedent disposition of openness to the horizon, message, and tone of the text. The impersonal curiosity of the physicist is not enough for the interpreter" (Meyer, 1989: 92).

How then does one balance the respective merits of a hermeneutics of trust and a hermeneutics of suspicion? It is tempting to resort to a paradoxical both/and solution and say that the text must be approached with both trust and suspicion. In fact, this is the correct answer, but we can be more precise than this and thereby avoid most of the contradiction. Trust is necessary in the initial phase, when the text is interpreted and its meaning is discovered. Suspicion enters during the second phase, the evaluative or critical phase, when the significance of the text for the modern community of faith is discerned. Ben Meyer makes a similar distinction and assigns a different hermeneutical disposition to each stage:

> The intrinsically appropriate stance of the interpreter is not doubt nor skepticism nor suspicion, but goodwill, empathy, the readiness to find truth, common understanding, agreement. . . . This initial stance does not foreclose critique. It supposes a distinction between understanding and critique, between their respective objects and requisites, and so between the stances appropriate to each. Finally, this view acknowledges accurate understanding as a *sine qua non* condition of valid critique. (1989: 22–23)

The latter sentence articulates an important principle: you cannot fairly critique a text that you have not first understood on its own terms. As Meir Sternberg remarks, "Even to judge against the text's grain, you must first judge with it: receptivity before resistance, competent reading before liberated counter-reading, poetics before politics" (1992: 473). This insight can be stated in a succinct, memorable maxim: *Suspicion must be suspended till the text is apprehended.* Vanhoozer makes a useful distinction between "letting the text have its *say*" and "letting the text have its *way*" (1998: 374–76). In the initial stage of interpretation, when trust and goodwill are primary, the reader must let the text have its say. In the latter stage, before letting the text have its way, a hermeneutics of suspicion critiques the text for any harmful ideology.

Thus both goodwill and suspicion are needed in the full task of herme-neutics. So Ricoeur wrote: "Hermeneutics seems to me to be animated by the double motivation: willingness to suspect, willingness to listen; vow of rigor, vow of obedience" (1970: 27). The combination of trust and suspicion is needed since, in addition to having respective merits, both dispositions have respective liabilities. The danger inherent in the hermeneutics of trust is naïveté about human fallenness; the danger inherent in the hermeneutics of suspicion is cynicism and contempt.

Even in the suspicion phase, however, trust is not excluded. Since the Scrip-tures have served the church over two millennia and have fundamentally shaped its faith and practice, our default posture throughout the hermeneutical task should be trust. Suspicion operates better as a radar than a rototiller, alerting the interpreter to the presence of a detrimental agenda more so than churning through the text in a deconstructive fashion. Suspicion guides the reader in identifying and, if possible, rehabilitating problematic texts. This immediately raises a key question: By what criteria does a text's meaning become problem-atic? My personal experience? The experience of the oppressed? Some broad overarching principle? This is one of the most important questions in biblical interpretation, but it awaits a later section of the book.

Must Exegesis Be Done in the Original Languages?

The original language of the New Testament was not English, despite the quip about the devout old-timer who said, "If the King James Version was good enough for Paul, it's good enough for me!" The New Testament's language is a specimen of Koine (*Koinē*) Greek, the common dialect of the period fol-lowing the conquests of Alexander the Great. A working knowledge of New Testament Greek is without question an advantage in the task of interpretation.

Yet this advantage should not be exaggerated. History is replete with persons who knew only vernacular translations and were used by God in powerful and effective ways. The ability to work with biblical languages is, therefore, not the litmus test of a faithful ministry. Recently I read the following claim by a Christian apologist: "Divinely inspired is precisely what Scripture is, and hav-ing a direct, unmediated encounter with the very words of God himself is the promise held by learning the biblical languages" (Akin, 2004: 33). Though I am always sympathetic to an argument in favor of biblical languages, this statement tends in the direction of a dictation theory of inspiration. Moreover, it ignores the fact that even the original languages clothe the message of Scripture in human language, culture, and thought. We will have "a direct, unmediated encounter with the very words of God himself" when we meet God in heaven, not before. In the meantime, however, learning biblical languages does enable the interpreter to move one step closer to the words of the biblical authors and thus, in the providence of the self-revealing God, we trust that we are a step closer to the truths that God would have us know.

In essence the reason for studying the New Testament in Greek is that it yields all the benefits you derive from studying it in English, only much more so. Every aspect of understanding a literary text—semantics, rhetoric, allusions, idioms, metaphors, morphology, verbal aspect, syntax, discourse, and so forth—can be done with much greater precision, power, and proximity via the original language. A few tasks, such as establishing the text through textual criticism, can really *only* be done via the original. Christian teachers and preachers should want the closest possible contact with the thought of the biblical writers. Reading the Bible in translation is like kissing your sweetheart through Saran Wrap. It's better than nothing, but direct contact is always more exciting.

The benefits of original language study are numerous:

1. *The ability to evaluate English translations.* The welter of English translations can be confusing. The person trained in Greek is able to compare them to the original and evaluate their success in rendering the thought and language of the biblical authors.

2. *Semantic precision.* The old adage that "something gets lost in the translation" is true and well known to anyone who has struggled to render one language into another. Although the most recent, standard translations are generally the responsible work of trained scholars, they sometimes err and frequently are forced to choose one among various nuances of the original. Knowing Greek enables you to uncover the errors and to enter into and understand the debates.

3. *The discipline of textual criticism.* English translations sometimes have footnotes identifying variant readings based on different Greek manuscripts. Our smooth vernacular renditions depend on a critical Greek text, which is itself the product of immense labor: sifting manuscripts, judging different readings, applying criteria, and so forth. The production and transmission of books in antiquity knew nothing of the fixity of texts that modern printing makes possible. One can scarcely make sense of these issues and understand how textual decisions were made without some knowledge of Greek.

4. *The use of scholarly tools.* Although many dictionaries, encyclopedias, commentaries, and monographs are usable by persons who do not know

biblical languages, the greatest benefit is gained by persons who are able to follow linguistic discussions and are not intimidated by the occasional excerpt in Greek or Hebrew. The more technical tools—Greek lexicons, theological dictionaries, grammars, Greek concordances, and so forth—require at least a working knowledge of the original language.

5. *The general benefit of attention to language.* It is a common experience among students that, in the course of their Greek study, they learn English. Nowadays students of the New Testament are often many years beyond their formal study of English grammar. They may begin Greek study while being a little fuzzy on predicate nominatives, the subjunctive mood, or even the basic parts of speech. Work in any language, particularly a highly inflected ancient language, forces one to recall the basic structures of language and the alternative ways of expression.

6. *The general benefit of slowing down.* Well-educated English readers breeze through most popular reading material (magazines, newspapers, fiction) with fluent ease. We can do the same with biblical narratives if we want to catch a quick overview, but if our purpose is careful study with a view to teaching or proclamation, then a slower, methodical pace is more appropriate. Working with the original languages guarantees this. We ponder sentence structure, word meanings, images, and phrases. Our attention is heightened, and our observations are more detailed. We see things in Greek that we do not see in English.

7. *Hearing the revelatory Word.* Finally, as the gestalt principle would assert, the whole of these benefits is greater than the sum of their parts. The result of a regular discipline of working with the original languages of the Bible is a heightened ability to hear in them the Word of God. God is revealed supremely in Jesus Christ, the incarnate Word, as well as through Scripture, the written Word. As human flesh constituted the earthly Jesus, so human language constitutes Scripture. Martin Luther recognized the biblical languages as a means to this lofty end: "The languages are the sheath in which this sword of the Spirit [Eph. 6:17] is contained; they are the casket in which this jewel is enshrined; they are the vessel in which this wine is held; they are the larder in which this food is stored; and, as the gospel itself points out [Matt. 14:20], they are the baskets in which are kept these loaves and fishes and fragments" (1962: 360).

In our culture generally and in education particularly, the trend of the last few decades has been pragmatic and utilitarian. We eschew learning that we deem to be for learning's sake only. We prefer to invest time in things that have an immediate and apparent payoff. The division of the theological curriculum into "practical" disciplines and "classical" or "historical" disciplines has the unfortunate effect of implying that the latter are impractical. This implication is false, however, since rigorous study of the Bible, including study of its original languages, has great potential to enrich both the content and the dynamics of one's interpretation and to transform the interpreter.

The amount of emphasis given to biblical languages in theological education varies widely among Christian denominations. Lutherans, Presbyterians, and some evangelical denominations often require a full course in Hebrew and/ or Greek. Among Catholics, Episcopalians, Methodists, and others, biblical language study is usually optional. Given that range of variation, the present book will employ Greek in transliteration in the hope that it will be usable both by persons with Greek language skill and by those without it, and in the hope that some of those without it might be moved to acquire it.

Exegetes have an impressive array of language tools on which to draw nowadays. In addition to the traditional hardcopy lexicons, grammars, parsing guides, and so forth, there are now several software programs with Hebrew and Greek texts, a wealth of translations, automatic identification of forms, and lexical assistance at the click of a mouse. These tools have made textual analysis much easier, and given that fact, there is no reason why serious interpreters of the New Testament should not have at least a lexical knowledge of Greek. The ability to read, translate, and do original exegesis of the Greek text is the ideal, but lacking that, the various computer tools available today enable the novice to make more intelligent use of the scholarly literature.

A Preview of the Method in This Book

An overview of the method presented in this book appears on page xlvii in the diagram titled "A Model for Biblical Interpretation." No one can propose such a model without being deeply indebted to others: former professors, colleagues, and scholars in the areas of hermeneutical theory, practice, and pedagogy. What follows is no exception. In particular I must acknowledge a debt to Robert A. Traina's *Methodical Bible Study* (2002), first published in 1952 and a classic in inductive Bible study method. Though the model presented here adapts, modifies, and supplements Traina, my indebtedness, especially in terminology, will be apparent to anyone familiar with that volume. The structure of the model is fourfold. In a sense the model moves in a circle, from the present time of the modern reader to the past of the ancient text, and eventually back to the modern reader's context. The four stages are as follows:

1. *Analyzing and preparing the interpreter.* The place to begin the interpretive process is with interpreters themselves. Although theorists will continue to debate just how large the role of the reader is and should be in interpretation, few would deny that the identity of the reader has an influence. We all read from some "place," and keen self-awareness about one's own location can enhance the process of reading, making one alert to one's own biases and sensitivities. Among the many things that one could reflect upon are one's social location, theological identity, and life experiences. Self-reflection will

lead to better engagement with the text, and this is especially true when the text involved is one that contributes to the reader's self-understanding.

2. *Analyzing the text (exegesis)*. In this second stage we turn to the text proper. Regardless of the identity of the reader, the text still presents us with hard data. The text has an objective quality, even though our observation and analysis of it necessarily occur through our own subjectivity. In this stage several discrete, analytical steps are involved. If interpretation is both a science and an art, this stage is the most scientific. Textual analysis involves a cyclical process of observation and interrogation. The interpreter poses a question to the text and then through the observation of the text's content, structure, language, and so forth, tries to answer that question. This process often raises other questions, leading to further observation. The importance of detailed, astute observation and analysis of the text can hardly be overemphasized. From this process the interpreter synthesizes an interpretation or explication of the text. At this stage the chief focus is historical: seeking the meaning intended by the biblical author and conveyed by the words. This is not the end of interpretation, at least for confessional readers, but it is an extremely important mediate stage. Before one moves to evaluating and contemporizing the text, the biblical author/text should be understood as fairly and objectively as possible (acknowledging the impossibility of doing this perfectly).

3. *Evaluating and contemporizing the text (hermeneutics)*. The third stage is distinguished from exegesis not so much by differentiating "what the text *meant*" from "what the text *means*" (cf. Stendahl, 1962: 419–20), but rather by taking the textual meaning and simply asking, What does the contemporary Christian community do with this? How do we receive the meaning of the text? *Can* we receive it? What is its significance for us in the twenty-first century? Needless to say, this hermeneutical stage is one of the most crucial in the interpretive process. Sharp disagreements between Christians nowadays, especially on divisive matters of ethics and public policy, often hinge on how one adjudicates the results of the exegetical phase. At this point, other criteria are brought in, what one might call "hermeneutical adjuncts." For although the Bible is an authoritative source for the faith and practice of Christians, its authority does not operate in a vacuum. If it did do so, we could adopt the Reformation motto *sola scriptura* in the most absolute sense and largely do away with this third step. But in fact, nearly all Christian traditions employ one or more additional criteria such as tradition, reason, and experience. A more realistic motto, then, would be *prima scriptura*: Scripture as the primary authority, but in conjunction with and mediated by other authorities. Both revelation and reason are gifts from God; indeed, they are interrelated gifts, since one cannot grasp a written, historical revelation without the use of reason. From this stage a contemporary interpretation of the text emerges.

4. *Appropriating the text and transforming the community*. In confessional contexts the ultimate goal of biblical study is the transformation of the

readers, their faith communities, and the world in which they live. Appropriation involves responding faithfully to the interpreted word. In appropriating Scripture, we make it our own. We follow its mandate; we heed its guidance; we reshape our lives in its light. All of this assumes that the previous stages have been carried out judiciously. If confessional readers are diligent in their study, are led by the Holy Spirit, and respond with a faithful performance of Scripture, then the results of their interpretation will tend toward the fulfillment of Jesus's prayer that "God's will may be done, on earth as it is in heaven" (cf. Matt. 6:9–10).

Finally, it must be acknowledged that the structure of the method presented here is somewhat heuristic. By that I mean that the precise sequence of the four steps in the overall method or of the dozen steps in the exegetical section (chapter 2) is useful as an aid to learning even if artificial in some respects. Experienced interpreters may skip steps, recognizing almost intuitively that some steps are irrelevant to certain texts or certain inquiries. Such experts may perform steps out of the order given in this book. Particularly vis-à-vis the overall method, one could argue that the separation of historical exegesis and contemporary hermeneutics into discrete stages is artificial. This is a valid cautionary note. As Brevard Childs observes, "Proper interpretation does not consist of an initial stance of seeking a purely objective or neutral reading to which the element of faith is added subsequently, but rather, from the start, the Christian reader receives a particular point of standing from which to identify with the apostolic faith in awaiting a fresh word from God through the Spirit" (1995: 10). The real-life praxis of biblical interpretation is more dynamic than a static, four-stage method implies. Nevertheless I argue that (1) there is a basic logic to most parts of the sequence; (2) the presentation of the method in a book is by necessity sequential, even if the actual implementation of the method may be more fluid; and (3) beginning interpreters in particular do well to ground themselves in an orderly method.

Discussion Questions

1. Consider the following modern example of a contested meaning. Martin Luther King Jr.'s famous "I Have a Dream" speech (1963) referred to King's longing for a day when people would "be judged not by the color of their skin but by the content of their character." In mid-1997 these words from Dr. King were cited by several politicians and litigants who were involved in legal battles over employment and college admissions issues to argue that affirmative action violated the ideal of a color-blind society. Others protested that King's words were being taken out of the context of his speech and life, that he would have supported affirmative action, and that this line was an extemporary comment, not part of

his manuscript. Was this use of Dr. King's words valid? If it was *not* in accord with his intention, was it a misinterpretation? Is the distinction between meaning/intention and significance/effect/application helpful here?

2. The Declaration of Independence contains the words: "We hold these truths to be self-evident, that all men are created equal." Since these words were written in 1776, what was originally meant by the final words: "All *men* are created equal"? If today we construe "men" generically to include men *and women* of all races, ethnicities, and socioeconomic levels, have we violated the intent of the original authors?

For Further Reading

Many books, essays, and articles have been cited in the parenthetical notes in this chapter. In addition to those resources, one may turn to a variety of reference works containing articles on the issues that have been raised. Here I can only mention a few of these.

The New Jerome Biblical Commentary (Brown, Fitzmyer, and Murphy, 1990) has major essays titled "Hermeneutics" and "Inspiration."

The Dictionary of Biblical Interpretation (Hayes, 1999) has the brief entries "Eisegesis," "Exegesis," "Hermeneutics," and "Meaning," as well as entries on a variety of interpretive methods.

The massive *Anchor Bible Dictionary* (Freedman, 1992) has lengthy articles titled "Biblical Criticism," "Exegesis," "Hermeneutics," "History of Interpretation," "Scriptural Authority," and "Word of God."

The assortment of technical vocabulary in biblical interpretation can be intimidating to the beginner. Helpful dictionaries include Coggins and Houlden (1990), Hayes (1999), and especially Tate (2006). For terminology related to general literary criticism, Macey (2000) is helpful. Finally, the *Dictionary for Theological Interpretation of the Bible* (Vanhoozer, 2005) is an exceptionally rich resource for confessional interpreters. It has entries titled "Exegesis," "Hermeneutics," "Meaning," "Objectivity," and entries on a wide variety of interpretive methods, movements, and individuals.

A Model for Biblical Interpretation

1	2	3	4
Self Awareness	**Exegesis**	**Hermeneutics**	**Application**
Analyzing and preparing the interpreter	Analyzing the text	Evaluating and contemporizing the text	Appropriating the text and transforming the community

Reflect on the social location, theological identity, and life experiences of the interpreter

Observation
⇧ **Text of Scripture** ⇩
Interrogation

Synthesis →

The meaning intended by the author and conveyed by the text

Correlation
⇧ **Truth of Scripture** ⇩
Evaluation

Synthesis →

The truth revealed by God through the human author

Responding to Scripture as God's Word for faith and practice

1. Survey
2. Limits of the passage
3. Original wording
4. Genre, form, and function
5. Context and structure
6. Language
7. Grammar
8. Textual connections
9. Backgrounds
10. Theology
11. Commentaries
12. Synthesis

1. Scripture
2. Tradition
3. Reason
4. Experience?

1

Analyzing and Preparing the Interpreter

A university professor wanted to illustrate the dangers of alcoholism to her science students. She set two petri dishes on the table before the class, one filled with water, the other with alcohol. She put an earthworm in the water, and within a few seconds it had wriggled out of the dish. She put a second worm in the alcohol, and it died almost instantly. Looking up at the class, the professor queried, "What do you learn from this experiment?" A hungover student in the back of the class raised his hand and said, "If you drink enough alcohol, you'll never have worms." The moral of the story? Interpretation may be influenced by the interpreter's identity; or perhaps in this case, interpretation may be *under the influence* of the interpreter's identity.

Literary critic Frank Kermode offers the startling judgment that "all interpretation proceeds from prejudice, and without prejudice there can be no interpretation" (1979: 68). Perhaps this is just the commonplace, postmodern denial of objectivity that we have seen before, now in starker dress. Kermode's basic point is similar to the oft-heard claim, "All knowledge is perspectival." There is a truth here, although Kermode's formulation of it is blunt and one-sided. Over against this pessimistic assessment, one needs to place James Barr's remark cited earlier that while complete objectivity is not attainable, a high degree of it is, and a high degree is much better than a low degree (1980: 24). If interpretation dissolves into nothing more than prejudice and opinion, then communication is thwarted, and the rationale for engaging in critical and methodical biblical study is undermined.

The partial and provisional character of our interpretations does not mean there is no truth "there in the text" to be disclosed, and it certainly does not constitute a denial of absolute truth. If God exists and is truth, then there is absolute truth. Human perceptions of truth may be partial and provisional (R. Brown, 1981: 4n8), but there is a huge difference between imperfect perceptions of absolute truth and a world void of absolute truth. The fact that all interpreters read from a certain location does not mean that we should despair of meaningful interpretation; nor does it mean that all interpretations are equally prejudiced and therefore equally valid (or invalid). It simply means that we must analyze the interpreter as well as the text.

Analyzing the Interpreter

Analyzing the interpreter refers to self-reflection leading to a better awareness of one's identity and perspective. Subjectivity is not inherently friend or foe. A person's social location can be a blind spot or a magnifying glass: it may obscure one's reading of the text or enhance it. The aim, then, is neither to repress one's subjectivity nor to revel in it, but to understand it, be aware of its effects on interpretation, and exercise it responsibly.

Several dimensions or domains of reflection could be relevant to the reader's self-understanding vis-à-vis the act of interpretation. Some aspects of a reader's identity pertain to group identity and have a taxonomic, check-the-box quality to them; others are highly individualistic. This reflects the obvious fact that one's identity is a function of both personal characteristics and the groups to which one belongs. Cultural critics nowadays sometimes speak of "identity politics," the idea that one's views are a function of one's group, especially one's socioeconomic group, race, ethnicity, gender, and so forth. This is true, but only to a degree. The same critics often point out that although members of such groups may display certain trends, they seldom walk in lockstep with one another. African-Americans, for example, do not all hold the same political views, and the diversity within that group should be respected. In a similar fashion, we must recognize the limitations of "identity hermeneutics." One's social location influences one's interpretation of Scripture, but not in a coercive or comprehensive fashion. It is quite possible for two white, married, college-educated, middle-class, middle-aged, heterosexual American men to have very different perspectives on biblical interpretation. In what follows, I hope that the combination of taxonomic categories and individual commitments and experiences will provide a sufficiently broad base for analyzing the interpreter.

The following three areas gather up the most important aspects of self-analysis: (1) *Social location*. By this I mean the basic categories of the interpreter's social identity, the sort of information that might be asked for on a census or application form. Such factors would include one's age, gender, race, ethnicity, socioeconomic background, educational level, and so forth. In recent years sexual orientation has also come to be seen as an important aspect of social location. (2) *Theological identity*. Given the obvious and pervasive religious content of biblical literature, one's religious identity can clearly have an impact on interpretation. Issues involved here would include one's broad orientation toward religion (Jewish, Christian, Muslim, secularist, agnostic, and so on), one's specific religious community (e.g., a denominational heritage), the specific tenets of one's faith and practice, and any particular or especially distinctive religious convictions and commitments. (3) *Life experiences*. Whereas most of the factors already mentioned are group characteristics, this last area involves more personal and individual characteristics. Here one could consider childhood experiences (either pleasant or traumatic), career experiences, relationships, health issues, cultural phenomena, marriage/divorce, childrearing, and so forth.

To illustrate the possible influence of the reader's identity, it may be helpful to consider some actual examples of how these factors have influenced interpretation.

Social Location

Romans 16:7 offers an example of the way gender can influence interpretation, in this case with distorting results. In verses 1–15 Paul greets friends and coworkers, among whom are several women: Phoebe, Prisca, Mary, Tryphaena and Tryphosa, the mother of Rufus, Julia, and the sister of Nereus. The New Revised Standard Version (NRSV) translates 16:7, "Greet Andronicus and Junia . . . ; they are prominent among the apostles." The name "Junia" denotes a woman. But a superscript letter in the NRSV refers the reader to a note that says, "Or *Junias*; other ancient authorities read *Julia*." The 1984 New International Version (NIV), in contrast, translates, "Greet Andronicus and Junias," construing both names as those of men, with no explanatory note attached. Can the original Greek be so ambiguous that translators are unsure of what the name is and whether it denotes a man or a woman?

There is a minor textual question concerning what Paul originally wrote. Among the many Greek manuscripts that lie behind Romans 16:7, only two have the name "Julia." Textual scholars rightly regard this as meager support and dismiss this reading as secondary. So the choice is between "Junia" and "Junias" because, some scholars say, depending on the accent, the name might be masculine, a shortened form of "Junianus." Are we then left with an unsolvable dilemma? Not at all, says New Testament textual critic Bruce Metzger, who notes that "the female Latin name Junia occurs more than 250 times in Greek and Latin inscriptions found in Rome alone, whereas the male name Junias is unattested." Second, Metzger points out that "when Greek manuscripts began to be accented, scribes wrote the feminine . . . ('Junia')" (1994: 475–76). What this means is that, although the earliest manuscripts of Romans had *no* accents and so were ambiguous, when accents began to be inserted, *every* extant witness construed the name as feminine.

Why then do so many modern translations of Romans 16:7 render the name "Junias"? It is hard to see any other reason than the translators' bias against the possibility that a woman could be an apostle, especially "prominent among the apostles." James Dunn's comment is apt: "The assumption that [the name] must be male is a striking indictment of male presumption regarding the character and structure of earliest Christianity" (1988b: 894). In this case the long tradition of biblical translation and interpretation by men who held skewed views of women's leadership has misrepresented both Paul's intention and the historical record. On Junia and Romans 16:7 one can now read the definitive treatment by Eldon J. Epp (2005).

Theological Identity

One's religious commitments obviously have the potential to influence interpretation, either by way of heightened alertness and perception or by way of distortion and resistance to textual meaning. Sometimes religious identity overlaps with racial/ethnic identity, as in the case of Jewish readers of Scripture. When Jews read the New Testament, they often have special sensitivities, both positive and negative, from which Christians could learn. Adele Reinhartz is a scholar of ancient Judaism and early Christianity, especially the Gospel of John, which speaks of "the Jews" pervasively and often negatively. "As a Jew," Reinhartz says, "the word 'Jews' jumps out at me in the Gospel of John" (1994: 562). Perceptive Christian readers notice this motif but would not likely feel the intensity and immediacy of its sting.

Among Christian interpreters, denominational affiliation can certainly exert an influence. The Catholic/Protestant distinction has sometimes been at the root of interpretive debates. In her commentary on the Gospel of John, Gail O'Day notes that John 6:51–58 has been variously interpreted as patently sacramental (alluding to the Eucharist) or as nonsacramental, often along denominational lines. The Catholic tradition, presumably more open to symbolic, especially liturgical, interpretations, sees a sacramental "fuller sense." Protestant interpreters, seeing John as a more spiritual or even existential Gospel, regard the sacramental view as contrary to the whole tenor of the Fourth Gospel. O'Day rightly observes that the debate tells us more about the interpreters than about John's Gospel. If our aim is to interpret the latter, we will seek the hard textual data, whether it coincides with our theological tradition or not (1995: 605–6).

A second example can be found in the meaning of the term "righteousness" in Matthew 5:6. Ulrich Luz notes that the two main possibilities are (1) righteousness as human acts of virtue, or (2) righteousness as the divine act of imputed, justifying grace (1989: 237). Again the debate falls largely along religious lines: (1) Catholics prefer the notion of sanctified behavior, and (2) Protestants argue for a more judicial concept of justification. In this case, Protestant interpreters may be guilty of reading Matthew through a Pauline lens.

Needless to say, a variety of other theological commitments may influence interpretation for good or ill. Pentecostal readers will be alert to the mention of the Spirit and charismatic gifts. Evangelical readers might be keen on texts having to do with discipleship, Christology, or eschatology. Pacifist Christians will not miss references to the nonviolent ethic of Jesus. In each of these cases, religious commitments may variously be assets or liabilities. Balanced and sound interpretations are more likely when conversation among interpreters crosses such boundaries.

Life Experiences

We interpret through what we live through. Life experiences, perhaps especially difficult and unpleasant experiences, imbue our perception and thinking like tinted glasses. Such lenses may be distorting, as in the case of rose-colored glasses, but this is not necessarily so. Tinted glasses sometimes sharpen one's vision by filtering out harmful elements. Mark Allan Powell notes that victims of spousal and child abuse will hear Jesus's teaching on nonretaliation differently from those of us who have never suffered physical violence. When the lector declares on a given Sunday morning, "If anyone strikes you on the right cheek, turn the other also" (Matt. 5:39), there will almost always be people present in the sanctuary who have recently been slapped or hit, and they "will hear the text with a poignancy you can scarcely imagine" (2001: 18).

The same scholar elsewhere relates a cross-cultural instance of the effect of life experience on one's reading of the story of the prodigal son (Luke 15:11–32). Using an exercise in which a person reads the story silently and then recounts it to someone else, Powell found that only 6 percent of American readers mentioned the famine that befell the land and contributed to the prodigal's destitution (15:14). In contrast, *all* of them (100 percent) recounted the prodigal's "squandering" of his property (15:13). Powell used the exercise again while on a sabbatical in Eastern Europe in 2001. He polled fifty residents of Saint Petersburg, Russia, and found that 84 percent mentioned the famine when recounting the story, but only 34 percent mentioned the squandering. Powell notes that in 1941 the army of Nazi Germany had besieged Saint Petersburg (Leningrad at that time) for about two and a half years, causing the death of 670 thousand people. The persons polled in the exercise were either survivors of the famine, their descendants, or immigrants who shared the collective memory. Presumably the American readers had never experienced a famine but were familiar with excessive, wasteful lifestyles! This does not mean that Russian readers would necessarily come up with an interpretation of the story of the prodigal son that was dramatically different from that of American readers, but it indicates that life experiences cause one to attend to the details of a text differently, and that can certainly influence interpretation (Powell, 2004: 265–68).

I offer one final example of a critical life experience that, while not tied specifically to biblical interpretation, illustrates the profound impact that experience can have on a person's religious outlook. Jesuit priest Michael Paul Gallagher tells the story of a meeting he had with a university student. While discussing a course assignment, the student aggressively blurted out, "I'm an atheist, you know." Gallagher didn't take up the gauntlet at that time, but a few days later he had another opportunity to talk with the student. Gallagher describes the tone as tense, as the student initiated the conversation:

> He started by announcing that there was something difficult he had to tell me about himself. He beat around the bush a little, then said, "I suffer from asthma." I thought this was an introduction to something bigger, but no: it was almost the whole story. Thank God I didn't laugh. Because asthma had ruined his childhood, had cut him off from a lot of life, and became something he was ashamed of, and deeply angry over. . . . I now assume that behind many an aggressive rejection ("I'm an atheist") there can live a softer reality of disappointment or hurt ("I suffer from asthma"). (1988: 39–40)

If a traumatic life experience can completely alienate a person from God, then such experiences can surely influence one's approach to and interpretation of Scripture. They may sensitize or desensitize a person to aspects of the text. They may create openness or resistance to the intended effect of the text. As Joel Green says, "Presuppositions enable our understanding, as well as disable it" (2007b: 24–25).

In the preceding discussion I have described ways that a reader's identity may *influence* interpretation, not *determine* it. If the reader's identity *determines* interpretation, then we necessarily have as many interpretations as we do readers, and we descend into the postmodern abyss of indeterminacy. Influences, on the other hand, may be welcomed or resisted, and judicious interpreters will try to discern when influences encourage attention to the text or distract from it. This point is made by Roger Kimball about literature in general:

> The idea that all reading is "ideological" has gained great currency in literary studies in recent years. Among other things, it implies that we are imprisoned by our point of view, that our language, our social or ethnic background, or our sex inescapably determine the way we understand things. But are we so imprisoned? Granted that such contingencies *influence* our point of view, do they finally determine it? (1998: 91)

Interpreters should strive, therefore, to be aware of both how their subjectivity may *hinder* faithful interpretation and how it may *enable* faithful interpretation. Social location, theological identity, and life experiences influence interpretation in diverse ways, sometimes blatantly, sometimes subtly, in manners that are sometimes predictable, but sometimes unexpected. Because of this, there is not necessarily any one privileged perspective from which to interpret Scripture. Some scholars speak of the "hermeneutical advantage" of the oppressed (Schneiders, 1991: 183), and there is reason for this. The marginalized are often able to see injustices to which others are blind, precisely because, as marginalized persons, they experience their effects. But the oppressed do not somehow escape subjectivity, and bias may afflict them as well.

There is no reason why white Euro-American male readers should produce inherently inferior interpretations of the biblical text, while minority ethnic, third-world, and feminist readers produce inherently superior ones. Social location is not bad for one group and good for another. The problem with white Euro-American male readers is not a uniquely disadvantageous social location but rather the fact that they have blind spots, and blind spots beset all readers. The best solution is not to demonize one group and to privilege another but to strive for diverse reading groups, whether in the academy or in faith communities, so that one reader's clearer vision will compensate for another's blind spot. This process of clarification works in all directions. Four people sitting in an automobile have different areas of sight and different blind spots. In a given situation any one of them might be able to correct the driver's deficient vision, or vice versa, based on an advantageous location. The key to enhanced understanding in biblical study is to read the Bible with people who are sitting elsewhere in the car. As Robert Wall has said, "I must try to listen to other interpreters, believing that true objectivity emerges out of a community of subjectivities" (Wall, 2002: 305; see also Green, 2007b: 66–79).

The Virtuous Reader

Self-awareness is perhaps the foremost quality to be cultivated among readers. Self-aware readers know their potential biases, are able to critique them, and are open to the critique of others, especially those who have significantly different social locations, theological identities, and life experiences. The integrity that readers need "consists not of having no presuppositions but of being aware of what one's presuppositions are and of the obligation to listen to and interact with those who have different ones" (Wright, 2005: 16). Vanhoozer identifies what he calls "interpretive virtues," each having to do with hearing and understanding the text's "enacted intention." He defines an interpretive virtue as "a disposition of the mind and heart that arises from the motivation for understanding, for cognitive contact with the meaning of the text" (1998: 376). Vanhoozer then lists the following four virtues: (1) *Honesty*. Honesty is "internal clarity," the acknowledgement of one's prior commitments, one's aims and interests. Thus Vanhoozer's first interpretive virtue is basically the same as what I have described in terms of self-awareness. Without honesty a reader is liable to act as a censor of the text, perhaps unwittingly. (2) *Openness*. The open reader allows the text to have its say, hearing its ideas without prejudice or ill will. Openness implies a willingness to change in accord with the text's intention. (3) *Attention*. The virtuous reader is observant, attending to the text and exercising patience, thoroughness, and care in reading. (4) *Obedience*. Finally, the virtuous reader follows the text's directions, not necessarily in terms of enactment, but at least in terms of reading. The obedient reader practices literary compliance, "reading history as history, apocalyptic as apocalyptic, and so on" (Vanhoozer, 1998: 377; see also Stylianopoulos, 1997: 85).

In addition to these virtues that would apply to almost any readers and any texts, I add a final virtue especially pertinent to reading Scripture in confessional contexts: piety. The pious reader hopes to encounter God in the text and be led by the Holy Spirit in discovering meaning and being transformed by it. It is unfortunate that the word "pious" sometimes carries disparaging nuances of hypocrisy or self-conscious religiosity. Needless to say, none of that is intended here. The pious reader is devoted to the God who inspired the text and is dutiful about fulfilling God's will as revealed through that text.

François Bovon, professor at Harvard Divinity School, is the author of a commentary on the Gospel of Luke in the prestigious Hermeneia series. In the preface of his first volume, he writes: "I wish to examine [Luke's] Gospel with the sober reserve of a scholar and with the confidence of a believer. For I hope in this manner to arrive at genuine understanding. I also realize that this becomes possible only if God leads me into his Word" (2002: xiii). In an online review of Bovon's commentary, Joel Green remarks, "This is itself a startling declaration in the preface to a contribution to a series that characterizes itself as 'critical and historical.' Where one would have anticipated assertions of scientific objectivity and scholarly neutrality, Bovon lays claim to his theological commitments and ecclesial location—not as hindrances to but as partners in the interpretive enterprise" (Green, 2003).

Bovon thus provides a good example of a virtuous reader: honest, open, attentive, obedient, and pious. Biblical interpretation in confessional contexts presupposes that Scripture is inspired by the Holy Spirit, even if the precise nature and effects of inspiration are variously understood. It is appropriate then to appeal to that same Spirit for guidance and illumination when the Scriptures are read in communities of faith.

Prayer

The most explicit way this appeal is made is through prayer. Indeed, some step-by-step plans for exegetical method include prayer as the first step. Although this is not a universal practice among Christian interpreters, it is nevertheless a salutary practice with a long history. Both medieval and Reformation interpreters put much emphasis on the reader's disposition when studying the

Bible. One needs to possess the proper frame of mind and spirit, pray dutifully, and seek the guidance of the Holy Spirit (Jasper, 2004: 46, 59). The sidebars below offer two sample prayers as examples of how one might begin the task of biblical interpretation and as a stimulus to the reader's own compositions.

Self-Awareness

A self-statement is a reflective exercise leading to increased self-awareness. When one has sufficient knowledge of oneself, coupled with sufficient human authenticity and a passion for God's truth, the Scriptures can mediate that truth in ways that transcend and transform one's experience, biases, and limitations.

There is danger in any self-revelation. The reaction of others to one's self-disclosure is never certain. You may find that not everything you learn about yourself is unqualifiedly encouraging. In addition, since one's self-statement changes with accumulating life-experiences, what one writes today may not be a fully accurate description of oneself tomorrow. Self-reflection is necessarily an ongoing process and one that may involve risk.

Since both interpretive acts (reading Scripture) and communicative acts (writing a book) involve situated agents, the reader may wish to know where I am situated. At the outset of her book on hermeneutics, Sandra Schneiders offers a brief account of her own intellectual and spiritual journey in order to "dispel that illusion of anonymous, objectively authoritative, and disinterested scholarship that written texts in general, and academic ones in particular, seem to generate" (1991: 4). It is, indeed, an illusion that a printed text represents a transcendent, disembodied voice of objective authority. Human beings, not heavenly voices,

A Prayer before Studying the Scriptures
(N. Clayton Croy)

God of truth and revelation,
> In many and various ways you spoke through the prophets in the past.
> Now you have revealed yourself supremely through your Son, Jesus.
> And through the Holy Spirit you recall to our minds and refresh what Jesus taught.
> We give thanks for your faithful servants who, under the inspiration of your Spirit, told stories, handed down laws, preserved prophetic utterances and sayings of the wise, recorded the words and deeds of our Lord and of his followers, exhorted the faithful, rebuked the wayward, and envisioned your ultimate victory.
> Reveal to us your truth through the sacred text. Grant that our eyes may carefully perceive, that our minds may soundly analyze, and that our lives may be joyously transformed by your living and active Word.
> Through the cleansing, empowering, and instruction of your written Word, make us better disciples of Jesus Christ, the incarnate Word, in whose name we pray. Amen.

A Prayer before Study
(St. Thomas Aquinas)

Creator ineffable, you who are in truth the fountain of light and wisdom, deign to shed upon the darkness of my understanding the rays of your infinite brightness, and remove far from me the twofold darkness in which I was born, namely, sin and ignorance. You, who give speech to the tongues of little children, instruct my tongue and pour into my lips the grace of your benediction. Give me keenness of apprehension, capacity for remembering, method and ease in learning, insight in interpretation, and copious eloquence in speech. Instruct my beginning, direct my progress, and set your seal upon the finished work, you who are truly God and truly human, who live and reign, world without end. Amen. (adapted from Christopher and Spence, 1943: 579–80)

write books. So that the reader may be assured that this book does indeed come from a very specifically situated, this-worldly writer, and in order to offer an example and stimulus, I offer my own self-statement (see the sidebar below). By reflecting on and taking ownership of my own social location, presuppositions, interests, and biases, I will practice what I have preached in the previous pages.

THE AUTHOR'S SELF-STATEMENT

Social location. I am a white, middle-aged, middle-class, heterosexual male. As such I may be less sensitive to narratives and images in Scripture that women, members of other racial groups, or gay persons might find offensive. Nevertheless, my professional training and experiences in faith communities tend to counter these influences. Although my family has never been wealthy by Western standards, I have never experienced poverty or suffered the lack of basic human needs. This makes me less aware of both the dimensions and causes of poverty, but again, education and experience can compensate for this. As a theological educator, I have many years of education and have earned a typical array of degrees for people in my profession. This training has obviously sharpened certain analytical skills. It has also alerted me to historical and cultural issues in biblical interpretation of which I was unaware as a youth. My upbringing was in a small town in Northern California, including some rural (farm) experience, but in recent years I have lived in large metropolitan cities of the South and Midwest.

Theological identity. I am a Wesleyan Christian. This makes me more attentive to themes in Scripture that my faith tradition emphasizes: social concerns, sanctification, the Holy Spirit, evangelism, ecumenism, and so forth. My upbringing and early faith experience were in an evangelical congregation of the United Methodist Church. As a result, I have a high regard for Scripture as revelatory of God and authoritative for faith and practice. On the other hand, my more recent faith experience has included many years in pluralistic settings, making me aware of the broad and diverse activity of God's Spirit in the world. Words like "inerrant" and "infallible" have never been of great importance to my understanding of Scripture. Although I believe that the Bible truthfully reveals the way of salvation and is an authoritative guide for the Christian life, my faith is not undermined by minor discrepancies or errors in historical and literary matters. Even for theological and moral issues, I believe the Bible must be studied critically and in its canonical and ecclesial contexts.

Life experiences. I was raised in a Christian home and a very functional family. Having loving, supportive parents made it easy for me to embrace the Christian faith, including the metaphor of God as Father. I had a conversion experience at age 11 and grew significantly as a Christian in my teen and early adult years. I attended college and seminary at evangelical institutions and became interested in theological education, especially Greek and New Testament studies. I have been married since 1977, but my wife and I do not have children. We have two cats, and I sometimes think of my relationship to them as loosely analogous to God's relationship to me. My current professional setting in a mainline Protestant seminary requires me to be sensitive to a wide variety of issues. I am grateful to have good health, good relationships with family, supportive colleagues and friends, and meaningful employment.

Exercises

1. Write a self-statement of about five hundred words describing who you are as an interpreter of Scripture. Give attention to at least three areas: social location (age, gender, ethnicity, sexual orientation, socio-economic background, educational background, urban versus rural, and so on), theological identity (denominational heritage, faith and practice, specific religious convictions and commitments), and life experiences (childhood experiences, career experiences, relationships, health issues, cultural phenomena, marriage/divorce, child rearing, and so on). For a more detailed description of such an exercise with a total of eighteen categories of questions, see Norman Gottwald's "Self-Inventory," which has been used at New York Theological Seminary (1995). On the general topic of the interpreter's self-reflection, see Robbins (1996a: 96–100).

2. Read an essay on biblical interpretation from a particular ethnic/social location other than your own. Summarize the essay and reflect on the ways that the perspective is similar to or differs from your own. Such essays can be found in the following sources:
   - In volume 1 of *The New Interpreter's Bible* (Keck, 1994), read the introductory essay, "Reading the Bible from Particular Social Loca-tions" (150–53) and one of the following essays: "Reading the Bible as African Americans" (154–60), "Reading the Bible as Asian Ameri-cans" (161–66), "Reading the Bible as Hispanic Americans" (167–73), "Reading the Bible as Native Americans" (174–80), or "Reading the Bible as Women" (181–87).

- In the *Dictionary for Theological Interpretation of the Bible* (Vanhoozer, 2005), read one of the following essays: "African Biblical Interpretation" (31–34), "Asian Biblical Interpretation" (68–71), or "Feminist Biblical Interpretation" (228–30).
3. Read an essay on biblical interpretation from a particular Christian perspective or historical era other than your own. Summarize the essay and reflect on the ways that the perspective is similar to or differs from your own. Such essays can be found in the following source:
   - In the *Dictionary for Theological Interpretation of the Bible* (Vanhoozer, 2005), read one of the following essays: "Catholic Biblical Interpretation" (102–6), "Charismatic Biblical Interpretation" (106–9), "Liberal Biblical Interpretation" (453–54), "Medieval Biblical Interpretation" (499–503), "Orthodox Biblical Interpretation" (554–58), "Patristic Biblical Interpretation" (566–71), or "Protestant Biblical Interpretation" (633–38).
4. Compose your own prayer to use when you begin to study Scripture, whether for teaching, proclamation, or personal enrichment.

Further Reading

Throughout this chapter I have referred to important literature in the parenthetical notes. These resources will provide a wealth of information on their respective topics. In addition, the articles listed in the above exercises provide brief but helpful synopses. Finally, there are a few volumes especially worthy of mention here. Fernando Segovia and Mary Ann Tolbert edited the two-volume set *Reading from This Place* (1995a, 1995b), which provides numerous examples of biblical interpretation from both Western and global perspectives. In a similar vein, Daniel Patte's *Global Bible Commentary* (2006) offers succinct treatments of every book of the Bible from varied perspectives. Uniquely structured and illuminating is *Return to Babel: Global Perspectives on the Bible*, edited by John R. Levison and Priscilla Pope-Levison (2004). This volume selects ten biblical texts, five from each Testament, and gathers brief essays on each text from Latin American, African, and Asian perspectives. A similar threefold arrangement, but within the American academic guild, can be found in *They Were All Together in One Place? Toward Minority Biblical Criticism*, edited by Randall C. Bailey, Tat-siong Benny Liew, and Fernando F. Segovia (2009). Randall Bailey's *Yet with a Steady Beat* offers a collection of essays on contemporary African-American biblical interpretation (2003), as does Cain Hope Felder's *Stony the Road We Trod* (1991). Feminist biblical interpretation constitutes a vast and growing body of literature. Two helpful entry points are *The Women's Bible Commentary* (Newsom and Ringe, 1998) and *The IVP Women's Bible Commentary* (Kroeger and M. Evans, 2002).

2

Analyzing the Text

When readers discipline themselves by self-reflection, cultivate the virtues of reading, and pray for the enlightenment of the Holy Spirit, they prepare themselves spiritually and intellectually for the task of biblical interpretation. The best internal preparation must be complemented, however, by a sound methodology. A certain amount of technical expertise, knowledge of principles, and access to resources is essential for thorough and methodical interpretation.

An essential part of interpretation is interrogation. There is significant agreement on this point among experts: "Biblical interpretation is the art of asking questions of texts" (Koester, 2001: 19). "Interpretation is an effort to meet questions that have arisen about a text. The questions that interpretation . . . seeks to answer are specifications of the general query, 'what does the text mean?'" (Meyer, 1989: 41) "The interpretive project begins with the proper formulation of the questions one wishes to ask of the text and the selection, from the repertoire of methods, of those that are useful for eliciting from the text the material for answering those questions" (Schneiders, 1991: 152).

James Dunn helpfully refines this basic point, however, by suggesting that a more complete model for biblical interpretation is dialogue rather than simply interrogation (2003b: 124). Both the interpreter and the text must be allowed to have their say. Granted, the text does not engage in dialogue the same way a friend sitting across the table from you does. But neither is the text entirely under the control of the interpreter, allowed only to answer questions that have been posed to it. The text is not like a hostile witness in a courtroom whose speech is limited to terse replies to the district attorney's questions. The text testifies freely, often in narrative form, sometimes answering our questions directly, but more often reflecting on matters in its own terms. Thus dialogue is even more apt as an image than interrogation.

How then do we generate suitable questions for the text? In accordance with Dunn's dialogue model, there must be reciprocity, a give and take with the text. Interrogation alternates with observation and creates a cycle of interpretation. One observes the textual data, their content, form, and structure, and formulates questions about their meaning and significance. One answers the questions by returning to observation, which in turn may raise more questions. The cycle is by no means a vicious one, however. Done properly it leads one deeper into the text.

Some questions arise immediately, almost spontaneously. Certain words or allusions are puzzling. Metaphors and intertextual references perplex you. Persons, places, or institutions are mentioned about which you lack knowledge. But other questions only result from more painstaking observation. How has the author used this word before? How does this passage fit into the work as a whole? What is the interrelationship of the constituent parts of this paragraph?

The observation/interrogation cycle will sometimes reach a dead end, occasionally because the question posed is inappropriate, other times because the text, like some human dialogue partners, just is not forthcoming. It is important, then, to know what kinds of questions are most beneficial. Literary scholar Wayne C. Booth distinguishes three types of questions that readers may pose: "those that the [text] seems to *invite* me to ask; those that it will *tolerate* or respond to, even though perhaps reluctantly; and those that *violate* its own interests" (1988: 90). Biblical examples of these types may be helpful here. The book of Jonah *invites* questions about the attitudes that God's people should hold toward their enemies; it *tolerates* questions about whether the book's genre should be understood as history, fable, or satire; and it is *violated* by questions about the genus and species of the sea creature that swallowed Jonah.

One might think that this tripartite division is rank ordered, such that questions that *violate* the text are to be avoided. This is often the case, but one should not overlook the need for the third type of question. As a general rule, interpreters should try to formulate questions of the first type, and sometimes the second, during the *interpretive* phase, when the primary goal is hearing the text on its own terms. However, during the *evaluative* or critical phase, questions of the third type may be very important. For example, in evaluating a text that calls for women to be silent in church (1 Cor. 14:33–35; 1 Tim. 2:11–15), one ought to pose such questions as, "Is this a mandate for the church today?" "Does this reflect God's will?" Such questions "violate" the text because they question the text's implicit assumptions. The texts just cited surely intend to communicate that their injunctions *should* be followed, that they *do* reflect God's will. But the full hermeneutical task is larger than the recovery of the historical meaning of a given text; it must include the evaluation of that meaning and its correlation with other passages within the canon of Scripture. Questions that violate the text, therefore, come into play especially when dealing with problematic passages. (Note: Yet perhaps some "violating" questions should be avoided since they neither address the text's historical intention nor are relevant to the evaluation of the text. The third example with Jonah above would be of this type.)

Observation is the process whereby the text is allowed to speak, to have its part in the dialogue. Observation obviously entails reading, but it is more than simply vocalizing the text. It is reading attentively, perceptively, and inquisitively (the last adverb anticipates the movement toward interrogation). Good observation is a skill to be honed. It goes beyond simple physical sight to include perception. You have observed something, not when its image forms on your retinas, but when its meaning and significance form in your mind.

Precision in observation is essential. A story is told about William Osler (1849–1919), an eminent Canadian physician, who was one of the great icons of modern medicine. Osler was especially known for his ability to diagnose diseases by means of precise observation. Wishing to impress upon a group of medical students the importance of such exactitude, he performed a small test. He showed the students a small bottle containing a specimen for analysis and informed them that the patient's disease could be determined by a precise test. Osler would perform the test. The students would observe him and then duplicate the procedure. The physician opened the bottle, dipped a finger into the contents, and then stuck a finger into his mouth. He then passed the bottle around the room, asking the students to do as he had done and try to diagnose the disease. With reluctance the students did so until Osler again held the bottle. After a few ideas had been propounded by the students, Osler drove home the point: "Gentlemen, if you had observed me carefully, you would have noticed that I put my index finger into the bottle but my middle finger into my mouth" (Traina, 2002: 32–33).

Sound interpretation also requires persistent and painstaking observation. Quick and casual observation produces modest and superficial insights. Fuller understanding only comes with meticulous study. Louis Agassiz (1807–73), professor of zoology at Harvard University and founder of Harvard's Museum of Comparative Zoology, provides an instructive example. An oft-repeated story tells how Professor Agassiz would assign his beginning students the task of examining a specimen of a fish, a smelly dead specimen extracted from a jar of yellowish alcohol. Typically students would study the fish for ten minutes and assume that they had seen all that could be seen. But Agassiz required them to persist at the task for three days, and he forbade them to do anything but examine the fish and record their observations. It was a common experience that students discovered new and pertinent information as a result of pushing themselves beyond the early stages of boredom and the presumption of mastery. (See appendix 7 for the full story.)

Agassiz's students observed many things, such as size, color, texture, structure, shape, symmetry. The things to observe in the biblical text are likewise manifold: individual words, syntactical units, literary context and structure, intertextual references, and so forth. These will be treated in detail in the remainder of this chapter. Bear in mind again that observation and interrogation constitute a continuing cycle. As your skill in observing increases, you will find yourself attending to things that you had previously missed. These observations will raise questions that will, in turn, force you back into the text to find answers.

Do not be put off by the mechanical aspects of exegetical method. Mechanics are a necessary part of mastery (Traina, 2002: 18). Concert pianists practice finger drills; professional soloists sing scales; master chefs often use cookbooks. Expert interpreters use the standard tools and established techniques of their trade. Mechanics may become second nature at some point on the way to mastery, but there is no shortcut that ignores them.

1. Survey the Writing as a Whole

Literary critics speak of something called the "hermeneutical circle." This refers to the fact that the knowledge of a text as a whole should inform one's study of its parts, but the study of the parts in turn informs one's knowledge of the whole. The argument need not become circular but rather can be a reciprocal and mutually enriching process. It is, therefore, beneficial to survey a writing before attempting a detailed analysis of any given passage, examining the macrostructure first, before the microstructure. This bird's-eye view gives one the lay of the land, a panoramic view that precedes a slow hike through the territory. Several different exercises can accomplish this. I will discuss the following five: guided reading, reading multiple translations, summary and outline, charts, and pictographs.

Guided Reading

The simplest way to gain a sense of a literary work is to read it in its entirety, in one sitting if possible, so as to gather a unified impression. Such a reading is best done under the guidance of some general questions that help readers attend both to the work and to themselves. Ideally these questions will vary slightly from one writing to the next, but many of them are broadly applicable. Here is a list of questions that can be used to "catch the big picture" of Paul's Epistle to the Philippians.

1. Read through the epistle to get a sense of its contents, structure, and argument. Write down your general observations and questions.
2. Be aware of yourself as a reader. Which parts of the letter interest, irritate, or perplex you? Why? Do any parts seem to be digressive, obscure, or irrelevant? Why?

3. What seems to be the mood of the letter? Does the mood change at any point(s)?
4. What do we learn about Paul from the letter? What do we learn about the Philippians? About Paul's relationship with the Philippians? (Answer these questions from only the letter. Do not consult secondary sources.)
5. Where are the major divisions in the epistle? Is there a clear introduction? A conclusion? Are there any digressions? What are the major themes of the epistle? Are there any peculiar shifts in the theme? What terms or ideas occur repeatedly?

With modifications, this list of questions could be easily used with other books of the Bible. Narrative writings, in particular, would require additional questions attending to time, locale, characterization, description, plot, point of view, and so on. Thus the reader of a Gospel needs to pose and answer genre-specific questions.

Reading Multiple Translations

This strategy is probably most fruitful for shorter passages, but it can also be employed for entire works. Read the text in two or more translations, such as the New Revised Standard Version (NRSV) and Today's New International Version (TNIV). In addition to the basic questions in the above list, ask the following: Does one translation have a different feel from the other(s)? Are there any differences in the portrayal of characters or issues? (These may be subtle and difficult to detect at the level of the writing as a whole.) Does one translation smooth over rough spots, use less (or more) offensive language, or employ less (or more) technical terminology? How are especially perplexing or critical passages handled by the different translations?

Summary and Outline

This is a tried-and-true exercise for gaining an understanding of a literary work. Mortimer Adler discusses it in his modern classic *How to Read a Book* (Adler and Van Doren, 1972: 75–95). A summary is a statement of the book's unity in a sentence or, at most, a short paragraph. What is the book about? What is its theme or main point? Some critics would object that a literary work, especially a narrative work such as an epic, a novel, or a biography, simply cannot be reduced to a sentence or paragraph. The concern is well taken but not insurmountable. When briefly summarizing a book, we must bear in mind that a summary does indeed *reduce* it, not just in scope, but also in force. In addition, it changes the genre. A single sentence is obviously not equal to a lengthy narrative or even to a poem. A summary statement does not aim to reiterate in full but to recapitulate in the shortest possible compass.

An outline aims to express the work's complexity. It sets forth the major divisions of the book, its subdivisions, sections, and subpoints. An outline shows how these parts are related to one another and to the work as a whole. Normally an outline would contain at least three levels (I. II. III., A. B. C., 1. 2. 3.), though short works might be adequately outlined with two levels. The parts of an outline may be either phrases or complete sentences. Phrases have the advantage of brevity; sentences have the advantage of predication, the expression of complete thoughts. An outline should draw from the data of the book itself; it should be inductive and summarizing. It should analyze, in the sense of identifying component parts, rather than interpret, in the sense of explaining the work conceptually or theologically. Finally, avoid being too clever in composing an outline since this may result in a loss of the outline's clarity or its ability to evoke the contents of the writing.

An important caveat about outlining biblical books: remember that chapter and verse divisions are *not* the work of the biblical authors. The oldest system of chapter divisions is that of a fourth-century manuscript known as Codex Vaticanus (Metzger and Ehrman, 2005: 34). The modern verse divisions are later still; they are the work of the French publisher Robert Estienne (Stephanus). The fourth edition of his Greek New Testament, published in 1551, contains the first such divisions. Chapter-and-verse divisions are not only the work of later scribes and editors; they are also sometimes ill chosen. An oft-repeated story about Estienne was that he marked verse divisions while riding on horseback, and the more infelicitous divisions were due to uneven roads or the jarring gait of the horse (Metzger and Ehrman, 2005: 150). When outlining a biblical book, therefore, one should pay attention to chapter-and-verse divisions but not slavishly so, lest your outline owe more to a sixteenth-century Parisian pothole than to the natural divisions of the text.

By these two tasks the reader can grasp both the unity of the book (by a summary) and master its complexity (by an outline). The order of execution is not rigid, and in a given instance it may seem easier or more natural to compose the outline first. Here again we see the hermeneutical circle: the whole informs the parts, the parts inform the whole. If one composes the summary first and then the outline, one might wish to go back and tweak the summary in the light of the outline, or vice versa. It goes without saying that one person's summary or outline will differ from another's. This does not necessarily indicate that one of them is incorrect. There are different ways, often equally valid, of expressing the same thought. Moreover, the work being summarized may not be fully coherent, such that well-meaning and capable readers struggle to express its unity. But this does not mean that summarizing or outlining a work is a free-for-all without rules. As Adler says, "Though readers are different, the book is the same, and there can be an objective check upon the accuracy and fidelity of the statements anyone makes about it" (Adler and Van Doren, 1972: 83).

The biblical author may give you help in discerning the unity of the book. John's Gospel, for example, has an unmistakable statement of purpose (John 20:30–31). Similarly, many scholars see Romans 1:16–17 as Paul's statement of that epistle's theme. A book's structure is usually more subtle, but various literary techniques may provide clues: transitions, repetition, inclusions, sectional summaries, enumerations, parallel passages, and so forth. On rare occasions the work itself may offer an outline of its contents, such as the threefold division suggested by Acts 1:8. Again Adler advises: "Do not be too proud to accept the author's help if he proffers it, but do not rely too completely on what he says in the preface either. The best-laid plans of authors, like those of mice

An Outline of Paul's Epistle to the Philippians

I. Epistolary opening (1:1–2)
   A. Senders (1a)
   B. Recipients (1b)
   C. Standard Pauline greeting (2)
II. Thanksgiving (1:3–11)
   A. The Philippians' partnership and Paul's affection for them (3–8)
   B. Paul's prayer for the Philippians' love, knowledge, and purity (9–11)
III. Paul's circumstances (1:12–30)
   A. Positive results of Paul's imprisonment (12–14)
   B. Preachers with mixed motives (15–18a)
   C. Departing to be with Christ or remaining to be in ministry (18b–26)
   D. Paul and the Philippians: believing in and suffering for Christ (27–30)
IV. Giving oneself for others (2:1–3:1a)
   A. The supreme example of Christ's humble self-emptying (1–11)
   B. Philippians work out salvation; Paul is poured out as a libation (12–18)
   C. The example of Timothy's concern for others (19–24)
   D. The example of Epaphroditus's risking his life (2:25–3:1a)
V. Paul's personal example versus the Philippians' opponents (3:1b–4:1)
   A. Faith in Christ, not confidence in the flesh (3:1b–11)
   B. Pressing on toward the heavenly call (3:12–16)
   C. Enemies of the cross versus citizens of heaven (3:17–4:1)
VI. Specific and general exhortations; Paul's thanks for their gift (4:2–20)
   A. Specific exhortation to Euodia and Syntyche (2–3)
   B. General exhortations to joy, peace, and honorable contemplation (4–9)
   C. Paul's contentment, whether well fed or hungry (10–14)
   D. Paul's commendation for the Philippians' generosity (15–20)
VII. Epistolary closing (4:21–23)
   A. Greetings (21–22)
   B. Closing wish (23)

A Concise Summary of Paul's Epistle to the Philippians

Paul thanks the Philippians for their love and support and urges them to live humbly and in the interests of others, following the example of Christ, Paul's coworkers, Paul himself, and the prior generosity of the Philippians themselves.

and other men, often go awry" (Adler and Van Doren, 1972: 80). Paul, for example, appears to be wrapping up in 1 Thessalonians 4:1 ("Finally, brothers and sisters . . .") and then continues for forty-five more verses (cf. Phil. 3:1).

Examples of outlines are manifold and can be found in most study Bibles, commentaries, and reference works. The sidebars above give a sample outline and a sample summary statement.

Charts

Charts are similar to outlines in that they display contents and structure in summary fashion. They differ from outlines in their visual and graphic dimensions and are thereby able to trace multiple themes through the work simultaneously. Charts may be employed to survey entire books or sections thereof. The empty framework of a chart can be generated easily by using one of many computer programs (e.g., Microsoft Word tables). The chart can then be filled in by hand, or the work can be done entirely on computer. The specific features of a chart should be adapted to the particular book, but certain standard features are helpful in framing the project.

I recommend two standard features for whole-book charts. After a title of some sort at the top, the first horizontal row should enumerate the chapters of the book. So, for example, a chart of the Gospel of John will have twenty-one boxes across the top row; a chart of the Epistle to the Hebrews will have thirteen. These boxes in the top row will be used for chapter titles. (As mentioned above, chapter divisions are later, scribal decisions and are not intrinsic to the work. Nevertheless, they provide the only universally available means of navigating through a biblical book.)

Assigning titles to chapters is a simple exercise in reflecting on the contents of the writing. It is a descriptive exercise; at this point you are not trying to be analytical or interpretive. The aim is to compose a title that will succinctly evoke the contents of that particular chapter. Sometimes this is easy, as when the chapter is homogeneous or clearly thematic. John 9, for instance, is a tidy, self-contained narrative about the healing of a blind man and its aftermath. Hebrews 11 is a glorious catalog of Old Testament heroes and heroines of faith. The contents of such chapters are unified and relatively easy to title. Other times, when the chapter's contents are diverse or the chapter division is badly chosen, it will be a challenge to assign a title.

   The following guidelines should be helpful in creating chapter titles.
(1) Titles should be short, generally in the range of three to six words. If
too many words are used, the pithy quality of the title will be lost; if too few
words are used, specificity may be diminished. A good title often sounds like
a newspaper headline: it captures the gist of the chapter concisely. (2) Whenever possible, concrete and descriptive language is better than abstract and
interpretive language. Thus for John 9, "Blindness Cured in Man, Not Pharisees," is better than "Progressive Revelation Meets Existential Obtuseness."
Often the language of the title can be drawn directly from the text. (3) Most
important, a chapter title should evoke the contents of the chapter, that is,
it should help you recall the specific material of the chapter. A good test of a
chapter title is to read it to someone else who is also making a chart or who is
well acquainted with the biblical writing in question. That person should be
able to say, "Oh yes, that refers to chapter __." Otherwise, either your title is
failing in its evocative function, or your test person needs a refresher course.
(4) A final and relatively less important characteristic of a chapter title is
cleverness or humor. If the title meets the first three guidelines *and* is clever,
you have achieved the home run of chapter titles. For example, for John 3,
in which the Pharisee Nicodemus comes to Jesus at night, the title "Nick at
Night" commends itself to some readers. Alliteration or allusiveness can also
make titles more memorable. Cleverness can backfire, however, especially if
the significance of the title is too esoteric. In such cases they become meaningful to their writer and no one else. I once had a student who composed
thirteen chapter titles for the Epistle to the Hebrews around the theme of
football. This almost worked for the chapters that had some athletic imagery
(e.g., Heb. 12:1–3), but elsewhere the law of diminishing returns prevailed.
The cleverness quotient of the titles was off the charts, but their ability to
evoke the specific contents of the chapters (to anyone but the person who
conceived them) was minimal.
   The row of chapter titles serves as a rough index of the contents of the
writing. The second row should display the intrinsic structure of the writing. Here one should freely disregard chapter divisions if the natural organization of the material so dictates. Though the chapter-title row should have
vertical lines dividing that row into the appropriate number of chapters, the
structure row should begin as one long, skinny rectangle. Vertical lines are
drawn in the structure row at the natural divisions and subdivisions of the
text, whether they correspond to chapter divisions or not. For example, it is
universally recognized that John's Gospel has a prologue consisting of John
1:1–18. This is the first division even though it is only about one-third of
that chapter. Other sections in John will span more than one chapter, such as
the Farewell Discourse of chapters 14–16. The structure row can sometimes
be layered very effectively to show large blocks of material as well as their
smaller component parts.

The remaining rows of the chart will vary according to the writing being displayed. For narrative works, it may be useful to devote a row to geography or chronology. Thus, at a glance, a chart of John's Gospel will show that the action shifts back and forth from Galilee to Judea. As a general rule, these lower rows on the chart may highlight any themes, terms, or dynamics whose importance is indicated by their repetition in the writing. The most relevant criterion for selection is usually simple: frequency. If an idea occurs once or twice in the writing, it may not be worth charting, unless it can be grouped with related ideas. Something found a dozen times is almost certainly worth displaying. Hence, the mention of miraculous signs or references to Jesus's "hour" would be suitable categories in John. References to suffering would be a highly appropriate category in a chart of 1 Peter.

When charting the thematic rows, you should include both the verse reference and a few words of description (space permitting). This adds both usefulness and visual appeal. A chart with little more than verse numbers has a scant appearance and lacks information that could easily be included. Rather than mark instances of miraculous signs in John with nothing more than verse numbers, one ought to include a few words of description, such as "Water Turned to Wine (2:1–11)." In general, one should avoid two extremes: a chart that is so busy and overwhelmed with information that it is confusing, or a sketchy chart with little more than chapter-and-verse numbers.

Finally, since part of the appeal and value of a chart is its visual impact, the use of color, variation in fonts, or the insertion of small symbols is often helpful. Color helps distinguish groups of data, even within a single row. In a chart on the Gospel of John, references to "Son of Man" and "Son of God" can be combined in a single row if they are distinguished by color, font, or location (at the top or the bottom of the boxes). Computer symbols (e.g., Word's Wingdings) often include images that can be inserted at appropriate places. (Hearts, e.g., can be inserted at the points one encounters the theme of love in 1 John.) A chart that is visually effective and packed with accurate information is more than an exercise in learning; it is a useful tool that you will refer to again and again whenever that particular book is studied. (A sample chart of Mark's Gospel can be found in appendix 5.)

Pictographs

Persons with an artistic bent might want to experiment with pictographs, which are basically charts in which small, cartoonlike drawings do much of the work of verbal description. Artistic talent helps, but even stick figures add a creative, visual dimension. Persons who are resourceful with computer graphics might be able to find enough ready-made images to create a pictograph. (Sample pictographs of Philippians and 2 Corinthians can be found in appendixes 3–4.)

Exercises

Select either the Gospel of Mark or 1 Corinthians and survey the writing by using one of the above-described methods.

2. Determine the Limits of the Passage

Before beginning to analyze a specific text, one ought to reflect on and, if possible, justify the passage as a unit. In other words, we should consider what makes the text a cohesive entity. Is the beginning of the text a natural division? Is the ending an appropriate close to the unit? This is an especially important step when you use a text determined by a lectionary. Sometimes lectionaries establish the limits of a text by liturgical or theological criteria as much as literary criteria. For example, a protracted narrative that has an inviolable literary integrity will, nevertheless, often be sliced into portions of suitable size to be read in worship. Similarly, verses are sometimes omitted to avoid digressions, shifts in tone, or offensive content. How often have the plaintive words of the Psalm 137 been read ("By the rivers of Babylon—there we sat down and there we wept when we remembered Zion") minus the concluding verse ("Happy shall they be who take your little ones and dash them against the rock!")? The awkward ending of Mark's Gospel is sometimes repaired cosmetically by stopping at Mark 16:7. Such liturgical and theological criteria are not to be swept aside, particularly in settings when the Bible is read aloud to a congregation. But if the lectionary passage is then interpreted in teaching or preaching, brief comments about its literary integrity or lack thereof might be appropriate.

Determining the limits of the passage is seldom rocket science. It often involves commonsense observations of transitions, shifts in topic, changes in grammatical subject, scene changes, and so forth. Narrative texts, in particular, usually form identifiable units via transitions in time or space, the entrance or departure of characters, changes of speaker, and so forth. But occasionally the determination of the unit will not be obvious, and it will be worthwhile to critique the lectionary's decision and modify it, if necessary, or at least to be aware of the liabilities of working with a debatable unit and the potential impact on interpretation.

Exercises on Key Texts

Select one of the following passages and evaluate the limits of the passage (the beginning and the ending). Are there natural divisions in the text? What clues in the writing suggest that the unit is properly delimited? Could the limits be construed differently? Don't be afraid of calling attention to the obvious. (Note: These texts will be repeated at several steps in the exegetical process.)

Mark 2:1–12 (Healing a Paralytic)
Mark 7:24–37 (A Syrophoenician Woman and a Deaf Man)
Acts 3:1–10 (Peter Heals a Lame Man)
1 Corinthians 12:1–11 (Spiritual Gifts)
1 Corinthians 15:1–11 (The Resurrection)
Revelation 4:1–11 (A Vision of Heavenly Worship)

3. Determine the Original Wording of the Text

The interpretation of ancient and medieval texts, meaning those produced before the invention of the printing press in the mid-fifteenth century, involves a step, indeed an entire discipline, that is usually unnecessary for modern texts. Since these texts were produced, copied, and transmitted entirely by hand, both accidental and intentional changes were introduced into the text. We do not have the original manuscripts of the New Testament (the autographs), and the manuscripts that we do have differ from one another. Hence, scholars must determine the original wording of the text by comparing and evaluating the textual readings of the thousands of manuscripts that have survived.

Textual criticism is probably the most complex and technical aspect of New Testament interpretation. Independent text-critical work requires, at a minimum, a working knowledge of both Greek and the critical apparatus of the Greek New Testament. The top experts in textual criticism usually know both Greek and several other languages of the early church: Latin, Syriac, Coptic, Gothic, Armenian, Ethiopic, and Georgian. In addition, textual criticism requires a knowledge of paleography, ancient scribal practices, and early Christian controversies.

If there is ever a case when the old cliché about "standing on the shoulders of giants" is true, it occurs in the simple act of picking up and reading a Greek New Testament. Add several more giants when you pick up and read a modern English translation. The establishment and refinement of a critical text of the Greek New Testament and the collation of thousands of textual variants were tasks of monumental scope, spread across approximately three centuries.

Given the complex and technical nature of textual criticism, one might wonder just how much the average religious professional (pastor, teacher, youth worker, missionary, or other student) needs to know about it. There is no one-size-fits-all answer to this question. Bible translators and scriptural scholars obviously have a greater need to engage textual variants than most others in Christian ministry, but anyone dealing with inquisitive laity should at least know the general history of the New Testament text and the basic principles by which textual decisions are made.

That is not to say that ministers need to examine in detail every variant in the texts on which they preach or teach. Not all textual variants are of equal importance. When a scribe makes a careless mistake that produces gibberish in the text (such as the inadvertent omission of several words), that reading can easily be dismissed as secondary. Other times a textual decision involves two or more truly competitive possibilities, but nothing of much significance hangs on the choice. An example of this would be the presence or absence of the definite article with a proper noun. English idiom does not distinguish between *Iēsous* (Jesus) and *ho Iēsous* ([the] Jesus), and the difference in the force of the Greek is usually negligible.

How then can the interpreter, especially the novice, determine which variants deserve special attention? Common sense is often sufficient: variants that make a difference in terms of translation and/or exegesis obviously are important. Along with one's intuition, the following guides are helpful. (1) Bruce Metzger's *Textual Commentary on the Greek New Testament* (1994) is by necessity selective. It would be impossible to offer even brief comments on all variants in the manuscript tradition of the New Testament, so Metzger identifies and comments on the ones he deems to be more significant. More recently Philip Comfort has provided a useful tool in his *New Testament Text and Translation Commentary* (2008). It is a large volume (900+ pages) with a very thorough treatment of the variants that impact translation and exegesis. It is similar to Metzger (1994) but more accessible to non-Greek readers. (2) The apparatus of the United Bible Societies Greek New Testament is similarly selective. It also uses a letter grade system {A, B, C, D} to indicate the relative degree of certainty for the reading adopted as the text (B. Aland et al., 1993: 3*). Readings assigned an "A" or "B" are relatively more certain, those with a "C" or "D" relatively less certain. These letters, then, give the interpreter a sense of whether the editors' decision was more or less unanimous or was strongly contested among the members of the committee. Finally, (3) the footnotes of standard English translations are another guide. Pastors and teachers should be ready to explain the textual variants mentioned in these notes since they are readily accessible to lay readers and may raise questions. These are usually variants that have exegetical payoff and are genuine contenders for the original wording.

The relationship between textual criticism and exegesis would seem to be straightforwardly sequential: one must establish the text before one interprets it. This is generally true, but there may also be a feedback loop from the exegetical process. In other words, the meaning that emerges from exegesis may assist the interpreter in deciding that one variant is more likely than the other(s), based on congruence with literary context, the author's theology, or other factors.

The importance of textual criticism in exegesis will vary greatly from one passage to the next. On the one hand, although nearly every verse of the New Testament would present multiple variants if one scoured the entire textual tradition, some passages have no *significant* textual issues, none in which the original text is a genuine conundrum and the choice among the variants is exegetically significant. On the other hand, the interpretation of some passages may be profoundly affected by a text-critical decision. An important part of the interpretive process is discerning the relative importance of the various exegetical steps vis-à-vis a particular passage. For some passages, a text-critical judgment may be the most decisive step in interpretation.

What then are the principles by which textual decisions are made? It is rightly said that "the most basic criterion for the evaluation of variant readings is the simple maxim 'choose the reading that best explains the origin of the others'" (Metzger and Ehrman, 2005: 300). Text critics have elaborated this simple rule into a series of criteria, traditionally grouped under two headings: external evidence and internal evidence. A brief discussion of these criteria follows. Fuller treatments are widely available (K. Aland and B. Aland, 1987: 275–311; Ehrman in Green, 1995: 127–45; Epp, 1997: 45–97, esp. 61–73; Metzger and Ehrman, 2005: 300–43). In what follows I am especially indebted to Metzger and Ehrman (2005: 302–4).

External evidence. (1) The general *quality or reliability* of a manuscript is of great importance. Reliability is closely related to the *date* of a manuscript, although other factors, such as the care with which the scribe worked, are also involved. Our oldest Greek manuscripts of the New Testament were written as early as 200 CE. The most recent manuscripts date from the time of the invention of the printing press, some even postdating its invention, such as the sixteenth century. As a general rule, a manuscript from the earlier period is less likely to have been substantially altered than one from the later period. Even more important than the date of the manuscript itself is the date of the text it contains. In other words, a ninth-century manuscript may have been carefully copied from a third-century exemplar and hence be an effective witness to the text of that century. (2) A textual reading with a *wide geographical distribution* is more likely to be original than a reading stemming from a single locale. To use this criterion, one obviously must know the provenance (origin) of the manuscripts and be reasonably certain that one's geographically diverse texts are also independent of one another. (3) The *genealogical relationship* of manuscripts is also important. If a large number of witnesses attest to a certain reading, but it is known that they all are dependent on a late and/or unreliable source, then their large number is meaningless. One early, reliable witness is of greater value than a hundred mutually dependent, unreliable ones. A maxim of textual criticism states it well: manuscripts must be weighed, not counted. In this sense, textual criticism is *not* a democratic endeavor. The majority does *not* necessarily rule; in fact, it usually does not.

Internal evidence. This evidence is of two types: transcriptional probability, having to do with the habits of scribes, and intrinsic probability, having to do with the habits of the author. Of the following criteria, the first five are transcriptional, the last is intrinsic. (1) The *harder reading* is generally more likely to be original. This is based on the commonsense assumption that scribes are more prone to improve or smooth out a text than to make it worse. As with all text-critical criteria, this one must be applied judiciously. A reading that is gibberish and contains no subtle logic is more likely to be an error. (2) The *shorter reading* is more likely to be original. This is based on the assumption that a scribe is more likely to add material than to delete some. Yet there are reasons why a shorter text might be secondary, such as an accidental omission or intentional censoring. (3) *Harmonizations* are more likely to be secondary emendations. Scribes were known to harmonize parallel texts, such as passages in the Synoptic Gospels, and to smooth out New Testament quotations of the Old Testament. Thus, rougher variants that are at odds with parallel texts or misquote the Old Testament are more likely to be original. (4) *Improvements in style* often reflect editing. Scribes would sometimes substitute more familiar words, more elegant diction, and more proper or more explicit grammar. (5) *Liturgical embellishments* are usually a telltale sign of a scribe's hand. A prayer, doxology, or epistle that lacked a concluding "amen" was hard for a scribe to leave alone. See, for example, the comments in Metzger (1994) on John 21:25, on Acts 28:31, and on the concluding verse of nearly all the Pauline Epistles. (6) *Vocabulary, style, and theology* that are typical of the author, as evidenced elsewhere in the writing, are more likely original. Departures from the author's usual mode tend to be the work of the copyist. This criterion cannot be rigidly applied, however, since all authors sometimes vary their vocabulary and style, and a scribe who is well acquainted with the author's work may emend the text to conform to the author's normal usage.

As I have already cautioned above, these criteria cannot be mechanically applied. Some of them have been called into question (see Epp, 1997: 62–63), and none of them should be routinely granted veto power over the others. Sometimes they will conflict with one another such that priority has to be given to one consideration over another, but this priority will shift from one textual decision to the next. Textual criticism is thus an art as well as a science (Metzger and Ehrman, 2005: 304).

Two manual critical editions of the Greek New Testament are currently in the widest use by English speakers:

The Nestle-Aland text. The Nestle-Aland series began in 1898 under the editorship of Eberhard Nestle. Although published by the Württemberg Bible Society in Germany, the edition has always borne the Latin title, *Novum Testamentum Graece*, suggesting its international scope. Indeed, a few years after its appearance, it was adopted by the British and Foreign Bible Society. Editorial leadership passed from Eberhard Nestle to his son, Erwin Nestle, and eventually to Barbara and Kurt Aland. Now in edition 27, this Nestle-Aland work (NA[27]) is the standard text for scholarly study of the Greek New Testament. The textual apparatus of the NA[27] text uses a system of symbols and abbreviations that takes some effort to learn, but it allows the editors to pack a lot of information into a small space. The introduction of NA²⁷, provided in both German and English, is tedious but essential reading for users of that edition (B. Aland et al., 2000: 44–83 for English).

The United Bible Societies text. The first edition of the UBS Greek New Testament appeared in 1966. The editorial committee included Kurt Aland, and for some years work on the two editions continued in parallel. The co-operative effort led to the adoption of the same Greek text for both edition 26 of the Nestle-Aland text and edition 3 of the UBS text. This text remains unchanged in the NA²⁷ and the UBS⁴ texts. The most important difference between the two editions is their intended readership. The UBS text is designed more for Bible translators than for scholars doing historical and theological research in early Christianity (although some persons obviously wear both hats). Because of its readership, the UBS apparatus is much more selective, being limited to variants that have given rise to significant differences in modern translations. Although fewer passages are treated in the UBS apparatus, the citation of witnesses is more complete for those passages. In addition, textual variants are cited in full, without employing the symbols and abbreviations used in the Nestle-Aland edition. This makes the UBS apparatus more user-friendly, although somewhat less informative overall. (For more on the UBS and NA Greek New Testaments, see the prefaces and introductions to B. Aland et al., 1993 and 2000, from which much of the above information has been derived. See appendix 6 in this book for a handy chart comparing NA²⁷ and UBS⁴.)

General Exercises

This brief introduction will not enable you to conduct detailed, independent analysis of text-critical problems. The aim of these exercises is, therefore, more modest: to acquaint you with the principles and practice of New Testament textual criticism through surveying the evidence and reading an expert commentator. For the latter, one may consult either Metzger's *Textual Commentary on the Greek New Testament* (1994) or Comfort's *New Testament Text and Translation Commentary* (2008). One might also consult critical commentaries on the Greek New Testament. In addition to many excellent, freestanding volumes, commentaries in the following series usually address text-critical problems: Anchor Bible, Baker Exegetical Commentary, Hermeneia, International Critical Commentary, New International Greek Testament Commentary, and Word Biblical Commentary.

1. *Major textual problems.* The two largest text-critical problems in the New Testament, those involving the largest amount of text, are both well-known passages. It happens that they both entail a dozen verses:

Mark 16:9–20 (the canonical ending of Mark) and John 7:53–8:11 (the story of the adulteress). Examine the apparatus for these passages, read Metzger or Comfort, and summarize the external and internal evidence for the judgment that they are not original.

2. *A liturgical elaboration.* Christians pray the Lord's Prayer every Sunday in a fuller form than that found in Matthew 6:9–13. Check the apparatus to see the various scribal additions. Read the remarks in Metzger, Comfort, or a critical commentary on Matthew. Why is it virtually certain that the shorter version is original?

3. *An important theological addition.* The most explicit reference in the New Testament to the idea of the Trinity is found in a longer version of 1 John 5:7–8 (see the King James Version [KJV]). This famous passage is known as the Johannine Comma. Examine the textual apparatus, read Metzger or Comfort, and explain why it is omitted in most modern English translations.

3. *Missing verses.* Several verses are missing from modern translations of the New Testament, such as Mark 7:16; 9:44, 46; 15:28; Luke 22:43–44; 23:17, 34; John 5:4; Acts 8:37; 15:34; 28:29. Choose one or more of these, consult the critical apparatus, and read the remarks of Metzger or Comfort. Why might these verses have been added in some manuscripts?

4. *Single words.* In Matthew 5:11 and Matthew 27:16–17 the presence of a particular word is in doubt. Describe the textual issue and explain why a scribe may have omitted or added the key word.

Exercises on Key Texts

Examine your key text in the apparatus of the Nestle-Aland and/or the UBS text. Are there any significant textual variants? Identify them, gather a sense of the manuscript evidence for the various readings, and then read Metzger (1994), Comfort (2008), or a critical commentary. Are any textual decisions crucial to the interpretation of the passage?

Mark 2:1–12 (Healing a Paralytic)
Mark 7:24–37 (A Syrophoenician Woman and a Deaf Man)
Acts 3:1–10 (Peter Heals a Lame Man)
1 Corinthians 12:1–11 (Spiritual Gifts)
1 Corinthians 15:1–11 (The Resurrection)
Revelation 4:1–11 (A Vision of Heavenly Worship)

4. Genre, Form, and Function

The genre of a biblical writing refers to its literary category or type. Determining the genre of a work is a crucial decision since genre provides a "context of expectation" that facilitates interpretation (Kermode, 1979: 162). When we recognize the genre of a writing, we immediately have certain expectations and understand the writings in ways that would not be appropriate if it belonged to a different genre. We do not expect a story that begins with, "The kingdom of God is like a person who scatters seed . . ." to be a historical narrative. But the preface of Luke's Gospel (Luke 1:1–4; cf. 3:1–2) leads us to expect that what follows is not sheer fiction. When we read "Paul and Timothy, servants of Christ Jesus, To all the saints in Christ Jesus who are in Philippi," we expect a more or less personal, occasional writing that addresses issues of common concern to the writer(s) and the addressees. If those words were followed by a bill of sale or an account of a surreal, otherworldly journey, we would wonder if some papyrus sheets had been misplaced.

The issue of genre and expectations can be illustrated by a modern phenomenon that combines multiple types of literature: the newspaper. Our expectations of a front-page article differ from those we have of the editorial page. When journalists writing a front-page story blatantly insert their own value judgments, we say that they are editorializing. Although opinions and facts are not always easy to distinguish from one another, we expect journalists to try. Vice versa, on the editorial page, we want writers to take a position and argue for it. We expect movie reviews to have a different style and tone from obituaries. We expect the business page and the sports page to have much more quantitative data than the leisure section.

Genre creates expectations for content, structure, style, and tone. It is not always the case that an author conforms fully to those expectations. Genre may function prescriptively: an author may produce a work while consciously conforming it to literary expectations. But genre is also a descriptive category in that scholars have observed numerous examples of a type and identified their common traits. A significant departure from generic expectations could be a sign of an author's incompetence, but more often it indicates an author's innovation and calls the reader's attention to important features of the writing.

Although some people use "genre" and "form" interchangeably, I prefer to distinguish the terms and thereby denote distinct ideas. By "genre," I mean the broad species of the literary work. There are probably only four or five genres in the New Testament: Gospel, historiography, Epistle, sermon, and apocalypse. I use "form" to refer to the many smaller units of material that are found within genres. An epistle, for example, might contain a vice list, a prayer, a creed, and a hymn. There are perhaps two or three dozen literary forms in the New Testament, depending on how one defines and enumerates them. Sometimes a writing in one genre may contain a short passage of another genre. For example, the book of Revelation contains seven miniepistles in chapters 2–3. The book of Acts quotes an epistle in Acts 15:23–29. Both Gospels and Epistles may contain apocalyptic passages. In short, genres serve as hosts, usually for literary forms, occasionally for smaller units of other genres, but forms do not host genres.

Much scholarship since the early twentieth century has been devoted to biblical genres and forms. Classic works include those by Bultmann (1963) and Dibelius (1935). More recent summaries include Aune (1987), J. Bailey and Vander Broek (1992), and Ralph (2003). In what follows, I will offer only a sketch of this decades-long history of scholarship.

Genres in the New Testament

Gospels

The Gospels have been variously classified in terms of genre. Justin Martyr, writing in the mid-second century, describes them as the "memoirs [Greek: *apomnēmoneumata*] of the apostles" (*1 Apology* 67.3). Something akin to this understanding prevailed up to the early twentieth century, but the form critics of the 1920s and 1930s came to regard the Gospels as collections of free-floating stories with no chronological coherence. (The Passion Narrative was an exception to this rule.) Form critics denied that the Gospels could be classified as biographies and argued that, since "gospel" (Greek: *euangelion*) means "good news," these writings should be understood as *kerygma*, as proclamation. Even into the 1960s and 1970s there was a general consensus that whatever the Gospels were, they were *not* biographies. Indeed, the Gospels were understood as constituting a unique class (sui generis) without literary precedent. The following quotes reflect the viewpoint of this era:

> [Gospels are] the sole literary form that is peculiar to Christianity. . . . The anonymous compiler of Mark unwittingly invented a new genre of literature. . . . The gospels have no literary ancestors. (Grobel, 1962: 449)

> The category of "biography" is not suitable to the Gospels. . . . [The Gospel] is the only wholly new genre created by the Church and the author of Mark receives the credit for it. (Wilder, 1971: 28)

A significant shift began in the late 1970s, however, with a reexamination of the Gospels in the light of various Greco-Roman genres, especially biography. The works of David Aune (1987: 17–76) and Richard Burridge (2004) have demonstrated that the genre of ancient biography was a broad and flexible literary form, with which the Gospels share numerous family traits. Certainly ancient biography must be distinguished from modern biography. The Gospel writers "were uninterested in Jesus' education, appearance, personality, motivations, and development" (Aune, 1987: 63). These would be serious deficiencies in a modern biography, but such omissions are within the range of ancient "lives."

Classifying the Gospels as biography has various implications for interpretation. A biography or "life" is obviously centered on an individual. The Gospels are concerned to relate the life and significance of Jesus, not just a series of stories for the purpose of entertainment. The Gospels contain teachings of Jesus, but they are not primarily compendiums of doctrines or ethics. In keeping with the aims of ancient biographies, the Gospels characterize Jesus and present him as a model to follow. As biographies, they were also written with historical intentions. This generic classification does not, however, prejudge the *reliability* of the evangelists' reporting, nor does it exclude elements of polemic, rhetorical exaggeration, or symbolism (Aune, 1987: 64–65). In other words, the task of describing the historical Jesus is not solved simply by classifying the Gospels as biographies, but this classification does suggest that the Gospels are appropriate material to be mined for historical data. By no means are the evangelists indifferent to historical factuality, as is sometimes claimed, even if their primary interest is in the life of Jesus as divine revelation and a paradigm of discipleship. (See also McGing and Mossman, 2006.)

HISTORIOGRAPHY

In the New Testament, the book of Acts stands out as a narrative work whose primary focus is *not* the career of Jesus. Despite its common authorship, parallel motifs, and similar style with the Gospel of Luke, Acts deserves to be considered on its own. Although it is volume 2 of Luke's overall project, its unifying purpose and theme are not God's revelation in Jesus or the course of his career, although these features obviously are not entirely excluded. Acts is rather about the power of the Holy Spirit operating through the disciples of Jesus. Since the careers of these disciples are the means to telling this story and not its end, Acts should not be seen as a series of "lives."

Brook Pearson and Stanley Porter outline three views of the genre of Acts: a romance or novel, a travel narrative or sea voyage, and a work of history (1997: 142–48). The evidence for the first two views is weak. The motifs that Acts has in common with Hellenistic novels and travel narratives are hardly probative of its genre. Engaging fiction and well-written history share many similarities of content: legal trials, imprisonments, travels, narrow escapes, reunions, tearful speeches, and so forth. Such episodes are the stuff of good narrative, whether historical or fictional. One very common feature of fiction, however, is lacking in Acts: a predictable, happy ending that resolves the tensions in the text (Croy, 2003: 60–63).

Historiography remains the best generic classification of Acts. In the preface of Luke's Gospel, which is recalled in the opening verses of Acts, the author claims to have used written sources and the traditions of eyewitnesses in the composition of an orderly account. Throughout both Luke and Acts, one finds repeated references to and interaction with religious and political leaders, many of whom are known from other sources (Annas, Caiaphas, Gamaliel, Herod, Claudius, Gallio, Crispus, Felix, Festus, et al.). As in the case of the Gospels, to classify Acts as a work of historiography is not to guarantee the successful execution of the author's historical intentions; but it does caution against facile recourse to novelistic parallels to explain what Luke is doing in a given passage. Again I must stress that I am speaking of *ancient* historiography, not modern. The fact that Acts contains passages that have apologetic, didactic, or homiletical aims is entirely within the range of functions for ancient historiography. No claim is made here that Acts' history is comprehensive (important figures and geographical areas are omitted), impartial (the author is obviously an adherent of the movement he describes), or infallible (a few passages contain statements that are notoriously difficult to reconcile with other historical sources). For a vigorous defense of Acts as a work of ancient historiography, see Hemer (1990).

EPISTLES

Of the twenty-seven writings of the New Testament, thirteen are Epistles attributed to Paul. Seven more writings attributed to various authors (James, 1–2 Peter, 1–3 John, Jude) bear most of the characteristics of the epistolary genre and are often called the Catholic Epistles, because their addressees are not specific congregations or individuals. (The latter does not strictly apply to 2 and 3 John, but because of their close association with 1 John they are normally grouped with the Catholic Epistles.) Letters are thus the most common literary genre in the New Testament.

In modern times, we have a wide variety of options for communicating with friends, family, and acquaintances at a distance. In antiquity the only alternatives were personal envoys or letters, and envoys often functioned as letter carriers since there was no public postal system. An important function of letters was to mediate the presence of the letter writer to the recipient. Seneca, a first-century-CE Stoic philosopher, wrote these words to his friend Lucilius:

> I thank you for writing to me so often; for you are revealing your real self to me in the only way you can. I never receive a letter from you without being in your company forthwith. If the pictures of our absent friends are pleasing to us, though they only refresh the memory and lighten our longing by a solace that is unreal and unsubstantial, how much more pleasant is a letter, which brings us real traces, real evidences, of an absent friend! For that which is sweetest when we meet face to face is afforded by the impress of a friend's hand upon his letter—recognition. (*Moral Letters* 40.1; cited in Stowers, 1986: 29; cf. Seneca, *Moral Letters* 67.2)

About a century ago Adolf Deissmann analyzed New Testament letters in the light of newly discovered papyrus documents from Egypt (Deissmann, 1901, 1927). Deissmann identified the language of the New Testament as Koine (*Koinē*) Greek, similar to that found in the papyri. He also made a strict distinction between the "unliterary" world that produced the papyri and the "literary" world of more formal writings, such as those of the classical era.

Part of this distinction was a division between two forms of epistolary writings: letters (private, nonliterary correspondence) and epistles (formal, literary productions). Based on this distinction, Deissmann classified the Pauline writings as letters.

Though Deissmann's description of New Testament language as Koine Greek has stood the test of time, his distinction between letters and epistles has not. Neither Greco-Roman nor Pauline letters fall neatly into these categories. Moreover, Deissmann's analysis was strongly influenced by a view of early Christianity that was distorted by nineteenth-century Romanticism. This artistic and philosophical movement preferred the personal and artless communication of the primitive common person over the impersonal, conventional, and artificial productions of literary sophisticates. Deissmann's distinction between "the real letters of Paul and the literary epistles of later Christianity corresponds to the myth of a genuine charismatic Christianity followed by a degenerating institutional Christianity" (Stowers, 1990: 198; see also Pearson and Porter, 1997: 149–51).

Another distinction sometimes made is one between "genuine" letters that address specific situations and broad, thematic essays that are epistolary only in form. This distinction highlights an important characteristic of many ancient letters, including those in the Pauline tradition: their "occasional" quality. This does not mean that Paul wrote letters every now and then, but rather that his letters addressed specific occasions. Paul's letters were prompted by particular situations: conflict in a congregation, the receipt of a gift, anxiety about current events, written inquiries from a congregation, travel plans, and so forth.

Despite the concrete circumstances that elicit Paul's correspondence, his letters are far from perfunctory communications of only antiquarian or philological interest. Paul seems unable to say "Thank you" or "Can't we all get along?" without waxing theological, grounding Christian life in the events of Christ's death and resurrection, citing Israel's Scriptures, and invoking the Holy Spirit. All this is profoundly to our advantage. Paul's highly developed reasoning and reflections enable modern Christian interpreters to find wisdom and truth in his letters, even when the historical occasion, or as we might say, the "presenting issue," is esoteric and scarcely related to our life and times. For example, Paul's counsel in 1 Corinthians 8 about eating food offered to idols (not a burning issue in most modern congregations) takes a jab at quasi-gnostic arrogance, affirms monotheism, acknowledges Christian freedom, and urges deference for weaker believers. Because Paul reflects deeply and theologically on this first-century issue, his response can be used to undergird and shape communal life even in twenty-first-century churches.

The structure of the New Testament Letters is variously seen as involving three, four, or five parts (Pearson and Porter, 1997: 151–52). The simplest outline is thus: opening, body, and closing. Paul typically includes a "thanksgiving" as part of the opening or as a transition to the body of the letter (e.g., 1 Cor.

1:4–9). Sometimes the thanksgiving serves as a précis or summary of the letter's content. The basic components can be further subdivided. The opening identifies the sender(s) and recipient(s) and offers a greeting. The body of the letter may have introductory or transitional formulas. The body of some Pauline Letters is divided into a theological section and a practical or ethical section. The closing typically has such features as a wish for good health, final greetings, a doxology, and a benediction.

The knowledge of these epistolary conventions can be important for interpretation, especially when an author deviates from them. As is often pointed out, the lack of a thanksgiving in Paul's Letter to the Galatians signals early on that the apostle is more than a little miffed with them (Gal. 1:6–9). Interpreters should be attentive to an author's adherence to, or departure from, the conventions of genre, such as the expansion, contraction, or other modifications of formal components. For more on letters, see Stowers (1986), Stirewalt (2002), and Klauck (2006).

SERMON

Some might debate the validity of the "sermon" as a New Testament genre, at least in part because there is at most one complete example in the canon. The so-called "Epistle to the Hebrews" may actually be neither an epistle nor written to the Hebrews. If not an epistle, its best generic classification is probably as a sermon. The epistolary classification is seen to be dubious as soon as one searches for the standard features mentioned above. The writing has no opening that identifies the sender or the recipients. There is no greeting; there is no thanksgiving section. Instead, Hebrews begins with an elaborate and artistic periodic sentence designed to please the ear and capture the imagination. However, Hebrews has several concluding epistolary features. The style changes to short, practical exhortations (13:1–6), references to community leaders (vv. 7, 17), a request for prayer (v. 18), a benediction (vv. 20–21), final appeals, a greeting, and a wish for grace (vv. 22–25). In short, Hebrews begins like a sermon but ends like an epistle.

The style of Hebrews is highly rhetorical, both in its artistry and in its argument. It makes frequent appeals in the first-person plural ("Let us . . . ": 4:1, 11, 14, 16; 6:1; 10:22–24; 12:1, 28; 13:13, 15), a common homiletical technique by which the speaker appeals to the hearers. The argument of Hebrews is elaborate and sustained, but also repetitive, which is an aid in hearing and understanding. The strategy of the sermon alternates back and forth between exposition (citing and explaining passages from the Old Testament) and exhortation (ethical and theological mandates rooted in the exposition). These characteristics support the hypothesis that "Hebrews probably originated as an orally delivered sermon" (Aune, 1987: 213). There is also internal evidence that this is the way the author conceived of the writing. In Hebrews 13:22 the work is described as "a word of exhortation." This phrase is used elsewhere in the New Testament only in Acts 13:15, where it seems to denote a synagogue sermon. Such a description suggests that some of the speeches in Acts might also be analyzed generically as sermons. The classification of Hebrews or other portions of the New Testament as sermons makes sense of their use of Scripture, their structure, and their artistic elements. Indeed, rhetorical criticism, an ancient discipline that has been "rediscovered" by biblical scholars in recent decades, is an extremely valuable tool in the analysis of sermonic material (J. Bailey and Vander Broek, 1992: 193–94; Kennedy, 1984).

APOCALYPSE

The final literary type represented in the New Testament is the genre of apocalypse, probably the most abused and the least understood of all the New Testament genres. Most people have written letters and heard sermons; many have read biographies and histories. But apocalyptic literature is foreign to the mind-set of many modern people. The primary New Testament representative of the genre is the book of Revelation, also called the Apocalypse. As one scholar laments, "Few writings in all of literature have been so obsessively read with such generally disastrous results as the Book of Revelation" (L. Johnson, 1999: 573). G. K. Chesterton (1874–1936), the British essayist and wit, once quipped that although the author of Revelation "saw many strange monsters in his vision, he saw no creature so wild as one of his own commentators" (quoted in Achtemeier, Green, and Thompson, 2001: 555–56). The "wild" interpretations of the book of Revelation often stem from an inadequate understanding of its genre.

Apocalypses flourished in the years from 200 BCE to 150 CE. The word means "uncovering," "disclosure," or "revelation," and the literary genre refers particularly to the revelation of divine truth through visions and other transcendent experiences. The worldview that gave rise to apocalypses was rooted in a radical dualism. It saw in the struggles of the religious community a much larger conflict, a cosmic battle with God, angels, and the faithful arrayed on one side and the devil, demons, and evil earthly powers on the other. It longed for deliverance, usually in the form of a dramatic intervention by God. The moment of deliverance was usually associated with a cataclysm that would vindicate the righteous, punish the unrighteous, and establish God's reign.

The genre of apocalypse has been helpfully sketched by John Collins (1979: 9). He offers the following definition: "a genre of revelatory literature with a narrative framework, in which a revelation is mediated by an otherworldly being to a human recipient, disclosing a transcendent reality which is both temporal, insofar as it envisages eschatological salvation, and spatial insofar as it involves another, supernatural world." At the heart of this definition are two "axes," both of which illustrate the dualism of the apocalyptic worldview. The temporal axis can be conceived as a horizontal timeline. At one end is the present, evil age; at the other end is the coming age of righteousness. The dramatic intervention of God is the turning point at which the coming age dawns. There is also a spatial axis, which might be conceived as a vertical dualism: the earthly realm versus the heavenly realm. Simultaneous with the present fallen order, there is a perfect celestial world, inhabited by God and the angels. The faithful belong to that world, even though they currently reside in the corrupt earthly realm.

The New Testament book of Revelation is unmistakably an apocalypse, but like other such writings, it serves as a host for other literary forms: hymns, oracles, prayers, visions, exhortations, benedictions, and even letters (chaps. 2–3). Indeed, the book of Revelation can be seen as an apocalypse within an epistolary framework (Rev. 1:4–8; 22:6–21; J. Bailey and Vander Broek, 1992: 205–7). One of the most common errors in interpreting Revelation is confusing the genre of apocalyptic with that of prophecy, particularly in the sense of prediction and fulfillment. While Revelation contains prophetic oracles and certainly anticipates the victory of God, it does not intend to give a timeline of future events. Indeed, research has shown that much of Revelation is deeply rooted in first-century political realities (Hemer, 2001).

A related error is the construal of Revelation's bizarre visions and images in highly specific (and often modern) ways. Rather than seeking the *identity* of, for example, the beast of Revelation 13:1–5, it is more useful to understand the character, actions, and function of the beast vis-à-vis God and God's people. Then the interpreter might see aspects of this character in a variety of historical manifestations. Thus one interprets through *analogy* rather than *identity*, through many potential *embodiments* of the image rather than a single *fulfillment* of it (deSilva, 2004: 927).

Finally, apocalyptic literature generally does not aspire to linear or logical consistency. This is perhaps especially true of the book of Revelation, with its bizarre, often-grotesque imagery. One should not be overly concerned about the strict sequence of events or the precise arrangement of visual elements. Thus in chapter 6 the end of the world seems to occur, but in chapter 8 more catastrophes are reported (see esp. 6:13; 8:12; and 12:4). To force such details into some kind of logical or chronological scheme is to misunderstand the genre of the writing. The power of an apocalypse has more to do with its emotional impact and its ability to sustain the faith and reaffirm the values of its readers and hearers than with its logical coherence.

Forms in the New Testament

As indicated above, I use "form" to denote the smaller, discrete units of material that are found within genres. Some literary forms, such as benedictions or chiasms, are as short as a single verse of Scripture. Others are several verses or several paragraphs long. In either case a literary form is a pattern of discourse that facilitates communication. Without the benefit of forms, we would encounter all discourse without any clues about its structure or type.

Discourse that fits previously existing categories, that *conforms* to recognized forms, can be understood more easily. If someone stood up in a group, without words of introduction and without the benefit of known categories of discourse, and began to say, "A priest, a minister, and a rabbi were in a rowboat," the hearers would not know whether the speaker was sharing a personal anecdote, relating a news event, reciting a poem, telling a joke, or giving nautical instructions. Formal categories of speech or writing help us understand the nature and likely content of what we are hearing or reading.

A literary form must have two things to be identified as such. First, it must have sufficient structure to cohere and be recognizable. Second, it must have sufficient representation in the literature to be more than an idiosyncrasy of a single author. But within those parameters, forms are relatively flexible. They occur throughout the New Testament, and although there are no strict rules about what genre of Scripture may use what particular forms, certain forms are more commonly found in narrative material (Gospels and Acts), others in epistolary material, and still others in apocalyptic. In the discussion below, the first seven forms are chiefly found in the Gospels and Acts, the remaining forms chiefly in the Epistles and Revelation. The large number of forms necessitates a relatively brief treatment of each. For fuller discussion, see Aune (1987), Blomberg (1992), J. Bailey and Vander Broek (1992), and the works cited below.

Parables

A parable is a "narrative or saying of varying length, designed to illustrate a truth especially through comparison or simile" (Danker, 2000: 759).

More precisely, in the New Testament, a parable is a metaphor that likens the reign of God to some aspect of everyday life, often rural and domestic images: agriculture, livestock, travel, nature, economics, social relationships, and so forth. It is the nature of parables to be simple, so that most readers can grasp their meaning at some level, yet simultaneously polyvalent, provocative, and paradoxical, such that it always invite deeper reflection. Interpreters should accept this invitation and allow the parables to function as "iconoclastic stories that shake up the world as we know it" (J. Bailey and Vander Broek, 1992: 112). Jesus's parables are numerous (ca. 45) and, for the most part, well known. A helpful list can be found in Snodgrass (1992: 595). The secondary literature on parables is vast. Classic works worth consulting include Dodd (1936) and Jeremias (1963). Recent commentaries with full bibliographies include Hultgren (2000) and Snodgrass (2008).

Sayings

This broad category includes a variety of subforms: aphorisms, proverbs, prophetic oracles, apocalyptic sayings, and so forth. An aphorism is a concise saying attributed to a specific individual that conveys that person's insight and authority. For example: "It is easier for a camel to go through the eye of a needle than for someone who is rich to enter the kingdom of God" (Mark 10:25). Aphorisms are most often declarative statements but may take the form of a question or a command. "For what will it profit them to gain the whole world and forfeit their life? Indeed, what can they give in return for their life?" (Mark 8:36–37). In contrast to the aphorism is the proverb or maxim, which is an unattributed saying that conveys collective wisdom of a more general nature (J. Bailey and Vander Broek, 1992: 98–99; D. Watson, 1992: 105–6). Prophetic sayings include both promises of blessing and pronouncements of judgment. A quick check of a concordance for the word "woe" will provide many examples of the latter. Prophetic oracles also include Jesus's predictions of the destruction of Jerusalem (Mark 13:2) or his own passion (Mark 9:31). Apocalyptic sayings will contain one or more of the characteristics discussed above under that genre: a spatial or temporal dualism, divine intervention through the coming of the Son of Man or Messiah, cosmic phenomena, visions, and so forth (see Mark 8:38; 13:24–29; Luke 21:34–36). Another category of Jesus's sayings is nearly unique to John's Gospel: "I am" sayings. These employ the Greek words *egō eimi*, an echo of the divine name in the Septuagint (LXX) translation of Exodus 3:14, and are used by the Johannine Jesus as metaphorical self-descriptions (e.g., John 6:35; 8:12; 14:6).

PRONOUNCEMENT STORIES

Also called apophthegms or paradigms, pronouncement stories are closely related to the previous form, since they are basically sayings set in a narrative context. A short story culminates in a climactic pronouncement by Jesus. The narrative preparation does more than just provide a spatial and temporal setting; it builds to and evokes the saying (e.g., v. 45 in Mark 10:41–45). Pronouncement stories may also be *controversy stories* when the climactic saying results from a conflict between Jesus and his opponents. Typical examples would be controversies over Jesus's associates (Mark 2:15–17), his actions on the Sabbath (Mark 2:23–28), his political views (Mark 12:13–17), and his treatment of sinners (John 8:2–7). For a full discussion and a list of subforms, see J. Bailey and Vander Broek (1992: 114–16).

MIRACLE STORIES

The name of this form is fairly self-explanatory: the power and authority of Jesus are demonstrated in an extraordinary way that implies divine action and defies normal understandings of cause and effect. The motive is benevolent, and the result is almost always redemptive and revelatory. (The cursing of the fig tree would constitute a partial exception: Mark 11:13–20; Matt. 21:19.) The following subforms can be distinguished: healings, raising the dead, exorcisms, and nature miracles. *Healings* involve the remedying of a disease or disability. They are usually immediate (Mark 10:46–52) but may be gradual (Mark 8:22–25). They may involve some means such as mud or saliva (Mark 7:33; 8:23; John 9:6) or no more than an authoritative word or touch (Matt. 8:1–3). They may be performed in Jesus's presence (John 5:1–9) or at a distance (John 4:46–53). Healing stories typically have an introduction with a description of the illness or disorder, the healing itself achieved by some word or action, and finally some verification of the cure with responses from those who witnessed it. *Raising the dead* might be considered the ultimate healing story, but for that reason they constitute a separate subform. Apart from Jesus's own resurrection, which is actually a miracle of a different order, there are three such stories in the Gospels: the daughter of Jairus (Mark 5:21–43), the son of the widow of Nain (Luke 7:11–17), and Lazarus (John 11:1–46). *Exorcisms* might also be considered a subtype of healings, but their form is distinct enough to be treated separately. Preparation for the exorcism usually highlights the detrimental effect of the demon (Mark 5:1–5). The encounter with Jesus often involves some recognition of his status on the part of the demon (Mark 5:6–7). After the exorcism there is usually a response on the part of the observing crowd (Mark 5:15). *Nature miracles* are generally of two types. Provision stories are narratives in which Jesus supplies food or drink in response to a situation of need. Feeding the five thousand, the four thousand, and turning the water into wine are clear examples (Mark 6:35–44; 8:1–9; John 2:1–11). The second type of nature miracle involves Jesus's exercising control over the forces of nature: calming a storm (Mark 4:37–41), walking on water (Mark 6:48–51), and perhaps the timing of a miraculous catch of fish (Luke 5:1–10; John 21:1–11). As in the case of parables, the literature on Jesus's miracles is extensive. Blackburn (1992) offers a useful summary. Fuller treatments include Kee (1983), Wenham and Blomberg (1986), Meier (1994), Twelftree (1999, 2007), and Achtemeier (2008).

Commissioning Stories

Also referred to as call stories, these narratives are modeled on the prophetic call stories of the Hebrew Bible. God confronts an individual, usually through an angelic intermediary or a heavenly voice, and commissions that person for a divinely ordained task. Typical components include an introduction, the divine encounter, the call proper, an objection, reassurance, and a confirming sign (Aune, 1983: 97–99). In the New Testament the clearest examples are probably the three Lukan accounts of the commissioning (traditionally, the "conversion") of Paul (Acts 9:1–9; 22:3–16; 26:9–18). It has also been pointed out that the Lukan annunciation story follows this pattern (Luke 1:26–38; R. Brown, 1993: 156–57, 630n148). The use of this literary form favors an understanding of Paul's Damascus Road experience as a commissioning to an apostolic ministry rather than a conversion to a new faith. The similarities between commissioning stories and the Lukan annunciation suggest that Mary's task of motherhood has overtones of a prophetic call.

Discourses

This form refers to sayings material of a more extensive nature. Here we find a wide variety of sermons and speeches. In the Synoptic Gospels the best examples are the Sermon on the Mount (Matt. 5–7) and the Sermon on the Plain (Luke 6:17–49). These are collections of sayings grouped by topic and/or form. It is likely that Jesus delivered portions of this material as it appears in the New Testament, since there is no more reason to deny an organizing instinct to Jesus than to the evangelist. But the macrostructure of these sermons is usually thought to be the editorial work of the evangelist. In the Gospel of John, the discourses of Jesus are different in both content and tone. Jesus engages in rather lengthy disquisitions, often employing symbolism and dualistic language, and usually pertaining to his own identity and role vis-à-vis God the Father. Moreover, the Johannine Jesus sounds a great deal like the Fourth Evangelist, and it sometimes is difficult to know where Jesus has left off and the evangelist has begun (e.g., John 3:15–21). Within the Gospel of John, the most extensive discourse is the Farewell Discourse of John 14–16. This discourse has been formally analyzed as a "testament," meaning the final speech of a departing leader, such as one of the Old Testament patriarchs. The testament form has been shown to contain a number of typical features, most of which are found in John's Farewell Discourse (R. Brown, 1970: 597–601; Kurz, 1990). A final example of discourse material would be the speeches in Acts, which are two dozen in number and account for about 20 percent of that book. Speeches in ancient history writing were not mere showpieces or digressions but served to interpret and reinforce the events being related. They complement the narrative and serve the ends of plot enhancement, clarification, and characterization. The sources that Luke used to construct the speeches in Acts are for the most part unknown, and many scholars would say that Luke had a significant hand in their composition, perhaps guided by the general circumstances of the speech and a knowledge of rhetorical, legal, and evangelistic conventions. Many of the speeches, especially in the first thirteen chapters, are evangelistic sermons addressed to Jews, but Paul addresses Gentile audiences in Acts 14:14–18 and 17:22–34. Finally, legal speeches dominate in chapters 22–26, where Paul is defending himself before various courts. For more details on the structure of speeches, see J. Bailey and Vander Broek (1992: 166–78). For a brief survey of scholarship on the Sermon on the Mount/Plain, see Stanton (1992). For the speeches in Acts, see the classic studies of Dibelius (2004) and Cadbury (1958) and the more recent commentary by Soards (1994).

GENEALOGIES

A genealogy is an account of one's ancestry, the history of the descent of an individual or a group. Biblical genealogies are patrilineal, tracing descent through the father. That fact in itself suggests that the mention of women in a genealogy is worthy of special attention (e.g., Matt. 1:3, 5, 6, 16). Whereas there are about two dozen genealogies in the Old Testament, there are only two in the New Testament, those of Jesus (Matt. 1:1–17; Luke 3:23–38). Genealogies serve various purposes. They establish the identity of the individual or group. They may validate one's professional status, as for a priest or king. They may demonstrate the character, explain the significance, or predict the destiny of the person involved (R. Brown, 1993: 64–66). The historical value of biblical genealogies is limited; their chief purpose is theological. Just as we say, "She's her mother's daughter" or "Like father, like son," the evangelists are primarily concerned to characterize Jesus by depicting his ancestry in a certain way. For more, see J. Bailey and Vander Broek (1992: 183–88), Huffman (1992), and M. Johnson (1998).

CREEDS AND CONFESSIONAL TRADITIONS

Creeds are concise affirmations of what early Christians believed. Modern Christians are familiar with the Apostles' Creed, the Athanasian Creed, and the Nicene Creed. Although the New Testament does not contain creedal affirmations as formal and comprehensive as these, there are snippets of early Christian beliefs embedded in several of the Epistles. This material is traditional, in the sense that it has been inherited or handed down. When Paul uses a creedal statement, he is more likely employing a formula from early Christian liturgical practice than composing something on the spot. The earliest Christian creeds are very brief and focus on the most distinctive and essential beliefs. A common component of a creed is an introductory word such as "confess" (homologeō) or "believe" (pisteuō). Thus, Paul writes in Romans 10:9, "If you confess with your lips that Jesus is Lord and believe in your heart that God raised him from the dead, you will be saved." In Philippians 2:11 the apostle speaks of God's intent "that . . . every tongue should confess that Jesus Christ is Lord." The First Epistle of John avers that "God abides in those who confess that Jesus is the Son of God, and they abide in God" (1 John 4:15). Such terse christological formulas, "Jesus is Lord" and "Jesus is the Son of God," may be the earliest Christian creeds. (See also Rom. 1:3–4; 1 Cor. 12:3; 1 John 5:5.) In addition to these concise affirmations, we find lengthier expressions of confessional material, again often introduced by special language. In 1 Corinthians 15:3–7 Paul reminds the believers of the fundamental teachings that he has received, teachings that he has in turn passed on to them. The language of "receiving" and "passing on" is the language of transmitting tradition (Danker, 2000: 763, 768). Paul uses the very same terms in 1 Corinthians 11:23–25, when he relates the institution of the Lord's Supper. Finally, in the Pastoral Epistles (1 Timothy, 2 Timothy, Titus) creedal statements are sometimes introduced with the words, "The saying is trustworthy" (pistos ho logos; cf. NIV: 1 Tim. 1:15; 4:9; 2 Tim. 2:11; Titus 3:8). For more on New Testament creeds, see R. Martin (1993a) and Kelly (1972: 1–29).

HYMNS

New Testament hymns are similar to creedal statements in that both tend to highlight foundational truths of the Christian story. They differ in mode, especially language and rhythm. The language of hymns is poetic and lyrical;

the language of creeds is prosaic and propositional. Hymns normally have a cadence or rhythm; they are patterned speech. Creeds obviously have structure, but there is generally less concern about measured patterns and balanced clauses. The difference is not rigid, and there may be instances when the classification could be debated (e.g., 2 Tim. 2:11). In addition to language and rhythm, the following characteristics of hymns have been identified. They often are introduced with a demonstrative or relative pronoun that is expanded by participial clauses. Thus, in perhaps the most famous New Testament hymn, Paul exalts "Christ Jesus, *who*, though he was in the form of God, did not regard equality with God as something to be exploited, but emptied himself" (Phil. 2:6–11). Hymns often have balanced clauses or strophes that can be set off in stanzas (see NRSV: Phil. 2:6–11; 1 Tim. 2:5–6; 3:16; 2 Tim. 2:11–13). Finally, the content of early Christian hymns varies. Ralph P. Martin (1993b: 421–22) identifies sacramental, meditative, confessional, christological, and ethical types. Of the various types, the christological hymns have received the most attention. A common pattern in these hymns is the advent, ministry, exaltation, and/or enthronement of Jesus. This may take the form of a two-movement pattern of descent/ascent or a three-movement pattern of preexistence/earthly life/exaltation. Hymns, like creeds, often fall into the category of traditional material, thus reflecting their primitive nature. If the so-called Christ hymn of Philippians 2:6–11 is traditional, from pre-Pauline tradition, then it constitutes a remarkably early example of a highly exalted Christology. Other texts that have been proposed as christological hymns include Colossians 1:15–20; 1 Timothy 3:16; and Hebrews 1:3–4. Even this short sketch of New Testament hymns cannot overlook the many hymns in the Apocalypse. Unlike the hymns embedded in the Epistles, which often must be teased out based on content, structure, and introductory formulas, the hymns in Revelation are unmistakable. They normally address God and/or Christ directly; they are supremely laudatory; and they are sometimes accompanied by explicit language of singing (Rev. 4:8–11; 5:9–10; 7:11–12; 11:16–18; 15:3–4). For useful surveys, see Wu and Pearson (1997), R. Martin (1993b), and J. Bailey and Vander Broek (1992: 76–82). For more extended treatments, see Sanders (1971) and Karris (1996).

BLESSINGS AND DOXOLOGIES

These are straightforward literary forms that can be easily identified by key terms. The term "blessed" (*eulogētos*) denotes one who is the object of praise and commendation. This term, not to be confused with "blessed, happy" (*makarios*), is used exclusively in the New Testament of God and Christ. So Paul writes, "Blessed be the God and Father of our Lord Jesus Christ, the Father of mercies and the God of all consolation" (2 Cor. 1:3). (See also Eph. 1:3; 1 Pet. 1:3.) Doxologies contain an ascription of glory (*doxa*) to God or to Christ. This is a way of recognizing and even enhancing the status, honor, and fame of the Deity (Danker, 2000: 257). So Paul concludes his Epistle to the Romans with the words, "to the only wise God, through Jesus Christ, to whom be the glory forever! Amen" (Rom. 16:27). (See also Rom. 11:36; Gal. 1:5; Phil. 4:20; 1 Tim. 1:17.) For a useful survey of these and related liturgical and epistolary forms, see O'Brien (1993).

CATECHETICAL MATERIAL

Catechism refers to basic instruction in the faith given to new converts. Christian catechism became formalized in the second and third centuries, but even within the first generation of the Christian faith, its leaders recognized the need for instruction that went beyond the initial proclamation of the gospel. When Christianity was basically an intra-Jewish movement, a core of Jewish teachings, both ethical and theological, could be assumed. When the church ventured into Gentile territory, it became necessary to instruct pagan converts, who did not share this cultural heritage. So in 1 Thessalonians, a letter thought to have a largely Gentile audience (see 1:9), Paul writes, "For you know what instructions we gave you through the Lord Jesus. For this is the will of God, your sanctification: that you abstain from fornication, . . . that no one wrong or exploit a brother or sister in this matter. . . . For God did not call us to impurity but in holiness" (1 Thess. 4:2–7). Hebrews 6:1–2 speaks of the need to move beyond a basic catechism. The latter is elaborated in terms of the teachings of repentance, faith, baptisms, laying on of hands, and eschatological doctrines of resurrection and eternal judgment. Though catechetical material is well represented throughout the Epistles, the so-called Pastoral Epistles (1 Timothy, 2 Timothy, Titus) are especially concerned with sound, orthodox teaching, as a quick concordance check of the word "teaching" (*didaskalia*) will attest. This reflects the initial steps of the second and third generation of the church, moving toward a simple catechism, especially to counter what was viewed as harmful and heterodox (1 Tim. 1:3; 6:3). For more details, see M. B. Thompson (1993) and Wilkins (1997).

PARAENESIS

Paraenesis is closely related to catechetical material; indeed, it may be regarded as a subdivision of that form. Paraenesis simply means moral exhortation, and so it is a very general category that includes several smaller, more-specific forms. (The next two categories—virtue and vice lists and household codes—are subtypes of paraenesis, but their literary forms are sufficiently distinct to merit separate treatment.) The simplest form of paraenesis would be an imperative verb form: a command to engage in proper behavior or a prohibition of wrongful behavior. Paraenesis may be gathered together in a concluding section of a letter (as in Romans, Galatians, Ephesians, 1 Thessalonians), or it may be scattered throughout (as in 1 and 2 Corinthians, Philippians, Hebrews, James). Paraenesis is often of a traditional nature; that is, there are conventional categories of moral exhortation called *topoi* (themes, topics). Therefore interpreters should be careful about using paraenesis as a window into the precise circumstances of the readers' lives. When a writer urges the recipients of a letter to "love one another" or "abstain from immorality," it may not indicate that this group was especially unloving or immoral. Such exhortations are generally appropriate and might be urged upon any group. Evidence of this is apparent when one reads Greco-Roman moralists and finds that they often issue exhortations similar to those of early Christian writers (Malherbe, 1986). The more specific paraenesis is, however, the more likely it may reflect actual circumstances in the lives of the readers. Common paraenetic *topoi* include duties to the state or city (Rom. 13:1–7), sexual behavior (1 Thess. 4:3–8), use of one's finances (Heb. 13:16), control of anger (James 1:19–20), propriety in speech (James 3:1–12), respect for leaders (Heb. 13:17), and so forth. For helpful surveys, see J. Bailey and Vander Broek (1992), M. B. Thompson (1993), and Wilkins (1997).

VIRTUE AND VICE LISTS

A common strategy among Hellenistic moralists was to list behaviors, traits, and dispositions that were to be practiced or to be shunned. Such lists might function descriptively, as in Romans 1:29–31, when Paul depicts the sins of the godless: "They were filled with every kind of wickedness, evil, covetousness, malice. Full of envy, murder, strife, deceit, craftiness, they are gossips, slanderers, God-haters, insolent, haughty, boastful, inventors of evil, rebellious toward parents, foolish, faithless, heartless, ruthless." While the primary purpose here is to portray the decadence of the wicked, such lists also function as a salutary warning to anyone who might be tempted to engage in such conduct. Conversely, virtue lists enumerate ideal behaviors and qualities of believers, either as the natural result of being in Christ or enjoined as desiderata for God's children. Thus, using the metaphor of clothing, Colossians 3:12–15 urges the proper attire for God's chosen ones: "Clothe yourselves with compassion, kindness, humility, meekness, and patience. . . . Above all, clothe yourselves with love." Virtue and vice lists can naturally be combined to give starkly contrasting portraits of behavior. So Paul combines the fruit of the Spirit and the works of the flesh in Galatians 5:19–23. For helpful surveys of virtue and vice lists in the New Testament and the Apostolic Fathers, see Kruse (1993b) and Reid (1997).

HOUSEHOLD CODES

This subtype of paraenesis refers to the various tables of exhortations to members of a Christian household. The exhortations are typically reciprocal, that is, addressed to both sides of paired individuals or groups, and they usually address three relationships: husbands and wives, parents and children, and masters and slaves. Colossians 3:18–4:1 and Ephesians 5:22–33 illustrate the form well. The sources and aims of the household codes are the topic of much debate. There are at least partial parallels in Jewish and Greco-Roman writings. The codes probably reflect a growing concern in early Christianity that the group appear respectable and well ordered to members of the dominant culture. While this in itself is a worthy goal, some have argued that a consequence, whether intended or not, was to inscribe in the Christian community, and simultaneously to provide a theological rationale for, the institution of slavery and a traditional hierarchy between men and women. While *mutual* love and submission are laudable qualities in a marriage relationship, some modern Christians find the distinctive roles assigned to husbands and wives to be an unfortunate adoption of a patriarchy that does not stem from the heart of the gospel message. The seemingly unperturbed acknowledgment of the institution of slavery has also caused much mischief in the history of New Testament interpretation. However, some modern interpreters have argued that certain aspects of the household codes moderate and even undermine the abusive potential of these relationships. In particular, the reciprocal nature of the codes tends to protect the subordinate party and limit the authority of the superior party (Achtemeier, Green, and Thompson, 2001: 387–88). For further discussion, see Philip H. Towner (1993, 1997).

AUTOBIOGRAPHICAL STATEMENTS

Paul's Letters are primarily pastoral and theological discourses as opposed to narratives, but they do contain a number of short, first-person narratives. These serve various functions: to demonstrate the gracious action of God in Paul's life, to establish Paul's credentials as an apostle, to reassure the recipients of the letter, or simply to relate Paul's circumstances. In writing to the Philippians, Paul reassures them of his well-being (despite his imprisonment) and at the same time attests to the advance of the gospel: "I want you to know, beloved, that what has happened to me has actually helped to spread the gospel, so that it has become known throughout the whole imperial guard and to everyone else that my imprisonment is for Christ" (Phil. 1:12–13). In another passage, Paul describes the consolation provided by God through the visit of a coworker: "For even when we came into Macedonia, our bodies had no rest, but we were afflicted in every way—disputes without and fears within. But God, who consoles the downcast, consoled us by the arrival of Titus" (2 Cor. 7:5–6). Paul's most extended autobiographical statement occurs in Galatians 1:11–2:14. Here Paul describes his life before meeting Christ, the revelation of Christ to him (although tersely!), and his first contacts with the apostles in Jerusalem. On one level, such passages are extremely important in reconstructing the life of Paul; on another level, since Paul's chief interest is not just to relate his life story, these texts illustrate the pastoral and theological use of Paul's autobiography. Always the missionary, Paul deploys his life's story for the sake of proclaiming the truth of the gospel.

MIDRASH

The word "midrash" derives from a Hebrew verb meaning "seek" or "investigate." There is much debate about the precise meaning of "midrash" in the context of Second Temple Judaism. A serviceable definition would be this: a type of literature that attempts to interpret a biblical text that is regarded as an authoritative, divine word by citing or alluding to this text and drawing out its contemporary significance (J. Bailey and Vander Broek, 1992: 42; Porton, 1992: 818). Thus midrash occurs when a writer interprets a canonical text with a view to making it relevant to the writer's community. Midrash in various forms was among the most common rabbinic techniques of interpretation. The New Testament, in its citations and interpretations of the Old Testament, offers several examples of midrash. The form involves a citation of or allusion to an Old Testament text, followed by the author's commentary on that text. J. Bailey and Vander Broek distinguish four subforms of midrash (1992: 43–46). *Running commentary* consists of the citation of several Old Testament texts alternating with the commentary by the New Testament author. Galatians 3 is an example. *Pesher* was the method of biblical interpretation used at Qumran. The name derives from the frequent use of the term in the Qumran Scrolls to introduce an interpretation of a biblical text (Dimant, 1992: 244). In the Qumran community's understanding, "what was written in the past, properly interpreted, is seen as being fulfilled in their own present. . . . Interpretation is based more upon what is perceived as divine revelation for the immediate situation than upon what we would call rational exegetical methods" (J. Bailey and Vander Broek, 1992: 44). Although pesher interpretation violates the axioms of modern historical criticism, it was fully accepted at Qumran, and similar interpretation can be found in New Testament authors. The author of Hebrews cites Old Testament texts that in their original contexts referred to Israel's king and freely reinterprets them as describing the exalted status of Jesus as God's Son (Heb. 1:5–14). Paul likewise can set aside the original context of an Old Testament passage and use it creatively for his own purposes. In 1 Corinthians 9:9 Paul quotes Deuteronomy 25:4, "Do not muzzle the ox that treads out the grain," to defend his right to compensation as an apostle. Though the analogy is clear and effective, the author of Deuteronomy (and presumably God) *were* in fact concerned about oxen, contrary to what Paul claims. But again, such an interpretative move was common and quite acceptable in Paul's day. Two final subforms of midrash are more specific. *Typological interpretation* involves the elaboration of a correspondence between an Old Testament person or event and its alleged New Testament counterpart. The Old Testament figure or event is the *type*, and it is thought to foreshadow its New Testament counterpart, the *antitype*. Examples include Paul's portrayal of Christ as a second Adam (Rom. 5:12–21) and Hebrews's likening of Christ to Melchizedek (Heb. 7). Finally, *allegorical interpretation*, although commonly employed by the Greeks, the rabbis, Philo, and others, is relatively rare in the New Testament. An allegory is an extended metaphor. An author finds a symbolic truth in an Old Testament person or event and elaborates its meaning. Thus an Old Testament character is not just a person but also a way of thinking; a character's behavior is not just an action but also represents the condition of the human soul, and so on. Allegorical interpretation was an especially useful way of dealing with problematic or embarrassing texts. A mundane or offensive literal meaning could be avoided by attributing a loftier, spiritual meaning to the text. The only explicit New Testament example is Paul's treatment of Hagar and Sarah in Galatians 4:21–31, in which the two women represent two different cities, two different covenants, and two different ways of relating to God. As in the case of other midrashic methods, allegory moves beyond the literal or historical sense to an individualized, spiritual sense. While modern critical interpreters are usually wary of allegory, it likely did not raise any eyebrows in Galatia when Paul employed it.

CHIASM

A chiasm is a reverse parallelism. Two or more elements are given, and then the series is reversed with the parallel elements given in the opposite order. The simplest chiasm consists of four elements in the order A-B-B′-A′. Sometimes a chiasm has an odd number of elements such that one is in the center as a pivot and has no parallel. Thus: A-B-C-B′-A′. Chiasms have been observed in both narrative and epistolary literature, both on the scale of a few lines and of units as large as a few chapters (see J. Bailey and Vander Broek, 1992: 49–54, 178–83). Romans 10:19 illustrates the form in brief.

A I will make you jealous
   B of those who are not a nation;
   B′ with a foolish nation
A′ I will make you angry.

On the one hand, a chiasm was a stylistic flourish, enabling the writer to wax rhetorical. On the other hand, it has some value in structuring one's thought. The paired elements sometimes help interpret one another. At times special attention may need to be given to the central, unpaired part of a chiasm. But the interpreter should also beware of overwrought interpretations. In scholarly literature there is a tendency to find elaborate chiasms that may exist more in the mind of the interpreter than the ancient author. As one scholarly wag put it, "Any literary critic worth his or her salt could fake a chiasm" (Gunn, 1993: 193). As long as caution is exercised, however, attention to chiasms can contribute to the appreciation of both a writer's artistry and meaning.

DIATRIBE

In vernacular English, "diatribe" refers to a harsh and abusive speech or writing, a tirade or harangue. As an ancient literary form, it has none of these connotations. In antiquity a diatribe was a discourse in which the speaker engaged in a debate with an imaginary opponent. The genius of a diatribe is that it has the appearance of a vigorous give-and-take in which the writer soundly defeats the opponent. Yet the debate is a fiction that is completely controlled by the writer, and the opponent serves only as a foil to advance the writer's argument. The two most common features of a diatribe are (1) direct address to the opponent in the second person, sometimes involving a vocative, "O, man!" or "O, fool!" and (2) objections and false conclusions (J. Bailey and Vander Broek, 1992: 38–39). The writer anticipates an objection to what has been said and poses a response, often a question, via the imaginary opponent. Scattered features of the diatribe have been identified in a few New Testament writings, but Paul's Letter to the Romans uses it extensively. The address to the opponent using "O man!" appears in Romans 2:3 and 9:20 (NIV; cf. 1 Cor. 15:36; James 2:20). Objections, questions, and false conclusions abound in Romans. For example, after Paul has discussed the abundant nature of divine grace in Romans 5, he anticipates an objection in 6:1: "What then are we to say? Should we continue in sin in order that grace may abound?" This patently mistaken notion is then slapped down with one of Paul's favorite retorts: "By no means!" (6:2; *mē genoito*; see also Rom. 3:4, 6, 31; 6:15; 7:7, 13; 9:14; 11:1, 11; 1 Cor. 6:15; Gal. 2:17; 3:21). Research on the diatribe form has shown that it was, among other things, a didactic tool in Hellenistic schools of philosophy. In other words, it was less an instrument of polemic against outsiders than a means of instructing insiders. The interlocutors in the diatribe are not necessarily real opponents, but rather rhetorical voices (D. Watson, 1993: 214). This fits Paul's Letter to the Romans, in which he wants to instruct a church composed of both Jews and Gentiles about the essence of the gospel that he preaches and to alert them to potential distortions of the same. The diatribe was well suited to this purpose. For more on the diatribe, see D. Watson (1993) and the important work of Stowers (1981).

HARDSHIP CATALOGS

These lists of afflictions and sufferings were a common technique used by Stoic and Cynic philosophers to commend themselves or their heroes. A chief value of Stoics and Cynics was serenity or imperturbability (*ataraxia*), the ability to be untroubled by dire circumstances. The hardships that the sage bravely endures function as a test of character. The stalwart sage endures them bravely, confident that outward sufferings do not impinge on the true self. Paul makes use of this literary form, especially in his correspondence with the Corinthian church (1 Cor. 4:9–13; 2 Cor. 4:8–10; 6:3–10; 11:23–28; 12:10; cf. Heb. 11:35–38). Some of Paul's lists are more abstract, speaking of perplexity and despair (2 Cor. 4:8–10); others are quite concrete and specific, describing imprisonments, scourgings, shipwrecks, and so forth (2 Cor. 11:23–28). It has been noted, however, that unlike the philosophers, Paul does not minimize the real impact of his sufferings, nor does he regard his endurance as evidence of his own strength.

The hardships are genuinely distressing for Paul, and he must utterly rely on the power of God to endure them (Kruse, 1993a: 19). At times Paul may sincerely appeal to his sufferings as credentials of his apostleship (2 Cor. 6:4), but when he flagrantly boasts about them, he openly acknowledges that he is engaging in rhetorical gamesmanship (2 Cor. 11:16, 21, 23, 30; 12:11). For more on hardship lists, see Hodgson (1983), Fitzgerald (1988), and Kruse (1993a).

Other literary forms could be mentioned, but those discussed above are the most commonly encountered. The benefits of attending to forms are similar to those derived from attending to genre. Familiarity with the range of forms enhances communication by helping the reader to perceive structure, composition, and function. It creates expectations in the reader based on the known characteristics of the form. In John's Gospel the high-priestly prayer of Jesus in chapter 17 comes at the end of the Farewell Discourse of chapters 14–16. Rudolf Bultmann, who at times was too eager to rearrange the text of John, thought that the many links between John 17 and John 13 were evidence that chapter 17 originally came immediately after 13 (Bultmann, 1971: 459–61). But as others have pointed out, farewell discourses are a well-defined literary form, and they often conclude with a prayer (R. Brown, 1970: 597–601; O'Day, 1995: 787). Knowledge of this form makes textual rearrangement of John 17 not only unnecessary but also inadvisable.

An acquaintance with the standard components of a literary form enables the interpreter to identify departures from or modifications of the typical pattern. As noted above, miracle stories typically have three parts: an introduction and description of the problem, the healing proper, and a verification of the cure, with responses from the witnesses. In John 11 the story of Jesus's raising of Lazarus expands the simple miracle form into a sprawling narrative of forty-six verses. When one observes that the miracle per se is narrated in verses 43–44 and the responses of witnesses are confined to verses 45–46, it becomes clear that the first component—the introduction of the scene and the characters; the death of Lazarus; and Jesus's interaction with Martha, Mary, and the other disciples—has been vastly expanded. The interpreter should infer that, as spectacular as the miracle is, the theological freight is borne by the narrative and dialogue in verses 1–42. In this case, the literary "preparation" contains the bulk of the theological revelation (Meier, 1994: 803).

Last, an understanding of literary forms also serves as a corrective against misinterpretations that might result from the failure to recognize patterns of discourse. In Mark 1:31, when Jesus heals Simon Peter's mother-in-law, the narrative concludes by saying "the fever left her, and she began to serve them." A knowledge of healing stories will help the interpreter see the last clause as proof of the cure rather than an argument for a woman's role as the servant of men. As a final example, in Luke's birth narrative the conception of Jesus is announced to Mary by the angel Gabriel. In Luke 1:34 Mary seems perplexed and asks, "How can this be, since I am a virgin?" Much ink has been spilled in trying to explain Mary's precise reasoning and inner psychology. But such speculation overlooks the fact that the literary form of an annunciation (and of a prophetic commissioning!) invariably has a statement of doubt or resistance on the part of the human recipient. In this case, Luke's account is more likely shaped by literary convention than a desire to reflect on Mary's inner musings (R. Brown, 1993: 307–8).

THE FUNCTION OF A PASSAGE

The function of a passage is a product of its form and content. Literary form reveals something about the generic function of a passage. Paraenesis aims to exhort; pronouncement stories highlight a climactic saying of Jesus; exorcisms showcase the authority of Jesus over the demonic; creeds distill the essence of the faith; and so forth. But to discern the function of a specific text, one must obviously attend to content as well. For example, what is the specific content of the exhortations in a paraenetical text? What warrants are given for the exhortations? What penalties are implied for disobedience? In an exorcism, how are demonic forces portrayed? How do they interact with Jesus? How is the authority of Jesus depicted, and what does it suggest about the function of the passage in the larger context of the Gospel?

The function of a passage is also a product of its rhetoric and its social situation. Rhetoric is the art of persuasion, so one could pose questions about the persuasive aims of the text. What do the words, phrases, images, and movement of the text seek to accomplish? What is the desired impact on the readers? Since biblical texts are, in varying degrees, the products of social groups and are intended for social groups, a variety of questions can be posed about the social situation of the text's production and purpose: How does the text function in terms of the early Christian community? Does it urge a certain group ethos? Does it encourage certain behaviors, attitudes, or group dynamics? How does the text contribute to Christian identity? Does it serve to characterize Christian community vis-à-vis other communities or help define its boundaries? Questions that probe the rhetoric and social situation of a text are based on the assumption that the Bible is about more than ideas (although ideas are obviously among its concerns). There are also social needs, norms, conflicts, interests, and ideologies at work. Interpreters should be careful not to *reduce* biblical writings to a network of ideological power plays, but neither should they be naively ignorant of a text's social and rhetorical aims. On the fertile and growing fields of rhetorical and sociological exegesis, see Kennedy (1984), Robbins (1996a, 1996b), Elliott (1981, 1993), Esler (1995), Malina (1996), and deSilva (2000a).

Exercises on Key Texts

Using one of the key texts, write a paragraph or two describing its genre, form, and function. Genre is nearly always a straightforward and simple classification. Literary form may be more complex, since authors sometimes combine and adapt forms and, at times, may employ discourse that does not correspond to any patterns that form critics have identified. The description of a text's function will present the greatest challenge since the possibilities are nearly infinite. Nevertheless, try to state the function in a few sentences. Such a statement will normally be constructed around one or more infinitive verbs, usually verbs that relate to the literary form: to exhort, to convince, to warn, to reinforce, to summarize, and so on. But this is only the skeleton, and the details of content, rhetoric, and social situation are needed to add muscle and sinew to the description.

Mark 2:1–12 (Healing a Paralytic)
Mark 7:24–37 (A Syrophoenician Woman and a Deaf Man)
Acts 3:1–10 (Peter Heals a Lame Man)
1 Corinthians 12:1–11 (Spiritual Gifts)
1 Corinthians 15:1–11 (The Resurrection)
Revelation 4:1–11 (A Vision of Heavenly Worship)

5. Literary Context and Structure

Identifying literary context and structure are essential steps in textual interpretation. Although related to one another, they are distinct ideas and deserve separate sections in an exegetical treatment of a biblical text. Briefly stated, context refers to the place of your passage—your pericope of a dozen or so verses—in the flow of the larger writing. Structure refers to the *internal* organization of your passage: its constituent parts and their interrelations.

Literary Context

Appeals to the importance of context are a rhetorical commonplace. One of the most familiar complaints of authors, politicians, or celebrities who have come under fire for something penned or uttered is, "You are taking my words out of context." This protest, whether desperate or defensible, is familiar to the point of being a tired cliché. Attention to context is, nevertheless, the single most important rule of biblical interpretation. Years ago I had a seminary professor who was fond of saying, "Context is everything." He abbreviated it by the acronym "CIE" and found frequent occasion to remind students of it. Someone would query in the middle of a class, "How do you know whether Paul means *x* or *y* when he uses this expression?" The professor, often without speaking, would turn to the blackboard and write "CIE." If a second such question arose in the same class period, he would just point to the letters. Initially I thought the appeal to "Context is everything" was an obvious hyperbole, maybe even a convenient dodge of a difficult question. Nowadays I'm not so sure. I see less and less exaggeration in my former teacher's mantra. If not quite everything, context is nearly so.

The word "context" needs closer definition since there are different types and levels of context. In this section I am concerned with literary or verbal context of both an *immediate* and *broader* sort. In large measure, the meaning of an utterance is determined by its context, by the surrounding discourse in which the utterance occurs. Usually the *immediate* context, what comes directly before and after the utterance, is of greatest importance; but the *broader* context up to and including the entire writing may also be relevant. Other types of context—historical, social, cultural, religious, political, and so forth—are also very important. (These matters will be taken up in the section beginning on p. 97.) Before I turn to some suggestions for the analysis of literary or verbal context, I offer two modern examples of the importance of context: one trivial, one tragic.

THE IMPORTANCE OF CONTEXT: A TRIVIAL EXAMPLE

Several years ago, I signed up to attend a weekend spiritual retreat. I received a list of things to bring. It included typical equipment for a retreat setting: sleeping bag, flashlight, insect repellent, and so forth. But one item stood out as odd: "shower shoes." I figured, "Okay. They have showers there that are used by a lot of people, so for hygiene's sake, they want you to wear sandals in the shower." This was the one item on the list that I did not already own, so some days before the retreat, I went to a drugstore and found a clerk, a young saleswoman, at the front counter. I requested the item by the term that I had always used while growing up: "Do you have thongs?" There was an awkward silence, and a look of disbelief crept over the woman's face. Eventually I realized that she was imagining me wearing skimpy swimwear . . . and she was traumatized by the thought. Finally I blurted out, "What I mean is sandals, flip-flops . . . shower shoes, for cryin' out loud!"

Communication had failed due to a lack of context. If I had prefaced the question with a statement like, "I'm looking for some inexpensive, waterproof footwear," I could have averted the misunderstanding. Likewise there might never have been a problem if I had been in a shoe store. Minus all verbal context or a particular social context, my brief utterance was ambiguous.

THE IMPORTANCE OF CONTEXT: A TRAGIC EXAMPLE

One of the most tragic cases in British legal history involved Derek Bentley and Christopher Craig. On November 2, 1952, these two boys were spotted breaking into a warehouse. When the police arrived, the boys tried to hide on the roof of the building. A policeman climbed a drain pipe to the roof and called for the boys to surrender. Craig, the younger boy, had a gun, which he began firing wildly. Bentley later testified that he did not know that Craig had a gun until he pulled it out on the roof.

The policeman called for Craig to hand over the gun and surrender. He then grabbed Bentley, who was nearby. Bentley broke free momentarily and called to his partner, "Let him have it, Chris!" Craig fired, wounding the policeman in the shoulder, who was still able to apprehend Bentley. By this time other police had arrived, entered the building, and climbed the interior stairway to the roof. With Bentley now in custody, one of these policemen emerged from the staircase onto the roof. Craig fired again, striking this officer in the forehead and killing him instantly.

At their trial both boys were charged with murder, even though Bentley had been under arrest when the fatal shot was fired. An important part of the prosecution's case was that the boys had acted in concert and so were both guilty of the crime. In particular, Bentley's shout, "Let him have it!" was interpreted as evidence of his violent intent and complicity. The defense interpreted the same remark as a plea to surrender the gun. Since Craig was a minor at the time, he was sentenced to life in prison. Bentley had an IQ that placed him in the bottom 1 percent of the population, but because he was 19, he was tried as an adult and sentenced to hang. Although the jury recommended mercy, Bentley was hanged on January 28, 1953. Forty-five years later, on July 30, 1998, Bentley's conviction was overturned by an appeals court. A movie made about the case was titled *Let Him Have It!*

What was the meaning of the terse utterance "Let him have it"? The verbal context would include any earlier comments by the two boys as well as the policeman's call for surrender of the gun. But given the ambiguity that remained, other considerations were equally pertinent. What were Bentley's intentions, knowledge, and general character? Did he have a history of criminal behavior and/or violent tendencies? Was he a docile youth under the pernicious influence of a companion, or was he an impetuous ringleader?

We see that the notion of "context" quickly becomes complex, embracing not just the verbal context but also personal histories and sociocultural factors. Although interpretive decisions related to biblical texts are seldom as trivial as the first example, nor as perilous as the second, the meaning of a given passage of Scripture may be crucial to our understanding of faith and practice, and the consideration of context, verbal and otherwise, is of great importance.

Suggestions for Analyzing Literary Context

Prior literary context is especially important. Since a reader normally experiences a text (whether visually or aurally) in sequence, a given statement will normally be intelligible in the context of the discourse that leads up to it. But since writers sometimes postpone climactic information like the punch line of a joke, and since ancient authors often assume knowledge that they shared with their ancient readers, the entire verbal context of a writing, both prior and subsequent, must be considered. Thus the relevant context for interpreting any passage in the Gospel of Mark is the entire Gospel. As a general rule, nearer literary context is more critical than more remote context. In other words, chapter 15 of 1 Corinthians will probably be more relevant to the interpretation of 1 Corinthians 15:1–11 than chapter 1 will be. A sound methodology will give particular attention to the immediate context but will also take into consideration the entire writing. (Indeed, *all writings* by a particular author could be relevant "context," but this anticipates the section "Consider Textual Connections," beginning on p. 88.) Here are some general questions to pose to your text:

- How does the immediately prior context relate to your passage? How does your passage connect (syntactically, logically, thematically) to what precedes?
- How does the immediately subsequent context relate to your passage? How does your passage connect (syntactically, logically, thematically) to what follows?
- Is your passage part of a larger division or subdivision of the whole writing? How does its location in the writing affect its interpretation?
- Have earlier portions of the writing prepared for your text?
- Does your text anticipate or prepare for passages that come later in the writing?
- What is the flow of the narrative or argument in this part of the writing, and how does your passage fit into it?
- Does your text constitute a pivot point? The beginning of a new section or theme? The conclusion of a section or theme?
- All the above are variations of the most basic question: How does the literary context of this passage illumine its meaning?

Exactly how does context illumine meaning? Some examples:

1. John 3:1–10 tells the familiar story of Nicodemus coming to Jesus at night. Nicodemus is described in 3:1 as "a Pharisee" and "a leader of the Jews," terms that at this point in the Gospel have not gained the strongly negative nuance that will come later. But suspicion has already been cast on Nicodemus by the prior context. In John 2:23–25 the evangelist warns that many in Jerusalem believed in Jesus because of the signs he performed. Nicodemus refers to Jesus's signs in his opening remark (3:2). The connection is even more evident in Greek. The last word of John 2 is *anthrōpos* ("man, human being"). The third word in 3:1 is the same term. Granted, this is a very common word, but it is used twice in the singular form in 2:25 and then immediately in chapter 3. The effect can be felt via a noninclusive translation: "Jesus needed no one to testify to him about *man*, for he knew what was in a *man*. Now

there was a *man* . . . " (cf. KJV). The verbal link leads us to believe that Nicodemus is a person of the type just described.

2. The temptation story in Matthew 4:1–11 is immediately preceded by the baptism of Jesus in 3:13–17. The climax of the latter scene is the declaration by a voice from heaven that Jesus is "my Son, the Beloved." We are probably safe in assuming that the heavenly speaker is God. (Once when I asked a classroom of students, "Who is obviously intended by this unnamed voice?" a student responded, "Someone *really* tall." Call me unimaginative, but I'm going to stick with God.) The declaration of Jesus's divine sonship prepares for the Matthean temptation story, in which the first two trials begin with the devil's statement: "If you are the Son of God" (Matt. 4:3, 6). The devil in effect assumes, for the sake of argument, the truth just conveyed in the baptismal scene. The point of the first and second temptations, then, is not whether Jesus is God's Son, a thesis that neither the evangelist nor the devil calls into question. Matthew 3:13–17 has established beyond all doubt the *fact* of Jesus's divine sonship (since God is a reliable character). The issue in Matthew 4:1–7 is the *nature* of Jesus's sonship.

3. Finally, Luke 11:9 contains the familiar saying of Jesus, "Ask, and it will be given to you; search, and you will find; knock, and the door will be opened to you." Read in isolation, this verse could be construed as advocating a life of voluntary poverty and begging, thus portraying Jesus as a Cynic-like philosopher. In the Lukan context, however, its meaning is unmistakable. It is embedded in a section on prayer (Luke 11:1–13) and encourages people to petition God for their needs. If anything, the exhortation urges those who are *already* poor to turn to God for the necessities of life, not to adopt a self-imposed poverty as a countercultural statement of utter independence from material goods (R. Horsley, 1994: 82–83).

Interpreting a New Testament text clearly benefits from (in fact, *demands*) careful attention to the immediate and broader literary contexts. Since we often engage Scripture in bite-sized chunks via the lectionary, we must resist the temptation to read our dozen or so verses and little more. To point out the obvious, there is great advantage in having done a survey of the entire writing (step 1 above) before analyzing the context of a given pericope. The interpreter will already have some sense of the whole, and placing the text in its larger context will be much easier. I offer below a sample analysis of literary context. For more on the general topic, see Gorman (2001: 69–71).

A Sample Analysis: the Literary Context of 1 Corinthians 13:1–13

First Corinthians 13 is situated between chapters that deal with spiritual gifts. The larger section clearly begins with 12:1, "Now concerning spiritual gifts . . ." (*peri de tōn pneumatikōn*) and ends with 15:1, "Now I would remind you, brothers and sisters." Chapter 12 deals with the unity of the gifts in terms of the Spirit, the Lord, and the God who activates them. The body metaphor in 12:12–31 furthers the idea of the unity of the gifts. The final verse of chapter 12 prepares for chapter 13 when it speaks of a "more excellent way."

The chapter itself clearly has unity around the theme of "love." The noun "love" (*agapē*) occurs nine times. (Earlier in 1 Corinthians, it appeared in 4:21 and 8:1. In 8:1 it is implied that love is superior to knowledge because it builds up the church.) The first verse of chapter 14 clearly picks up where 12:31 left off. It echoes the theme of chapter 13—"Pursue love"—but then resumes the discussion of spiritual gifts, repeating the verb of 12:31a, "strive for," and the noun of 12:1, "spiritual gifts."

Chapter 14 continues the treatment of spiritual gifts with a nearly exclusive focus on prophecy and speaking in tongues. These two gifts and their relative merits dominate the chapter, which argues for the greater communal value of prophecy. The chapter concludes with a call to orderly worship. As mentioned above, 15:1 is a clear transition to a new topic.

Structure

Structure pertains to the arrangement and interrelationships of ideas. One can speak of structure at different levels. We have already discussed macrostructure above under "Survey the Writing as a Whole." There we were concerned with major divisions and subdivisions of an entire biblical book. At the other end of the spectrum, one can analyze the highly detailed structure of individual sentences, clauses, and phrases. This would fall under grammatical analysis (pp. 79–88). In the present section we are concerned about an intermediate level of structure: the structure of the pericope, generally a passage of suitable length for in-depth study, proclamation, or liturgical reading.

Structural analysis often raises the question of authorial intent. Two extremes should be avoided. Avoid the objectivist certainty that says there is only one right structural outline or analysis of a text. Seldom is the structure of a passage so unambiguous that all contending analyses but one are ruled out. On the other hand, interpreters should with equal aversion shun the notion that structure is entirely imposed on a text, that it is only in the interpreter's head. Beauty may be in the eye of the beholder, but structure, for the most part, resides in the text. If one wishes to assert that the modern mind has an organizing instinct that "imposes" structure on a text, there is no reason to deny the ancient author the same instinct. The clarity of a text's structure, just like the determinacy of its meaning, will obviously vary according to genre, authorial skill and purpose, and other factors. But the default assumption should be that authors structure their thoughts, and this assumption should only be abandoned when a text utterly defies it.

The analysis of structure begins with the identification of the component parts. This might be as simple as counting the clauses or sentences. (Obviously, this is a much more precise exercise if done with the Greek text. English translations of the New Testament sometimes alter the sentence structure of the Greek, usually by necessity.) Beyond tallying the number of clauses and sentences, one must discern the logical relationships between them. Does one clause state an effect of which another is the cause? Does one sentence make a general statement that is then illustrated by specific examples in later sentences? Here are some basic questions to pose to your text:

- How many constituent parts are there in your passage? How many sentences in your English translation? How many sentences in the Greek text?
- How do these constituent parts relate to one another? What are the logical connections between the various sentences or verses?
- Moving to the next finer level, what are the main clauses? What are the subordinate clauses? How do they relate to one another?
- How does the logic of the argument or the flow of the narrative unfold?

It may be useful to describe some of the structural relationships that govern biblical (or any literary) texts. These relationships operate at the macrolevel of structure, the pericope level, and in some cases at the level of sentences and clauses. Our chief concern here is the intermediate level of the pericope. In what follows I am especially indebted to Traina (2002: 36–68).

REPETITION

The most basic indicator of what is important to an author is repetition. When an author repeatedly uses the same terms or similar terms, they obviously reveal an important theme in that pericope or book. Repetition in itself does not always constitute a structuring device, but the next step would be to determine how the repeated elements relate to one another. Do they build toward a climax? Do they alternate with contrasting elements? Do they appear in a chronological sequence? Sometimes repetition jumps out at the reader. Who can read Hebrews 11 or 1 Corinthians 13 and not detect the respective themes of faith and love? Other times repetition is more subtle and may depend on the Greek text, as in the repetition of the Greek root *phil-* (love) in Heb 13:1–6. Observing repetition is often a good way to begin analyzing a text.

COMPARISON/CONTRAST

This is one of the most basic ways we structure our thoughts: by pointing out similarities and differences. Comparison associates like things, contrast associates dissimilar things. The words "like" and "as" often signal comparisons: "Everyone then who hears these words of mine and acts on them will be *like* a wise man who built his house on rock" (Matt. 7:24). "Everyone who does what is right is righteous, just *as* he is righteous" (1 John 3:7). Note the introduction to many parables: "The kingdom of God/heaven is *like* . . ." (e.g., Matt. 13:44–45). When these words are negated, a contrast may be expressed: "But the free gift is *not like* the trespass" (Rom. 5:15). "For he taught them as one having authority, and *not as* the scribes" (Mark 1:22). Needless to say, comparisons and contrasts are often implicit and do not involve these markers. Regarding contrast, there are both contrasting ideas and contrasting perspectives. In the former, two mutually exclusive ideas are contrasted: loving one's brother versus hating one's brother (1 John 2:10–11 NIV). In the latter, the meaning is the same in both parts; only the point of view changes: "God is light and in him there is no darkness at all" (1 John 1:5). "I am speaking the truth in Christ—I am not lying" (Rom. 9:1).

CLIMAX

An author may arrange material so that it builds toward a climax. This may involve as few as three steps but could contain more. In Matthew 5:22 (NIV) Jesus warns about liability to legal judgment, to the Sanhedrin, and ultimately to the fires of hell. Similarly in Matthew 5:25 there is an escalation of judgment that moves from accuser to the judge to a guard to imprisonment. In the parable of the evil tenants, there is a progression of violence against slaves, violence against a larger group of slaves, and eventually against the landowner's son (Matt. 21:33–40). A more-positive movement toward a climax occurs in Romans 5:3–5, in which Paul describes a progression from suffering, through endurance, character, and hope, culminating in the love of God through the Holy Spirit.

PIVOT

Material may be structured such that it turns or pivots at a given point. The tenor or the characteristic issues leading up to the pivot point are different from those that follow. The whole of Mark's Gospel can be understood as pivoting on the confession of Peter at Caesarea Philippi (Mark 8:27–30). On the scope of a pericope, the Christ Hymn of Philippians 2:6–11 has a rather clear structure of two movements: the downward abasement of Christ in verses 6–8 and the exaltation of Christ in verses 9–11. The pivot point consists of the final words of verse 8: "even death on a cross."

ALTERNATION

This technique consists of the alternation of (often contrasting) elements in an A-B-A′-B′ pattern. The interchange of the elements may serve to enhance the contrast. Examples of relatively large-scale alternation include the following: (1) the interweaving of the birth of John the Baptist with the birth of Jesus in Luke 1–2, producing a pattern of John, Jesus, John, Jesus; (2) in John 18:28–19:16 the alternation between scenes outside the praetorium and scenes inside the praetorium, producing a pattern of Pilate with the Jews, Pilate with Jesus, Pilate with the Jews, Pilate with Jesus, and so forth; and (3) the interchange through much of the Epistle to the Hebrews between exposition (citation and treatment of Old Testament texts) and exhortation (urging certain action based on the treatment of the Old Testament texts).

General to Particular/Particular to General

Sometimes an author will state a general principle or issue an appeal and then illustrate it with particular instances. This movement is called particularization. Discourse that moves in the opposite direction—from specific examples to a broad statement—is called generalization. Particularization occurs in Matthew 6:1–18. In 6:1 Jesus warns against performing acts of piety so as to be seen by others. What follows are three specific examples: almsgiving (vv. 2–4), prayer (5–15), and fasting (16–18). Romans 8:35–39 is similar; it moves from a rhetorical question, "Who will separate us from the love of Christ?" (the thrust of which is the affirmation, "Nothing will separate us") to a series of circumstances exemplifying the truth of the opening claim. Colossians 3:11 might be seen as an example of generalization on a very small scale. After listing various identities that are transcended in Christ, the verse concludes with the general principle: "Christ is all and in all!" Luke 6:32–36 moves from a series of examples of strictly reciprocal charity to a broad imperative to be merciful as God is merciful. A good aid to observing generalization or particularization is simply to be alert to any listing of specific examples or instances. Then look to see if the list is introduced or concluded with a statement of the general principle. It is possible that the list of examples might even be enclosed with a general statement both fore and aft (see James 2:14–26).

Causation/Substantiation

One of the most basic organizing principles of the human mind is to relate things as cause and effect. Stated in that order, you have causation. If the effect is stated first, and then the cause, explanation, or reason thereof is given, we have substantiation. Though these structuring techniques are sometimes implicit, more often they are explicitly marked with adverbs or conjunctions such as "because," "since," "therefore," "consequently," and so forth. Interpreters should be alert to the use of these "function words," which express grammatical relationships more than lexical meaning. As the old saying goes, "Whenever you see the word 'therefore,' you should stop to see what it's there for." Obviously, then, there are numerous small-scale examples of these relationships. On a pericope scale, see Romans 1:18–32 for an example of causation and Hebrews 2:5–18 for substantiation.

INSTRUMENTATION

This structuring technique involves the statement of an instrument or means and the desired end or purpose. As in the case of causation/substantiation, this is a very common relationship on the small structural scale of clauses. The words "in order that" or "so that" often follow a clause expressing means and introduce a clause expressing purpose: "I have said this to you, *so that* in me you may have peace" (John 16:33). The Gospel of John contains a statement in 20:30–31 asserting that several miraculous "signs" were recorded in the Gospel (the means) "so that" the readers might "believe that Jesus is the Messiah, the Son of God" (the purpose).

PREPARATION OR INTRODUCTION

Often the opening verses of a pericope, especially a narrative, serve to orient the reader to what follows. Characters, locale, or time may need to be identified. Background information that is necessary to understand the story is provided. The healing in John 5:1–9, for example, is introduced by verses 1–3, which give the geographical and religious setting, the specific locale, its name, a structural detail, and the fact that many disabled persons are present. Indeed, in this passage some scribes thought that not enough preparation had been given! They supplied verse 4, which is textually suspect but quite helpful in understanding the unfolding narrative.

SUMMARIZATION

Sometimes an author will provide a short summary or compendium of a section. Such a summary not only serves to underscore (and sometimes reiterate) key points; it may also serve to mark a transition in a narrative or discourse. The author of Acts likes to summarize the narrative of the expanding Christian movement with brief descriptions of their communal life, evangelistic successes, and miraculous events (Acts 2:42–47; 4:32–37; 5:12–16). The author of Hebrews seems to acknowledge the complexity of that writing's argument by providing an explicit summary statement of the main point of the discourse at about the midpoint of the book (Heb. 8:1–2).

INTERROGATION

The normal mode of discourse is declarative: making statements that declare, assert, or explain something. Alternative modes include imperative discourse (issuing commands), optative (expressing a wish or desire), and interrogative (asking questions). The latter is our concern here. On the one hand, questions posed by an author may be rhetorical, in which case they are the equivalent of an assertion, and no answer is expected. We saw above that the literary form of the diatribe often employed rhetorical questions (Rom. 6:1). On the other hand, questions may be real, in the sense that they are genuinely open and anticipate a response. In its fullest form, the author may supply both the questions and the answers. This is a common way of presenting information nowadays, especially in brochures and websites. The ubiquitous acronym FAQ is a handy structuring technique. (Note that a question-answer format was used in the introduction to this book.) Interrogation of this type occurs in Hebrews 3:16–19.

TEMPORAL PROGRESSION

A common way to structure material is chronological. This indeed is the standard method for most narrative. Even though the New Testament Gospels are often faulted (not without reason) for being unconcerned with chronology, this is not true at the macrolevel. John the Baptist's ministry precedes that of Jesus. Jesus's baptism and temptation precede his public debut. Much of the central portion of Jesus's career is not sequence-sensitive, but his triumphal entry into Jerusalem marks the beginning of the end in all four Gospels. Needless to say, Jesus's betrayal, arrest, trial, crucifixion, death, burial, and resurrection could scarcely be told in any other order. The Acts of the Apostles is similarly chronological in its treatment, despite being perspectival and selective. The structuring technique of temporal progression is not limited to narrative works, but may also be found in narrative sections of the Epistles (Gal. 1–2; Heb. 11) and in speeches within narratives (Acts 7). The genealogies of Jesus (Matt. 1:1–17; Luke 3:23–38) also employ temporal progression, in both directions!

SPATIAL PROGRESSION

A structural technique closely related to chronology is spatial progression, with its obvious emphasis on geography. Again, this is chiefly used in narrative works. It is often pointed out that Acts 1:8 uses spatial progress to sketch the expansion of the early Christian movement (and arguably of the book of Acts itself). Spatial progression seems especially important in the so-called travel narrative of Luke's Gospel (9:51–19:27), in which Jesus resolutely marches toward the city of Jerusalem. John's Gospel makes a point of the geography of Samaria as a necessary "thruway" between Judea and Galilee (John 4:1–6). In rare cases, nonnarrative works may employ spatial progression as a structural technique. For example, the vision of the heavenly throne room in Revelation 4 has spatial aspects. The throne itself is central; twenty-four elders are seated around the throne; before the throne are seven torches and a sea of glass; four surreal creatures encircle the throne. The description may seem overwrought and confusing, but spatial features at least play a role in the depiction. (Cf. the vision of the new Jerusalem in Rev. 21:9–27.)

CONDITIONS

A final technique to be considered is the condition. A condition is a premise or prerequisite to the realization or fulfillment of something else. In simple terms, it is an "if-then" statement. The "if" clause states the prerequisite; the "then" clause states the outcome to be realized. This structural technique is exceedingly common on the small scale of sentences or verses. It is unusual for either the "if" clause or the "then" clause to be extended beyond a sentence in length, although each clause may have several components. (See, e.g., 2 Chron. 7:14.) An author may, however, use a series of conditions to reinforce or elaborate a point (Mark 3:24–26; 1 John 1:6–10; Rev. 22:18–19). Explicit conditions are easily recognized by the word "if" (Greek: *ei* or *ean*). Implicit conditions, such as participial constructions, lack such explicit clues (D. Wallace, 1996: 632–33). How does the interpreter identify them? CIE.

The analysis of structure is an essential part of interpretation. Content does not operate alone in the communication of meaning; it is assisted by structure. Sometimes structure can clarify content that is ambiguous. In Luke's infancy narrative, the idea of a virginal conception is usually seen in Luke 1:34, when Mary responds to the angel Gabriel, saying, "How can this be, since I am a virgin?" But occasionally it has been argued that Luke's story has no explicit claim of Mary's virginity up to the birth of Jesus, akin to Matthew 1:25, and therefore that Luke 1:34 could refer to Mary's condition at the time of the annunciation, with the conception of Jesus occurring at a later time via sexual intimacy with Joseph. But Raymond Brown rightly argues that the structure of Luke 1–2 demonstrates Jesus's superiority to John the Baptist. Since John was conceived by aged parents through divine intervention, Jesus could not be conceived by normal means to young parents. The structure of Luke's narrative requires that 1:34 be understood as implying the virginal conception of Jesus (R. Brown, 1993: 299–301).

Below is a sample analysis of literary structure. For a highly detailed model of structural analysis called "Sentence Flow," see Gordon Fee (1993: 65–80). This sort of analysis, akin to sentence diagramming, will be considered in the section "Examine the Grammar" below.

A SAMPLE ANALYSIS: THE STRUCTURE OF 1 CORINTHIANS 13:1–13

The internal structure of 1 Corinthians 13 is threefold, as reflected in the paragraphs in the NRSV. Verses 1–3 consist of a series of conditional sentences: "If I speak," "And if I have," and "If I give away." All three conditions include in the protasis ("if" clause) the words "but do not have love." The apodosis ("then" clause) of each condition gives a negative result, especially evident in the second and third: "I am nothing" and "I gain nothing." The first two conditional sentences foreshadow the themes of chapter 14: tongues and prophecy.

The second paragraph consists of verses 4–7. Verses 4–5 are marked by a series of short affirmations and denials about love. They are strung together without conjunctions of any kind (asyndeton). There are two positive affirmations about what love does; then there are seven denials about what love does not do. Verse 6 seems at first to continue the denials, but it is in fact an antithetical pair: "[Love] does not rejoice in wrongdoing, but rejoices in the truth." Verse 7 is a quartet of affirmations, each beginning with *panta* (all things) in Greek.

The third paragraph is less rigidly structured than the first two, although there is a clear contrast between love on the one hand and prophecy, tongues, and knowledge on the other, again preparing for chapter 14. Love is "perfect" or "complete." Everything else is partial. The closing verse highlights the Christian virtues of faith, hope, and love, but upholds love as the "greatest of these," a verbal echo of 12:31a, suggesting that love is not only the more excellent way (12:31b) but also the greatest gift.

Exercises on Key Texts

Analyze the literary context and structure of one of the key texts listed below. Pose to your text the bulleted questions that were listed above in the sections "Literary Context" and "Structure." Look for the structural techniques that were discussed. Write a few paragraphs on both the context and the structure of your chosen text.

Mark 2:1–12 (Healing a Paralytic)
Mark 7:24–37 (A Syrophoenician Woman and a Deaf Man)
Acts 3:1–10 (Peter Heals a Lame Man)
1 Corinthians 12:1–11 (Spiritual Gifts)
1 Corinthians 15:1–11 (The Resurrection)
Revelation 4:1–11 (A Vision of Heavenly Worship)

6. Examine the Language

Historical philology was one of the first and most important contributions of the Renaissance, the humanistic revival of the fourteenth to seventeenth centuries, which led to the flowering of the study of language and literature. The seventeenth-century precursors of modern biblical scholarship such as Hugo Grotius (1583–1645) and Richard Simon (1638–1712) achieved major advances in the study of biblical languages (Baird, 1992: 29). The philological and grammatical method was further refined in the eighteenth century by Johann August Ernesti (1707–1781) and Johann Salomo Semler (1725–1791). The latter asserted that "hermeneutical skill depends upon one's knowing the Bible's use of language properly and precisely, as well as distinguishing and representing to oneself the historical circumstances of a biblical discourse" (quoted in Frei, 1974: 109).

In the eighteenth century, Friedrich Schleiermacher (1768–1834), often considered the founder of modern hermeneutics, urged that careful attention be given to the historical meaning of words: "A more precise determination of any point in a given text must be decided on the basis of the use of language common to the author and his original public" (quoted in Dunn, 2003b: 112n51). The foundational work of these scholars has been refined and elaborated, but their intellectual heritage remains formidable. Biblical texts are to be interpreted with careful attention to their language and linguistic contexts. Historical philology is part of the unavoidable heavy lifting of sound biblical interpretation.

Interpreters should receive this heritage as the bountiful gift that it is. Our current philological resources—lexicons, dictionaries, theological wordbooks, grammars, electronic data banks and search engines, and so forth—represent the vast accumulated wisdom of nearly four centuries of toil by thousands of scholars. We should not be put off by the technical detail and occasional aridness of these tools. Since words are a medium of divine revelation, their study is indispensable. As the nineteenth-century Scottish theologian A. M. Fairbairn said, "No [one] can be a theologian who is not a philologian. [The one] who is no grammarian is no divine" (A. Robertson, 1934: x). Lexical resources often reward and even surprise the dutiful interpreter. The Anglican biblical scholar Edwyn Hoskyns waxed poetic in a sermon, "Can we rescue a word, and discover a universe? Can we study a language, and awake to the Truth? Can we bury ourselves in a lexicon, and arise in the presence of God?" (quoted in Bockmuehl, 2006: 144) Overstated? Theatrical? Perhaps. But anyone who has experienced the transcendent and transforming power of the Word (or even "words," in the plural and without capitalization) will attest to the connection between discourse and divine revelation, perhaps best expressed in the opening words of the Gospel of John.

Etymology, Usage, and Context

How then do we probe into the meaning of words? That actually may not be the most helpful way to conceive of the task, for individual words are not the primary bearers of meaning. The locus of meaning is to be sought in units of discourse certainly no smaller than a sentence. As a general rule, the paragraph is the basic unit of communication (Louw, 1982: vii). Words do, at least in the popular sense, have meanings; indeed, morphemes, which are only small parts of words, have meaning. (The letter "s" has meaning when as a suffix it forms the plural of a noun. The letter "a" has meaning when as a prefix it denotes the negative or absence of something, as in "atheist.") The point here is a variation of one made earlier: context is decisive in determining meaning, or as my former professor said: "Context is everything." We will consider the importance of context momentarily; first I will discuss two other factors that may contribute to meaning but are scarcely determinative: etymology and usage. It is important to understand what etymology and usage do and do *not* tell us, for their misuse involves certain logical fallacies.

ETYMOLOGY

Etymology refers to the history of the development of a word from its origin to its current usage (Louw, 1982: 23–31; Barr, 1961: 107–60). This usually involves analyzing the word's component parts and tracing the cognate forms of the word in other languages, especially an ancestral language. It is often fascinating to learn about the origin and history of a word, and etymology sometimes contributes to meaning. But it is a lesser contribution, and in some cases etymology is quite far removed from the contemporary, contextual meaning of a word. A handful of English examples will suffice to illustrate the point. In the columns below, the word on the left has an etymological connection to the word or words on the right.

amethyst	remedy against drunkenness
assassin	hashish user
cretin	Christian
hysteria	womb
manure	to work with the hand
nice	ignorant, not knowing
orchid	testicle
subtle	weaving of textiles
testicle	witness
veterinarian	old

Numerous other examples could be given to show how a word's meanings can stray far from its origin. It is, therefore, ill advised to speak of the "root meaning" of a word. If a root has a meaning at all, it is not necessarily close to the contemporary semantic range of the word. Moreover, knowledge of the root meaning or etymology of a word is scarcely needed in order to use it intelligently. How many English speakers could explain the etymology of the words "butterfly" and "honeymoon" without recourse to a reference dictionary? Yet we use these words with ease. "It is a basic principle of modern semantic theory that we cannot progress from the form of a word to its meaning. Form and meaning are not directly correlated" (Louw, 1982: 29).

In John 12:6 and 13:29 the Greek word *glōssokomon* is used. It refers to the "money bag" or "common purse" that Judas kept for the disciples, but originally the word meant a protective case for a reed or mouthpiece of a flute (*glōssa*, "tongue" + *komeō*, "tend, care for"). It eventually comes to mean any sort of container, including a box for money. Its development is similar to the English term "glove compartment." Who keeps gloves in a glove compartment anymore? Yet the name has stuck.

The failure of etymology reliably to supply the meaning of a word has led scholars to speak of the *etymological fallacy*: the mistaken notion that etymology is the key to meaning. Etymology is still valuable for understanding the history and origin of words, but it is of relatively less importance for textual interpretation, in which the primary concern is a word's meaning in a particular literary context. A partial exception to this principle occurs when the word in question has very limited usage in the literature (Barr, 1961: 158). When a word is rare, there are fewer contexts for discerning its meaning. In such cases etymology becomes more important, but even here it must be used with caution. A New Testament example is the word *theopneustos* (2 Tim. 3:16). This passage contains the only New Testament occurrence of the word. By analyzing the form of the word, we can at least discern that it is related to the notions of "God" and "breathing." Hence, the common translation "inspired by God" or "God-breathed." Another example is *harpagmos* in Philippians 2:6. Much scholarly energy has been expended on this single word, in part because this is the only instance of it in the New Testament. Again, scholars have turned to analysis of its apparent root and its cognate forms, though even with these aids the precise meaning remains somewhat elusive.

Usage

Usage refers to the variety of meanings that a word might have in a variety of contexts, its semantic range. The notion of "usage" underscores the semantic principle that words do not have a single meaning or a root meaning; rather, they have a range of meanings, each one elicited by a particular context. The technical term for this is "polysemy." As J. P. Louw points out, "Polysemy is a matter of the economic utilization of forms. A language would be quite unwieldy if it had a separate word for everything in existence. To overcome this problem different things are denoted by the same form" (1982: 40). Polysemy implies, then, that a word does not have a meaning apart from a linguistic context, but only a range of possible meanings.

As a general rule, the linguistic context of a word will determine which of the possible meanings is intended. Biblical scholars have sometimes erroneously argued that a New Testament author intends by the use of a particular Greek word all the possible nuances of the Hebrew term that lies behind it (Barr, 1961: 187–88). But it is a fallacy to think that a word bears all its possible meanings in a single context or that this enriches communication. In fact, "words signify only *one* meaning in each specific context in which they are used, except for rare instances where a speaker purposely intends a play on meanings" (Louw, 1982: 35). James Barr (1961: 218) has a term for this: "The error that arises, when the 'meaning' of a word (understood as the total series of relations in which it is used in the literature) is read into a particular case as its sense and implication there, may be called 'illegitimate totality transfer.'" Despite this term's precision, I find "illegitimate totality transfer" rather cumbersome. I prefer the *dump-truck fallacy*. Imagine an interpreter driving a semantic dump truck throughout the literary landscape, tossing heaping shovelfuls of meaning into the truck at each of several stops. Then the interpreter backs the truck up to the passage under consideration, hits the lever, and "transfers the totality in an illegitimate fashion," unloading it all into one text. Authors scarcely ever intend this; interpreters should try to discern the intended meaning of the word in its context as precisely as possible.

Scholars are not the only ones to fall prey to the dump-truck fallacy. I once received an exegesis paper on a passage in Philippians, where Paul writes that he wants to "be found *in* [Christ]" (3:9). In explicating the preposition "in," the student wrote that by the use of this phrase, "Paul indicates that he wants to be with, near, within sight of, and in the arms of Jesus Christ. Additionally Paul wants to be within Jesus, as well as around and near him." I was encouraged that the student had obviously consulted a lexicon to learn the word's usage, but one can only hope that the poor, overworked preposition survived this wringing to be used another day.

The dump-truck fallacy errs by importing a word's entire usage into one text. There is another error related to usage, what one might call the *statistical fallacy*. When the contextual meaning of a word is unclear or problematic, some interpreters are tempted to rely on the meaning that is statistically most common. For example, one scholar found the verb "know" in the account of the destruction of Sodom and Gomorrah to be problematic: "And they called to Lot, 'Where are the men who came to you tonight? Bring them out to us, so that we may *know* them'" (Gen. 19:5). This scholar argued that "know" in this context probably does not mean "know sexually" since only fourteen times out of 943 instances does it have that meaning in the Hebrew Bible (D. Bailey, 1955: 2–4). But as John Oswalt asserts, "This interpretation is astonishing. Odds have nothing to do with linguistic usage. Context determines meaning" (Oswalt, 1979: 73).

In a similar fashion, another scholar was troubled by Mark 2:26, in which Mark seems to name the wrong high priest when he says, "[David] entered the house of God when Abiathar was high priest" (*epi Abiathar archiereōs*). In 1 Samuel 21:1–6 the priest in this episode is clearly identified as Ahimelech. Again the argument is made that the meaning of a particular word (*epi*) is highly unusual. In 18 of the 21 places where Mark uses this preposition with the genitive case, it refers to location rather than time. So, the argument goes, the translation "when" is not very likely (Blomberg, 1987: 193). This scholar asserts that the preposition must be quasilocative rather than temporal. The meaning must be, "[David] entered the house of God *in the passage of Scripture concerning* Abiathar the high priest," since Abiathar was a more important high priest who figures prominently in the narrative of 1 Samuel shortly after the Ahimelech episode. There are several weaknesses in this argument, but for our present purposes I simply note again: statistics do not determine meaning; context does, and context in this case favors a temporal sense. For more on this particular text, see Danker (2000: 367, 18a) and France (2002: 146n52).

CONTEXT

So we return to the importance of context as the determining factor in the meaning of individual words as well as the meaning of larger units of discourse. I once read a promotional flyer for a book titled *The Words of Jesus* (Lewis, 1998). The advertisement claimed that the book

> strips away all but the essence of Jesus' thought and lets the reader go right to the heart of the sayings. It presents every one of Jesus' words, as recorded in the New Testament, without the intervening stories and other dialogue. Now, for the first time, every saying and parable is allowed to stand on its own, without comment, without adornment. . . . It's a new way to study Jesus' teachings. It presents Jesus' words—words heard over and over in one particular context—but now without the benefit (or the burden) of familiarity.

The editors of this volume seem to operate by a different version of the CIE principle: Context is extraneous. One might be able to argue that selected sayings of Jesus have a freestanding and aphoristic quality, but even in these cases the biblical context provides an interpretive framework by which to understand the sayings, and that context is an aid to interpretation, not a hindrance. Context does not clutter; it clarifies.

Yet context has many aspects: linguistic, historical, social, religious, political, and so forth (Vanhoozer, 1998: 250–51). In the section "Consider Textual Connections" below, we will examine the broader context that extends to historical events, social phenomena, religious institutions, and political dynamics, but here our chief concern is the linguistic or discursive context: the language of the text we are studying and of other relevant literature. In terms of linguistic context, the interpreter should bear in mind the *rule of proximity*. Simply stated it claims, "The closest context is the most relevant context." When interpreting a passage in Paul, the most important context is the immediate context, the surrounding verses, the paragraph or two that precede and follow the text under study. From there one may branch out incrementally. Think in terms of a series of concentric circles. The smallest circle is the immediate context. The next level might be a subdivision in the book, then a major division, then the entire writing. From there one might move to other works by the same author, or in the case of Matthew, Mark, and Luke, to the other Synoptic Gospels. The next larger circle would be the New Testament, then the entire Bible (i.e., incorporating the Septuagint), then Greek literature that is roughly contemporary with the New Testament, and finally all ancient Greek literature.

All of this is to say that, while a passage in Homer (750 BCE?) might shed some light on the meaning of a word in the Gospel of Mark (70 CE?), that is *not* the first place an interpreter should look. A sound principle is that Mark is the best interpreter of Mark, Paul of Paul, John of John, and so on. This principle is ancient. Aristarchus, head of the library in Alexandria in the mid-second century BCE, articulated the principle that one ought to "explain Homer from Homer" (*Homēron ex Homērou saphēnizein*; Sodano, 1970: §56). In other words, "The best guide to an author's usage is the corpus of [that author's] own writings, and therefore difficulties ought to be explained wherever possible by reference to other passages in the same author" (Reynolds and N. Wilson, 1974: 13). So in studying Mark, turn to Homer only after more proximal sources have been exhausted.

Among the writings *outside* the New Testament that most often have value for interpretation, pride of place clearly goes to the Septuagint. Even though the writings of the Septuagint were translated from Hebrew (or in some cases written originally in Greek) between one hundred to three hundred years before the production of the earliest Christian writings, they nevertheless emerge from approximately the same social, religious, and cultural matrix that Jesus and his earliest disciples inhabited. In addition to the Septuagint, two authors deserve special mention: Josephus, the Jewish historian, and Philo, the Jewish statesman and philosopher of Alexandria. Both of these authors flourished in the first century CE, Philo chiefly in the first half, Josephus in the latter half. Philo was a resident of the Jewish Diaspora, Josephus a resident of Palestine. Extensive bodies of writings survive from both men. Because of both cultural and chronological proximity, the value of Philo and Josephus for understanding the New Testament and early Christianity can hardly be overstated.

If exegesis is a process of interrogating or conversing with a text, what questions can we pose to the text in order to analyze its language? The first issue is the selection of words for study. Here are some initial questions:

- What words in the text are especially important and deserving of further study? (The average interpreter cannot realistically study every word of the text in depth, nor does every word merit equal attention.)
- What words or similar terms are *repeated*? (Remember that repetition is one of the most basic ways an author reveals emphasis.)
- What words bear the most *semantic* freight by virtue of their part of speech? (E.g., nouns and verbs, especially less-common ones, are usually important. Adjectives and adverbs may be worth examining. Function words, such as articles, prepositions, and personal pronouns, usually have less significance. Obviously there may exceptions to this rule. In rare cases a definite article might be critical to interpretation.)
- What words bear the most *theological* freight? (E.g., when Paul writes, "God was in Christ, reconciling the world to himself" [2 Cor. 5:19: cf. versions], the participle "reconciling" is worthy of special attention because of its theological importance. Repetition also flags this word as highly significant in this context.)

From there move on to more focused questions.

- What are the basic *characteristics* and *qualifiers* of the important words? If a noun, is it singular or plural? Do any adjectives or clauses further describe the noun? If a verb, what is its subject? What is (are) its object(s), if any? Do any adverbs or phrases further define the nature of the verb's action?
- What is the *range of possible meanings* for the word as indicated by the dictionary?
- What does a concordance reveal about the *distribution* of the word in the New Testament? In this particular author? In this particular writing?
- What is the range of the word's *meanings* in this particular author?
- What is the most likely *contextual meaning* of the word in this specific text?

Three brief examples of lexical study will illustrate some of the points made above.

In Luke 2:35 the elderly Simeon blesses Mary and the infant Jesus and warns that the child is destined to be a sign that will be opposed, "so that the inner *thoughts* of many will be revealed." The word "thoughts" translates Greek *dialogismoi*. The etymology of the word suggests a neutral meaning: "thoughts, reasoning, ruminations." But the New Testament usage reveals a pejorative tendency: "schemes, machinations, doubts, disputations, vanities." In particular, Luke's five other uses of the word refer to "thoughts hostile to Jesus or questioning him" (R. Brown, 1993: 441). More important, the context in Luke favors this since it speaks of opposition, power struggles, and Mary's related grief. The word's usage, especially in Luke, combines with context to favor a pejorative sense of *dialogismoi* in Luke 2:35.

In Matthew 19:28 (roughly paralleled by Luke 22:30) Jesus informs his disciples that "at the renewal of all things, when the Son of Man is seated on the throne of his glory, you who have followed me will also sit on twelve thrones, *judging* the twelve tribes of Israel." The participle "judging" (Greek: *krinontes*) could be read in a negative fashion: Jesus's followers will "sit in judgment" on Israel, will examine them judicially and condemn them. But biblical usage of the verb *krinō* and the related Hebrew term *shafat* often convey the sense of "rule," "govern," even "vindicate," in the sense of "administer justice" in behalf of the oppressed, rather than against perpetrators. Examples abound in the Psalms: 10:18; 35:24; 43:1; 72:4; 82:3; and so on. This may very well be the contextual sense in Matthew 19:28 and Luke 22:30. In the former passage, the context speaks of the time of renewal. Is this not the messianic age in which the people of God (the tribes of Israel) are vindicated? The context in Luke is even clearer. The disciples will receive a "kingdom," with messianic imagery of eating and drinking at the table. In both Matthew and Luke, "thrones" suggest a context of government rather than judgment. The authority to be conferred on the disciples is, therefore, not the judicial role of punishment but that of governing so as to effect justice (R. Horsley, 1994: 86–87).

Finally, in John 15:2 we find the image of God as a vinegrower or tenant farmer. God is said to "remove" or "take away" every branch in Jesus that bears no fruit. The Greek verb is *airō*, and every beginning Greek student learns that this word means "I take away, I lift up." The latter meaning is attractive here. Could God be seen as one who "lifts up, props up, supports" the ailing branch to enable it to become fruit bearing? This meaning is more redemptive and less harsh than the sense of "remove, take away, cut off." But the remedial sense is not contextually supported. The larger passage (15:1–8) describes a stark contrast between branches that do and do not abide in the vine, that do and do not bear fruit. John 15:2a is the negative outcome that contrasts with the positive outcome in 15:2b. Verse 6 makes it clear that branches that do not abide in the vine (and thereby bear fruit) are discarded and burned. In keeping with the stark dualism so typical of the Fourth Gospel, *airō* in John 15:2 is to be read as "remove."

As a final caveat before we turn to the specific tools to be employed, the student of the New Testament must always be alert to authorial quirks and tendencies. Granted, this comes only with extended exposure to a writer's style or with study of relevant secondary literature. A particular possibility to be aware of is *stylistic variation*. Some authors may vary vocabulary, shifting back and forth between rough synonyms, for no reason other than a desire to avoid repetition. The interpreter who teases out subtle distinctions in the use of such words might be conjuring up nuance where it does not exist. The Fourth Evangelist is particularly fond of varying vocabulary for stylistic effect. On the one hand, John has two words for "love," two words for "send," and two words for "sheep," with no apparent difference in meaning (see John 20:21; 21:15–17). On the other hand, John has two words for "life," between which he maintains a strict distinction. Careful study of an author's usage and style in such cases is necessary to discern whether the variation is semantically significant (Turner, 1976: 76–77).

Tools for Lexical Study

The types of tools for lexical study, already alluded to above, are threefold:

1. the lexicon or dictionary (especially the standard, authoritative works);
2. theological dictionaries and wordbooks (often multivolume sets); and
3. concordances.

Because of their special importance, these resources are listed here, with brief annotations, as well as in the bibliography.

Lexicons and Dictionaries

The old saying "A dictionary is obsolete as soon as it is published" reflects the continual evolution of a living language. This is less of a problem with a dialect of an ancient language that has a fixed and limited textual basis. Nevertheless, other things being equal, a comprehensive and up-to-date lexicon of New Testament (NT) Greek is better than one that is abridged or several decades old. The following resources are recommended. Standard abbreviations are given in parentheses after the bibliographical data.

F. W. Danker, ed. 2000. *A Greek-English Lexicon of the New Testament and Other Early Christian Literature.* 3rd ed. Based on a German lexicon edited by Walter Bauer and on previous English editions by W. F. Arndt, F. W. Gingrich, and F. W. Danker. Chicago: University of Chicago Press. (BDAG) This is the standard lexicon for NT study. Up-to-date and unsurpassed, it has a wealth of references to primary and secondary literature. It is indispensable for serious study of the Greek NT.

J. P. Louw and Eugene A. Nida, eds. 1988. *Greek-English Lexicon of the New Testament Based on Semantic Domains.* 2 vols. New York: United Bible Societies. (L&N) This lexicon is the product of recent linguistic study. Words are arranged by semantic domains, as clusters of words with similar meanings, and not alphabetically. It lacks the wealth of citations and bibliography that BDAG has but is full of insights about synonyms and is particularly helpful to translators. Not a rival to BDAG but an excellent complement.

Horst Balz and Gerhard Schneider, eds. 1990–93. *Exegetical Dictionary of the New Testament.* 3 vols. Grand Rapids: Eerdmans. (*EDNT*) This set moves in the direction of the theological dictionaries but, unlike the latter, it includes every word in the Greek NT. The discussion of exegetical and theological problems is sometimes concise, but sometimes fuller than BDAG.

Theological Dictionaries

These resources usually make no attempt to treat every word in the NT, but they provide lengthy discussions of theologically significant words. The first two resources below are edited collections of studies authored by scores of German scholars. The third item is the work of one prodigious French scholar.

G. Kittel and G. Friedrich, eds. 1964–76. *Theological Dictionary of the New Testament.* Translated by G. W. Bromiley. 10 vols. Grand Rapids: Eerdmans. (*TDNT*) The *TDNT* or "Kittel" is a monumental reference work and a source of information without equal. The arrangement is alphabetical, but the essays draw together clusters of etymologically related words. Thus, "faith" (*pistis*) and "believe" (*pisteuō*) are covered in the same essay. The structure of a typical essay moves from classical Greek to the Septuagint (LXX), Philo and Josephus, the pseudepigrapha and rabbinic literature, ending with the NT and other early Christian usage. Christian usage alone is available in a highly abridged, one-volume format, the "little Kittel" (Kittel and Friedrich, 1985). The linguistic method of the *TDNT* has been criticized (Barr, 1961: 206–62), and concerns have been raised about the political sympathies of Kittel himself, who was a supporter of the Nazi party. Although the latter is surely to be condemned, it should be noted that Kittel edited only the first four volumes and authored only a small fraction of the essays in those volumes. Kittel was capable of sober, historical scholarship, and his politics did not necessarily taint everything that he wrote. Nevertheless, one should always read critically, and some German biblical scholarship of the 1930s and 1940s requires special scrutiny (Ericksen, 1985: 28–78; Meeks, 2004).

Colin Brown, ed. 1975–85. *New International Dictionary of New Testament Theology*. 3 vols. plus an index vol. Grand Rapids: Zondervan. (*NIDNTT*) This work is arranged in English alphabetical order, making it user-friendly for persons without a knowledge of Hebrew and Greek. Like Kittel, it traces the usage of words through classical Greek, the Old Testament, rabbinic writings, and the NT. Unlike Kittel, it sometimes groups words that are semantically but not etymologically related (a method that is arguably more linguistically sound). Volume 1 includes a helpful "Glossary of Technical Terms." Finally, the *NIDNTT*, although translated from German, has been revised and significantly enlarged in its English version, including several new articles by British and American scholars.

Ceslas Spicq. 1994. *Theological Lexicon of the New Testament*. Translated and edited by James D. Ernest. 3 vols. Peabody, MA: Hendrickson. (*TLNT*) Spicq's aim is self-consciously theological, but he illustrates the language of the NT with a wide range of literary texts, papyri, and inscriptions. The *TLNT* treats many words that receive summary treatment in Kittel.

Related Greek Lexicons

The following resources are invaluable tools for specific bodies of literature. While they occasionally shed light on early Christian usage (especially the first three items), they are not, strictly speaking, lexicons of NT Greek. They are a reminder that Greek has a long history, with several centuries of literary production both before and after the writings of the NT.

James Hope Moulton and George Milligan. 1930. *The Vocabulary of the Greek Testament Illustrated from the Papyri and Other Non-literary Sources*. Grand Rapids: Eerdmans. (MM) In the late nineteenth and early twentieth centuries, many nonliterary papyri were discovered, dating to a period roughly contemporary with the writings of the NT. This volume does not try to provide a complete lexicon of the NT but rather shows how these papyri, as well as Greek inscriptions, shed light on its language. Since most of its citations are not translated, MM requires some expertise.

J. Lust, E. Eynikel, and K. Hauspie, eds. 1992–96. *A Greek-English Lexicon of the Septuagint.* 2 vols. Stuttgart: Deutsche Bibelgesellschaft. The general aim of this volume is concise, rather than exhaustive, treatment. All LXX words are included, but most entries are brief and typically provide "translation equivalents" rather than extended discussions of meanings. A brief introduction and bibliography are included.

T. Muraoka. 2009. *A Greek-English Lexicon of the Septuagint.* 3rd ed. Leuven: Peeters. This is a full-fledged lexicon of the LXX, not merely a glossary. It includes helpful information on synonyms, antonyms, idioms, and syntactical constructions. Even function words such as prepositions and conjunctions are fully analyzed. References to relevant scholarly literature are also included.

Henry G. Liddell and Robert Scott. 1940. *A Greek-English Lexicon.* 9th ed. Revised and augmented by Henry S. Jones. With a 1968 supplement. Oxford: Oxford University Press. (LSJ) Referred to as LSJ (the initials of its primary editors), this is the standard lexicon for ancient Greek. It is a reference work of vast erudition, with over a century and a half of refinement and expansion. The sweep of authors and writers incorporated in its entries is breathtaking, from Homer (eighth century BCE) to late antiquity (fifth century CE), with the greatest concentration on the fifth to third centuries BCE. The structure of most entries is chronological, beginning with the oldest attested usage. Although there are numerous citations of the LXX and NT, students of early Christianity need to be mindful of the work's broad historical range. A word with one meaning in the Gospel of John may have had a quite different meaning in Homer or Plato. Remember the "rule of proximity."

Geoffrey W. H. Lampe, ed. 1961. *A Patristic Greek Lexicon.* Oxford; New York: Clarendon. (PGL) As the name implies, this is the standard lexicon for Greek Christian writers of the postapostolic age. The time period spans approximately seven centuries from Clement of Rome, who was contemporary with the later writings of the NT, to Theodore of Studios (759–826). It thus covers the era of the creeds, councils, and doctrinal disputes. Words that are important in the development of Christian theology, spirituality, liturgy, and church structure receive especially full treatment. In part, PGL serves as a companion to LSJ in that it treats all words used in the church fathers, whether of theological importance or not, that are not included in LSJ. Contrariwise, words that are treated in LSJ that have no special significance in the Greek fathers are not included in PGL, even though they may be attested in those authors. In this way PGL aims not to duplicate

LSJ but to complement it. While PGL does not treat NT usage, it often provides the trajectory for NT words, such as how *martys* develops from "witness" to "martyr"; how *euangelion*, "proclaimed good news," becomes "a writing dealing with the life and teaching of Jesus"; how *episkopos*, "overseer," evolves into the formal office of "bishop"; and how *prosōpon*, "face," develops into "a person of the Trinity."

CONCORDANCES

A concordance is an alphabetical index of the words in a given corpus of writings. Concordances exist for hundreds of authors and writings from antiquity through modern times, and the Bible is no exception. Indeed, most major translations of the Bible have occasioned the production of new concordances, since concordances are text-specific. Thus there are concordances of the Hebrew Bible, the Greek NT, Latin and Syriac Bibles, the Septuagint, and scores of modern translations including the NRSV and the NIV (Danker, 2003: 1–21). Concordances of English translations are helpful in locating specific verses when only a key term or two are remembered. They also help a reader locate texts on a given topic, such as "patience," "joy," "fasting," "divorce," and so forth. The minister who wants to preach a sermon series on "the heart" can consult a concordance and quickly find a wealth of texts from which to develop ideas (700+ passages in the NRSV). There are, however, limits to the use of English concordances, since a translation imperfectly reflects the word choices of the original author. If one wants to study Paul's idea of "sanctification," the greatest precision will be obtained by selecting a cluster of closely related Greek terms (perhaps by using Louw and Nida, 1988) and then gathering data on the relevant words by using a Greek concordance.

Concordances are wonderful for generating raw data. This is both their strength and their weakness. They are the least interpretive tool one can use in studying the Bible. They will lead a reader to all passages relevant to a particular theme, along with some that may be irrelevant, and provide a bit of context in each case. But the data is unprocessed, uninterpreted, and must be sorted, weighed, and construed by the user. Nowadays computer software is making hardcopy concordances obsolete. Electronic texts can be searched in myriad ways by software that spews back results and even tells you what fraction of a second elapsed while generating them. (As one person quipped, "Now we can make bad exegetical decisions at lightning speed.") Biblical texts have been searchable for many years now, and other ancient writers, such as Philo and Josephus, have also become available.

With an increase in technological capacity seems to come a decrease in patience. Some years ago I learned how to use one of the most amazing tools ever created for studying ancient Greek texts: the *Thesaurus Linguae Graecae*, a searchable CD-ROM database of all ancient Greek literature from Homer to

600 CE, and many additional texts up to the fall of Byzantium in 1453. I told my doctoral adviser about the helpful data that I was gathering on my trips to the computer lab in the main university library. He said that he had been curious about a particular word and asked me to conduct a "global search" for him (i.e., a search of the entire CD-ROM rather than selected authors) the next time I was in the lab. I hesitated somewhat and lamented out loud, "But global searches can take up to sixty minutes, professor—!" I caught myself midsentence, realizing with some chagrin that what he had asked me to do could not have been accomplished in sixty *years* when he had been a graduate student. So for those who retain enough fortitude to invest an hour or more in the use of a concordance, electronic or otherwise, I list the following tools for both Greek and English Bibles.

Edwin Hatch and Henry A. Redpath, eds. 1998. *A Concordance to the Septuagint: And the Other Greek Versions of the Old Testament.* 2nd ed. Grand Rapids: Baker Academic.

John R. Kohlenberger III and Edward W. Goodrick. 1999. *The NIV Exhaustive Concordance.* 2nd ed. Grand Rapids: Zondervan.

John R. Kohlenberger III, Edward W. Goodrick, and James A. Swanson. 1995. *The Exhaustive Concordance to the Greek New Testament.* Grand Rapids: Zondervan. (The citations are given in Greek, with the key Greek word in boldface.)

John R. Kohlenberger III, Edward W. Goodrick, and James A. Swanson. 1997. *The Greek-English Concordance to the New Testament.* Grand Rapids: Zondervan. (The citations are given in the NIV. The English word that translates the key Greek word is in boldface.)

John R. Kohlenberger III and Richard E. Whitaker. 2000. *The Analytical Concordance to the New Revised Standard Version of the New Testament.* Grand Rapids: Eerdmans; New York: Oxford University Press.

W. F. Moulton and A. S. Geden. 1978. *A Concordance to the Greek Testament.* Revised by H. K. Moulton. 5th ed. Edinburgh: T&T Clark. (First ed., 1897. Moulton and Geden was a standby for many generations, is still very usable, but perhaps is succeeded by Kohlenberger, Goodrick, and Swanson, 1995.)

There are several software packages for Bible study, most of which have numerous texts and translations (Hebrew, Greek, English, etc.) and the capacity to do simple and complex word searches. Among the most popular are the following:

Accordance 7.1. (Oriented toward Mac but will run on Windows with a provided Mac emulator. Swift and efficient; well-designed; offers a variety of packages, some rather pricey.) Website: www.accordancebible.com.

BibleWorks 8.0 for Windows. (A focus on the original languages; fast and capable of complex searches; one basic package with a variety of optional modules; a good value for what one gets; some beginners find that it has a steep learning curve.) Website: www.bibleworks.com.

Logos/Libronix. (Integrates Bible software with a large electronic theological library; a huge and growing assortment of optional resources; several different packages are available; some users find it not as speedy as the others.) Website: www.logos.com.

Technological resources for biblical study are a burgeoning field. New start-up companies are legion, and some of them "shall be like the morning mist or like the dew that goes away early" (Hos. 13:3). The three resources mentioned above have been around for a while, have undergone many improvements and new versions, and are likely still to be there in the near future. Bible software, like a major reference work, is a big investment, and it is wise to ask around and do a little research before making a commitment. I have found the website *Bible Software Review* to be a helpful resource (www.bsreview.org). There is also a helpful appendix in Hayes and Holladay (2007: 213–30) that discusses both software packages and internet websites.

The beginning interpreter could easily be overwhelmed by the mass of information available in the resources described in the last few pages. Although one will certainly encounter discussions whose relevance to one's immediate needs seems remote, the reader should not think that the standard linguistic tools contain nothing more than stale, antiquarian data. Deep theological and even homiletical insights can be found by the resourceful exegete. While preparing a sermon on Matthew 16:13–26, I looked up the Greek word *satan* in the standard NT Greek lexicon (BDAG), even though I already knew full well its meaning and etymology. I encountered this tidbit: "Peter is called Satan by Jesus, because his attempt to turn Jesus aside fr[om] his divine assignment to accept the consequences of his involvement with humanity has made him a tempter of a diabolical sort, who might thwart the divine plan of salvation" (Danker, 2000: 916–17). With just a little editing, this theological jewel fit neatly into the finery of my sermon. Such gems await the diligent user of our rich lexical resources. For a more detailed discussion of concordances, lexicons, their history, and their use, see Danker (2003: 1–21, 109–47).

Exercises on Key Texts

Read your key text with a view to identifying its important words. Look these up in the standard Greek lexicon (Danker, 2000) to get a sense of both their usage and their likely meaning in your passage. Pick one or two of the words you consider most critical to understanding the text and look them up in a theological dictionary.

Mark 2:1–12 (Healing a Paralytic)
Mark 7:24–37 (A Syrophoenician Woman and a Deaf Man)
Acts 3:1–10 (Peter Heals a Lame Man)
1 Corinthians 12:1–11 (Spiritual Gifts)
1 Corinthians 15:1–11 (The Resurrection)
Revelation 4:1–11 (A Vision of Heavenly Worship)

7. Examine the Grammar

Grammar is the study of words, their forms, and their relationships to one another in the formation of phrases, clauses, and whole sentences. Analysis of grammar is, in effect, structural analysis at the most detailed level. We have already talked about structure at the level of the entire writing and at the level of the pericope. When we zero in on the structure of individual phrases, clauses, and sentences, we are studying grammar.

A traditional way of analyzing English grammar, popular for generations in elementary schools and high schools, was sentence diagramming. (It wasn't by chance that such institutions were sometimes called "grammar" schools.) Using this method, students would show in graphic form both the basic structure of a sentence (e.g., subject—verb—direct object) and its more detailed components (adjectival and adverbial modifiers, prepositional phrases, relative clauses, etc.). Some people will find sentence diagramming a helpful tool for analyzing and displaying the grammatical structure of biblical passages, whether in English or in Greek. Others may find that the benefits of diagramming are at least partially outweighed by its costs. In effect, diagramming is a graphic technique that must first be learned and then employed on specific texts. Some people may find that they understand the grammatical relationships apart from their graphic presentation, and mastering the latter only steepens the learning curve. The approach here will focus on individual grammatical phenomena that are exegetically significant. Persons who find that sentence diagrams facilitate their learning may wish to consult Fee (1993: 65–80). In addition, some computer software programs provide assistance in diagramming.

The finer one's structural analysis, the greater the need to work with the Greek text. English translations frequently, and often necessarily, break up Greek sentences, turn subordinate clauses into main clauses, rearrange word order, supply words that are implied, and make other changes to the structure of the Greek text. Although one obviously can glean a great deal of important information about the meaning of a text by studying it in translation, detailed study of structure may go astray if based only on the English.

The components of Greek grammar are many, as a perusal of the table of contents of any standard reference grammar will indicate. The most important areas of grammar for exegesis are the following four: the case function of nouns, the tense and mood of finite verbs, the usage of the infinitive and participle (nonfinite forms), and the diverse types of subordinate clauses. Some common interpretive questions for each of these four are listed below. Individual illustrations will be given, and then an example of a more holistic grammatical analysis will be given by using 1 Corinthians 13, which was also used above (pp. 63–64) to illustrate structural analysis at the level of the pericope.

Grammatical Analysis of Nouns

- What are the case, number, and gender of the noun in question? (Case is the most significant characteristic for exegesis since it reveals the relationship between the noun and other words in the sentence.)
- What is the precise function of the case? This will depend on the combination of at least three factors: (1) the basic meaning(s) of that case, sometimes called the "unaffected" meaning (D. Wallace, 1996: 37, 76–77, 139–40, 177–78); (2) the lexical meaning of the noun in question; and, most important, (3) the literary context.
- Are any other features significant (the gender or number of the noun, other words in the close context that govern or are governed by the noun, the possibility of an idiomatic expression, and so forth)?

An Illustration of Case Function

In Revelation 3:14 Jesus is referred to as *hē archē tēs ktiseōs tou theou*, "the beginning [or, "ruler"] of God's creation" (NRSV mg. note). The noun *ktiseōs* (creation) is in the genitive case. The phrase might be construed as calling Jesus the first part of creation: the first created being. This interprets the genitive *ktiseōs* as expressing the whole, of which the *archē* is the part. This is linguistically possible (Danker, 2000: 138), but *archē* here more likely refers to the "first cause." As a noun of action (cf. the cognate verb *archō*, "begin, rule"), the meaning of *archē* is probably "the one who is the originating cause of [or, "the one who rules"]" creation. In this way the genitive *ktiseōs* is understood as the object of the action implied in *archē*. This is supported by the theology of the entire writing. Nowhere in the book of Revelation is Jesus regarded as part of the created order, whereas his regnant role is often highlighted (1:5; 11:15; 17:14; 19:16; 20:4). In Revelation, Jesus is only "the beginning" in conjunction with being "the end," an overarching expression of totality that leaves little room for regarding him as the first part of the creation (22:13; cf. 1:17; 2:8).

Grammatical Analysis of Finite Verbs

- What are the tense and mood of the finite verbs in the passage? (These are generally the most exegetically significant characteristics.)

- What time and type of action are expressed by the verb tense (if indicative)? This will normally be a function of three things: (1) the basic significance of the tense (the so-called "unaffected meaning"; D. Wallace, 1996: 497, 499–504); (2) the lexical meaning of the word in question; and (3) the literary context. Although the Greek verb tenses have a basic significance (linear, undefined, or completed action), there are various nuances of each of the tenses that will be revealed by the lexical meaning of the word and the context. Thus a present tense might denote action that is attempted, iterative, ongoing, instantaneous, customary, and so forth.

- For nonindicative verbs, what is the significance of the mood? Most important here are the subjunctive and imperative moods. The optative mood was in decline in the Hellenistic period and is relatively infrequent in the NT (D. Wallace, 1996: 447, 461–93).

An Illustration of Verbal Analysis

In 1 Corinthians 15:3–5 the apostle Paul passes on traditional tenets of the Christian faith in a creedal statement. In a highly formulaic declaration, he employs four verbs to sum up the passion and resurrection of Christ: he died, he was buried, he was raised, and he appeared. Most English translations imply that all four actions are simple past-time events, but attention to the Greek tenses of the verbs reveals a nuance that is lost in translation. "Died," "was buried," and "appeared" are all in the aorist tense. The basic significance of the aorist tense (in the indicative mood) is to denote simple or undefined action in past time. The aorist affirms the action of the verb without describing its nature or duration. The verbs in question denote actions that can naturally be summed up by the aorist. But for the action of the resurrection, the perfect tense is used: *egēgertai*. The significance of the perfect tense is that it denotes an action that was completed in the past but has an effect or result that continues to the present, to the time of speaking. The implication is that, whereas the death and burial of Jesus were simple past events, his resurrection has an enduring effect. This is difficult to translate with economy of words, but one could paraphrase: "He died, . . . he was buried, . . . and his resurrection was accomplished such that now he is the risen one, . . . and he appeared. . . ." Of these four actions, the raising of Christ is portrayed as having a result that persists to the time of Paul's writing to the Corinthians, indeed to the "present" of all believers. It is often the case, as in 1 Corinthians 15:3–5, that the *departure* from the aorist tense in past-time narration is exegetically significant.

Grammatical Analysis of Infinitives and Participles

- Infinitives are verbal nouns, and as such they have both verbal and nominal qualities. One of the first questions to pose about an infinitival construction is this: How does it function in the sentence? Is the infinitive primarily verbal or nominal in its function? (See D. Wallace, 1996: 587–611.)

- Discerning the function of an infinitive may be facilitated by noting various "function words" that are closely related to it. Does the infinitive have an article? If so, what is the case of the article? Is the infinitive part of a prepositional phrase? If so, what is the preposition? Is there a conjunction with the infinitive such as *hōste* or *hōs*? These words will often limit the range of possible functions for the infinitive. Observation of the function words, together with careful scrutiny of the literary context (always the most important factor!), will usually make the function of the infinitive clear.

- Participles are verbal adjectives, and as such they have both verbal and adjectival qualities. Modern students of Greek often find participles one of the most challenging aspects of Greek grammar, in part because of their wide variety of uses. Again, the most basic question to pose is this: What is the function of the participle in its clause or sentence? Is its function primarily adverbial, adjectival, or nominal? (See D. Wallace, 1996: 612–55.)

- A variety of basic questions will help narrow the range of possible functions. Does the participle have an article? If the participle has an article, are they both in a construction with a substantive? The presence of an article is often a helpful structural clue, but even when the article is present (and especially when it is absent), context looms very large in the analysis of participles. Along with determining its function, always be sure to parse the participle fully. Identify its subject, any direct objects, adverbial modifiers, and so forth.

Illustrations of the Analysis of Infinitives and Participles

In James 1:27 the author defines religion that is pure and undefiled. He defines it in terms of two infinitival clauses: "to care for [*episkeptesthai*] orphans and widows in their distress" and "to keep oneself [*heauton tērein*] unstained by the world." Neither infinitive has an article, but both have direct objects and prepositional modifiers. The function of the infinitives is to identify the essential qualities of the noun "religion" and thereby define it. Grammarians refer to this as the appositional infinitive. James's point, then, is that pure and undefiled religion necessarily consists of these two qualities: one directed outward, toward persons in need; and one directed inward, toward conforming one's own life to God's law and avoiding the profane.

The Great Commission in Matthew 28:19–20 contains three participles that are strategically related to the main verb in the sentence. Most English translations render the opening words as, "Go therefore and make disciples," or something similar. The only finite verb in verse 19, however, is the imperative "make disciples." This clearly identifies it as the central thought, the primary action to which the participles are somehow related. Obviously, "going" is an antecedent action to "making disciples," particularly in the original social context in which the disciples were being commanded to take the gospel to all nations. The "going" does not identify the time, manner, means, cause, purpose, condition, and so forth of the main verb; it is simply an accompanying action, what grammarians call a participle of "attendant circumstance." Participles of this type often pick up the flavor of the main verb. Hence, "going" (*poreuthentes*) becomes a command in translation. The other two participles follow the opening imperative: "baptizing them . . . [and] teaching them." These are not simply accompanying acts that necessarily go along with the making of disciples. (One could imagine a religion that makes disciples by some very different entrance ritual.) Baptizing and teaching are likely the specific *means* by which Christian disciples are made, so these participles are instrumental in function. One makes disciples *by* baptizing persons into the faith and teaching them the commands of Jesus (D. Wallace, 1996: 645).

Grammatical Analysis of Clauses

- Since clauses are of many different types, the questions to be posed to them are manifold. The most important distinction is independent versus dependent. An independent clause can stand alone; it is not subordinate to another clause. It will contain a subject and a predicate. A dependent clause is grammatically subordinate to another clause (often the main clause) or some other part of the sentence. A dependent clause is not a complete thought and does not constitute a stand-alone sentence.

- In grammatical analysis of a sentence or larger unit of text, one must identify the independent (main) clauses and the dependent (subordinate) clauses. What is/are the main verb(s) in the sentence? What is/are the subordinate clause(s)? What sort of conjunctions link them together? Do these conjunctions simply tack one thought to the next, or do they subordinate one thought to another? Are the clauses related by contrast, cause and effect, inference, explanation, disjunction, or some other relationship? Again, we are often assisted by so-called function words, which primarily express relationship rather than semantic content.

- Greek grammar is like a computer operating system in that there are often several ways of accomplishing the same task. Redundancy is thus built into language. Purpose clauses, for example, can be expressed with the infinitive, the subjunctive, or an adverbial participle. Clauses can thus be analyzed according to their structure (e.g., a clause constructed with the conjunction *hina* + a subjunctive verb) or according to their function (e.g., a clause expressing the purpose of some other action). Attention to a clause's structure is often helpful in determining its meaning, but identifying the function or syntactical relationship is the chief exegetical goal. One could note, for example, that a computer operation was performed by a "double click." It is more important to note that the person thereby opened a file so as to edit a document.

Illustration of the Analysis of Clauses

In Acts 5:27–32 the apostles are brought before the council in Jerusalem after violating an order not to teach in Jesus's name. Peter speaks on behalf of the apostles, but angry opposition persists. Gamaliel, a respected teacher of the law, offers a counsel of wisdom and moderation. In 5:38–39 Gamaliel utters two conditional statements that offer contrasting assessments of the apostles' ministry: it may be of human origin or it may be of divine origin. Most English translations do not distinguish between the conditions, but the Greek grammar preserves a nuance of difference. In verse 38 the alternative of human origin is a third-class condition, which implies the uncertainty, though possibility, of the protasis (the "if" clause). The alternative of divine origin in verse 39 uses a first-class condition in Greek, which assumes, at least for the sake of argument, that the "if" clause is true. The two conditions are distinguished by different Greek words for "if" and different verbal moods in the protasis (subjunctive in v. 38, indicative in v. 39). A paraphrase would be something like: "If this should turn out to be of human origin . . . , but if, in fact, it is from God . . . ." Whether the historical Gamaliel actually spoke words that gave the benefit of the doubt to the divine origin of Christianity is beyond our knowledge. (He would have spoken Aramaic, not Greek.) But it is certainly the case that Luke *portrays* Gamaliel as being favorably disposed toward the new movement, and there is no question that *Luke* regards its origin as divine (Bruce, 1990: 178).

Tools for Grammatical Analysis

In these few pages we have only skimmed the surface of a discipline to which some scholars have devoted a lifetime. As in the case of all major reference tools, we are the beneficiaries of their extensive labors. The computer tools listed above under "Tools for Lexical Study" (pp. 77–78) provide a wealth of morphological information, meaning the identification of noun and verb forms, and sometimes offer grammars as add-on modules. The standard hardcopy tools for grammatical analysis include the following resources, grouped according to size and purpose:

Full-Reference Grammars

F. Blass and A. Debrunner. 1961. *A Greek Grammar of the New Testament and Other Early Christian Literature*. Translated and edited by Robert W. Funk. Chicago: University of Chicago Press. This was the standard Greek grammar in German for most of the twentieth century. Funk translated and supplemented it with notes from Debrunner. It is a valuable repository of grammatical information, although its arrangement in some places is awkward.

James Hope Moulton et al. 1908–76. *A Grammar of New Testament Greek.* Edinburgh: T&T Clark. Vol. 1, *Prolegomena*, 1908; vol. 2, *Accidence and Word Formation*, by W. F. Howard, 1929; vol. 3, *Syntax*, by Nigel Turner, 1963; and vol. 4, *Style*, by Nigel Turner, 1976. This set is the most thorough treatment of Greek grammar by British scholars. The volumes on syntax and style will usually be of greatest interest to NT interpreters.

A. T. Robertson. 1934. *A Grammar of the Greek New Testament in the Light of Historical Research.* 4th ed. Nashville: Broadman. This is a massive work (1454 pp.) by a scholar of immense learning. Part 1 sketches the modern history of Greek grammars, the development of the Greek language, and the relationship between Koine Greek and its world. Part 2 treats accidence and word formation. Part 3 devotes over 800 pages to syntax proper. Because of its bulk, Robertson is accessible to exegetes primarily through its indices.

Herbert W. Smyth. 1920. *Greek Grammar.* Cambridge, MA: Harvard University Press. This is the most thorough Classical Greek grammar in English. It is arranged well and has numerous indices, but must be used with care by students of biblical Greek since the latter often diverges from Classical usage.

Daniel B. Wallace. 1996. *Greek Grammar beyond the Basics.* Grand Rapids: Zondervan. This is probably the best advanced grammar available today. It often bridges the gap between the study of syntax and theological exegesis. Some of its extended treatments of individual passages have more grammatical information than many commentaries. For a book full of technical detail and specialized vocabulary, Wallace is surprisingly readable.

Student Grammars or Handbooks

J. A. Brooks and C. L. Winbury. 1979. *Syntax of New Testament Greek.* Washington, DC: University Press of America. This is perhaps the best of the handbook-sized grammars. It is user-friendly, well organized, and amply illustrated with NT examples.

H. E. Dana and Julius R. Mantey. 1927. *A Manual Grammar of the Greek New Testament.* Toronto: Macmillan. This is an older but still useful handbook, indebted to the work of A. T. Robertson. It uses an eight-case system for nouns that some may find disconcerting.

A. T. Robertson and W. Hersey Davis. 1977. *A New Short Grammar of the Greek Testament.* 10th ed. Grand Rapids: Baker Academic. This student grammar grew out of the massive research that informed Robertson's larger grammar, but with less than a third of the bulk of that larger volume. Its many editions speak to its perceived value through much of the twentieth century.

Maximilian Zerwick. 1963. *Biblical Greek Illustrated by Examples.* Adapted by Joseph Smith from the 4th Latin ed. Rome: Pontifical Biblical Institute

Press. This manageable handbook-sized grammar (185 pp.) was originally written in Latin by a Jesuit scholar. Its dual system of paragraph numbering can be confusing, but its discussions are generally learned and helpful.

OTHER TOOLS

Ernest DeWitt Burton. 1900. *Syntax of the Moods and Tenses in New Testament Greek*. Chicago: University of Chicago Press. Reprint, Grand Rapids: Kregel, 1976. With over two hundred pages, this volume is still one of the best treatments of the verbal system. Its format is visually pleasing, and it is replete with NT examples.

C. F. D. Moule. 1959. *An Idiom Book of New Testament Greek*. 2nd ed. Cambridge: Cambridge University Press. As the title implies, this is not a full grammar per se. Along with sections on the standard topics—tense, mood, voice, cases, prepositions, adjectives, and so forth—it has brief chapters on word order, Semitisms, Latinisms, and style.

Max[imilian] Zerwick and Mary Grosvenor. 1996. *A Grammatical Analysis of the Greek New Testament*. 5th, rev. ed. Rome: Pontifical Biblical Institute Press. Beginning, intermediate, and even advanced students will find this a very useful aid. It begins with a brief glossary of grammatical terms, but the remainder of its 800+ pages is arranged canonically. Chapter by chapter, verse by verse, it provides a terse grammatical commentary on the Greek NT, identifying word meanings, parsing verb forms, explaining idioms, and providing etymological information. It packs a huge amount of data into a volume only slightly larger than the average Greek NT.

Other works could be mentioned, but the above have stood the test of time and proved their value. In addition, lexicons and theological dictionaries, particularly Danker (2000), often contain grammatical tidbits. Needless to say, commentaries that are based on the Greek text usually attend to grammatical matters when they are significant for exegesis.

As important as grammar is, it is not a magical key to unlocking meaning. Correct parsing does not guarantee correct interpretation. However, interpretation easily goes astray if forms are incorrectly identified or syntax is misconstrued. Sound grammatical analysis is an essential stone in building one's exegetical method, if not quite the capstone. What follows is an analysis of 1 Corinthians 13. Like other types of analysis, grammatical study can generate a great deal of data, not all of which will wind up in one's final interpretation. Bear that in mind as you wade through the details in the following paragraphs.

A Grammatical Analysis of 1 Corinthians 13:1–13

The first three verses consist of three third-class conditional clauses. Such clauses are introduced with *ean* and normally contain a subjunctive verb in the protasis. The apodosis ("then" clause) of a third-class condition may contain any tense and mood. In 1 Corinthians 13:1–3 we find the subjunctive in each protasis and the indicative in each apodosis. Third-class conditions assume a situation that is capable of fulfillment, although in practice this can range from a present general condition, to a future probable condition, to a condition that is purely hypothetical (D. Wallace, 1996: 696–99). Verse 1 speaks of human and angelic tongues, activity that is within Paul's experience (1 Cor. 14:18). Verse 2 speaks of the possession of prophetic gifts and special knowledge, but the latter is stated with such hyperbole as to be a theoretical condition. Verse 3's images of utter poverty and martyrdom are conditions that could be realized but are not presently true for Paul. Thus the conditional clauses seem to combine scenarios that are quite capable of fulfillment with scenarios that are largely hypothetical. Verse 2 adds a result clause to one of its conditions ("so as to move mountains"), clearly a conceived result rather than an actual one (Dana and Mantey, 1927: 215; Burton, 1900: 149; Robertson, 1934: 1090).

The second paragraph (vv. 4–7) is characterized by a scarcity of conjunctions, known as asyndeton (Robertson and Davis, 1977: 203). In forty-three words of text there is a single conjunction (*de*, v. 6). All fifteen verbs in this paragraph are present indicatives. They are all aphoristic in the sense of stating general, timeless truths about what love does or does not do. The first two verbs could be classed as stative, meaning that they predicate a quality of love more so than an action. Note that the first two verbs in verse 4 are positive. The next three verbs in verse 4, all the verbs in verse 5, and the first verb in verse 6 are negated with *ou* or *ouk*. The second verb in verse 6 and all four verbs in verse 7 are again positive. Thus love is characterized both positively and negatively: by what love is/does and by what it is not/does not do. The use of the definite article *hē* ("the") with "love" in verse 4 is contrary to English idiom but common Greek usage with abstract nouns. Verse 7 is a series of terse, staccato statements, each beginning with the direct object *panta*.

The final paragraph (vv. 8–13) is framed by statements of love's persistence. Verse 8 describes love as never failing; verse 13 speaks of love as the greatest of the abiding qualities. Verses 8b–9 contrast the persistence of love with the temporality of prophecy, tongues, and knowledge. The latter is expressed with the disjunctive particle *eite* in the construction "whether *x*, or *y*, or *z*." In each case the passing nature of the particular phenomenon is stressed. Verse 9 is an explanatory clause (*gar*), explicating the previous verse. Prophecy, tongues, and knowledge will ultimately pass away because they are at best partial and incomplete gifts. Verse 10 mentions the perfection that contrasts with the incompletion stressed in verse 9. The phrase *to ek merous* in verse 10 is an anaphoric use of the article with the repeated phrase from verse 9. Verses 11 and 12 are roughly parallel in contrasting two time periods: *hote . . . hote* (v. 11), and *arti . . . tote* (twice in v. 12). Verse 11 appropriately uses four imperfect tenses to describe habitual actions when one was a child ("I used to speak, . . . I used to think"). The adult phase is expressed with two perfect tenses: "having become a man/adult, I have set aside childish things." The perfect tense appropriately denotes completed action and a resultant state. Verse 12 is also an explanatory clause (*gar*). Childish ideas are set aside when one reaches adulthood because adulthood brings enhanced perception and understanding. Verse 12b skillfully employs three verb forms based on *ginōskō*. All three voices are used (active, middle, passive), as well as present, future, and past (aorist) tenses. Of special interest is the use of *epiginōskō* in the second and third instances. The prefixed preposition (*epi*) has perfective or intensive force, meaning "to know fully" (Robertson, 1934: 564, 600; Danker, 2000: 369 1a). Moulton's paraphrase of verse 12 is as follows: "Now I am acquiring knowledge which is only partial at best: then I shall have learnt my lesson, shall *know*, as God in my mortal life knew me" (Moulton, 1908: 113; see also Robertson, 1934: 827). In verse 13 a singular verb accompanies a threefold subject. Here *menei* either agrees with the nearest singular subject, *pistis*, or more likely, with the neuter plural *ta tria tauta*. Finally, in verse 13 the comparative *meizōn* ("better") is used as a superlative (greatest) (Dana and Mantey, 1927: 121; Zerwick, 1963: 49), and the article with *agapē* in verse 13 is anaphoric (Zerwick and Grosvenor, 1996: 525; Turner, 1963: 177).

Exercises on Key Texts

Read your key text with a view to identifying significant grammatical constructions such as unusual case functions, less common uses of verbal tenses, and participial clauses. Try to distinguish between routine items (e.g., an accusative direct object) and things that may be more exegetically significant (e.g., a subjective vs. objective genitive). Pose the kinds of questions suggested above. In a more perfunctory vein, you can consult the Scripture indices of the grammars listed above to see if they comment on your passage. Be aware that some of the data gleaned in this way will be esoteric and only modestly useful.

Mark 2:1–12 (Healing a Paralytic)
Mark 7:24–37 (A Syrophoenician Woman and a Deaf Man)
Acts 3:1–10 (Peter Heals a Lame Man)
1 Corinthians 12:1–11 (Spiritual Gifts)
1 Corinthians 15:1–11 (The Resurrection)
Revelation 4:1–11 (A Vision of Heavenly Worship)

8. Consider Textual Connections

No text is an island, untouched by all other human discourse. The writings of the New Testament are unquestionably influenced by previous literature and are frequently in touch with contemporary movements and ideas. An important aspect of New Testament interpretation, therefore, is the identification and analysis of comparative texts, especially when there are significant cultural or theological parallels. From the very beginning, the Christian movement showed both cultural continuity and cultural creativity. The early Christians shared a vast literary and cultural heritage with Judaism. Hellenistic philosophy contributed significantly to language, literary forms, rhetorical practices, and ethical precepts (Nock, 1972: 676–81). However, the church also engaged in genuinely creative reflection in such areas as Christology and soteriology. So when one considers "intertextuality," as this sphere of study is called, one should expect both significant points of similarity and areas of divergence and innovation.

Textual connections can be broadly divided into two groups: *intra*textual and *inter*textual. Intratextual connections refer to comparative passages within the same writing. If one is interpreting Paul's thought in 1 Corinthians 13, any other verse or paragraph in 1 Corinthians might be a relevant intratextual connection. Intertextual connections refer to comparative texts that fall outside the writing that you are studying. This is obviously a huge literary expanse, with multiple levels. Again, if you are studying 1 Corinthians 13, intertextual connections would certainly include any relevant texts in other Pauline Letters, including disputed (deutero-)Pauline Letters. They might also include other writings of the New Testament, the Septuagint, contemporary Jewish or Greco-Roman writings (e.g., philosophical reflections on love), and ultimately all the various corpora of ancient Mediterranean literature.

As you might suspect, the investigation of *inter*textual connections can become overwhelming. If one regards as a parallel any text that has a similar word, phrase, or idea, the parallels will quickly engulf the original passage, and meaningful analysis will become impossible. A related danger is that the interpreter may read too much into the parallels, finding literary dependence where none exists. Samuel Sandmel has warned against these dangers in a celebrated and aptly named article titled "Parallelomania." Sandmel defines "parallelomania" as "that extravagance among scholars which first overdoes the supposed similarity in passages and then proceeds to describe source and derivation as if implying literary connection flowing in an inevitable or predetermined direction" (1962: 1).

Parallelomania hinders meaningful analysis of texts and contexts. One must resist the temptation to run amok among superficial parallels that have been lifted from their contexts. "Detailed study ought to respect the context and not be limited to juxtaposing mere excerpts. Two passages may sound the same in splendid isolation from their context, but when seen in context reflect difference rather than similarity" (Sandmel, 1962: 2). None of this is to deny that relevant parallels exist between the New Testament and other bodies of literature. There is simply a need for attention to context (Do I need to say

CIE?) and especially for caution in positing direct derivation. Again, the need is for *caution*, not complete skepticism, for we will see that direct derivation is sometimes obvious. For more on the misuse of parallels, see Donaldson (1983) and Ferguson (2003: 1–4).

There are three types of intertextuality among bodies of literature. First, there is the use by New Testament authors of other writings in the New Testament. (That statement entails an anachronism, of course, since when those writings were used, they were not yet canonized.) It is universally agreed, for example, that there is some literary connection between the Synoptic Gospels: Matthew, Mark, and Luke. There are passages between two or three of these Gospels that are verbatim the same, passages that are nearly verbatim, and passages that seem to be more loosely related. There are various explanations for these similarities, but the degree of verbal identity is sufficient to require literary derivation in some direction. Also in this category would be parallels and possible instances of borrowing within the Pauline canon (e.g., between Colossians and Ephesians), and the parallels between Jude and 2 Peter.

A second, and quite obvious, type of intertextuality is the New Testament's use of the Old Testament (likewise a somewhat anachronistic statement since the canon of the Hebrew Bible was not rigidly fixed at the time). Sometimes this is explicit, as when Matthew cites the Old Testament by using an introductory formula, "This was to fulfill what had been spoken by the Lord through the prophet" (Matt. 2:15). At other times the connection is minimal and implicit, consisting of no more than a few words or a similar expression. Sometimes the parallel consists of an allusion to an Old Testament character, scene, or incident, without significant borrowing of specific language. The use of the Old Testament by the authors of the New Testament is the most important type of intertextuality, and there is a raft of scholarly literature discussing it.

Finally, in a small number of passages, scholars have detected borrowing on the part of New Testament authors from extracanonical sources. The best-known examples from a Jewish source are Jude's use of the apocryphal work *1 Enoch* (Jude 6, 14–15; see Charles, 1997). There are also three places in which New Testament authors quote Classical Greek literature. The familiar adage "Bad company ruins good morals" is quoted by Paul in 1 Corinthians 15:33 and derives from Menander or Euripides, who themselves probably derived it from an earlier author. In Titus 1:12 the ethnic insult, "Cretans are always liars, evil brutes, lazy gluttons," apparently stems from Epimenides. Finally, Paul's speech at Mars Hill (Acts 17:22 KJV) includes a quotation from the poet Aratus: "For we too are his offspring" (17:28; Aratus, *Phaenomena* 5). There are many other similarities and parallels, of both large and small compass, between New Testament writings and Greco-Roman writings, but none that one can confidently describe as a quotation (Renehan, 1973).

When considering the significance of these or any other parallels, it is helpful to bear in mind the distinction between analogical and genealogical parallels

(Donaldson, 1983: 198–201). Analogical parallels may be no more than similar expressions, born of our common human nature and circumstances. Analogical parallels do not necessarily have any derivative relationship: one author need not be borrowing from the other. Genealogical parallels are interrelated such that one can posit influence and, usually, its direction. Obviously, good evidence is needed to be able to assert that author x is borrowing from author y, and the tendency of some scholars is to posit influence or derivation too quickly. As Dale Allison warns, "Near meaningless parallels between two texts can always be uncovered if one puts in the effort." Allison goes on to quote the wry critique of Ihab Hassan: "Learned and meticulous essays have been written to demonstrate the influence of everything on anything" (Allison, 2000: 9).

In particular, there is an occasional tendency to look too far afield for the source of a New Testament author's ideas. Some scholars pursue red herrings in Homer when the quarry that they seek lies much closer at hand. Though there is no question that fascinating analogical parallels exist between New Testament texts and other writings of the Hellenistic world, there is only one body of literature that New Testament authors repeatedly quote, allude to, echo, paraphrase, and whose language colors their expressions at every turn: the Old Testament. No other body of literature even comes close in terms of intertextual significance. Moreover, New Testament authors are often quite explicit about this; there are scores of Old Testament citations that are un-disputed and many more that are quite likely. Karl Sandnes rightly speaks of New Testament authors as "advertising" or "broadcasting" their practice of intertextuality (2005: 728–32). Homer and other Greco-Roman authors may occasionally provide loose parallels to the Gospels, but the evangelists seem much more intent on showing connections between the life of Jesus and the sacred texts of Judaism.

Unfortunately, there is no standardized terminology for intertextuality (Porter, 1997b). Scholars speak of explicit quotations, formal quotations, allusions, echoes, parallels, comparative texts, and cross-references. Suffice it to say that intertextuality exists across a spectrum from explicit to subtle, from deliberate to unconscious, and we often have to content ourselves with probable judgments. Despite the extensive research done on the topic, there is no perfectly objective scientific method for determining allusions (Allison, 2000: 13).

So what criteria are available for discerning intertextuality? How do in-terpreters know if they are actually dealing with an intertextual allusion? Fortunately, this step is often unnecessary. Sometimes intertextuality is ob-vious, as when the author uses an explicit introductory formula, or when a quotation is apparent even without an introduction. In such cases one can move directly to the function and significance of the quotation. But when intertextuality is less obvious, the interpreter needs principles by which to judge its likelihood. Richard Hays (1989: 29–33) and Dale Allison (2000:

10–14) have offered helpful discussions on the matter, and I am especially indebted to them in what follows.

How Do We Identify Intertextuality?

Assuming that the instance under consideration is not patently obvious, the following criteria may be applied: (1) *Availability*. Obviously a literary work from which borrowing or influence occurs must antedate the borrower. Chronology thus rules out some alleged allusions. Complicating this otherwise simple rule is the fact that the date of a writing may be decades or even centuries later than the traditions that the writing preserves. Many Gospel scholars have highlighted similarities, if not necessarily influence, between the teachings of Jesus and those of the rabbis recorded in the Mishnah. The latter is usually dated to about 200 CE, but it purportedly preserves traditions of rabbis contemporary with or even earlier than Jesus. In addition to chronology, availability has to do with geographic and cultural proximity. The idea of Jesus's being influenced by the teachings of Confucius (551–479 BCE) would be conceivable in terms of chronology, but one would have to show evidence of the awareness of Confucian philosophy in first-century-CE Palestine. (2) *Verbal identity*. To establish conscious intertextuality, there must be sufficient verbal identity: similar vocabulary and/or similar syntax. Allison (2000: 11–12) points out that the case is weakened if the vocabulary in question is quite commonplace. The collocation of a few unusual terms in a similar pattern is stronger evidence than a lengthier phrase that is ubiquitous. (3) *Consistency*. If the author has elsewhere shown knowledge of and interest in the text to which one suspects an allusion, the case for that allusion is strengthened. Thus, if you know that Paul has used the Genesis narrative of Abraham in his Epistle to the Romans, it increases the likelihood that a suspected allusion elsewhere is valid. (4) *History of interpretation*. If other readers of the passage—ancient, medieval, and modern—have discerned a possible instance of intertextuality, that increases the odds that you have not created it *ex nihilo*. Neither precritical nor postcritical readers are infallible, but the more widespread an observation is, the greater the likelihood that there is some objective basis for it. (5) *General plausibility*. The assertion of intertextuality should be generally plausible for the ancient writer and his or her audience. As Richard Hays warns, we should be "wary of readings that turn Paul into (say) a Lutheran or a deconstructionist" (Hays, 1989: 30–31). Intertextual allusions or influence should fit what we know about the writer, the readers, and the times. (6) *Rhetorical effectiveness*. In the simplest terms, does the proposed intertextual allusion work? Is it consonant with the author's argument and tenor? Does the (sometimes rather subtle) allusion enhance what the text says explicitly? Does the proposal of an intertextual connection render a satisfactory interpretation?

Having Identified an Instance of Intertextuality, How Can We Discern Its Function and Significance?

Once one has determined that intertextuality is likely, either because the author has advertised the fact, or because the above criteria suggest it, then one can move to the important task of determining the function and significance of the quotation or allusion. The following questions are helpful guides. Beale and Carson (2007: xxiv–xxvii) offer a fuller discussion of these issues.

1. *What is the New Testament context of the quotation or allusion?* Careful study of the New Testament context will enable you to see what has prompted an appeal to the Old Testament and what use is made of the Old Testament source. This step is very similar to number 5 below, but it is appropriate to have the author's argument in the forefront of your mind throughout the analysis.
2. *What is the Old Testament source of the quotation or allusion?* Is the New Testament author citing or alluding to a particular Old Testament book? Is there possibly a conflation of more than one Old Testament text (e.g., Mark 1:2–3)? If the wording is imprecise, are there multiple possibilities for the Old Testament source? In the case of a vague allusion, is it possible that the New Testament author does not have a specific Old Testament text in mind?
3. *If you are able to identify a specific Old Testament source, does a particular textual tradition seem to be used?* Does the New Testament author quote the Hebrew (Masoretic Text)? the Septuagint? an Aramaic translation (targum)? Does the New Testament author have a textual tradition that is no longer available to us? Is it possible to tell? The Septuagint sometimes differs sufficiently from the Hebrew text such that a New Testament quotation can be confidently traced to one or the other, but this is not always the case. (See Matt. 1:23/Isa. 7:14 for an example of an important difference between the MT and the LXX.)
4. *Do other Christian or Jewish authors quote or allude to the same Old Testament text?* How is their use of the text similar or different? Again, in Matthew 1:22–23 the evangelist interprets Isaiah 7:14 as a messianic prophecy. It might be of significance to know whether this was a common understanding in contemporary Judaism. If there are important differences in the way Jews and Christians have interpreted an Old Testament text, can we account for the differences?
5. *Most important, how does the New Testament author use the Old Testament text?* Are key terms appropriated? Did the New Testament author seem to have in mind particular images? Does the New Testament author comment on the text? If so, what words or images are highlighted? Is anything modified in the Old Testament text? What direction does the New Testament author take the Old Testament text?

Is the Old Testament context honored, or is the text significantly recontextualized by the New Testament author? For example, New Testament
authors may take Old Testament texts that originally referred to God
or to Israel's king and apply them to Jesus (e.g., Heb. 1:5).

The work of identifying and analyzing quotations, allusions, and analogical
parallels in the New Testament continues. New Testament interpreters should
give careful attention to the explicit quotations and should investigate the
more subtle and debatable allusions with appropriate caution.

Bibliography on Intertextuality

The literature on intertextuality is burgeoning. There are broad literary
treatments, case studies in biblical intertextuality, theological essays, and practical tools. A brief survey of intertextuality in early Christian literature can
be found in Swartley (1997). Slightly broader and more theoretical introductions include O'Day (1999), Wall (2000), and Koptak (2005). C. Evans (2004)
and Porter (2006) are helpful collections of essays. Robbins (1996a: 40–70)
discusses multiple types of "intertexture," including cultural phenomena and
historical events. The essays in Beale (1995) and Berding and Lunde (2008)
grapple with the hermeneutical validity of the New Testament's use of the
Old Testament. Finally, an excellent reference work with full discussions of
every New Testament book's use of the Old Testament has been provided
recently in Beale and Carson (2007).

Practical tools for locating comparative texts are of several types. Parallels
between the Gospels are conveniently displayed in any Gospel synopsis, such
as K. Aland (1985) or Throckmorton (1992). Parallels within the Pauline
corpus can be found in the standard work of Francis and Sampley (1992)
or in the recent contributions by W. Wilson (2009) or Terrell (2009). Lexical
parallels anywhere in the Bible can often be discovered by the use of hardcopy
concordances or the various computer programs (see pp. 77–78 above). Additional sources of parallels include the marginal notes in the Nestle-Aland
Greek New Testament (B. Aland et al., 2000), the notes of most study Bibles,
and the standard lexical resources and technical commentaries. Finally, two
very handy lists regarding the use of the Old Testament in the New Testament, "Quotations" and "Allusions and Verbal Parallels," can be found in the
United Bible Society's *Greek New Testament* (B. Aland et al., 1993: 887–901;
cf. B. Aland et al., 2000: 772–808).

The search for New Testament parallels outside the biblical canon has
stretched over centuries. In the early era, the only way to locate them was to
read ancient writings extensively, and that is still the means by which the most
meaningful parallels are discovered. A major landmark in the eighteenth century was the critical edition of the Greek New Testament by J. J. Wettstein

(1750–51), which became more famous for the copious parallels cited in its notes than for the Greek text and its apparatus. The twentieth-century counterpart to Wettstein was an ambitious project launched shortly before World War I that was eventually named the *Corpus Hellenisticum Novi Testamenti*. The task turned out to be so vast that rather than produce a complete collection of parallels in a single work, the researchers published a series of volumes treating individual Hellenistic authors. (See the brief history and bibliography in Horst, 1992a). A more accessible treatment of Greco-Roman parallels is the *Hellenistic Commentary to the New Testament* (Boring, Berger, and Colpe, 1995). Nonliterary texts such as papyri and inscriptions are treated in the ongoing series *New Documents Illustrating Early Christianity* (G. Horsley, 1981–89; Llewelyn, 1992–2002). Rabbinic parallels are discussed in two classic sets. Strack and Billerbeck (1922–61) is a massive resource for those who read German (but see the important critique in Sandmel, 1962: 8–10). English readers may consult the dated but still useful commentary by John Lightfoot (1979; reprint of a seventeenth-century work). More accessible treatments of the rabbinic material can be found in Lachs (1987) and in the recently launched work by David Instone-Brewer (2004–), projected to be six volumes.

An Illustration of Intertextual Analysis: Hebrews 12:5–6

Hebrews is one of the richest writings in the New Testament for the study of intertextuality. No other New Testament book is so permeated with explicit quotations, allusions, echoes, images, and narratives from the Old Testament (Guthrie, 2007: 919). There are approximately three dozen explicit citations of the Old Testament and many more subtle borrowings. One of the explicit quotations occurs in Hebrews 12:5–6. In Hebrews 11 the author has recited a litany of faith heroes and heroines, mostly from the Old Testament but implicitly extending beyond that into the era of the Maccabean martyrs (11:35). In Hebrews 12:1–3 the list of exemplars is brought even more up-to-date with the example of Jesus. These persons, including Jesus, serve as paradigms of forward-looking faith, patient endurance, and the disregard of society's shame. In 12:3b–4 the author turns directly to the experience of the readers. Verse 4 implies that despite the intensity of their sufferings (see 10:32–36), they have not yet experienced martyrdom. They need to construe their hardships in a new light, not as meaningless adversities, but as the discipline of the Lord. This leads into a quotation from the Old Testament.

The quotation is from Proverbs 3:11–12. The wording in Hebrews 12:5b–6 follows the Septuagint (LXX) closely, with one slight exception. The author of Hebrews has added "my" to the opening word "son." This word (Greek: *mou*) is omitted in a handful of manuscripts of Hebrews, perhaps by judicious scribes who knew their LXX well. The Hebrew text, on the one hand, does have the endearing possessive "*my* son." On the other hand, the Hebrew has a stronger phrasing of the second line of Proverbs 3:11, something like "Do not have loathing or disdain for his reproof," rather than the Greek's "Do not grow weary being reproved by him." The Hebrew text of 3:12a is faithfully rendered by the LXX, but verse 12b differs. The Hebrew uses a simile: "as a father the son in whom he delights." The LXX has made 3:12b fully parallel to verse 12a by adding a verb: "and *chastises* every son whom he receives." This probably involves a misreading of the Hebrew by the LXX translator (Guthrie, 2007: 987). The upshot of this is that the author of Hebrews quotes the LXX except for adding "my" in the opening words. That slight variation could be either a faint memory of the Hebrew text or, I think more likely, an unconscious alteration to make the tone more intimate.

Proverbs 3:11–12 is not explicitly quoted in any other New Testament text, but one could argue that Revelation 3:19 is an allusion to verse 12. In that passage the Christ of the Apocalypse says to the church at Laodicea, "As many as I love, I reprove and discipline" (cf. KJV, NRSV). With the substitution of *phileō* for *agapaō*, there are three terms here in a configuration similar to that of Proverbs 3:12. The words that follow in Revelation 3:19 call for the church to "be earnest . . . and repent." Within the LXX, Proverbs 3:11–12 may also be echoed in Job 5:17 and *Psalms of Solomon* 3:4, although in both cases the connection is more thematic than lexical. Outside the biblical canon, the Jewish philosopher Philo explicitly cites Proverbs 3:11–12 in *On the Preliminary Studies* 177. His quotation of verse 11 differs slightly in word order from the LXX. The quotation of verse 12a differs only in the substitution of the verb *elenchei* for *paideuei*. Philo is describing the adversity of Esau, the experience of slavery that befell Esau as a result of his folly and belligerence. Finally, in rabbinic literature Proverbs 3:11–12 is quoted twice. The Babylonian Talmud (*Berakhot* 5a) asserts that adversity that cannot be traced to misconduct or neglect of the study of the Torah must be understood as a "chastisement of love." Proverbs 3:12 is then cited as a scriptural precedent. Elsewhere in this Talmud (*Megillah* 31b), the people on days of fasting are enjoined to read the blessings and curses of Scripture without interruption. The basis of this rule is found in the citation of Proverbs 3:11. It is apparent that these verses from Proverbs were well known in late antiquity and served to give meaning to a variety of adverse circumstances (Guthrie, 2007: 986–87; Croy, 1998: 210–13).

Most important, we turn to the particular use that the author of Hebrews has made of this quotation. In Hebrews 12:7–11 we have a substantial amount of data to consider: ninety-eight words of commentary on twenty-two words of Old Testament text. The author cites two full verses from Proverbs but makes highly selective use of the citation. The terms that are repeated in verses 7–11 are "discipline" (*paideia*) and "son" (*huios:* made inclusive in the NRSV as "children" in vv. 7a and 8, and as "child" in v. 7b). The word *paideia* and the related verb *paideuō* have approximately the same semantic range as the English word "discipline," conveying either a regimen of educative hardship or punishment for wrongdoing. The author of Hebrews exploits these words, while passing over the harsher, unambiguously punitive *elenchō* ("punish, correct"; v. 5) and *mastigoō* ("whip, chastise"; v. 6). This is consonant with the argument that has preceded. Neither the exemplars of faith in chapter 11 nor Jesus in 12:1–3 are being punished for sin; rather, they are enduring hardship, suffering, and shame for the sake of obedience to God and the joyous reward that lies ahead. The author's use of Proverbs 3:11–12 has recontextualized it in a way that serves the rhetorical aim of the epistle (Croy, 1998: 198–208).

Exercises on Key Texts

What types of intratextual and intertextual connections exist between your text and

1. the larger writing of which it is a part,
2. the larger corpus of writings by that same author (if any),
3. closely related texts in the New Testament such as other Gospels,
4. the New Testament as a whole,
5. the Bible as a whole,
6. significant and culturally proximate texts such as Josephus, Philo, and certain Greco-Roman philosophers, and finally
7. the broad range of ancient corpora of Hellenistic writings?

Use the practical tools and methods mentioned above: a Gospel synopsis, a Pauline parallel, marginal notes in your Greek New Testament, footnotes of a study Bible, concordances, computer searches, and commentaries. Needless to say, you will need to identify the connections most relevant to the interpretation of your passage and not be distracted by more-dubious literary echoes.

Mark 2:1–12 (Healing a Paralytic)
Mark 7:24–37 (A Syrophoenician Woman and a Deaf Man)
Acts 3:1–10 (Peter Heals a Lame Man)
1 Corinthians 12:1–11 (Spiritual Gifts)
1 Corinthians 15:1–11 (The Resurrection)
Revelation 4:1–11 (A Vision of Heavenly Worship)

9. Consider the Historical, Cultural, Religious, and Political Environment

Virtually every New Testament introduction that has been written has one or more chapters on early Christian backgrounds or some such topic. This reflects the rather obvious fact that the mantra "Context is everything" applies not just to semantics and literary contexts but also to broader historical and social contexts. Some scholars object to the term "background," and not without reason. If this metaphor, taken from the theater, is understood as implying that the broader historical milieu is relatively static cultural scenery against which the action of early Christianity is played out, then the term "background" disserves us, and it might be preferable to use "environment," "milieu," or "context" (Ferguson, 2003: 1). Early Christianity, part of a lively and multifaceted religious environment, was enduring an uncertain and evolving relationship with Judaism and an often-competitive relationship with traditional religions, mystery religions, the emperor cult, and gnosticism. Early Christian communities had to interact with commercial systems, political and military institutions, social hierarchies, and cultural phenomena that were not of their own making. They embraced some of these realities, rejected others, and accommodated themselves to still others. Suffice it to say, when we use the word "background," we do not imply a static view of the ancient world.

This aspect of New Testament interpretation is a vast world of its own, to which whole sections of libraries are devoted. Much of the literature of antiquity contributes to our understanding of the environment of early Christianity, obviously some writings more directly and relevantly than others. In this way, the present section of the book is closely related to the previous one, "textual connections." Comparative texts are often the source of helpful background information, even when no quotation or allusion is involved. By simply providing fuller detail on a topic, such as the synagogue or Stoicism, ancient texts enrich our understanding of the New Testament.

In addition to ancient texts, there is the whole arena of material culture. Material culture pertains to any kind of concrete remains of a society, the material record as it has been shaped by human beings. It includes archaeology, architecture, coinage, pottery, lamps, cooking vessels, weapons, tools, writing instruments, furnishings, weights, figurines, statuary, glass, and epigraphy (inscriptions). The study of material culture enables us to reconstruct and visualize the past more fully. It has the potential to corroborate details from literary sources, but more often it serves to fill out the larger picture of daily life in certain settings. It illuminates the general rather than the specific, the typical rather than the atypical. The study of material culture has, for example, confirmed the existence of certain historical persons mentioned in the New Testament, such as Pontius Pilate and Gallio, but rarely will it elucidate the specific acts of those persons narrated in the New Testament.

New Testament backgrounds are sometimes divided into two broad areas: Jewish backgrounds and Greco-Roman backgrounds. (In graduate school I had a semester-long seminar on each of these topics.) But the division is admittedly a heuristic aid to learning, not a partition that stands up under scrutiny. As already indicated above, the environment of early Christianity was by no means compartmentalized. It would generally be true that Jewish backgrounds loom larger in importance when one is studying religious life in Jerusalem, and Greco-Roman backgrounds assume greater significance when one investigates Paul's speech in Athens. But even in these examples, there is no strict division. Many studies have shown that Hellenistic culture had penetrated Palestine, including Jerusalem, in the centuries before Jesus (e.g., Hengel, 1974), and Diaspora Judaism made its presence felt during the same years throughout the Mediterranean world via synagogues, Jewish enclaves, and political dealings (Barclay, 1996; Collins, 2000).

Although the world of New Testament backgrounds is vast and overwhelming, it is paradoxically true that we are often frustrated by what we do *not* know about the ancient world. As Harold Attridge cautions, "The beginning of sober exegesis is a recognition of the limits of historical knowledge" (1989: 5). So the wise New Testament interpreter will vigorously pursue the lines of evidence that are promising but will also exercise appropriate humility when evidence is not forthcoming.

The importance of the historical, cultural, religious, and political (the list of adjectives could be extended) environment is probably self-evident, but a few examples may be beneficial. So simple an affirmation as "Jesus is Lord" can take on various shades of meaning in different historical contexts. For the modern, middle-class Christian living in the West, it may chiefly mean that Jesus reigns over my life and personal decisions. In the first century it had (and in some countries today it still has) profound social and political implications. For Christians in the Pauline churches, the affirmation of Jesus's lordship implied that no other earthly ruler held that honor (Rom. 10:9; 1 Cor. 12:3; Phil. 2:11; cf. Acts 25:26). "Jesus is Lord" meant "Caesar is not." Finally, the very same affirmation in the mouth of a twelfth-century crusader bent on slaughtering Muslim enemies had a very different political function and certainly a different ethical value (Work, 2002: 62).

An understanding of ancient Mediterranean culture is often critical in New Testament interpretation. One interpreter of the wedding in Cana (John 2:1–11) observed that the ceremony was attended by Jesus, his disciples, and his mother. The interpreter remarked: "When two generations are present at a wedding it is almost always a family affair. I have never attended a wedding with my mother except when it was the wedding of a relative. The only time my mother and my closest friends were at a wedding together with me was my own wedding!" He went on to note that the mother of Jesus was oddly concerned about the supply of wine, and finally queried suggestively: "Is this an echo not fully suppressed of the tradition of Jesus's marriage?" (Spong, 1992: 192). A more judicious reader of the same text has pointed out that a Jewish wedding in first-century Galilee was "a whole village affair, and quite probably a several-villages affair. Nazareth and Cana were close neighbours. It is highly likely that whole families in one village would go to a whole-family wedding in the next one" (Wright, 1992c: 91). The relevant background for interpreting the wedding in Cana is obviously Jewish practices of the first century, not Christian practices of the twentieth century.

A similar kind of anachronistic confusion has sometimes clouded the interpretation of Hebrews 11:11. In this passage it is at first unclear whether the faith of Abraham is being extolled (NIV, NRSV) or the faith of Sarah (TNIV, RSV). The chief difficulty is the interpretation of an expression meaning something like: "received the power for the laying down of a seed." Many modern interpreters consider this function necessarily to be that of the male in procreation. But again, the relevant background for interpreting Hebrews 11:11 is the *ancient* understanding of procreation, not the modern. Studies of ancient medical and philosophical texts have confirmed that the woman's role in reproduction was often understood in this way. The theory that both the man and the woman contributed a seed was widely held in the Hellenistic era. There is, therefore, no need for the strained syntactical construals of Hebrews 11:11 that reduce Sarah to a parenthesis. The author apparently meant what he wrote (see Horst, 1992b; and Croy, 2007).

Gaining a thorough acquaintance with the world of early Christianity should be regarded as the goal of a lifetime. There is no substitute for broad reading in both the primary, ancient texts and the secondary scholarly literature. However, we often have short-term, proximate goals, such as figuring out who in the world the Epicureans were by Sunday morning. So while serious students of the New Testament may commit themselves to a lifetime of study, they also need quick access to information on discrete topics. The latter is the purpose of a good reference work, several of which are listed below.

This step in the exegetical process could be posed as the following question: What aspects of the historical, cultural, religious, or political milieu of this writing, its author, and its readers may shed light on the interpretation of this passage? In the simplest, most pragmatic terms, the question might be formulated this way: What topic is *mentioned, implied, or presupposed in this passage* that I might profitably look up in a Bible dictionary or encyclopedia? Obviously, the study of New Testament backgrounds is more complex than this, but the interpreter must start somewhere, and the short-term goal of interpreting a specific text may be aided by posing just such a practical question. An example may be in order.

In Mark 12:18–27 some Sadducees approach Jesus with a question about the resurrection. They describe an elaborate, hypothetical case in which a widow marries a succession of her deceased husband's brothers. Then they pose the question: "In the resurrection whose wife will she be? For the seven [brothers] had married her." Jesus responds with Old Testament words of divine speech, "I am the God of Abraham, the God of Isaac, and the God of Jacob," a quotation from Exodus 3:6, 15–16. This narrative might prompt a person to look up a variety of dictionary entries, most obviously, an article on the Sadducees. There one would learn that the Sadducees "accepted only the written law of Moses as authoritative and rejected the oral law of the Pharisees. . . . Even the prophets and writings, although not rejected, were not treated as a source of doctrine" (Ferguson, 2003: 520; see also Bromiley, 1979–88: 4:279–80). When asked about the resurrection, Jesus might have appealed to Daniel 12:1–3, the most explicit Old Testament text on the topic. But such an appeal would not likely have been persuasive with the Sadducees, so Jesus responds with a quotation from "the book of Moses," words that the Sadducees could not easily dismiss.

Bibliographic Resources for New Testament Backgrounds

So where does one turn for a guide to the complex world of New Testament backgrounds? I often direct people to what I consider the best single volume on the topic: Everett Ferguson's *Backgrounds of Early Christianity* (2003). This is a hefty (648 pp.) but well-written and manageable treatment. It covers the gamut of political history, society and culture, Greco-Roman religions, philosophy, Judaism, and archaeology. The fact that it is in its third edition speaks to both its longevity and up-to-dateness. The book has numerous illustrations, frequent bibliographies for further study, and a helpful subject index that enables the user to zero in on specific topics. Another excellent but smaller (322 pp.) and more accessible work is Albert Bell's *Exploring the New Testament World* (1998). Written by a classicist for a "lay readership," this book is stronger on Greco-Roman backgrounds than Jewish, but it is well illustrated and has extensive bibliographies.

An outstanding tome in both usefulness and comprehensiveness of coverage is the *Dictionary of New Testament Background* (C. Evans and Porter, 2000). As the name implies, the work is arranged alphabetically, covering topics from "Adam and Eve" to the "Zenon Papyri." The volume's arrangement and size (1328 pp.) clearly identify it as a reference work. Though one might actually read through Ferguson's *Backgrounds* or Bell's *Exploring the New Testament World*, one "consults" the *Dictionary of New Testament Background*.

Beyond these handy resources, the bibliography is legion. Craig Evans provides a very helpful guide to the primary literature in *Ancient Texts for New Testament Studies* (2005). C. K. Barrett collects the most relevant ancient sources in *The New Testament Background: Selected Documents* (1995). A readable survey of the earliest Christian period is available in F. F. Bruce's *New Testament History* (1969). Two more excellent resources whose coverage extends into the patristic era are the *Encyclopedia of Early Christianity* (Ferguson, 1998) and the two-volume set *The Early Christian World* (Esler, 2000).

Much of the more specialized literature can be divided according the admittedly heuristic Jewish/Greco-Roman distinction. On the Jewish side, one can turn to Larry Helyer's *Exploring Jewish Literature of the Second Temple Period: A Guide for New Testament Students* (2002). More-advanced treatments include the updated classic Emil Schürer's *The History of the Jewish People in the Age of Jesus Christ* (1973–87); the highly informative collections by Safrai and Stern, *The Jewish People in the First Century* (1974–76); and Stone, *Jewish Writings of the Second Temple Period* (1984). A new reference work likely to become a standard text is *The Eerdmans Dictionary of Early Judaism*, edited by Collins and Harlow (2010). A reliable guide to the literature of the period can be found in George Nickelsburg's *Jewish Literature between the Bible and the Mishnah* (2005). Many of the texts discussed in all these volumes, along with excellent introductions, notes, and bibliography, can be found in *The Old Testament Pseudepigrapha* (Charlesworth, 1983–85).

On the Greco-Roman side, one may turn to James Jeffers's *The Greco-Roman World of the New Testament Era: Exploring the Background of Early Christianity* (1999). A standard reference work dealing with the Greco-Roman world is *The Oxford Classical Dictionary* (Hornblower and Spawforth, 1996). This impressive volume is written for the general reader and covers a swath of Mediterranean history, literature, and culture from the late Bronze Age to the patristic era. Its 6200+ entries include bibliographies and many references to ancient sources. Even more comprehensive is the seven-volume *Oxford Encyclopedia of Ancient Greece and Rome* (Gagarin, 2010). On the specific topic of Greco-Roman religions, one may profitably consult Hans-Josef Klauck's *The Religious Context of Early Christianity: A Guide to Graeco-Roman Religions* (2003), the work of Burkert (1985) on Greek religions, and Beard, North, and Price (1998) on Roman religions.

Finally, in the last few decades the investigation of New Testament culture has enjoyed considerable attention. Issues such as honor and shame, patronage, purity, kinship, and ancient notions of personality have proved to be very useful lenses through which to view early Christianity and its writings. Two helpful introductions to these phenomena, especially in the New Testament world, are the works of deSilva (2000a) and Malina (2001).

Perhaps the most obvious and readily available resources for probing into New Testament backgrounds have not yet been listed: Bible dictionaries and encyclopedias. As noted above, such tools are of immense value in that they permit quick access to information on specific topics. I have written a few entries for reference works, and it occurred to me afterward that I might spend a week or two researching and writing a medium-sized article, the fruits of which a reader could then gain in thirty minutes of reading, as well as find guides for further study. A well-crafted Bible dictionary or encyclopedia is thus a treasure trove, a repository of knowledge from an army of contributors, and scrutinized by a team of editors.

There is a wealth of biblical reference works. Some are written for the laity, some for pastors, students, and scholars. Those listed below are all serious scholarly works, but most of their articles are accessible to a general readership. For a brief survey of the most recent theological and biblical dictionaries, see

Green (2005b). For a history of biblical reference works from the sixteenth century to the mid-1970s, see Smith (1979).

One-Volume Bible Dictionaries

J. D. Douglas and Merrill C. Tenney, eds. 1999. *New International Bible Dictionary*. Rev. ed. Grand Rapids: Zondervan.

David Noel Freedman, ed. 2000. *Eerdmans Dictionary of the Bible*. Grand Rapids: Eerdmans.

I. Howard Marshall et al., eds. 1996. *New Bible Dictionary*. 3rd ed. Downers Grove, IL: InterVarsity.

Mark Allan Powell, ed. 2010. *Harper Collins Bible Dictionary*. Rev., 3rd ed. San Francisco: HarperCollins.

Multivolume Bible Dictionaries

Geoffrey W. Bromiley, ed. 1979–88. *The International Standard Bible Encyclopedia*. Rev. ed. 4 vols. Grand Rapids: Eerdmans.

David Noel Freedman, ed. 1992. *The Anchor Bible Dictionary*. 6 vols. New York: Doubleday.

Katharine Doob Sakenfeld, ed. 2006–10. *The New Interpreter's Dictionary of the Bible*. 5 vols. Nashville: Abingdon.

Merrill C. Tenney and Moisés Silva, eds. 2009. *The Zondervan Encyclopedia of the Bible*. Rev., full-color ed. Grand Rapids: Zondervan.

A Unique Set of Complementary but Self-Contained Volumes

Craig A. Evans and Stanley E. Porter, eds. 2000. *Dictionary of New Testament Background*. Downers Grove, IL: InterVarsity.

Joel B. Green, Scot McKnight, and I. Howard Marshall, eds. 1992. *Dictionary of Jesus and the Gospels*. Downers Grove, IL: InterVarsity.

Gerald F. Hawthorne, Ralph P. Martin, and D. G. Reid, eds. 1993. *Dictionary of Paul and His Letters*. Downers Grove, IL: InterVarsity.

Ralph P. Martin and Peter H. Davids, eds. 1997. *Dictionary of the Later New Testament and Its Developments*. Downers Grove, IL: InterVarsity.

There may be a temptation to forego the heavy lifting of historical study when reading Scripture. Admittedly, the Bible's basic message can be grasped without extensive research, and generations of believers, some of them illiterate, have heard and responded to the biblical message with relatively little knowledge of its original context. But those who help chart the course of twenty-first-century churches, both professional theologians and leaders of local congregations, will do well to attend to that original context. "The better one sees and knows *the background*, the more clearly that person can see *the cutting edge* of Christianity" (Ferguson, 2003: 4, with added emphasis).

Exercises on Key Texts

The investigation of historical, cultural, religious, and political backgrounds can be both enormously enriching and practically overwhelming. From a simple reading of your passage, what are the phenomena that commend themselves for further study? What individuals, groups of persons, geographical places, religious practices, ethnic customs, material objects, social institutions, and so forth are relevant to the interpretation of the passage? Consider both things that are explicitly named and things that are assumed. Look up the most important three or four items in some of the resources listed above.

Mark 2:1–12 (Healing a Paralytic)
Mark 7:24–37 (A Syrophoenician Woman and a Deaf Man)
Acts 3:1–10 (Peter Heals a Lame Man)
1 Corinthians 12:1–11 (Spiritual Gifts)
1 Corinthians 15:1–11 (The Resurrection)
Revelation 4:1–11 (A Vision of Heavenly Worship)

Excursus on Narrative Criticism

The discipline of biblical interpretation has often been enriched by borrowing insights from ancillary fields. Over the last few decades, one example of this is the development of what has come to be called narrative criticism. Needless to say, this method focuses on the portions of the New Testament that are in story form: the Gospels and Acts. Narrative critics analyze these texts, using insights drawn from the field of modern literary criticism. These scholars generally acknowledge that New Testament narratives are *referential*: they refer to real time-and-space events outside themselves. But such critics insist that New Testament narratives are also *poetic* in that they create their own story world and seek to achieve certain effects in their readers by drawing them into that world.

Narrative critical analysis sheds light on textual dynamics that other modes of criticism will only intimate. With respect to the steps discussed in this chapter, narrative criticism has points of contact with analysis of genre, form, function, context, structure, language, and intertextuality. Nevertheless, it is a method with its own integrity and deserves brief treatment. It is not entirely clear where this excursus would best fit, but I have chosen to insert it here, after the many steps with which narrative criticism shares commonalities and before the discussion of theological reflection, which is an essential step in confessional communities, regardless of what interpretive method(s) one uses. Narrative criticism attends to several literary dynamics. The following fourfold scheme—events, characters, settings, and discourse—draws on the work of Powell (1990) and Resseguie (2005).

1. Events are obviously those incidents that occur in the narrative. They may be examined in terms of order, duration, and frequency. Order is important because narrative criticism assumes that a story is to be read in sequence and in its entirety. Thus earlier events prepare for later ones. Duration pertains to the amount of space given to the narration of an event. It is not accidental, for example, that the Gospel of Mark devotes five full chapters (11–15) to the last week of Jesus's public ministry. By such duration, Mark is indicating that these events are highly significant and deserving of detailed treatment. Frequency is another way of calling attention to significant events. Why is the "conversion" of Paul narrated three times in the Acts of the Apostles (9:1–22; 22:4–16; 26:9–18) if the author does not see this as one of the most critical events in the first generation of Christianity? Other dynamics related to events include cause-and-effect links, pivotal points, the creation or resolution of conflict, and culmination. All of these dynamics pertain to how the story unfolds, the pace and logic of the plot. Here are some questions that can be posed to a text with regard to events. For more on events, see Powell (1990: 35–50) and Resseguie (2005: 197–240).

- What event takes place in your passage?
- What has prepared for this event? How does it prepare for what follows?
- Is the event narrated in normal sequence? As a flashback? As a prediction?
- How detailed is the narrative? Does the author hurry through some aspects of the story and linger over others?
- Are similar events narrated elsewhere in the writing, or is this story unique? If there are similar stories elsewhere, are there significant differences in the way they are told?
- How does this event contribute to the overall plot of the writing? Does it advance the plot or serve as a digression? Does it heighten conflict or alleviate it?

2. Characters are the *dramatis personae*, the actors in the story, and they may be of different types. A proper understanding of characters and characterization is essential to discerning the intended effects of a story. Narrative critics speak of round characters and flat characters. Round characters are complex: they may have multiple, even contradictory, traits. Flat characters, as the adjective suggests, are two-dimensional. Whether an individual or a large group, they normally represent a unified and fairly simple perspective. Flat characters exhibit a single trait or a relatively narrow range of traits: legalistic scribes, greedy rich people, religiously compromised Samaritans. Expectations can be subverted, of course, when an author introduces a judicious scribe (Mark 12:28–34), a gener-

ous rich person (Luke 19:1–10), or a compassionate Samaritan (Luke 10:30–37). Characters may be static, remaining largely the same throughout the narrative, or dynamic, evolving in response to events. Characters are distinguished by their words, deeds, and perceptions, as well as by what the narrator or other characters may say about them. For more on characters and characterization, see Powell (1990: 51–67) and Resseguie (2005: 121–65). Here are some questions that can be posed to a text with regard to characters:

- Who are the characters in your story? Do they appear elsewhere in the larger narrative?
- What do you learn about the characters from their words, deeds, and perceptions? What does the narrator reveal about them? Do other characters in the story provide further characterization?
- Are the characters round or flat? Static or dynamic? Are they stereotypical characters, or do they exhibit unexpected qualities?

3. Settings are the times and places in which the events occur. It makes a difference whether an event transpires in the wilderness or in the temple precinct. In Gospel narratives, it often is critical that an event occurs on the Sabbath. Settings may also involve certain social, cultural, or religious occasions. The same locale, such as a small village, will have a different significance if the occasion is a wedding, a harvest festival, or a funeral. Some settings may have symbolic significance. The wilderness may evoke the exodus generation; the Jordan River may symbolize the threshold of the promised land. Settings in narratives are akin to staging in plays. Features such as lighting, time of day, locale, scenery, background, furnishings, props, and so forth may all be pertinent to understanding the story. For more on settings, see Powell (1990: 69–83) and Resseguie (2005: 87–120). Here are some questions that can be addressed to a text regarding settings:

- How is the story "staged" in terms of time, place, and social settings?
- What is the relationship between the event(s) and these settings? Are these settings common in the large narrative, or are they unique to this passage?
- What aspects of the physical setting are important? How might they affect the characters?
- How is the time, day, or season of the story identified? Could the time be symbolic?
- What cultural or religious factors elucidate the social setting?

4. Discourse refers to a variety of narrative features such as point of view, irony, intercalation, and figures of speech. Point of view is especially impor-

tant in discerning the intended impact of a narrative. Plots invariably involve conflict, and conflicts entail different points of view. It is critical for the reader of a narrative to discern which points of view are reliable and which are not. In New Testament narratives, reliable points of view include, on the one hand, God, Jesus, angels, prophets, and the narrator. On the other hand, the points of view of the crowds, the religious leaders, and even the disciples are not always trustworthy. Complexities may arise, however, as when unclean spirits, who are generally unreliable, may make truthful affirmations about Jesus (Mark 1:23–24). Irony occurs in different forms, but a common feature, especially in John's Gospel, is "dramatic irony," in which a character in the narrative makes a statement that conveys truth recognized by the readers but not by the characters themselves (e.g., 11:49–53). Intercalation or "sandwiching" refers to the technique of embedding a narrative within a narrative in an A-B-A′ pattern. Mark seems to be fond of this device, as when he frames the cleansing of the temple with Jesus's cursing of the fig tree (11:12–24). Here the barrenness of the fig tree may provide a commentary on the temple. Other figures of speech are too numerous to treat individually. Resseguie offers an especially thorough discussion (2005: 41–86). For more information on aspects of narrative discourse, see Powell (1990: 23–34) and Resseguie (2005: 41–86, 167–96). Here are a few questions on issues of discourse:

- In your passage, which speakers are to be trusted? Whose words may be unreliable?
- Does irony occur in the story? What meanings might the author want readers to grasp, even if the speakers in the narrative are oblivious to them?
- What other structural patterns or figures of speech occur in the story? How do they contribute to the meaning and intended effects of the story on the reader?

In addition to the full-scale works of Powell (1990) and Resseguie (2005), one may consult the more concise treatments in Powell (1995, 1999) and Bartchy (1997). All of these resources have helpful bibliographies.

10. Reflect Theologically on the Text

Theological reflection might be omitted by interpreters whose interests are solely historical, but it is an essential aspect of scriptural interpretation in confessional contexts. The former group brackets out theological concerns as inappropriate for the academic study of religion. At most these researchers would speak of the theologies held by specific persons or communities: Pauline theology, Johannine theology, apocalyptic theology, and so forth. For them, the discipline of New Testament study should be "a strictly secular phenomenological study, in which a Christian theological interpretation can have no part" (Bockmuehl, 2006: 56).

But there is more than a little irony in the insistence that theological interests be bracketed out of scriptural interpretation. To do so is to exclude theology from the analysis of writings whose raison d'être is theological, whose subject matter is theological, whose authors' motives were theological, whose use and collection and preservation and canonization were theologically driven, whose implied readers have theological interests, and the vast majority of whose real readers have read them for theological reasons, believing that they communicate divine revelation (Green and Turner, 2000: 8–9). One might as well study the history of wine without reference to the fact that people drink it.

It should be clear that I embrace a confessional approach to Scripture. I have defined "confessional readers" in the preface as communities of persons who affirm the authority of Scripture and the faith of the classic creeds. These are persons who have embraced the distinctive faith that is grounded in the New Testament and further developed in the first few centuries of the Common Era. These readers consider it quite appropriate to study Scripture with a keen interest in theology, not just theology as a historical phenomenon, but also theology as a contemporary, living reality. One might say that these persons regard theological reflection on the New Testament as an *organic* activity: a wholly natural approach, integral to the larger task of hermeneutics, in which the interpreters respond to the invitation of the text itself and embrace the commitments and perspectives presupposed by the text. As Vanhoozer puts it, "The strongest claim to be made for theological interpretation is that only such reading ultimately does justice to the subject matter of the text itself" (Vanhoozer, 2005: 22; see also Stylianopoulos, 1997: 215).

When we reflect on the New Testament theologically, we are engaging it in a manner that builds upon but transcends description of the text. If we never move beyond the descriptive phase, we are, as one scholar put it, only "occupy[ing] the foyer in the house of hermeneutics" (L. Johnson, 1995: 162). Someone with strictly historical interests might go as far as asking, "What was Paul's or John's understanding of God, Jesus, the human dilemma, salvation, justice, the future, and so forth?" Theological interpreters do not just ask Paul and John these questions; but they also ask these questions *along with* Paul and John. Readers with theological interests push beyond descriptive analysis and engage the questions that engaged the biblical authors. They read a passage in the New Testament and ask not only about its meaning but also about its truth; they ask not only about its logic in the first century but also its theological significance in the twenty-first century (L. Johnson, 1995: 163).

Theological interpretation, in various forms, has been the dominant mode of biblical interpretation since antiquity. In the beginning was the Word, and the Word was read by people with theological interests. But "theological interpretation of Scripture" has also experienced a renaissance of sorts in recent years, particularly in the academy. There are several reasons for this, but two philosophical developments stand out as especially important. First, the critical assumption of complete objectivity and a dispassionate, scientific approach to Scripture, as we saw in chapter 1, turned out to be a fantasy. (Yet that does not discredit objectivity as a goal nor critical methodology as a desideratum.) Second, postmodernism has leveled the playing field for ideological readings, with the result that theology, having been escorted out the front door by modernism, returned by the back door of postmodernism (Green and Turner, 2000: 8–9).

Theological interpreters do not, however, have to resort to an argument that says, "Anything goes nowadays, so theology is in." There may be different opinions about what constitutes the best vocal talent, but that does not mean that anybody who shows up can be a soloist in the choir. All comers—historians, literary scholars, theologians, and others—must demonstrate exegetical rigor and coherence, and this means that we must preserve the best of traditional (i.e., modernist) exegetical theory and practice (Spinks, 2009: 3). But we should remember that theological interpreters have been singing in this choir for the last two millennia. Postmodernism has allowed us *back* in after a period of exile from some quarters of academia. Theological interpreters can therefore claim to have had dominance in the premodern era, a peripheral presence in the heyday of scientific criticism, and a renewed presence in the postmodern era. In this way theological interpretation is the once-and-future method of reading Scripture.

Theological interpretation, as newly resurgent in the academy, is variously defined. One simple definition is that theological interpretation means "interpreting the text of the Bible *as Scripture*, the 'word of God,'" in some sense a divine communication (D. Martin, 2008: 21). Others would speak of reading the Bible with a concern for its enduring significance (Moberly, 2000: 64–69), although this might be possible with the reading of any classic work of literature. One of the most impressive new volumes on theological interpretation, a groundbreaking reference work, defines it as "biblical interpretation oriented to the knowledge of God," meaning, "the knowledge of what God has done in Israel and in Jesus Christ for the good of the world." This is more than an intellectual exercise, although the intellect is certainly engaged. Such knowledge of God is "restorative and transformative" because it issues in loving obedience to the God who is known (Vanhoozer, 2005: 24).

Theological interpreters find themselves necessarily dealing with the obstacles that create distance between text and interpreter, even more so than those interpreters who restrict themselves to historical description. This is so because theological interpretation is concerned to span that distance, as far as possible, so as to join with the biblical authors in the task described by Saint Anselm (1033–1109) as *fides quaerens intellectum* ("faith seeking understanding"). Theological interpretation is already moving toward appropriation (see chapter 4 below), because it assumes an interpretive context that is broader than the horizon of the ancient author and readers, now to include contemporary communities of confessional readers. It is telling that one of the new commentary series that aims at theological interpretation is called Two Horizons (Eerdmans).

So the distance between text and interpreters is not fatalistically conceded and surrendered to, but honestly acknowledged and negotiated. The gulf is neither unbridgeable, nor is it the primary reality of a theological approach to interpretation. That primary reality is twofold: trust and solidarity. Confessional interpreters trust that God speaks through Scripture to the people of God in all ages. They also affirm a solidarity with the people of God in all ages. Their hermeneutical motto is that "the community within which the biblical texts were generated, the community who came to regard these books as canonical, and the community now faced with the need to interpret these texts as Scripture *are the same community*" (Green, 2005a: 125, with added emphasis). Confessional interpreters do not minimize the difficulties of appropriating an ancient text, but rather they negotiate those difficulties by combining the rigorous exercise of the relevant scholarly tools and methods with attentiveness to the God who speaks through Scripture and God's people, who have been shaped by Scripture through the centuries.

How to Engage in Theological Reflection

How, then, does one engage in theological reflection on the biblical text? The specific questions that one might pose to the text are manifold. Some aim at the big ideas in the text. Some provoke you to follow the text's imaginative trajectory. Some aim at the effects of the text on you as a reader. The genre and content of the text are the guides as to what specific questions are relevant in a given case. Here are three possible avenues of inquiry:

1. One could think in terms of classic doctrines of the Christian faith: God, Christology, pneumatology, creation, anthropology, sin, soteriology, ecclesiology, eschatology, and so forth. The following questions could be posed, but obviously not every question will be pertinent to every text:

- What does this text suggest about the character of God? The will of God? God's dealings with human beings, whether redemptive or remedial?
- What does it suggest about the person of Jesus? His relationships with various groups, institutions, and individuals? His demands of his disciples? His values and priorities?
- What does the text reveal about the nature and work of the Holy Spirit?
- What does the text contribute to a Christian understanding of creation? A Christian view of the body? A view of society? A view of history or the future?

- What does the text say about human beings, their virtues and vices, their obligations to God and to other human beings? What dilemmas and difficulties do humans face? What remedies to these dilemmas and difficulties does the text offer?
- What does the text contribute to our understanding of God's people, the body of Christ, its functions, its mission, its structure?

The above questions have some value in that Christian theology ought to start with Scripture and be shaped by it. Systematic theology serves as the distillation of the biblical witness, combined with the insights of philosophy and percolated through centuries of Christian reflection and liturgical practice. But while it is valid for Scripture to inform theology, it is anachronistic for the categories of theology to be the primary determinants of the questions we pose to the biblical text. So though theological reflection may use such questions, it should not be limited to them.

2. Perhaps a more useful avenue of inquiry would be questions about the biblical imagination. By that I mean, what sort of reality does the biblical text imagine? Joel Green describes it well in terms of three levels: "What sort of world, what sort of community, and what sort of person is this text constructing?" (Green, 2005a: 126). Here are those questions expanded slightly:

- How does the text make you view the world differently? How does it envision the reign of God? How does it guide, encourage, and empower you to pursue that vision? What would the world look like if the vision of this text were realized?
- How does the text envision the community of God's people? How would leadership be different? What would relationships look like? How would God's people on earth order their communal life differently if this text's vision were realized?
- How does the text form and inform Christian discipleship? At what points of living, doing, thinking, and being does it challenge persons today?

3. The meaning of a text can be understood in terms of its effects as well as its communicative intention. Thus a text's meaning is not limited to matters of information, and certain kinds of texts—such as poetry, hymns, and apocalyptic visions—do not primarily function as communicators of information. So one could pose a different set of questions:

- What longings, fears, or dreams does the text inspire in you? What visceral responses does it evoke? What passions does it stir? What convictions does it arouse?

- What moods does the text prompt? Contentment? Joy? Gratitude? Awe? Indignation? Hope? A sobering sense of obligation?
- Toward what actions does the text propel you? Prayer? Confession? Singing? Service to others? Advocacy? Praise? Repentance? Reconciliation with an enemy?

Bibliographic Resources for Theological Reflection

Finally, what scholarly tools are available for those who would engage in theological reflection? On this topic the vast array of modern, academic resources is of uneven value. Not all commentators are concerned with theology, although some devote attention to it. As it turns out, two fairly recent trends in biblical scholarship are especially promising for those who would engage in theological interpretation of Scripture: (1) commentaries that glean relevant excerpts from the premodern era, and (2) commentaries that are overtly theological, often written by systematic theologians rather than biblical scholars per se. The former collections of patristic and medieval reflections are inherently theological since the use of Scripture in those centuries was almost always related to the life of the church. The latter series of commentaries, while not ignoring the fruits of historical scholarship, deliberately move beyond it to reflect on the broad theological issues raised by the text. Both of these contributions are welcome developments for students of the Bible who see theological inquiry as an organic part of interpretation. To conclude this section, therefore, I will list these commentary series as well as some other resources for persons who want to read the Bible so as to know, love, and obey God more fully.

RESOURCES ON THE HISTORY OF INTERPRETATION

A growing body of scholarship is concerned with recovering the vast sweep of premodern interpretation. To gather insights from this millennium and a half of exegetical and homiletical literature requires expertise that is beyond most of us. But the exhausting spadework done by a number of scholars gives biblical interpreters access to the best hermeneutical gems of the patristic and medieval periods. The following are two commentary series that collect such material:

The Ancient Christian Commentary on Scripture. 1998–2009. Edited by Thomas C. Oden et al. 29 vols., also on CD-ROM. Downers Grove, IL: InterVarsity. This series is now complete for both the Old Testament and the New Testament.

The Church's Bible. 2003–. Edited by Robert Louis Wilken. Grand Rapids: Eerdmans. As a recently launched series, only a few volumes are currently available.

The above commentaries are the most helpful resources for finding premodern insights on specific biblical passages. For thematic and historical discussions of biblical interpretation in these centuries, the following books are useful:

Charles Kannengiesser. 2006. *Handbook of Patristic Exegesis: The Bible in Ancient Christianity*. Leiden: Brill.

John J. O'Keefe and R. R. Reno. 2005. *Sanctified Vision: An Introduction to Early Christian Interpretation of the Bible*. Baltimore: Johns Hopkins University Press.

John L. Thompson. 2007. *Reading the Bible with the Dead: What You Can Learn from the History of Exegesis That You Can't Learn from Exegesis Alone*. Grand Rapids: Eerdmans.

D. H. Williams, ed. 2006. *Tradition, Scripture, and Interpretation: A Sourcebook of the Ancient Church*. Grand Rapids: Baker Academic.

Resources on Theological Interpretation

There are also two new commentary series that very intentionally bring theological interests to the study of the Bible. The third item below is a single-volume commentary on the entire Bible.

The Brazos Theological Commentary on the Bible. 2005–. Edited by R. R. Reno. Grand Rapids: Brazos Press. Currently about a dozen volumes are available, and more are being published each year.

The Two Horizons New Testament Commentary. 2005–. Edited by Joel B. Green and Max Turner. Grand Rapids: Eerdmans. A more recent series, only a few volumes are currently available. (Its Old Testament counterpart, The Two Horizons Old Testament Commentary, is edited by J. Gordon McConville and Craig Bartholomew.)

Theological Bible Commentary. 2009. Edited by Gail R. O'Day and David L. Petersen. Louisville: Westminster John Knox. Handy but terse in its treatment.

In addition, two important journals are devoted to the theological interpretation of Scripture:

Ex auditu: An International Journal for the Theological Interpretation of Scripture. 1991–. Eugene, OR: Wipf & Stock.

Journal of Theological Interpretation. 2007–. Winona Lake, IN: Eisenbrauns. Joel Green offers an introduction to it (2007a).

Finally, several volumes address various issues in theological interpretation. Some of these also have essays that exemplify the approach by way of specific biblical texts:

A. K. M. Adam, Stephen E. Fowl, Kevin J. Vanhoozer, and Francis Watson. 2006. *Reading Scripture with the Church: Toward a Hermeneutic for Theological Interpretation.* Grand Rapids: Baker Academic.

Craig Bartholomew et al., eds. 2000. *Renewing Biblical Interpretation.* Scripture and Hermeneutics 1. Grand Rapids: Zondervan.

Markus Bockmuehl and Alan J. Torrance, eds. 2008. *Scripture's Doctrine and Theology's Bible: How the New Testament Shapes Christian Dogmatics.* Grand Rapids: Baker Academic.

Ellen F. Davis and Richard B. Hays, eds. 2003. *The Art of Reading Scripture.* Grand Rapids: Eerdmans.

Stephen E. Fowl, ed. 1997. *The Theological Interpretation of Scripture: Classic and Contemporary Readings.* Cambridge, MA: Blackwell.

————. 1998. *Engaging Scripture: A Model for Theological Interpretation.* Malden, MA: Blackwell.

Joel B. Green and Max Turner, eds. 2000. *Between Two Horizons: Spanning New Testament Studies and Systematic Theology.* Grand Rapids: Eerdmans.

I. Howard Marshall. 2004. *Beyond the Bible: Moving from Scripture to Theology.* Grand Rapids: Baker Academic.

Gary T. Meadors, ed. 2009. *Four Views on Moving beyond the Bible to Theology.* Grand Rapids: Zondervan.

D. Christopher Spinks. 2007. *The Bible and the Crisis of Meaning: Debates on the Theological Interpretation of Scripture.* New York: T&T Clark.

Daniel J. Treier. 2008. *Introducing Theological Interpretation of Scripture: Recovering a Christian Practice.* Grand Rapids: Baker Academic.

Kevin J. Vanhoozer, ed. 2005. *Dictionary for Theological Interpretation of the Bible.* Grand Rapids: Baker Academic.

Exercises on Key Texts

Review the questions listed in sections 1, 2, and 3 above and address them to your specific passage, recognizing that some will obviously have more pertinence than others. Read the commentary on your verses from a volume in one of the explicitly theological series. Find a commentary that has gathered remarks from the patristic and/or medieval eras and see what insights can be gleaned from the premodern period. Rather than just probe the biblical text like a specimen in a laboratory, try to think along with the biblical author. How does your text speak to and reveal life as it should be lived in God's presence?

Mark 2:1–12 (Healing a Paralytic)

Mark 7:24–37 (A Syrophoenician Woman and a Deaf Man)

Acts 3:1–10 (Peter Heals a Lame Man)
1 Corinthians 12:1–11 (Spiritual Gifts)
1 Corinthians 15:1–11 (The Resurrection)
Revelation 4:1–11 (A Vision of Heavenly Worship)

11. Consult the Commentaries

As I turn my attention to this penultimate step, I'm aware of the fact that I have already mentioned a few commentary series above. Here we see the difficulty of a sequential method of exegesis. Despite that slight foreshadowing, there is a good rationale for putting commentaries near the end of the exegetical process. One of the perils in the use of commentaries is the temptation to turn to them too quickly and rely on them too heavily. In this way, you short-circuit your own learning and thereby deprive your readers, your audience, and yourself of your own creative insights.

Commentaries are the most interpretive kind of tool. With a view to drawing out historical, literary, and theological meanings, they employ the various analytical methods discussed earlier in this chapter. In effect, they have done something much like what you do when you interpret a text. Concordances, dictionaries, and Synoptic parallels are relatively less-interpretive tools. They provide raw data that requires interpretation. Thus turning to the commentaries too quickly taints the exegetical evidence and makes it difficult for you to analyze it with an open mind.

There is, however, an opposite error too: largely ignoring the commentaries. Giants have preceded us in the enterprise of biblical interpretation, and the fruits of their labors should by all means be deployed. If you do your own work first and with due diligence, then you can engage the giants in a manner that is critical and informed rather than simply derivative. By all means, stand on the shoulders of giants, but do not ride along in their pockets. Vanhoozer offers this caveat about scholarly tools in general: "Critical tools have a ministerial, not magisterial, function in biblical interpretation" (2005: 22). More specifically and bluntly stated, commentaries are guides, not gods.

If commentaries only enter the exegetical process near the end, what is their function? They function in at least the following four ways:

1. *Confirmation.* Commentaries will often corroborate what you have discovered on your own. Although biblical interpretation does not always permit certainty, a conclusion that is reached independently by several interpreters has a greater claim to validity.
2. *Correction.* Needless to say, sometimes you won't get it right. This is true of both novices and more-seasoned exegetes. A commentator may alert you to evidence you have overlooked or a line of reasoning that

is faulty. The best commentaries are usually written by persons with significant expertise, both of a general sort (good training and years of experience) and specific (expertise in a particular author, genre, or methodology). Sometimes a major commentary is the crowning work of a scholar who has studied a writing, say Romans or the Gospel of Mark, for decades. It is to be expected, then, that a well-researched commentary will turn over stones that you did not know existed. On the other hand, no commentary is infallible and beyond questioning. One scholar advises exegetes to "bristle when a critic says 'unconvincing,' without demonstrating why the adverse decision is made. You may be exposed to a cheap shot" (Danker, 2003: 305). Commentators are human and, therefore, subject to bias and partisanship.

3. *Complement.* You may consult a commentary and find that it does more than just confirm your conclusion; it also adds to it and makes your argument more complete, more nuanced, or better reasoned. A commentary may cite a parallel text or phenomenon making much the same point that you made by citing a different text or phenomenon. It may strengthen your case or show its broader significance in ways that do not duplicate your research but rather supplement it.

4. *Conversation partner.* The combined effect of these functions is that the commentator becomes your conversation partner rather than just a tutor. It may still be the case that the commentator has far more training and expertise than you. But if by your own exegetical spadework you have discovered the most important data and acquainted yourself with the basic issues in a passage, then you can read the experts with much more understanding; you may, on occasion, even have reason to challenge their conclusions. One might ask, if a particular "fact" is there in the commentaries, why should I waste my time discovering it? First of all, there is intellectual satisfaction, even excitement, in discovering things firsthand. Second, not every assertion in a commentary is factual, and some assertions that are basically true could be better articulated or more convincingly established. When commentators become conversation partners rather than tutors, there can be give and take in the interpretive process.

The amount of secondary literature available nowadays on the Bible is overwhelming. In its quantity, it is an embarrassment of riches. In its quality, some of it is just an embarrassment. The commentaries, monographs, articles, devotional reflections, and study guides range from the profound to the shallow, from jewels to junk. Although the best commentaries reflect years of meticulous study and expert analysis, others are of more modest value.

The interpreter should distinguish three levels of commentaries: (1) critical and technical works written for scholars and advanced students; (2) serious works for a broad but educated readership, including pastors, students, and laity; and (3) devotional commentaries for the broadest possible readership. The third kind is not necessarily inferior to the first and second, but the aims of each should be borne in mind. For professional and semiprofessional interpreters (e.g., scholars, pastors, students, church educators, youth ministers, et al.), commentaries of the first and second types should be their mainstay. There are not strict dividing lines between these categories, but commentaries in the first group will be based on the original-language text and will seriously engage the scholarly secondary literature. Commentaries in the second group may be based on an English translation (e.g., the NRSV, NIV) but are usually written by scholars who consult the original and are conversant with the scholarly issues.

In addition to academic level, commentaries may be distinguished by depth, method, and ideology. By depth, I mean the sheer quantity of commentary devoted to the biblical text. Several one-volume Bible commentaries are listed below. It goes without saying that a thousand-page work on the entire Bible will not have the depth of discussion on Matthew's Gospel that a thousand-page commentary on Matthew will have. Serious students of the Bible should own a one-volume commentary as a handy reference, but a more-thorough work is needed for in-depth study. As for method and ideology, I refer to the fact that the diversification of reading strategies in recent decades has given rise to commentaries that employ a particular methodology or interpret the text with the concerns of particular readers in mind. Some of the more prominent types include narrative commentaries, sociorhetorical commentaries, reader-response commentaries, feminist commentaries, postcolonial commentaries, and so forth. We should not infer that commentaries that do *not* fall into any of these categories therefore have *no* methodology or *no* ideology, but rather that they do not foreground methodology or ideology.

Below I list some of the best and most recent whole-Bible commentaries, including several that articulate some of the more-recent perspectives. After that I list several commentary series. A caveat: almost every series is uneven. A series may have some of the best commentaries on particular books, a number of solid but less spectacular volumes, some mediocre volumes, and a few clunkers. In addition, some older series are periodically updated with new editions or even entirely new volumes that replace older ones. By listing a series below, I am commending its general quality, not necessarily every volume within it. Last, the reader should not forget the theological and patristic/medieval commentary series mentioned above, and should bear in mind the fact that some excellent commentaries are freestanding, not part of a series. For more on commentaries and their use, see Green (2005a) and Danker (2003: 282–307).

ONE-VOLUME BIBLE COMMENTARIES

Tokunboh Adeyemo, ed. 2006. *Africa Bible Commentary*. Grand Rapids: Zondervan.

John Barton and John Muddiman, eds. 2001. *The Oxford Bible Commentary.* Oxford: Oxford University Press.

Brian K. Blount et al., eds. 2007. *True to Our Native Land: An African American New Testament Commentary.* Minneapolis: Fortress.

M. Eugene Boring and Fred B. Craddock. 2004. *The People's New Testament Commentary.* Louisville: Westminster John Knox.

R. E. Brown, J. A. Fitzmyer, and R. E. Murphy, eds. 1990. *The New Jerome Biblical Commentary.* Englewood Cliffs, NJ: Prentice Hall.

James D. G. Dunn and John W. Rogerson, eds. 2003. *Eerdmans Commentary on the Bible.* Grand Rapids: Eerdmans.

R. T. France et al., eds. 1994. *New Bible Commentary: 21st Century Edition.* Downers Grove, IL: InterVarsity.

Catherine Clark Kroeger and Mary J. Evans, eds. 2002. *The IVP Women's Bible Commentary.* Downers Grove, IL: InterVarsity.

James L. Mays et al. eds. 2000. *HarperCollins Bible Commentary.* Rev. ed. San Francisco: HarperSanFrancisco.

Carol A. Newsom and Sharon H. Ringe, eds. 1998. *The Women's Bible Commentary.* Exp. ed. Louisville: Westminster John Knox.

Daniel M. Patte, ed. 2006. *Global Bible Commentary.* Nashville: Abingdon.

Fernando F. Segovia and R. S. Sugirtharajah, eds. 2007. *A Postcolonial Commentary on the New Testament Writings.* London: T&T Clark.

COMMENTARIES SERIES—CRITICAL AND TECHNICAL WORKS (LEVEL 1)

The following comments are generally quoted or adapted from the publishers' descriptions:

Anchor Bible. 1956–2007. Garden City, NY: Doubleday. Continued as Anchor Yale Bible. 2007–. New Haven: Yale University Press. International and interfaith in scope, it "aims to present the best contemporary scholarship in a way that is accessible not only to scholars but also to the educated nonspecialist." Employs both traditional and more recent methodologies. Covers Old Testament, New Testament, and several apocryphal books.

Baker Exegetical Commentary on the New Testament. 1994–. Grand Rapids: Baker Academic. Informed evangelical scholarship that blends "scholarly depth with readability, exegetical detail with sensitivity to the whole, and attention to critical problems with theological awareness." Aims to address the needs of persons involved in "the preaching and exposition of the Scriptures as the uniquely inspired Word of God."

Hermeneia. 1971–. Philadelphia/Minneapolis: Fortress. A technical, historical commentary "designed for the serious student of the Bible." International and ecumenical in the selection of authors, it will eventually cover Old Testament, New Testament, and some apocryphal and pseudepigraphical works.

International Critical Commentary. 1895–. Edinburgh: T&T Clark; New York: Scribner. Begun in the late nineteenth century, the ICC is steadily being updated. Generally technical and detailed, it employs textual, linguistic, historical, literary, and theological aids to exegesis. The older volumes are of mixed value; the recent replacement volumes are often excellent.

New International Greek Testament Commentary. 1978–. Grand Rapids: Eerdmans; Milton Keynes, UK: Paternoster. The New Testament is nearly complete. It offers "exegesis that is sensitive to theological themes as well as to the details of the historical, linguistic, and textual content." Based on the Greek text and thoroughly engaged with the scholarly literature.

Word Biblical Commentary. 1982–97. Waco/Dallas: Word. Continued, 1998–. Nashville: Nelson. Nearly complete on the entire Old Testament and New Testament, this series offers "the best in critical scholarship firmly committed to the authority of Scripture as divine revelation." Excellent sectional bibliographies, textual notes, verse-by-verse commentary, and summarizing explanations.

COMMENTARIES SERIES—SERIOUS WORKS FOR A BROAD, EDUCATED READERSHIP (LEVEL 2)

Abingdon New Testament Commentaries. 1996–. Nashville: Abingdon. Compact and critical, written for theological students, but also for undergrads, pastors, and other religious leaders. They "exemplify the tasks and procedures of careful, critical biblical exegesis."

Augsburg Commentary on the New Testament. 1980–. Minneapolis: Augsburg. Written for laypeople, students, and pastors. Includes introductions and section-by-section commentaries. Heavy use of technical terms is avoided. Authors are ordained, seminary professors who affirm the centrality of Scripture for the life and faith of the church.

Black's New Testament Commentary. 1993–. Peabody, MA: Hendrickson. "A reliable and enlightening exposition" of the author's own, fresh translation. Combines historical, literary, and theological treatment. Designed for pastors, students, scholars, and general readers.

Catholic Commentary on Sacred Scripture. 2008–. Grand Rapids: Baker Academic. "Combines outstanding biblical scholarship with lively faith." "Responds to the desire of Catholics to study the Bible in depth and in a way that integrates Scripture with Catholic doctrine, worship, and daily life." Interprets Scripture "in its canonical context and in the light of Catholic tradition and the analogy of faith."

Chalice Commentaries for Today. 2004–. St. Louis: Chalice. "Designed to help pastors, seminary students, and educated laity who are open to contemporary scholarship claim the Bible in their personal lives and in their engagement with the crucial issues of our time." Aims to offer "a better understanding of the biblical challenges to the values, beliefs, and behaviors in today's world as well as our own world's challenges to the values, beliefs, and behaviors in the biblical world."

Interpretation: A Bible Commentary for Teaching and Preaching. 1982–. Atlanta/Louisville: John Knox/Westminster John Knox. Scholarly commentaries "written specifically for those who interpret the Bible through teaching and preaching in the church." Authors are both scholars and teachers/preachers. Integrates historical and theological exegesis.

Interpreting Biblical Texts. 1981–. Nashville: Abingdon. Aims "to help serious readers in their experience of reading and interpreting by providing guides for their journeys into textual worlds." Focuses "not so much on the world behind the texts or out of which the texts have arisen as on the worlds created by the texts in their engagement with readers."

IVP New Testament Commentary Series. 1991–. Downers Grove, IL: InterVarsity. Designed for pastors, Bible study leaders, and teachers, the series offers expositions "informed by the best of recent evangelical scholarship." Authors are committed "to the authority of Scripture for Christian faith and practice."

New American Commentary. 1991–. Nashville: Broadman/Broadman & Holman. "For the minister or Bible student who wants to understand and expound the Scriptures." Based on the NIV translation, but with scholarly exegesis that attends to the original language. Emphasizes the theological unity of the book and of Scripture as a whole.

New Cambridge Bible Commentary. 2003–. Cambridge and New York: Cambridge University Press. Aims to "elucidate the Hebrew and Christian Scriptures for a wide range of intellectually curious individuals." Employs rhetorical, social scientific, narrative, and other new interpretive strategies. Accessible and free of jargon, it includes the text of the NRSV. Only a few volumes are currently available.

New International Biblical Commentary. 1988–. Peabody, MA: Hendrickson. Offers "the best of contemporary scholarship in a format that both general readers and serious students can use with profit." Based on the NIV, it offers section-by-section exposition. More technical notes are gathered at the end of each section.

New International Commentary on the New Testament. 1951–. Grand Rapids: Eerdmans. Provides users with "an exposition that is thorough and abreast of modern scholarship and at the same time loyal to the Scriptures as the infallible Word of God." Begun in the 1950s but regularly updated. New Testament is nearly complete.

New Interpreter's Bible, The. 2003. Nashville: Abingdon. A twelve-volume commentary on the Old Testament, New Testament, and Apocrypha, along with several introductory essays on different genres. Ecumenical and international, it aims "to bring the best in contemporary biblical scholarship into the service of the church to enhance preaching, teaching, and study of the Scriptures." Includes full text of the NIV and NRSV with commentary and reflections.

New Testament Library. 1963–. Louisville: Westminster John Knox. Offers authoritative commentary, fresh translations, and critical portrayals of the historical world in which the books were created. Pays careful attention to literary design and presents a theologically perceptive exposition of the text.

Paideia: Commentaries on the New Testament. 2007–. Grand Rapids: Baker Academic. Explores how New Testament texts form Christian readers by attending to the ancient narrative and rhetorical strategies that the text employs, showing how the text shapes theological convictions and moral habits, commenting on the final, canonical form of each book, focusing on the cultural, literary, and theological settings of the text.

Pillar New Testament Commentary. 2002–. Grand Rapids: Eerdmans; Nottingham: Apollos. "Designed both for serious students and for general readers of the Bible," this series interacts with critical issues but "avoids undue technical detail." Blends "rigorous exegesis and exposition, scholarship and pastoral sensitivity, with an eye alert both to biblical theology and to the contemporary relevance of the Bible."

Reading the New Testament. 1978–. Macon, GA: Smyth & Helwys. Presents "cutting-edge research in popular form that is accessible to upper-level undergraduates, seminarians, seminary educated pastors, and educated laypeople, as well as to graduate students and professors." Focuses "on a close reading of the final form of the text." Concerned with both "the communication strategies and the religious message of the text"

Sacra Pagina. 1991–. Collegeville, MN: Liturgical Press. Written by an international team of Catholic scholars for scholars, students, clergy, and religious educators. Aims to provide "sound, critical analysis without any loss of sensitivity to religious meaning."

Smyth and Helwys Bible Commentary. 2000–. Macon, GA: Smyth & Helwys. Aims "to make available serious, credible biblical scholarship in an accessible and less intimidating format." Includes not only commentary but also "images, photographs, maps, works of fine art, and drawings that bring the text to life." Sensitive to the needs of a visual generation of believers. Draws from the history of interpretation not only in traditional commentary but also in literature, theater, church history, and the visual arts. Every volume includes a CD-ROM.

Westminster Bible Companion. 1995–. Louisville: Westminster John Knox. Assists "pastors and students in their study of the Bible as a guide to Christian faith and practice. Each volume explains the biblical book in its original historical context and explores the text's significance for faithful living today."

ANNOTATED BIBLIOGRAPHIES

Finally, since it is impossible here to offer evaluative remarks on individual commentaries, the prospective buyer should consult annotated bibliographies. D. A. Carson's *New Testament Commentary Survey* (2008) and Jim Rosscup's *Commentaries for Biblical Expositors* (2006) will provide helpful lists and descriptions. Other bibliographies worth consulting but broader in scope than commentaries alone include David Bauer's *An Annotated Guide to Biblical Resources for Ministry* (2003) and John Glynn's *Commentary and Reference Survey* (2007). Various websites also offer reviews of commentaries. In addition to the website of the *Review of Biblical Literature* (www.bookreviews .org), one may profitably consult www.bestcommentaries.com. These tools, combined with the recommendations of peers and professors, should enable a person to judiciously build a library of resources.

Exercises on Key Texts

The extensive bibliographical section above is an indication of the vastness of the resources for this step, and I have limited the list to resources in English! How much work one does at this stage depends on one's context and aims. The graduate student writing a major thesis should consult a broad range of literature. The Christian leader preparing a weekly study or sermon may only have time to consult a few commentaries. For the present exercise, read the relevant portions of at least two commentaries on your passage. How do these authors confirm, correct, or complement your own exegetical spadework? How can you engage them in conversation on the basis of your own research?

Mark 2:1–12 (Healing a Paralytic)
Mark 7:24–37 (A Syrophoenician Woman and a Deaf Man)
Acts 3:1–10 (Peter Heals a Lame Man)
1 Corinthians 12:1–11 (Spiritual Gifts)
1 Corinthians 15:1–11 (The Resurrection)
Revelation 4:1–11 (A Vision of Heavenly Worship)

12. Synthesize

Once you have carried out the above steps with respect to a particular biblical passage, you will have generated a raft of data, observations, explanations, and connections. You have not yet achieved the goal of exegesis, however, which is a well-informed, coherently constructed interpretation of the passage (Hayes and Holladay, 2007: 178). Even if you have interpreted some of the data along the way, you still need to synthesize the results of your study and state them with clarity and force.

These twelve steps (including the synthesis) are steps in the exegetical *process*, not sections of an exegetical *paper*. In other words, the final write-up of your interpretation need not, indeed, normally *should* not, have exactly these twelve component parts. The structure of an interpretive essay may take different forms and is to be guided by the text in question, not by a rigid outline. Even the actual unfolding of the exegetical *process* usually has more flexibility than is implied by the above enumerated steps. As one handbook puts it, "The various exegetical procedures are not related to one another in any strict architectonic fashion" (Hayes and Holladay, 1987: 132). There is no rigid twelve-step program for recovering eisegetes.

Nevertheless, a process with relative merit is better than no process at all. It is easier to have a plan from which one may vary than to bring order out of sheer chaos. The methodical approach presented in this chapter may at first seem mechanical, rigid, even stifling of creativity. Is there no role for imagination, intuition, or the guidance of God's Spirit in biblical interpretation? Certainly there is, and an orderly method need not suppress such gifts. But the method presented here offers at least two advantages.

First, creativity is at its best when it is disciplined. Ingenuity and originality are powerful engines of new knowledge, but durable knowledge is seldom created without reference to existing knowledge, forms, and canons. Discipline properly tempers and guides creativity, ultimately making it more effective. Interpreters whose creativity soars without discipline may break free from certain forms of imprisonment like Icarus of Greek mythology with his waxen wings. But like Icarus, they may find that their creations eventually disintegrate and no longer bear them aloft.

Second, a methodical approach has the advantage of constancy. The responsibilities of biblical interpretation for teaching and preaching can be relentless and at times tedious. An orderly method can be employed, even when the imagination grows dull and inspiration wanes. An orderly method is especially helpful in the early stages of one's training. A novice chef needs a good cookbook and disciplined devotion to the task. A master chef, whose skills are honed by years of experience, gains a certain panache that, while not replacing the cookbook, may on occasion free the chef from strict adherence to it. If you are a beginner, learn to cook by the book. When your skills are honed by practice, then you can create more freely, occasionally skip a step, and add just the right ingredients without always having to consult the directions.

The key to an effective synthesis is deploying your results, not just reporting them (Hayes and Holladay, 2007: 185). By "deploy" I mean that you *marshal the data meaningfully in the service of a goal*, that goal being an interpretation of the biblical text that is disciplined, creative, and faithful. More specifically, such deployment usually involves the following.

(1) *Eliminate less-meaningful data.* Not everything that you discover will be significant, so winnow the data and use what best serves your goal. There might be ten interesting parallels for a certain idea, but two or three are most relevant. An effective discussion of those two or three will do more to make your case and less to weary your readers than a catalog of all ten.

Closely related to this is (2) *develop a sense of proportionality.* Give prominence to material in proportion to its importance. Discern what lines of inquiry had the greatest payoff. Was there a significant text-critical problem in the passage? Then a discussion of the variants and the rationale for the chosen reading will be important parts of the final interpretation. Did certain key terms bear significant theological freight? Then an analysis of the text's language is in order. Were specific historical persons, places, institutions, or practices central to a narrative? Then you will need to incorporate the results of some background study. Critical issues should receive several paragraphs of text. Ancillary matters may deserve a sentence or two. A tangential idea may be relegated to a footnote.

(3) *Make proper use of scholarly resources.* As noted previously, there is a wealth of secondary literature on the Bible, and a good interpretive essay will make use of it. But a good essay will not be overpowered by the secondary literature. In other words, the framework of the essay and the bulk of its content must be your own original work. It may be accented by the work of others but not overwhelmed by it. An essay that is little more than a patchwork quilt of quotations and paraphrases gleaned from the experts should be avoided. Good exegesis requires your own creative engagement with the biblical text. No one expects you to perform intellectual parthenogenesis, the creation of something with no fertilizing input from anyone else. But neither is exegesis a kind of surrogate motherhood, in which you deliver something to which you have no genetic relation.

(4) *Let the structure of the body of your paper arise from the biblical passage.* A common structure, such as is found in many commentaries, moves verse by verse through the text. In some cases, this is a workable structure for an exegetical paper. But the best guide for the body of an interpretive essay derives from the structure of the passage in question. Since the paragraph is the basic unit of thought, your essay might work through the passage paragraph by paragraph. In some cases, a thematic approach might commend itself, so that you approach the passage via the analysis of its key motifs. Usually the best way to deal with a text from the Gospels or Acts is to follow its narrative structure. What are the elements of the story? Is there a series of scenes? Is it structured by the give and take of dialogue? Is there alternation between action and discourse? In every case the interpreter should look to the biblical text for the most appropriate way to structure the essay.

The previous paragraph concerns the *body* of an interpretive essay. Normally, in addition to the core that constitutes the bulk of the paper, you should have some introductory matter and a conclusion. Again, there is flexibility as to what goes into these parts of an essay and just how long they should be. In effect, *an exegetical paper is a modern literary form* used in theological education, and as in the case of all literary forms, there are typical characteristics as well as the possibility for innovation. Having acknowledged that flexibility, I find that most beginning interpreters are happy to have some guidelines. I recommend the following basic components for an exegetical essay. If the length of the paper is in the range of twelve to fifteen pages, the guidelines suggested below may be helpful. Yet when individual instructors have different expectations, they should be followed. Finally, if one is doing original-language exegesis, the interpreter's own translation will often serve as a preface to the paper.

A Suggested Outline for an Exegesis Paper

A. Introduction—one-half to one full page

- The introduction should orient the reader to the passage you will be interpreting. I urge students *not* to introduce the writing as a whole by rehearsing matters of date, authorship, recipients, themes, and so forth. The introduction may begin with a sentence or two about the writing as a whole but it should move quickly to the text in question.
- The introduction should offer the reader a concise preview of the issues in the paper without giving away too much. If the introduction is rhetorically effective, the readers will have a general idea of what is to come, and their curiosity will be piqued. Often the introduction is best written last, when the overall shape, substance, and outcome of the paper are known.

B. Literary Context—one-half to one full page

- This section is precisely what was discussed above. In fact, a well-written paragraph or two from that step in the exegetical process can often be imported into the paper with light editing. The function of this part is to locate the text meaningfully in the context of the writing, with particular attention to the immediate context: what comes before and what comes after your verses.

C. Literary Structure—one-half to one full page

- Again, the paragraph(s) that you composed in step 5 can be inserted here, perhaps with light editing. Here the focus is not on the surrounding text in the larger writing but on the internal structure of your passage. This section is strategically located here in the essay because it will usually serve as the guide for the arrangement of the following section: the commentary.

D. Commentary—about ten pages

- The commentary is thus the core and the largest portion of the exegetical essay. Whether proceeding verse by verse, paragraph by paragraph, by theme, or by a narration, the structure of the commentary should present the material of the text in the most appropriate fashion. As discussed just above (in C), let the structure of the body of your paper arise from the passage itself.
- The commentary will thus contain a rich variety of materials that were generated in the exegetical process: text-critical observations, lexical insights, grammatical data, historical backgrounds, relevant information about social, cultural, economic, political, and religious matters, and so forth. As noted above, deploy this information. Do not simply report and catalog it. Craft these diverse data into a clear and persuasive essay, in which everything serves the goal of interpreting the text.

E. Conclusion—one to two pages

- The conclusion might serve various functions. While you certainly want to draw together the strands of the argument and seal the deal, the best way to do that may *not* be to rehearse the paper point by point. A good conclusion is more than a summary. State the results of your exegesis clearly, especially the theological and/or practical fruits of your study. Move beyond the details of individual verses and reflect on the larger ideas that your passage addresses. Show how this particular text relates to and informs the faith and practice of Christian communities.

So far the assumption has been that a traditional exegetical paper is the most likely material product of the exegetical process. In theological education, that is still generally true, although the nature, definition, and goals of exegesis are much debated. We should acknowledge, however, that exegetical study could form the foundation for a variety of products or activities: a sermon, a session of an adult education class, a personal quest for understanding, an article for publication, a background paper for a denominational study, an activity for a youth retreat, or even a dramatic production based on a biblical story. It is not possible to discuss and illustrate each of these and other possibilities, but there is one other model that most of my students have found useful as they prepare for their ministries: the exegetical brief.

The Exegetical Brief

The exegetical brief is an attempt to provide a model that can be employed in real-life ministry settings. I am enough of a traditionalist to believe that there is still significant value in writing a standard exegesis paper of twelve to fifteen pages, but I am enough of a realist to know that this model cannot be easily transported to ministry contexts as a regular practice for teaching and preaching. There may not be sufficient resources in one's personal library to do a thorough, traditional exegetical paper. Likewise, there often is not enough time in a busy minister's schedule to devote the requisite hours to a full-blown exegetical study. But that concession to real-life demands and limitations is not an excuse to be slack in one's preparation. Thus what I am calling an exegetical brief is a compromise effort, incorporating most of the activities discussed in this chapter but in an abbreviated format that can be practiced in real-life settings.

The format for an exegetical brief is a condensed version of the outline for an exegetical paper. I give students a specific format and detailed instructions pertaining to form and ask that they follow them closely, although the contents obviously vary according to the biblical text. The typical length of an exegetical brief will be 1,300 to 1,500 words or 2–2.5 pages, single spaced. An exegetical brief does not purport to be a full-fledged exegetical treatment. Although the extent of one's research will vary, I normally ask students to use at least three sources: a lexical resource (e.g., Danker, 2000), a good study Bible with notes and introductions, and at least one critical commentary. This ought to be the *minimum* regimen for a Christian leader's weekly preparation. Going beyond the minimum can only enrich one's personal benefit and better serve one's constituents. Here are the four sections of an exegetical brief and the recommended format:

1. *Context and structure*: Normally one medium-sized paragraph for each of these topics suffices. The paragraph should begin with the word "Context" or "Structure," in italics and followed by a colon.
2. *Exegetical notes*: In these notes the interpreter moves through the passage methodically, making observations on the most pertinent matters: lexical, textual, intertextual, historical backgrounds, and so forth. The snippet of the text on which one comments in the note should appear first, using italics and followed by a colon. It is not necessary to excerpt the entire text in these snippets. Given the limitations of space, the interpreter may have to pass over some phrases. The exegetical notes will normally occupy about half the space of the brief.
3. *Theological comments*: Here the interpreter should highlight two or three of the "big ideas" in the text for theological reflection. Depending entirely on the passage, these ideas might have to do with Christology,

healing, social justice, prayer, religious practices, eschatology, and so on. Each paragraph should begin with an italicized word or short phrase that identifies the topic, followed by a colon.

4. *Ideas to profess, practice, and proclaim*: In this final section one should move toward the ways of appropriating or performing the text. The terms "profess" and "practice" obviously refer to beliefs and religious practices toward which the text points. "Proclaim" refers to a third type of reflection, not necessarily exclusive of the first two: the homiletical use of the text. How might the exegetical work inform and shape a sermon on this passage?

A sample exegetical paper and a sample exegetical brief appear in appendixes 1 and 2.

3

Evaluating and Contemporizing the Text

We are now at a bridge between two major stages in the interpretive method outlined in this book: "Analyzing the Text" and "Evaluating and Contemporizing the Text." These two stages correspond respectively to historically grounded exegesis and contemporary hermeneutics. The theological reflection that was discussed above as one of the last steps (step 10) in exegesis actually serves as a link between the two major stages. Through historically oriented analysis we gain insight into the meaning that was intended by the author and conveyed by the text (recognizing that there will be limitations on the success of that task). The meaning that the text likely had in its original context is not the sum total and only possible meaning of the text, but any extended, fuller, or symbolic meanings that are posited should be related to the historical meaning.

Exegesis thus provides a foundation for further theological reflection and appropriation of Scripture's meaning(s). Contemporary relevance is obviously of great importance. Indeed, that is almost always the ultimate goal of confessional readers, and it is clearly the goal of the method presented in this book. But as Raymond Brown cautions, contemporary relevance "must be related to (but not confined to or necessarily identical with) the meaning intended and conveyed by the evangelists to their audiences" (1994: 7; cf. Stylianopoulos, 1997: 223–24, 227). Luke Timothy Johnson also warns that historical exegesis must not be swallowed up in hermeneutics, and he illustrates this error by reference to highly individualistic and modernistic interpretations of apocalyptic literature. In such cases, "the conviction that God's Word speaks directly to every age has not been accompanied by the appreciation that it does so as mediated through its initial historical expression" (1999: 574).

The move from the exegesis of Scripture to its contemporary relevance often happens naturally and intuitively. Through the centuries, the majority of Christians have read Scripture without analyzing it according to the criteria of modern biblical criticism, and they have been shaped by it in their values, beliefs, and practices. What, then, is the need for a methodical discussion of the ways Christians move from interpreting to applying Scripture? It is not that Scripture cannot achieve its effects without such a method, since it has done so in the past and still does for most Christians who read and study Scripture for personal guidance. The reason for reflecting on this hermeneutical move is that confessional communities need a method for forming their identities and maintaining their ethos. In other words, individual Christians can and do study Scripture in rather informal and individualized ways all the time, usually with benign results, sometimes not. But Christian *communities* that struggle to discern the will of God and the leading of the Holy Spirit should not apply Scripture willy-nilly. A principled and consistent system for moving from individual texts to a coherent theology and a biblically informed practice is essential for the well-being of the larger church.

This chapter, therefore, will deal with some of the most challenging aspects of that "complex and contested enterprise" described at the beginning of this book. Precisely how does Scripture form and inform the faith and practice of Christians? In particular, what else besides Scripture may be involved? And how do we relate the different sources of authority for Christian theology and discipleship? R. W. L. Moberly gives this succinct, threefold description of the task: "Questions of how to understand the Bible in its own right, of how to understand the Bible in terms of contemporary categories, and of how to relate these perspectives are *the* questions of biblical interpretation" (2000: 76, with original emphasis). Chapter 2 of this book was primarily devoted to a process by which we may understand the Bible in its own right. We now turn to the second and third parts of Moberly's description.

Sola Scriptura or Prima Scriptura?

The title of this book, *Prima Scriptura*, is a fairly transparent play on the Reformation slogan *sola scriptura* (Scripture alone). The slogan implies that the Reformers made a sharp distinction between Scripture and tradition and then drew solely upon the former. But several historians and theologians point out that in practice *sola scriptura* did not exclude other sources. David Steinmetz clarifies: "While it is true that the reformers were at first optimistic that it would be possible to teach and preach a theology that was wholly biblical, they rarely intended to exclude theological sources that were non-biblical.

Sola scriptura generally meant *prima scriptura*, Scripture as the final source and norm by which all theological sources and arguments were to be judged, not Scripture as the sole source of theological wisdom" (2002: 129; see also Whidden, 1997: 216–23; Mathison, 2001; Charles, 2002: 143n58; Olson, 2003: 53; and M. M. Thompson, 2008: 13). *Sola scriptura* was meant to exclude "only what is contrary to Scripture, not everything except what is explicitly written in Scripture" (Hinlicky, 1999: 395).

So the thoroughgoing, exclusivist notion of *sola scriptura* was not actually what the mainstream Reformers practiced. Luther and Calvin frequently appealed to the church fathers and the creeds, for example, as authentic expressions of the apostolic faith (McGrath, 1999: 153). It is true that some of the more radical proponents of the Reformation rejected tradition outright, but their movement quickly degenerated into ideological chaos precisely because their theology, lacking the moorings that tradition could provide, spun off in a multitude of directions. Alister McGrath distinguishes these "radical Reformers" from the "magisterial Reformers," noting that the latter "had a very positive understanding of tradition" (McGrath, 1999: 154). They were "painfully aware of the threat of individualism, and attempted to avoid this threat by stressing the church's traditional interpretation of Scripture where this traditional interpretation was regarded as correct" (McGrath, 1999: 155). Tradition was rejected only when it contradicted or went far beyond Scripture.

An exclusive appeal to Scripture was untenable for a number of reasons. First, tradition (in the sense of the theology and practices of the church in the first few centuries) was directly involved in the creation and delimitation of Scripture. Although Scripture has shaped the church and extended its influence from the first century onward, it was the church that first gave birth to sacred texts and then gave shape to the canon. Based on standard dating of New Testament documents, the church existed for about two decades without epistolary writings and for about four decades without a written Gospel. Based on the timeline of the canonization process, the church existed for three centuries or more without the precise collection of writings that we call the New Testament (although the core of the New Testament was already coalescing in the first half of the second century). To the person who says, "The Bible alone is my authority, *not* tradition," one could pose the question, "By what authority do you know which books are biblical?" The answer can only be "Tradition!" One cannot rely on Scripture without simultaneously relying on the generative and shaping forces of the early church.

Second, Scripture does not function in a vacuum (Hays, 1996: 209). As we saw in chapter 1, everyone reads from a certain location, through certain lenses, and in the light of a particular tradition and life experiences. Though objectivity is always the goal, we cannot transport ourselves back to the first century and read the New Testament as if the intervening millennia had not occurred. We are steeped in tradition, whether consciously or unconsciously.

This is true even for those who say they have "no creed but the Bible." All Christians, whether they belong to the Catholic tradition going back two millennia or to a denomination of much more recent vintage, have "historic and contemporary figures who have exercised powerful, formative influences over their interpretation of Scripture" (Whidden, 1997: 213). These mentors are part of the reason for the theological pluralism that exists in Christianity. Indeed, even "among groups that strenuously profess fidelity to the Bible as their sole authority," there is a "bewildering array of doctrinal options" (Whidden, 1997: 214). An exclusivist notion of *sola scriptura* does not produce theological uniformity precisely because the influence of tradition is everywhere at work. The point is forcefully made by Whidden: "No Bible-believer is strictly *sola Scriptura* in any arena of theological discourse—and this includes the most stridently fundamentalistic persons in the most conservative traditions of independent, Bible-oriented American churches" (1997: 220). Tradition shapes us all.

Finally, the scholarly dimension of the Christian tradition is what makes it possible for us to read the Scriptures today. It is absurd to think that one can bypass churchly tradition and scholarship in studying the Scriptures since any act of interpreting presupposes a long tradition of scholarly endeavors. The modern study of Scripture presupposes centuries of scholars who transmitted and established the New Testament text and did the linguistic and literary work of translating the text. In this sense, no one interprets from scratch.

It therefore is incoherent to reject the role of ecclesiastical tradition in the interpretation of Scripture (Hinlicky, 1999: 395). One could even argue that the long-term effect of an exclusivist version of *sola scriptura* was harmful because it removed biblical interpretation from its natural context: the church. The final result of divorcing Scripture from its ecclesial context was "the complete secularization of Scripture itself" (Hinlicky, 1999: 395). This is especially apparent in public universities in the United States, but its effects are also seen in some private and even church-related institutions. Paul Hinlicky laments this separation and its destructive effects:

> There is now no way of perceiving the Bible any longer as the written form of the one Word of God, centering in Jesus Christ the saving Lord. All this has actually taken place in the historical criticism of the Bible in modern Protestantism. The principle of "Scripture alone" has self-destructed, because it has set aside the relation of Scripture to the Holy Spirit and the church. The radical opposition between the Word of God and human tradition has taken its vengeance on the Scripture itself. (1999: 395–96)

Some scholars seem prepared to write the obituary of *sola scriptura*. It would be preferable, however, to rehabilitate and clarify the principle along the lines of *prima scriptura*. Even some who would retain the traditional language recognize the need to correct distorted versions of the concept. Lutheran theologian Carl Braaten, for example, argues for the continuing affirmation of *sola scriptura*, but "not as a battle-cry *against* the church and its tradition. Rather, 'sola scriptura' means that everything essential in the original apostolic preaching which founded the church is written down in Scripture, and that no later tradition can negate or supersede it" (1981: 194, with original emphasis). Later traditions sometimes reinforce the gospel and sometimes undermine the gospel. The criterion that the church must use to judge these traditions is Scripture.

If we adopt *prima scriptura* in lieu of *sola scriptura*, we should not think that Scripture has thereby been demoted or devalued. Scripture is still the primary authority for Christian faith and life. If ever there is a conflict between Scripture and tradition, Scripture must have priority (Charles, 2002: 143). As one theologian put it, "In matters of theological development and debate, tradition should get a vote but never a veto" (Olson, 2003: 54). The classical statement of this quality of Scripture is *norma normans non normata* (apparently all classical statements must be in Latin): Scripture is "the norm or standard that regulates [all else, but is itself] not regulated [by any]." Scripture is what constitutes Christian identity and shapes Christian faith and practice. It has pride of place in Christian moral and theological deliberation.

It is an encouraging sign that Christians of different stripes are beginning to recognize the need for *both* Scripture *and* tradition, while usually understanding the latter as serving the former. Historically, Catholics stressed the role of tradition, while Protestants asserted the superiority of Scripture. One scholar likens this old Reformation divide to an out-of-court divorce settlement. "She gets the house while [he] keeps the car and furniture" now becomes "They [the Protestants] get the Scripture while we [Catholics] keep Tradition and the Magisterium." But surely the two should be inseparable: "Thus, the proper interpretation of Scripture must be done in the Church, for the Church, and by the Church" (Hahn, 2003: 179). With the encyclical letter of Pope Pius XII *Divino Afflante Spiritu* (1943), Catholic biblical scholars gained greater freedom to engage in the critical study of Scripture, a freedom that was reaffirmed at the Second Vatican Council (1962–65). Since Vatican II, Catholics have been gaining greater appreciation for Scripture, and since the late twentieth century, Protestants, especially evangelicals, have begun to turn again to the rich resources of tradition, especially the patristic era (Ray, 1997; Colson and Neuhaus, 2002; Williams, 2005). These are welcome developments.

So the role of Scripture and its relationship to tradition are better captured by the phrase *prima scriptura* than *sola scriptura*. Scripture is the primary authority, but its authority does not operate alone. I also remind the reader of a point made earlier: Scripture's authority is *derived* rather than inherent. It is derived from God, who alone is the supreme authority over life and creation. "As important as canonical Scripture is in the Church, it is not its ultimate authority. That capacity belongs to *the* Word, the person of Jesus Christ, who is more than a text" (Work, 2002: 258). So Scripture derives its authority from God, and among the means commonly employed by Christians to discern the will and ways of God, Scripture is primary. But the word "primary" implies other means of discernment with a secondary or supportive role. So what are they?

Quadrilaterals, Trapezoids, and Triangles

From the patristic era onward, virtually all Christian communities have employed tradition along with Scripture in their theological and ethical deliberations. Some have done it deliberately; some have done it almost unwittingly, all the while claiming, "No creed but the Bible." On rare occasions tradition has been given equal footing with Scripture; more often Scripture has been seen as having primacy.

Although most formal hermeneutic systems employ both Scripture and tradition, they typically include one or more additional criteria. My own Wesleyan tradition is famous for the so-called Wesleyan Quadrilateral, a four-part method that employs Scripture, tradition, reason, and experience. The language is not John Wesley's, but Wesleyan theologians would generally say that these four elements were operative in his thinking. The term was coined by Albert C. Outler, who himself was not fully satisfied with it (Oden and Longden, 1991: 21–37; Chilcote, 2005: 22; see also Langford, 1991: 75–88, 154–61). For one thing, it leaves unclear how the sides are related to one another. Are Scripture, tradition, reason, and experience of equal importance, such that the quadrilateral is in effect a square? Or should Scripture be viewed as foundational, with the other sides being of lesser magnitude, in which case the quadrilateral may become a trapezoid? If a fifth criterion is proposed, should we speak of a pentagon? And should one have to have a college minor in geometry to understand biblical hermeneutics?

If Wesley himself had been asked about the appropriateness of the quadrilateral model, he probably would have asserted, as he often did, that he was, indeed, a *homo unius libri*, "a man of one book." But "this reliance on Scripture as *the* fount of revelation was never meant to preclude a concomitant appeal to the insights of wise and saintly Christians in other ages" (Oden and Longden, 1991: 25). Wesley might have added that "experience" was valuable, not as a material contributor to faith, but as a confirmatory result of faith. "Christian experience adds nothing to the substance of Christian truth; its distinctive role is to energize the heart so as to enable the believer to speak and do the truth in love" (Oden and Longden, 1991: 25). With these qualifications, Wesley probably would have embraced the quadrilateral. This system "preserves the primacy of Scripture, it profits from the wisdom of tradition, it accepts the disciplines of critical reason, and its stress on the Christian experience of grace gives it existential force" (Oden and Longden, 1991: 26).

Other models have utilized a threefold scheme and opted for a different metaphor. The Anglican tradition, in which Wesley was ordained, has often spoken of a three-legged stool or a threefold cord, referring to Scripture, tradition, and reason. This image suffers from a deficiency similar to that of the quadrilateral: Are the three legs of equal length, and if not, won't the stool tilt? The latter image of a threefold cord can at least appeal to biblical precedent (Eccles. 4:12). This tripartite system has some claim to go back to Richard Hooker (1554–1600), an early Anglican theologian (Borsch, 1984: 7). Again, the precise language of a "three-legged stool" is not found in Hooker, but he does appeal to Scripture, reason, and tradition, in that order: "What Scripture doth plainly deliver, to that the first place both of credit and obedience is due; the next whereunto is whatsoever any man can necessarily conclude by force of reason; after these the voice of the Church succeedeth" (*Laws of Ecclesiastical Polity* 5.8.2; Keble, 1888: 34; cf. Hooker, 1977: 39). For a critique of the propriety of calling this an Anglican hermeneutic and especially of its contemporary use under the aegis of Richard Hooker, see Seitz (1993: 88–93; 2001: 59–61) and Sykes (1978: 87–100). Jeremy Taylor (1613–67), another Anglican divine, described his method in this way: "Scripture, tradition, councils, and fathers, are the evidence in question, but reason is the judge" (Cross and Livingstone, 1997: 66; cf. Underhill, 1966: 332). In Taylor's formulation, the third and fourth terms—councils and fathers—simply elaborate on "tradition." This threefold method, however loosely articulated and implemented, was bequeathed to the early Methodists. The fourth element, "experience," was Wesley's distinctive emphasis.

Some hermeneutical systems add other elements. Catholic Christians look to the magisterium, the teaching authority of the church. Formal definitions and pronouncements of the pope are viewed as contemporary supplements to the tradition: "They are monuments, that is, embodiments of Tradition" (Nichols, 1991: 248). Such pronouncements obviously draw upon and interpret Scripture and earlier tradition, yet they have a force in the lives of faithful Catholics for which there is no complete parallel in Protestant Christianity. Some Protestant Christians have invoked the Holy Spirit in theological and moral debates, perhaps simultaneously appealing to incidents in Scripture that they understand as illustrating the Spirit's overturning of earlier precedents (Adams, 1996). Such appeals have the power to introduce radically new paradigms, but whether an appeal to the Spirit should be a trump card to override the witness of Scripture is a question to which I will return below.

Other hermeneutical models could be mentioned (Seitz, 1993: 88n4), but with the exception of the Catholic magisterium, no other criterion has gained a large following. The use of Scripture and tradition is ancient, and the introduction of reason as a formal criterion dates back at least as far as the sixteenth century. Indeed, the *informal* use of reason in interpretation is as ancient as biblical interpretation itself. The introduction of experience *as a formal criterion* is characteristic of the Wesleyan movement of the eighteenth century, although again, informal appeals to religious experience are ancient. Without necessarily canonizing these four criteria or ruling out the possibility of others, the longevity of Scripture, tradition, reason, and experience justifies the brief treatment of them that follows. For more on the quadrilateral, see Thorsen (1990), Newbigin (1996), and Gunter (1997). For the three-legged stool, see Bauckham and Drewery (1988).

The Rule of Scripture

Scripture is primary among the criteria because it transmits the foundational narratives of the faith (Israel's story, the life, death, and resurrection of Jesus, and the early Christian movement) as well as the earliest and normative interpretation of those events. In contrast, later traditions, such as the writings of the patristic and medieval eras, tend to be referential and interpretive: they point back to and try to explain or elaborate Scripture.

Although Scripture might be regarded as the earliest phase of tradition, the difference is more than chronological; it is also qualitative. James B. Torrance helpfully distinguishes between apostolic tradition, meaning the apostles' preaching of the gospel and its embodiment in the New Testament, and ecclesiastical tradition, which derives from the apostolic tradition and is subordinate to it:

> When the Church drew up the Canon it was making precisely this distinction. On the one hand, she wanted to preserve the Apostolic tradition from being lost or misinterpreted, regarding it as the norm for all faith and practice. On the other hand, she was humbly subordinating herself to the authority of Holy Scripture, so that the Norm was not herself, not ecclesiastical tradition, but the Gospel. (1987: 249–50; see also Küng, 1980: 17)

The primacy of Scripture is aptly expressed in the volume written by Stephen Gunter and others: *Wesley and the Quadrilateral: Renewing the Conversation*. After a historical introduction, a chapter is devoted to each of the sides of the quadrilateral, with a subtle variation in the heading (which I have borrowed here). The titles speak of "The *Rule* of Scripture" but then of "The *Role* of Tradition," "The *Role* of Reason," and so forth. What might almost seem to be a typographical error is clearly intended to distinguish the function of Scripture vis-à-vis the other elements. Scripture has the dominant position; tradition, reason, and experience have a dependent role (Gunter et al., 1997). Paul Chilcote has suggested that a mobile or wind chime might be a more helpful image than a quadrilateral, precisely because the base of the mobile or chime can represent Scripture, with the other elements suspended from it, literally "dependent" (2005: 23).

An important point to make about Scripture is that the entirety of the canon must be considered. Although an interpreter can obviously read and study individual passages with much benefit and insight, when one studies Scripture with a view to forming and informing the corporate life of the church, it is important to hear the full range of the biblical witnesses. If we are seeking the biblical perspective on a given topic, we obviously should consult all the texts that address that topic or imply something about it. One could, for example, cite passages that imply the acceptance or even endorsement of slavery, holy war, or polygamy. Other texts could be adduced that call God's people to ameliorate, transcend, or reject such practices.

A possible outcome of consulting the entire canon must be frankly acknowledged here. When we seek the biblical perspective on topic x, we may very well find that there are biblical perspectives (plural). Though the desire to harmonize disparate views in Scripture is natural and not always wrongheaded, we must allow each biblical witness to speak with its own voice. It is true that the entire canon serves as a guide for interpreting the individual writings, yet this function must not be coercive: "This text *must* mean such-and-such because of what this other text says." Nor should the canon function restrictively: "This text *cannot possibly* mean that because of what is said elsewhere." Rather, the canon provides the literary and theological arena in which interpretation is played out.

To switch metaphors, taking the canon into account does *not* mean that we make Mark sing tenor if in fact Mark is a baritone. First, we must appreciate Mark's distinctive voice on its own merits. For example, Mark's Suffering Servant Christology should be allowed its full force. As a second step, we should blend Mark's voice with the rest of the canonical choir so as to discern the harmony of the whole. So Mark's Suffering Servant Christology is combined with John's glorious, triumphant Christ. The harmony that arises from the combination of such voices creates a richly diverse (and not necessarily contradictory) theology.

Another important reason for attending to the canonical whole is the fact that affirmations about Scripture's authority are affirmations about the whole. Robert Traina poses the provocative but essential question, "Is each biblical statement authoritative for faith and practice, or does biblical authority reside in the entire scriptural corpus, which is self-correcting and even self-transcending?" (1982: 89) The answer is surely the latter. The authority of Scripture is a function of the canon as a whole. It is difficult to affirm the authority of every individual verse of Scripture severally, given the fact that individual verses can be found endorsing practices that Christians rightly reject (e.g., capital punishment for disrespectful children; Exod. 21:17). There is also the problem of biblical statements that stand in strong tension, if not contradiction, with other biblical statements (e.g., Exod. 34:6–7 and Ezek. 18:19–20). This does *not* mean that authority never attaches to individual affirmations; it simply means that authority does not automatically attach to every individual statement of Scripture. But when the canon as a whole is considered, Scripture has the capacity to correct and transcend itself. Thus a statement like Galatians 3:28 ("There is neither Jew nor Greek, there is neither slave nor free, there is neither male nor female, for you are all one in Christ Jesus") provides a principle for interpreting those texts that otherwise might undergird Jewish exclusivism, the institution of slavery, or the subordination of women. When Scripture is taken as a whole, the resulting canonical message is the normative Word of God that is mediated by the human words of Scripture.

This requires interpreters to look for patterns, progressions, and trajectories in the biblical witness, to consider foundational narratives and themes (creation, fall, covenant, redemption, cross, resurrection, Pentecost, justification, sanctification, the body of Christ, and so on) as guides to interpret the more obscure and problematic passages. The so-called gestalt principle from the field of psychology is useful here in that the canon of biblical writings is greater than the sum of its parts. Since Scripture is both a divine word and a human word, it partakes of the qualities of both agencies. If certain passages are particularly encumbered by lesser human qualities, it is only in the canonical witness as a whole that Scripture can transcend itself. In this way Scripture is able to provide its own checks and balances (Vanhoozer, 1998: 179, 193n172).

The Role of Tradition

G. K. Chesterton understood the role of tradition: it gave a voice to the past that only arrogance would deny to it. Chesterton saw democracy's extension of a franchise to all persons living in the present as having a counterpart in tradition's extension of a franchise to those who lived in the past:

> Tradition means giving votes to the most obscure of all classes, our ancestors. It is the democracy of the dead. Tradition refuses to submit to the small and arrogant oligarchy of those who merely happen to be walking about. All democrats object to men being disqualified by the accident of birth; tradition objects to their being disqualified by the accident of death. Democracy tells us not to neglect a good man's opinion, even if he is our groom; tradition asks us not to neglect a good man's opinion, even if he is our father. (1959: 48)

Our fathers (and mothers), in the ecclesiastical sense, have a role in biblical interpretation, and a proper reverence for tradition grants them that role. Tradition must have a voice in our ethical and theological deliberations. As noted earlier, tradition does not have veto power over Scripture, nor is Scripture outvoted by lining up enough mystics, monks, and divines with a contrary view.

Protestants would generally say that the authority of tradition is derived from Scripture and the earliest apostolic testimony. In terms of the Latin formulation given earlier, tradition would be *norma normata*, the norm or standard that is regulated or established (by Scripture).

Tradition as a criterion of Christian faith and practice is not to be equated with Christian history in general (Gunter et al., 1997: 64–65). Needless to say, not everything that Christians have done over the last two millennia is normative or to be imitated. Tradition rather refers to the treasured body of beliefs and practices that have been deliberately chosen and handed on to future generations to shape their identity and guide their living. It consists of those aspects of a community's life that are valued, selected, interpreted, transmitted, and appropriated (Schneiders, 1991: 70–71).

Tradition thus implies normative content. By this understanding, it becomes clear that the classic creeds of Christianity (e.g., the Apostles' Creed and the Nicene Creed) are extremely important depositories of tradition. Creeds are formal, authoritative statements of Christian doctrine, and the classic creeds are the result of extended deliberation, successive versions, and liturgical use. Creeds typically avoid the whimsical and eccentric. On the contrary, they aim to distill what is essential, ancient, and consensual. Although the claim that the Apostles' Creed was jointly composed by the original twelve apostles is clearly legendary, the core of that creed's affirmations nevertheless enjoys great antiquity, including support in the New Testament (cf. Matt. 28:19). As early as the fourth century, creeds were used as baptismal confessions, a fact that clearly indicates their function as identifying what is obligatory and constitutive. Christians might believe many things not contained in the creeds, but the creedal affirmations were deemed to be binding on those who would assume Christian identity.

Creeds and the canon of Scripture are complementary and interdependent. The classic creeds can be criticized for omitting the life and ministry of Jesus, skipping from his conception and birth to his execution and burial. But the rich ethical, exemplary, and paraenetic resources from the life of Christ are supplied by the New Testament. The concise, orderly, and developed formulations of faith are supplied by the creeds. With a bit of oversimplification, one might say that the creeds define Christian orthodoxy, while the canon defines Christian orthopraxy. In this way Christian faith and practice are deeply rooted in both Scripture and tradition.

The value of tradition in hermeneutics must be emphasized because of three types of biases that tend to undermine it: the biases of Protestantism, modernism, and historical criticism. (As a modern Protestant trained in historical criticism, I need to hear this as much as any of my readers.) The sixteenth-century Reformers were suspicious (not without reason) of medieval church traditions. They understandably distinguished between the witness of Scripture and that of tradition. But as we saw above, the magisterial Reformers by no means dismissed the entirety of the church's witness through the centuries. Regrettably, the more radical Reformers did draw a bright line between the two, and the spiritual descendants of even the magisterial Reformers have sometimes drawn that line too boldly. It is only a bit of an exaggeration to say that some Protestant Christians seem to operate with the assumption that the Spirit of God was dormant from the end of the first century to the beginning of the sixteenth.

Modernity compounds this bias with its assumption that our generation is the only one worth listening to. If, as modernity assumes, there is a steady and inevitable progress in human reason, then more recent thinking must be better. David Hall has called this "the Dogma of Evolutionism": "Evolutionism is not the scientific theory of Evolution, but the philosophical theory that human thought is continually progressing so that the ideas of today are necessarily an improvement on the ideas of yesterday" (1990: 3). In the area of biblical interpretation, this bias manifests itself in the facile devaluation of tradition.

Finally, the historical-critical approach to Scripture provides a third kind of bias against tradition. Although many believing scholars use historical criticism and derive many benefits from it, as a method it was developed precisely to provide an approach to Scripture that was *free from* traditional constraints. By the application of an objective, scientific method, Scripture could be analyzed without the suffocating influence of the church. In the introduction we saw that this view involved self-deception and an unwarranted denigration of the ecclesial context of interpretation. But its effects are still sometimes evident, as when historical-critical scholars tend to dismiss patristic and medieval interpretation.

What, then, is the positive function of tradition in the interpretation of Scripture? Historically, tradition was helpful in countering heresies of the first few centuries. Since heretics would often appeal to the same Scriptures that orthodox believers used, it was apparent that some guiding framework was needed for interpretation. Several church fathers referred to the "rule of faith" or "rule of truth" as a shorthand expression for this traditional framework. The rule of faith summarized the content of apostolic preaching and functioned as a hermeneutical key for interpreting Scripture (Greene-McCreight, 2005: 703). Irenaeus used a vivid metaphor of a mosaic to critique the heretics' misuse of Scripture. A mosaic contains a beautiful image of a king, but someone comes along and destroys the mosaic, rearranging the stones into an inferior image of a dog or fox, and then claims that this is the work of the original artist. In a similar way, the heretics violate the natural order of Scripture and reject the pattern that is supplied by the rule of faith, meaning the tradition (*Against Heresies* 1.8.1; Unger, 1992: 41).

In more recent times, the benefit of engaging the tradition is that it broadens the conversation. Into our study circle we invite Christian interpreters from other eras. It goes without saying that those interpreters approached the texts with a different set of skills and strategies as well as a different set of presuppositions (although the latter were not always so far removed from those of modern believers). If in fact we all read from some location, and if a modern or postmodern, Western location has both strengths and liabilities, then we should be open to the possibility, indeed the likelihood, that we can learn something from Origen, Augustine, Anselm, and Aquinas. F. F. Bruce offers the following admonition: "To jettison tradition as such is to reject the inherited wisdom of the past and thereby suffer incalculable impoverishment" (Bruce, 1988: 36). Tradition reminds us of the plurality of the interpreting community. When we interpret Scripture, the "we" involved should be transtemporal and transspatial, incorporating Jesus's followers from other eras and places (S. Davis, 2006: 102).

More specifically, the role of tradition is to corroborate, elaborate, clarify, and systematize the truths of Scripture. The Bible does not address every situation that Christians encounter, certainly not in an explicit, systematic manner. Tradition is, in large part, the endeavor to relate the foundational revelation of Scripture to the manifold and changing circumstances in which Christians find themselves. In that way tradition serves to "fill in doctrinal lacunae not specifically addressed in Scripture" (Thorsen, 1990: 127). Three examples will illustrate the complexity of this task: the Trinity, infant baptism, and certain doctrines about Mary.

The doctrine of the Holy Trinity—God as a triune being of three persons, Father, Son, and Holy Spirit—is a thoroughly orthodox tenet of Christianity. But the doctrine is not explicitly stated in the New Testament, certainly not in the creedal forms articulated at the first ecumenical Councils of Nicaea (AD 325) and Constantinople (AD 381). The divinity of Christ is affirmed in a small number of New Testament texts (e.g., John 1:1; Phil. 2:5–11), and the divine nature of the Holy Spirit is often implied. The trio of Father, Son, and Holy Spirit occurs only in the baptismal formula of Matthew 28:19. (The most explicit trinitarian formula in the New Testament, 1 John 5:7–8 in the KJV, is a later scribal addition to that writing.) Despite the fact that the Trinity is at best implicit and embryonic in the New Testament, the tradition has elaborated this doctrine in response to crises of the early fourth century, and the mainstream church has regarded it as a faithful expression of the trajectory of the New Testament. Today any Christian who recites the Nicene Creed affirms a Christology rooted in both Scripture and tradition.

Somewhat more controversial is the matter of infant baptism. As the early Christians developed liturgical, theological, and ecclesial traditions, they had to establish mechanisms or rituals by which persons joined their communities. Who could become a member of the church? What actions or confessions would be required of them? Was adult status a requirement? The New Testament offers no explicit authority for the administration of baptism to infants, but it was widely practiced from the third century to the Reformation. In the sixteenth and seventeenth centuries some Christians such as the Anabaptists and Baptists rejected the practice, preferring to associate baptism with a conscious confession of faith on the part of the baptized (Cross and Livingstone, 1997: 831–32). Although there is no explicit reference to infant baptism in the New Testament, Jesus welcomed children and said that the kingdom of God belonged to them (Mark 10:14). Paul associates baptism with circumcision as an entry rite, and the latter was performed on infants (Col. 2:11–12). Finally, given the fact that in antiquity, religious conversions tended to occur by households, not by individuals, the baptism of infants or young children may be implied in some New Testament stories (Luke 19:9; John 4:53; Acts 11:14; 16:31; 18:8). Here again, tradition has supplemented Scripture by establishing a Christian practice that is widespread, though not universal, and is usually thought to be consonant with the New Testament witness.

Even more controversial are the distinctive Catholic doctrines concerning Mary, the mother of Jesus. These include the perpetual virginity of Mary, the assumption of Mary, and the immaculate conception. The perpetual virginity of Mary—the idea that she remained a virgin through and after the birth of Jesus and bore no children thereafter—dates from the late second century and was widely accepted from the fifth century onward. The assumption of Mary—the belief that at her death Mary was taken up body and soul into heaven—seems to have originated in the fourth century. The doctrine of the immaculate conception of Mary—that from the moment she was conceived, Mary was kept free by divine grace from the stain of original sin—was a matter of debate throughout the Middle Ages, became more widely accepted in the fifteenth century and following, and was formally defined in 1854 (Cross and Livingstone, 1997: 117–18, 821–22, 1047–49). Such doctrines have slender support at best in Scripture, and so Protestant Christians have not regarded them as authoritative teachings. Catholic Christians would see them as rooted in ancient tradition and reasonably extrapolated from the biblical narrative.

Such issues raise the question of the precise relationship between Scripture and tradition as sources of authority. Must Scripture contain the seed of all later doctrines, or can the tradition step in where Scripture is completely silent? Needless to say, different confessional communities have offered different solutions in this complex and lengthy debate. Here I can only briefly outline four major views, drawing on a helpful article by A. N. S. Lane (1975; cf. Bauckham, 1988: 117–27). Lane identifies the following four views, which emerged in this historical order:

1. *The coincidence view*, prevalent from the second century onward, argued that Scripture, tradition, and church teaching were in full agreement with one another. There was no reason to appeal to Scripture against the tradition since the two coincided. Scripture was *materially* sufficient in that its content did not need to be supplemented by tradition, but it was

formally insufficient in that it required the authoritative interpretation of the church. The church was thus the custodian and official interpreter of Scripture.

2. *The supplementary view* evolved next and gained popularity in the Middle Ages. It posits, in effect, two sources of revelation. Tradition is needed to supplement Scripture because certain teachings and practices of the church could not find explicit warrant in the Bible. According to this view, Scripture is not only *formally* insufficient, but *materially* insufficient as well, since the fullness of revelation is to be found only in the combination of Scripture and tradition. The supplementary view was especially strong at the time of the Reformation as a way to counter the *sola scriptura* emphasis.

3. *The ancillary view* was that of the Protestant Reformers, who asserted that tradition was an aid in interpreting Scripture but did not materially supplement it. Scripture alone provided the norm, although tradition might be helpful in understanding it. Using the norm of Scripture, the Reformers generally judged the church in the patristic era to be theologically sound but to have grown increasingly corrupt thereafter. Neither the tradition nor the teaching authority of the church possessed an authority that could not be challenged by an appeal to Scripture.

4. *The unfolding view* is Lane's name for the modern Roman Catholic view (Lane, 1975: 47–48), the seeds of which lay in the sixteenth century, though it became prominent in the nineteenth century. Tradition had previously been understood as a rather static phenomenon. Now it was acknowledged that doctrine, far from being static, developed over time. Tradition came to be understood as "the process by which the full meaning of the apostolic message is gradually unfolded" (Bauckham, 1988: 124). Since some doctrines might at best be implicit in Scripture, the Roman Catholic magisterium became even more important as the official developer and interpreter of the faith. Under this view Scripture could be regarded as *materially* sufficient, but only in the sense that Scripture contained at least a faint hint of the doctrines that later unfolded. But the *formal insufficiency* of Scripture thereby became all the more evident.

In the last several decades there has been a narrowing of the rift between Catholic and Protestant views of the relationship between Scripture and tradition, such that some scholars have spoken of an "ecumenical convergence" (Bauckham, 1988: 125n18). Catholics have striven to demonstrate connections between Scripture and church teachings. Protestants have experienced a newfound appreciation for tradition. The Reformation fissure has not been bridged, but there has been some movement toward the center and an increasing mutual respect for one another's positions.

Much more could be said about the interplay of Scripture and the Christian tradition. For further reading, see the classic study by Catholic scholar Yves Congar (1967; cf. also his briefer treatment in 1964); the ecumenical anthology edited by Hagen (1994); and the evangelical treatments by Williams (1999 and 2005), Vanhoozer (2003), and Marshall (2004: 33–54).

The Role of Reason

Galileo, who had some experience with reason conflicting with religious authority, said, "[The notion] that the same God who endowed us with senses, reason, and understanding, does not permit us to use them, . . . *that* it seems to me I am not bound to believe" (Gebler, 1879: 48). Over the centuries Christian faith has had a fickle relationship with reason, as Galileo's case demonstrates. A Renaissance scientist who was himself a believer (he had earlier considered the possibility of monastic life), Galileo clearly felt that reason and scientific inquiry were compatible with religious faith; but the very church to which he was devoted summoned him before the Inquisition and forced him to recant his view of a heliocentric cosmology (Cross and Livingstone, 1997: 650–51). Sadly, the church has had such contradictory impulses as sometimes to prompt inquisitive action and other times to prompt inquisitional reaction.

The Scriptures themselves provide some impetus toward a favorable relationship between faith and reason. Wisdom literature in particular extols the virtues of reason and understanding, although with a moral nuance somewhat different from strict rationalism. "Happy are those who find wisdom, and those who get understanding" (Prov. 3:13). "My child, be attentive to my wisdom; incline your ear to my understanding, so that you may hold on to prudence, and your lips may guard knowledge" (Prov. 5:1–2). "Happy is the person who meditates on wisdom and reasons intelligently" (Sir. [Ecclus.] 14:20). Other texts of Scripture value wisdom and understanding while construing them more as divine gifts than as human achievements. "We have not ceased praying for you and asking that you may be filled with the knowledge of God's will in all spiritual wisdom and understanding" (Col. 1:9). "We know that the Son of God has come and has given us understanding so that we may know him who is true" (1 John 5:20). As Christians began to engage and interact with their pagan environment, the need for a carefully reasoned witness became evident. Thus, in 1 Peter 3:15 believers are urged to be prepared to offer a defense to anyone seeking the reason for their hope. (Such a defense came to full flower among the second-century writers known collectively as the apologists.) Finally, it is worth noting that in response to a question about the greatest commandment, Jesus elaborates slightly on Deuteronomy 6:4–5 by the inclusion of the intellect: "You shall love the Lord your God with all your heart, and with all your soul, and with all your *mind*, and with all your strength" (Mark 12:30). "Heart," "soul," and "strength" are present in the Hebrew text and the Septuagint. "Mind" (*dianoia*) is in neither, and yet it is in each of the three Synoptic versions of the saying (cf. Matt. 22:37; Luke 10:27). Does this reflect a very early recognition of the need for a reasoned faith?

On the other hand, the limitations of human reasoning are recognized in Scripture, even in Wisdom literature. "Thus they reasoned, but they were led astray, for their wickedness blinded them" (Wis. 2:21). "For the reasoning of mortals is worthless, and our designs are likely to fail" (Wis. 9:14). Human beings are fallen creatures, and their intellectual capacities do not escape the effects of the fall. Paul states this plainly. "For though they knew God, they did not honor him as God or give thanks to him, but they became futile in their thinking, and their senseless minds were darkened" (Rom. 1:21; cf. Pss. 14:1–3; 53:1–3). "There is no one who has understanding, there is no one who seeks God" (Rom. 3:11). Again, the moral and revelatory aspects of this reasoning are obvious. Paul's concern is not with the mere capacity of rationality but rather with reasoning *in faith*. Indeed, Paul implies that to divorce reason from faith is to render the former worthless.

The complex relationship between faith and reason that is reflected in Scripture is still very much with us. Part of the problem is that there are different understandings of what reason is. In the broadest sense, reason is the pursuit of truth: the exercise of the mind by analyzing evidence, reflecting, and making correct inferences so as to reach true conclusions and form true beliefs. But from antiquity there have been at least two schools of thought about how reason operated, schools embodied in the figures of Plato and Aristotle. On the one hand, Plato believed that the transcendent realm of ideas or nonmaterial reality was primary, and the mind had access to this reality by way of theoretical reasoning. So by rather abstract reflection, persons could attain understanding about the divine, the nature of human beings, truth, beauty, goodness, and so forth. Plato's theory of knowledge can thus be seen as containing the seed of the nineteenth-century movement known as rationalism. Aristotle, on the other hand, championed the approach that much later was known as empiricism: the reliance on observation of phenomena through the senses and experience. Thus, one reasons by observing data, analyzing and ordering it, making inferences, and thereby gaining knowledge (Clark, Lints, and Smith, 2004: 8–9, 19–20, 70–71).

There are, however, few persons who are pure rationalists or pure empiricists. When we interpret Scripture, we employ both types of reason, although the empiricist approach may be more obvious. Like empiricists, we interpret the data of Scripture, its words, phrases, images, and idioms; but like rationalists, we also rely on axiomatic, seemingly innate understandings of God and the world. John Wesley had a strong preference for the empiricist school of thought, but he also spoke of "spiritual senses" that gave one access to the transcendent realm (Gunter et al., 1997: 84–93). This insight of Wesley's finds support in broader theological themes. If, in fact, we are made in the image of a rational God and are endowed with a conscience, we have some access to divine truth that does not stem solely from our senses and experience. We are rightly wary of the person who says, "This is true because God told me so," but we should also be careful not to rule out intuitive reasoning and spiritual discernment as *components* of the larger interpretive process. Obviously the surest interpretation results from the combination of both types of reason.

How then does reason relate to faith? How do they work together in biblical interpretation? These are vital questions, as one Greek Orthodox scholar has stated plainly: "The most burning problem in hermeneutics is the proper *relationship between faith and reason* in examining the contents of Scripture and in assessing what elements of those contents are of abiding significance" (Stylianopoulos, 1997: 84). I would begin by rejecting two extremes: fideism and strict Enlightenment rationalism.

Fideism is the belief that Christian faith is independent of reason, that religious truth is to be sought solely through Scripture and tradition apart from the benefit of reason. Needless to say, this is a jaundiced view of reason, but there have been times in history when the values and practices that accompanied reason were such that Christians felt they had grounds for rejecting it. Tertullian (ca. 160–ca. 225) is an early figure associated with fideism. He found himself in a polemical situation of having to defend Christianity against both pagan slander and gnostic heresies. Because of these adversarial relationships, Tertullian distrusted philosophy and its claim to reason. Nevertheless, Tertullian was well acquainted with rhetoric, law, Stoicism, and other intellectual currents of his day. He employed them when they were useful, but he did not trust them as sources of truth. Tertullian's faith was exclusively rooted in God's revelatory acts (Cross and Livingstone, 1997: 1591–92). His famous rhetorical query, "What does Jerusalem have to do with Athens?" disassociated Christian faith (Jerusalem) from Greek philosophy (Athens). Tertullian's answer to his own question was emphatic: "Nothing" (*Prescription against Heretics* 7; Tertullian, 1954: 193; Greenslade, 1956: 36).

Bernard of Clairvaux (1090–1153) provides a medieval and monastic example of fideism. His letters reveal a persistent effort to restrict the use of reason in theology. In particular, Bernard was a harsh critic of the philosophical rationalism of Peter Abelard (1079–1142). Their classic confrontation, which led to the condemnation of Abelard, has been called "the greatest episode of the twelfth century." Bernard allegedly refuted the errors of his opponent's *rationalism* with such *clarity and force of logic* that Abelard was unable to make any reply (Gildas, 1913: 500). One has to wonder if the irony was lost on Bernard.

Other well-known figures in the history of Christianity occasionally denigrated reason, usually owing to their particular historical circumstances. In his last sermon delivered at Wittenberg, Martin Luther famously said, "Reason is the devil's whore" (Luther, 1959: 376–77). This acerbic remark, combined with many others, earned for Luther a reputation as an irrationalist, but the charge was undeserved (C. Brown, 1990: 149). Luther was addressing the wrongful use of reason, particularly its usurpation of revelation. His invective against reason must be set alongside his reputed statement in the most dramatic scene of his career. When Luther was brought before the Diet of Worms in 1521 and told to recant his views, he responded: "Unless I am convicted by scripture *and plain reason*, . . . my conscience is captive to the Word of God. I cannot and I will not recant anything, for to go against conscience is neither right nor safe. [Here I stand; I cannot do otherwise.] God help me. Amen" (Bainton, 1950: 185, with added emphasis). It is often pointed out that the order—first Scripture, then reason—is deliberate, but even so, Luther affirms a role for reason in his theological convictions (Marty, 2004: 177; Lohse, 1986: 159–63).

Similarly Blaise Pascal (1623–62), French scientist and mathematician, exemplified a faith that was Christ-centered and experiential. Pascal's famous wager, that it was better to take the risk of faith in God than to choose the contrary, demonstrates an abandonment to God and a response of the heart as much as of the mind. Pascal was critical of the philosophers of his day and often spoke of the philosophers' god as opposed to the God of the Bible (Clark, Lints, and Smith, 2004: 65–66). His perspective is reflected in his famous remark, "The heart has its reasons of which reason knows nothing" (Kreeft, 1993: 231). Nevertheless, the identification of Pascal as a fideist, as with Luther, requires considerable qualification. Both of them were well-educated persons and leading intellectuals of their day. An excessive rationalism and an accompanying denigration of faith account for their negative comments about reason. Neither Pascal nor Luther denied reason a role in religious deliberations, provided that reason was illuminated by faith. In this way, they anticipated the church's later struggle during the Enlightenment.

Mention of the Enlightenment leads us to the other extreme to be avoided: Enlightenment rationalism. If fideism is the view that faith is primary and reason is subordinate to faith, then Enlightenment rationalism is the view that reason is primary and faith is subordinate to reason. The Enlightenment refers to the philosophical movement of the eighteenth century that elevated reason above tradition and churchly authority. Its leading figures—John Locke, Voltaire, Denis Diderot, David Hume, Immanuel Kant—were a diverse group, including atheists, deists, and Christians. Their common ground was an appeal to reason in the pursuit of knowledge and the betterment of society.

The more militant figures of the Enlightenment staunchly opposed traditional Christianity and saw the church as an oppressive institution. They rejected miracles in the sense of divine intrusions into a closed system of natural causation. They also vehemently opposed the notion of predictive prophecy. David Hume was an especially vigorous critic of miracles. Even so eminent a figure as Thomas Jefferson "believed that miracles were an abhorrence to reason and so [he] desupernaturalized the Bible" (Clark, Lints, and Smith, 2004: 19). At the same time, some leaders of the Enlightenment preserved the existential truths of Christianity, its ethics, and resultant social benefits.

Enlightenment rationalism was a logically coherent system. It assumed that the universe operated strictly in accordance with natural law, so anything that violated that premise was disallowed. But the view of the universe as a closed system and the rejection of theism are themselves cultural constructs that reflect Enlightenment axioms. Marcus Borg describes his struggle in his thirties with the "modern worldview" (a product of the Enlightenment perspective): "I saw that most cultures throughout human history have seen things differently. I realized that there are well-authenticated experiences that radically transcend what the modern worldview can accommodate. I became aware that the modern worldview is itself a relative cultural construction, the product of a particular era in human intellectual history" (Borg and Wright, 1999: 10–11).

The Enlightenment was clearly a huge step forward when it countered irrationality, superstition, and abusive ecclesiastical authority, and Christians should be grateful for its intellectual advances and other salutary results. But Enlightenment rationality overreached itself when it implicitly claimed to circumscribe the entirety of human experience, let alone all reality, within a strictly natural system. Illumination is good, but we must be careful not to be benighted by the Enlightenment.

In addition to the miraculous events reported in biblical narratives, there are also several basic tenets of the Christian faith that, while not necessarily contrary to reason, certainly go beyond it, such as the Trinity, the incarnation, the atonement, and the Eucharist. These are not irrational ideas; they are suprarational, transcending rational explication. There is irreducible mystery in Christian theology, so we should not think that every element of our faith can be rationally analyzed without remainder.

The history of Christianity thus alerts us to two errors: faith that excludes reason, and reason that excludes faith. There is, therefore, broad support—Catholic, Protestant, and Orthodox—for an understanding of authority and a biblical hermeneutic that involve both: "Faith and reason are like two wings on which the human spirit rises to the contemplation of truth" (John Paul II, 1998: 7). But what is reason's precise role? Many would say that reason's role is instrumental: it is a tool for gaining knowledge from Scripture and tradition rather than an independent source of knowledge. That was certainly the view of John Wesley (Gunter et al., 1997: 77–79; Thorsen, 1990: 246), as well as that of early Anglicanism. "Reason helped the church to understand Scripture and tradition, not to challenge their authority by means of a rival authority" (Bauckham, 2002: 51). It is a virtually inescapable conclusion that reason has at least this minimal function. How can one seriously study Scripture and the traditions of the church without using reason?

Reason's instrumental function is used every time an interpreter ponders the meaning of a word, discerns an intertextual echo, perceives structure, or investigates the historical background of a passage. Reason is employed in both the construal of a text's meaning and in the consideration of its continuing relevance. Reason helps us resolve contradictions, struggle with morally offensive texts, and avoid literalist readings of rhetorical devices such as hyperbole and metaphor (Stylianopoulos, 1997: 91–92). Thus when we read in Mark 1:5 that "all Jerusalem" went out to see John the Baptist, we need not think of the city as completely vacated. Sometimes the function of reason may be akin to common sense. When Jesus calls his first disciples, and they drop everything, abandoning families and careers to follow him (Mark 1:16–20), we may reasonably assume that they had a developing relationship with Jesus before this point, even if Scripture makes no mention of it.

Nevertheless, some want to claim more than this, that reason is also *a material source* of religious truth. This may be true in a limited way. Theoretical reflection (Plato's mode) or sense perception of the created order (Aristotle's mode) may contribute some content to our theology, but such input usually would require the testing and clarification that Scripture and tradition provide. A complex question facing modern Christians is how the natural sciences and social sciences contribute to theology in such areas as anthropology, ecclesiology, ethics, or cosmology. Such contributions are certainly possible, and the church must remain open to insights from secular disciplines. If all truth is God's truth, then Christians should not fear the bona fide discoveries of science.

But we must also be alert to the danger of making a category error. The various natural and social sciences are designed to create knowledge of a particular kind, and while such knowledge may certainly inform Christian faith and practice, it is not always knowledge that contributes materially to theology per se. For example, medical science has greatly increased our understanding of alcoholism, particularly its physiological and psychological dimensions. But it would be a category error to take these scientific results and conclude that drunkenness is no longer a moral issue as well. Science should inform pastoral care for alcoholics, but its contributions are medical and psychological, and they must be incorporated into the moral and theological framework provided by Scripture and tradition. Similarly, the natural sciences have shed much light on the origins of the universe and forms of life within it. Christians should not fear scientific findings that are grounded in responsible methods, careful reasoning, and sound evidence. But science is obviously not equipped to evaluate theological claims about God as the creator, the purpose of creation, or the nature of providence.

For more on the vast topic of reason and faith, see Kreeft and Tacelli (1994: 27–44), Morris (1994), Stylianopoulous (1997: 88–100), John Paul II (1998), Clark and Lints and Smith (2004: 18–19, 27–28, 78–80), Wagner and Brown (2005), and Boa and Bowman (2006).

The Role (and Problematic Nature) of Experience

Experience, the last component of the quadrilateral, is the most difficult to define and the most problematic to apply. As noted above, John Wesley seems to have been the first Christian leader to emphasize experience *as a formal criterion* for defining Christian faith and practice (Thorsen, 1990: 201). This is by no means to suggest that Christians had not been guided by experience prior to John Wesley. Indeed, one of the earliest crises in Christianity—the question about what to require of Gentile converts—arose precisely because of the experience of Christian missionaries (Acts 8–10), and later that same experience was adduced as *part of* the rationale for formulating the church's policy (Acts 15:6–21). But Wesley was especially intentional about incorporating experience into his hermeneutical system.

Unfortunately, Wesley himself used the term "experience" in a variety of ways (Gunter et al., 1997: 108–12, 136), and so it is sometimes misunderstood even by Wesley's heirs. Experience is not only difficult to define; by its very nature it is also subjective and individualistic. Among the various criteria, therefore, experience is "most in danger of feeding the postmodern tendency toward relativism" (Robinson, 2003: 3). I once heard a pastor quip from the pulpit, "Please excuse me for relating so many personal experiences in my preaching, but those are the only kind that I have ever had."

There still is some value in attempting a generic definition of experience, one that will highlight both its subjective nature and the limits on that subjectivism. Nichols provides an insightful discussion of experience as an aid in the evaluation of Scripture and tradition (Nichols, 1991: 235–47). Drawing on Edward Schillebeeckx, Nichols defines experience as the "ability to assimilate perceptions" (235). In other words, when we experience something, we must process a complex array of sensations of many types: sensory (sight, sound, smell, and so on), bodily (pain, pleasure, hunger, and so on), and psychic (fear, boredom, anger, and so on). Nichols notes that there are two poles to experience: the objective pole of the thing or phenomenon, independent of ourselves, that we are perceiving; and the subjective pole of our sensations, which depend on our personal histories, our state of mind, our culture and language, and so forth. Thus every experience is at the same time subjective and objective. Two different persons' experiences of the same perception can be very different based on the subjective element, but the objective pole remains a controlling factor.

Experience may inform biblical interpretation in rather practical, commonsense ways. In John 14:13, Jesus says, "And I will do whatever you ask in my name, so that the Son may bring glory to the Father" (NIV). In the experience of most Christians, prayers are not that uniformly and positively answered. That does not mean that Jesus's promise is false, but rather that its truth must be carefully discerned in its literary context and probably involves implicit conditions and rhetorical force more than a mechanistic quid pro quo. Similarly, when we read New Testament texts about the parousia, or second coming of Christ (Mark 9:1; 1 Cor. 7:29–31; Phil. 4:5; 1 Thess. 4:15; James 5:7–8; among others), experience tells us that we are on the same side of this hope that the early church was. Some early Christians likely expected that Jesus would return in their lifetime, and when we exegete texts that express this hope, we must deal frankly with that fact. But at the hermeneutical stage, when we are seeking contemporary significance, our experience leads us to revisit that expectation and incorporate the delay of the parousia into our eschatology.

A second way that experience may function is to confirm the truths of Scripture in our lived reality. Thus most people would say that experience confirms the fallen state of human beings. If one asks how God brings about justification and sanctification in the lives of persons, one may certainly turn to Scripture, but the texts of human lives also bear witness to God's methods of redemption. This confirmatory role of experience was often employed by John Wesley, as when he appealed to experience to substantiate believers' assurance of their salvation (Thorsen, 1990: 202–3; Gunter et al., 1997: 123).

A third function of experience is as an evaluative tool for texts with harmful effects or a detrimental history of interpretation. For example, texts that condone slavery or the subordination of women (or that have been used to that end) are in need of the critique and evaluation that *other parts* of Scripture, as well as tradition, reason, and experience, can supply. Here is the place where ideological criticism and a hermeneutic of suspicion may be usefully employed. As I have said before, historical exegesis aims to construe the meaning intended by the author and conveyed by the text. That is *not*, however, the final goal of interpretation in confessional contexts, and it is not the chief aim of ideological criticism.

> [Ideological criticism's] aim is not primarily, much less exclusively, the simple elucidation of the meaning of the text, which has been the agenda of scholarly research since the Renaissance. Ideological critics are interested in changing the power arrangements in the academy, in society, and in the Church. (Schneiders, 1991: 121)

Persons who experience discrimination and abuse due to gender, race, ethnicity, economic status, and so forth bring that experience to the interpretation of Scripture. It is part of who they are, and they cannot divorce themselves from it. While there is good reason to hold the influence of that experience in abeyance *during the exegetical phase*, it has a valid function in the hermeneutical phase. Experience sometimes enables us to question Scripture more deeply, to be mindful of how other readers might receive its message, and to be alert to ways that it might be harmfully construed or applied. (See Schüssler Fiorenza

[1995: 1–22] for a programmatic statement of the role of women's experience in feminist interpretation.)

Ideological criticism has the capacity to rescue genuine biblical values from their ancient cultural entrapment. Richard Bauckham notes that "traditional doctrines of the ministry, . . . including its limitation to men, must be subject to the suspicion of being self-justification for those who propounded them. Modern ideology criticism *here proves an ally* of important New Testament concerns" (Bauckham, 1988: 138, with added emphasis).

However, experience can also be a problematic factor when it is elevated to the level of primacy and particularly when experience becomes a criterion that is independent of Scripture's critique. If an interpreter uses an evaluative criterion that is not itself informed by Scripture and, in using it, overrides the consistent witness of Scripture, then that criterion, rather than Scripture, has become the authority by which the interpreter operates. But our experience and ideology must also be subject to Scripture's critique. Luke Timothy Johnson warns that "the premise that sacred texts must always confirm and never challenge contemporary ideology is perhaps the most problematic aspect of this approach [of censoring offending texts]" (1989: 421).

This task of discerning, by means of one's experience, when a text is harmful and must be relativized in consideration of other Scriptural passages, tradition, and reason—this task is delicate. For example, feminist interpreters often decry the emphasis that certain biblical texts place on gentleness, submission, and endurance in suffering. There is a vital word of warning here inasmuch as such texts have sometimes been applied primarily or exclusively to certain groups: slaves, women, victims of violence, and so forth. It is important to hear the feminist challenge and reject gender-based and class-based uses of such texts. Neither should these Scriptures be so generalized and stripped of their contexts as to underwrite a kind of doormat discipleship. But part of judicious interpretation is recognizing when the baby is being thrown out with the bathwater. When uniformly applied to all Christians and balanced by the call to justice, qualities such as gentleness, submission, and endurance in suffering are still needed virtues, perhaps especially so in a modern culture of self-centeredness, aggression, and vindictiveness (Charry, 1993).

N. T. Wright points out that the elevation of experience as one's primary source of authority is in some ways both ancient and postmodern. Self-discovery and awakening to one's identity were central to ancient gnosticism. It is also central to some postmodern forms of Christianity. "If the point of the religious quest is to discover the divine spark within one's own self, to pay attention to that inner experience will—must!—trump any appeal to any other supposed source of authority" (Wright, 2006: 128). But it is precisely this elevation of experience to the position of final arbiter that creates such chaos, for experience "always and inevitably comes up with several simultaneous and incompatible stories" (Wright, 2005: 102). It does not, therefore, provide a reliable criterion for faith and practice.

In addition to being ineffective, there is a significant danger in enthroning experience as one's primary authority: the fathomless human ability to justify one's own experience. Kevin Vanhoozer warns that "there is a constant temptation to rewrite those parts of Scripture that sound most dissonant to our culture" (Adam et al., 2006: 61). N. T. Wright argues that experience, both individual and ecclesial, "is itself *that over which and in the context of which the reading of scripture exercises its authority*" (2005: 102, with original emphasis). In other words, our experience is ultimately subject to Scripture's authority, not vice versa. In this way we can be addressed by a word that is not simply an echo of our own voice.

All Christians are liable to the danger of their experience becoming a cultural blinder. A few years ago I heard a lecture by Jim Wallis, a prominent Christian author and political activist. In a provocative statement, Wallis said that conservative Christians, in backing the U.S. war in Iraq, were acting as Americans first and as Christians second. The comment elicited an assenting response from the mainline Protestant audience. As a Christian of conservative leanings, I thought that the remark was a challenging shot across the bow of evangelicalism. I also thought it was mostly justified. Some evangelicals are admittedly prone to an uncritical nationalism that loses sight of the gospel call to peacemaking and the global reach of God's redemptive mission. But in a similar fashion, some progressive Christians who are eager to normalize and sacralize homosexual unions may be guilty of acting as socially liberal Americans first and as Christians second. No one is immune to the distortions of personal experience and cultural assumptions.

Experience as a criterion in the evaluation of biblical texts can perhaps be rehabilitated if we understand it not as the subjective experience of an isolated individual but as broadly based human experience that is multinational and multiethnic. By this I mean something more precise than listening to voices of the oppressed, although that is certainly part of it. I mean listening to Christians of other cultures, especially those very different from one's own. Christians in the global west and north need to listen to Christians in the global east and south, and vice versa.

The rationale for broadening the notion of experience is in part practical: it is a hedge against error. Democracy is not a perfect political system, but it is generally superior to monarchy in that a broad swath of humanity is less likely to make an egregious error of judgment that a single individual is. Likewise, the cumulative human experience of the global body of Christ is a surer foundation for theological and ethical discernment than that of an individual believer. The rationale is also theological. "Although truth is comprehensive and certain in terms of God's knowledge, human perception involves finite, not to mention fallen, perspectives. Accordingly, at any given time and place we see only partially" (Treier, 2008: 202). Therefore we see more fully when we read Scripture in communion with others, both living readers around the world and sainted readers through history. In this way, experience honors the communion of saints geographically as tradition honors it chronologically.

Finally, the experience that helps us interpret God's revelation is particularly experience *in Christian community*, more so than generic human experience. Catholic scholar Aidan Nichols asserts that "the Catholic Christian as an experiencing subject is never separate from the life of the Church. He or she is nourished experientially by this life, which consists in a celebration of faith and of the sacraments of faith together with all those who co-participate in such celebration" (Nichols, 1991: 244). This statement would be equally true if the word "Catholic" were replaced by "Protestant" or "Orthodox." Experience is an aid in discerning God's revelation when that experience is communal: situated in and informed by the confessing, practicing community.

Before proceeding to the challenge of adjudicating theological and moral issues by means of Scripture, tradition, reason, and experience, it might be useful to summarize some of the key points made so far.

1. Scripture is the primary source of authority for the Christian life and the primary *material* source for matters of faith (theology) and practice (ethics). It does not operate alone, however, and so it is insufficient to claim the Bible as one's only creed.
2. Tradition has a subordinate but extremely important role. It can also be a *material* source for theology, especially in that it corroborates, elaborates, clarifies, and systematizes the truths of Scripture.
3. The role of reason is primarily *instrumental* in that it is the means by which Scripture and tradition are construed. Reason can also be a material source of information, but that information is usually ancillary to divine revelation. In other words, the information that reason supplies enables us to gain a more nuanced understanding of theological issues, to see how those issues relate to secular disciplines, and to shape our approach to a number of pastoral and ethical situations.
4. Experience chiefly has a *contextual* function in that our life before God in Christian community is the context in which Scripture exercises its authority. It may also have a *confirmatory* or *illustrative* function, as when it validates the truth of Scripture or demonstrates how the work of God is accomplished in real-life situations.

Appealing to Scripture and the "Hermeneutical Adjuncts"

The hermeneutical work of evaluating and contemporizing Scripture remains. We must move beyond the description of the sides of the quadrilateral and consider how they are interrelated and, especially, how we make decisions about Christian faith and practice by appealing to them. I think of tradition, reason, and (to a lesser extent) experience as hermeneutical adjuncts, important ancillary resources in the discernment of God's will, but subordinate to Scripture. Adjunct instructors in a university are essential to the operation of the whole, even if they have a status different from that of full-time, permanent faculty. Likewise, tradition, reason, and experience contribute to the interpretive process, though not on a par with Scripture.

As I noted in the introduction, it is widely acknowledged that Christians today should not embrace *every* teaching in the Bible. We do not execute our children for reviling their parents (Exod. 21:17). We do not put to death persons guilty of adultery (Lev. 20:10). Most Christian churches do not flatly prohibit women from speaking in church, although some restrict their roles (1 Cor. 14:34). Even the most traditional Christians understand intuitively, though not always systematically, that the legal and religious prescriptions of antiquity are not *wholly* transferable to the present. But it is crucial that we do not adopt a whimsical, smorgasbord-type approach to Scripture, selecting what suits the tastes of our generation or our tradition, passing over those teachings and commands that we find inconvenient or too demanding. What we need is a responsible method of contemporizing the text, a consistent hermeneutic by which to operate.

When I was a young Christian and first began to wrestle with the difficult texts of Scripture, I thought it was largely a matter of distinguishing those passages that had timeless, universal messages from the ones that were culturally conditioned. While the impulse behind that thinking was not necessarily wrongheaded, I eventually came to realize that if we discard all biblical passages that are culturally conditioned, we will have nothing left to interpret. *All human discourse* is necessarily conditioned by the culture (language, philosophy, intellectual horizons, social structures, and so forth) in which it was generated (Green, 2005a: 127). Cultural conditioning does not disqualify a text from being God's Word. It simply necessitates careful study to understand the text's cultural milieu and to judge whether that milieu is a limiting factor in appropriating the text's message.

In chapter 2 above, "Analyzing the Text," I highlighted the importance of interrogation, posing questions to the text in pursuit of historical meaning. A similar process is to be employed in the hermeneutical phase, only now questions are posed bearing on the entire canon of Scripture, as well as the respective contributions of the hermeneutical adjuncts, all in pursuit of contemporary significance. What, then, are the questions that should be considered at this point? Scores of volumes have been written to suggest principles for the complex movement from scriptural texts to contemporary faith and practice. The list of questions that I offer below is scarcely novel. I am especially indebted to Richard Hays (1996: 208–13) and Robert Gagnon (2001: 341–42).

Questions Related to the Exegetical Phase

- What biblical texts are relevant to the matter at hand? (Consider both texts that explicitly address the issue and those that address the larger picture or related issues.)
- How frequently is the issue addressed and by what range of biblical authors? (Be aware that while high frequency and a wide range of authors almost certainly reveal an issue of significant concern, the opposite is not necessarily true. Relatively infrequent mention may indicate that there was widespread agreement on the issue and only unusual circumstances prompted its discussion.)
- Is the message of Scripture clear and consistent? In particular, is there continuity on the matter from Old Testament to New Testament?
- Are there contrary texts that offer a counterperspective? Do these texts reflect irresolvable disagreement, developing thought, or different circumstances?
- What is the qualitative message of the relevant texts? Do they present the issue as one of great importance or minor importance? Of ongoing significance or temporary significance?

Questions Related to the Hermeneutical Phase

- What is the contribution of tradition? What do the historic creeds and teachings of the church through the centuries contribute? Has the church spoken consistently on the matter?
- What have the great theologians of the church said (Irenaeus, Origen, Jerome, Augustine, Anselm, Aquinas, et al.)? What is the contribution of the Reformers and founders of various Protestant traditions (Luther, Calvin, Wesley, et al.)?
- Is the issue addressed in Scripture similar to the one faced by the church today? Is the similarity at the level of the presenting circumstances and/ or the underlying principle?
- What does reason, in the general sense of logic and rationality, contribute to the issue?
- What does reason, in the particular sense of modern academic disciplines (history, the natural sciences, medicine, the social sciences), contribute?
- If the message of Scripture is clear and consistent, are there compelling reasons that would justify abandoning or changing the biblical view?
- In terms of Christian experience, does the life of confessing, practicing communities of faith shed light on the matter? How does this

interpretation of Scripture promote (or hinder) faithful Christian discipleship in both personal and communal contexts?

Metacriteria, Levers, and Touchstones

Biblical interpreters sometimes find that even after rigorous exegesis and careful contemporary reflection, uncertainty remains. The canon of Scripture does not always articulate a uniform perspective on a given topic. Sometimes it canonizes diverse viewpoints (e.g., views toward the secular state). Sometimes it only speaks to a modern problem in the most indirect way. Such difficulties have often led interpreters to seek some evaluative principle, some metacriterion by which to evaluate Scripture's statements and to resolve the uncertainty, particularly on the more vexing questions of Christian faith and practice.

What metacriterion would be sufficiently sound and reliable for such an important function? Some would assert that *experience*, or more often the particular experience of an oppressed group, is just such a metacriterion. Elisabeth Schüssler Fiorenza, in critiquing the patriarchy of Scripture, suggests that "the revelatory canon for theological evaluation of biblical androcentric traditions and their subsequent interpretations *cannot be derived from the Bible itself* but can only be formulated in and through women's struggle for liberation from all patriarchal oppression" (Schüssler Fiorenza, 1983: 32, with added emphasis). Here the authority of a particular group's experience has become the metacriterion, and Scripture is subordinated to it. Some liberation theologians would make a similar claim on behalf of the socially and economically oppressed.

Although the impetus to end the oppression of women and the poor is certainly honorable and indeed an imperative for Christians, we have already seen that the use of experience as a metacriterion is problematic, particularly when experience is independent of Scripture and immune to its critique. A weakness of all such systems is locating the metacriterion for the interpretation of Scripture in a principle *outside of* Scripture. In such cases the metacriterion becomes the final court of appeal for Christian faith and practice.

As early as Augustine, the principle of *love* was suggested as a metacriterion for interpreting Scripture. In *Christian Instruction*, Augustine writes: "So anyone who thinks that he has understood the divine scriptures or any part of them, but cannot by his understanding build up this double love of God and neighbor, has not yet succeeded in understanding them" (1.36.40 [86]); Augustine, 1996: 49). Thus the dual love of God and neighbor serves as a check on biblical interpretation.

But while love may have served Augustine well in the early fifth century, it is a more problematic criterion in the twenty-first-century West, in part because of the debasement of the word in popular discourse. Richard Hays warns that love "has lost its power of discrimination, having become a cover for all manner of vapid self-indulgence. . . . One often hears voices in the church urging that the radical demands of Christian discipleship should not be pressed upon church members because the 'loving' thing to do is to include everyone without imposing harsh demands" (Hays, 1996: 202). An example of this is the claim of one scholar who, in articulating a "love ethic," asserts that "the fulfillment and end of scriptural interpretation is the love of God and neighbor; any interpretation that does not accord with this principle is invalid no matter how 'correct' or 'accurate' the interpretation might seem to be, based on historical assumptions" (M. Wallace, 2006: 73). The author goes on to argue for an accepting attitude toward homosexual unions, claiming that "without the guidance of this love ethic, the Bible threatens to pull apart in a centrifugal explosion of hopelessly backward and contradictory messages" (81). I can appreciate Stanley Hauerwas's observation that "the ethics of love is often but a cover for what is fundamentally an assertion of ethical relativism. . . . In such a context love becomes a justification for our own arbitrary desires and likes" (Hauerwas, 1974: 124).

Justice has been another proposal for an overarching hermeneutical principle. Here again the same problem arises: How is the content of justice defined? Is the concept primarily defined by Scripture, or are modern Western notions of jurisprudence or fairness the chief determinants? As much as the Enlightenment promised to deliver a rationality and a related concept of justice that were transcultural, it has to be judged a failure, even before the onset of postmodern skepticism. For example, is it just or fair for one person to have many possessions and another to have few? If not, what does justice require us to do to rectify the disparity? Capitalist and Marxist notions of justice would give starkly different answers and remedies.

Perhaps it goes without saying that combinations of metacriteria are not likely to be successful. In 1991 a Presbyterian task force on human sexuality produced a document proposing that sexual relations be judged by the norm of "justice-love," a term they coined as an overarching principle by which to adjudicate the ethics of sexuality (Ellison and Thorson-Smith, 2003: ix–xii). But this would seem to compound the difficulty. Are Christian justice and love to be defined by a particular swatch of the twenty-first-century Western intelligentsia? Is that definition then adequate to evaluate the claims that Scripture makes on the Christian community?

There is a risk in making any particular principle or value outside Scripture the touchstone for Scripture's authority. Richard Hays asks, "If the Bible is dangerous, *on what ground do we stand* in conducting a critique of scripture that will render it less harmful?" (Hays, 1997: 218, with added emphasis). I would like to exploit the language I have italicized in Hays's question and use the images of ground and standing as a way to think about coping with Scripture's more difficult texts. In particular, when we encounter problematic passages of Scripture, where do we stand, and what are the lever and the fulcrum by which we negotiate such texts?

Archimedes, the Greek mathematician, understood the power of the lever, a simple machine by which an individual could move an enormous weight. He famously said, "Give me a place to stand, and I'll move the world" (*dos moi phēsi pou stō kai kinō tēn gēn*; Pappus of Alexandria, *Synagogue* 8; in Hultsch, 1876–78: 3.1060, lines 1–4). The full formulation of Archimedes' boast would necessarily include two additional premises: "Give me a place to stand, *a lever, and a place to put a fulcrum.*" This image of Archimedes and his lever can serve as a metaphor, particularly for the task of interpreting difficult texts of Scripture.

The critical issue in hermeneutics is not necessarily, as postmodernists tend to think, the place one stands when interpreting the text. We all stand outside the world of the text, all of us at a chronological distance from it and at varying degrees of linguistic and cultural distance. (This problem is at least partially overcome when study groups include readers standing in different places so as to challenge, correct, and complement one another. One might also say that it is partially overcome by the fact that *confessional* interpreters actually stand in close *spiritual* proximity to the text, since they have responded to its religious invitation.) In dealing with problematic texts of Scripture, the most critical issue in hermeneutics is, what is the *fulcrum* by which one leverages texts? That is, where does one find the pivot or principle, the metacriterion, by which one engages and evaluates troublesome texts? By what fulcrum—by what reliable, stationary support—does the interpreter pry and lever some texts to the center and others to the periphery?

My proposal is that the Archimedean fulcrum ought to be *within* Scripture rather than outside it. Let Scripture evaluate Scripture; indeed, let Scripture *correct* Scripture. In this way our interpretation of specific biblical texts is itself shaped by the biblical hermeneutic of the canon. On a number of issues there is an intracanonical debate that must be heard. One may employ a concept of justice to resolve these debates, provided that one's concept of justice is informed by Scripture itself rather than by a secular philosophy, whether Marxist, capitalist, laissez-faire, or anything else. The same could be said of love, compassion, reconciliation, faith, mission, even inclusiveness, so long as these guiding principles are biblically informed. The texts of Scripture that condone slavery or the subordination of women must be evaluated in the canonical context of other texts of Scripture that counter, relativize, correct, and transcend them.

If the fulcrum of biblical interpretation is located outside the canon of Scripture, such as in our experience or in a culturally defined ideal, then we risk losing the ability to hear a critique from outside ourselves. Joel Green expresses this idea well: "The capacity of the Bible to function as Scripture depends in part on its capacity to expose and thwart our own limited, historical horizons. . . . In this sort of scriptural engagement, communities of interpretation are challenged and formed with respect to their practices; they find their theological horizons expanded, their moral imaginations assaulted and sculpted" (2005a: 127).

How then does one adjudicate between divergent voices in Scripture? How does one let Scripture interpret Scripture? David Thompson offers an unpretentious maxim: "Let Jesus be the judge" (D. Thompson, 1994: 65–84). This maxim, akin to the popular "What Would Jesus Do?" slogan, "will not end all questions, nor should it be made a cliché substitute for careful observation and clear thinking" (79), but it contains an important hermeneutical principle: Scripture is to be evaluated christologically, through the lens of the person and work of Jesus Christ. Since Jesus is the Word of God incarnate, ultimate authority resides in him, and he is the highest court of appeal for the adjudication of Scripture (Work, 2002: 258). Thus, what Jesus embodied, lived, and taught, both in broad strokes and finer details, serves as the metacriterion for interpreting Scripture. Note that I am *not* speaking here of the "historical Jesus" in the sense of that minimalist, scholarly construct that strict historians have devised on the basis of criteria of historicity. That figure is both too diminished and too unstable to serve as the ultimate hermeneutical principle. I refer instead to the full-fledged figure we find in the Gospels, with all its attendant complexities. This Jesus—the living Lord of the *kerygma*, who is in continuity with Jesus of Nazareth—is the metacriterion for biblical interpretation. Communities that confess Jesus as Lord must be attuned to him and interpret Scripture accordingly. They should be wary of ethical and theological commitments that are contrary to the person and work of Christ, commitments that are unable to find even a hint or trajectory in his mission and message.

If a further metaphor can be tolerated, one might speak of a touchstone. A touchstone is a black, flintlike stone formerly used to test the purity of precious metals. In theory, gold or silver, if genuine, would leave a particular streak on a touchstone, and so the word came to mean a test or criterion by which one would assess the genuineness of a thing. To say that "Jesus is the judge" is to say that he is the touchstone. If any text of Scripture is to be relativized or set aside, such action can only be taken if the text's "genuineness" has not met the test of the dominical touchstone.

For Further Reading

Many books, essays, and articles reflect on the complex move from Scripture to contemporary faith and practice. In addition to those cited throughout this chapter, one may wish to consult the following: W. Brown (2002), Burridge (2007), Cosgrove (2002), Hays (1996), Johnson (1996), Johnston (1985), Kelsey (1975), Marshall (2004), Meadors (2009), O'Collins and Kendall (1997), Marxsen (1993), Siker (1997), Verhey (1984), and Wink (1973).

4

Appropriating the Text and Transforming the Community

The work of Scripture is not complete until interpreters and their communities respond to its message and are transformed. This may occur for an individual reader as a simple and sincere response to the witness of the sacred text. For such readers, "transformation hinges more on inner receptivity and the action of the Spirit rather than on the accuracy of exegetical and interpretive knowledge as such" (Stylianopoulos, 1997: 216). This certainly is not to devalue the careful work of exegetes, whose labors have informed the faith and life of the church through the centuries and whose toil has been especially essential when the church has faced theological and ethical crises. Indeed, the greater the dilemma encountered by the confessional community, the greater the need for sound hermeneutical work.

The transformative step is not of interest to all readers. "For those who do not accept the revelatory character and claims of the biblical witness, talk about a transformative level is meaningless" (Stylianopoulos, 1997: 215–16). The historical and literary levels are where some interpreters of the Bible begin and end. Such modes of analysis have contributed greatly to our understanding, and they are fine as far as they go, but the confessional reader will recognize that such interpretation stops short of Scripture's deepest significance. Markus Bockmuehl likens this approach to the traveling exhibits known as "Body Worlds," which feature preserved bodies in displays that are highly revealing of human anatomy and yet reveal relatively little about human existence. Such anatomical study is akin to the modernist critical excesses of twentieth-century professional guilds: poking and dissecting the biblical text on "educational" or "scientific" pretexts before publishing the carcass of "assured results," Gunther von Hagens-like, "plastinated" in contrived pseudo-lifelike positions that tended to bear little demonstrable relation to the human struggles and stories with God that actually animated these bodies and that alone can account for what they were and are. (Bockmuehl and Torrance, 2008: 7)

I am reminded of Gary Larson's *Far Side* cartoon in which two entomologists in a field come upon an exotic butterfly. One says to his colleague, "An excellent specimen, . . . symbol of beauty, innocence, and fragile life; . . . hand me the jar of ether" (1982). The beauty, vitality, and transformative power of Scripture are often neglected, and sometimes even sedated or euthanized, by the narrow type of historical criticism that eschews theology and contemporary religious relevance.

The premodern era of biblical interpretation had its own foibles, but it was usually keen in its perception of the ultimate goal of scriptural study. Saint Bonaventure (ca. 1217–74) warned against the inadequacy of "reading without unction, speculation without devotion, investigation without wonder, observation without joy, work without piety, knowledge without love, understanding without humility, endeavor without divine grace, reflection as a mirror without divinely inspired wisdom" (*The Soul's Journey into God*, Prologue 4; in Cousins, 1978: 55–56).

The idea of reading Scripture so as to practice its truth is ancient. James famously urged his readers, "Be doers of the word, and not merely hearers who deceive themselves" (1:22). The Mishnah passes down the words of Simeon, son of Rabbi Gamaliel: "All my days have I grown up among the Sages and I have found naught better for a [person] than silence; and not the expounding [of the Law] is the chief thing but the doing [of it]; and [the one] that multiplies words occasions sin" (Mishnah, *Aboth* 1.17; Danby, 1933: 447). Given my egregious failure to keep silent and my wanton multiplication of words in this book, I can only hope that this final chapter rescues my hermeneutical effort by crowning it with at least a verbal consideration of the "doing of Scripture."

First, we might note the variety of the terminology used to describe this step. One of the oldest and simplest terms is "application." After we interpret a passage of Scripture, we do our best to apply it to our lives. Although the word "apply" is serviceable and understood by most people, it has been criticized as superficial, as suggesting "the affixing of one complete substance (like a decal) to another complete substance (like a window)" (Schneiders, 1991: 161). This is a cautionary note worth hearing. We certainly ought to mean more by applying the Bible than a superficial add-on to an otherwise integrated and functioning system, like an add-on module to a computer software program.

To press the metaphor, being transformed by Scripture ought to be more like having the code for your central processing unit rewritten.

To avoid the charge of superficiality, others have suggested terms like appropriation, embodiment, enactment, performance, transformation, and integration. (See, e.g., the fascinating discussion of "Performing the Scriptures" in Lash, 1986: 37–46; cf. Green, 2007b: 67.) I am less concerned about arguing for specific terminology than I am about stressing the general point toward which all these terms aim: we must make Scripture's revelatory Word *our* script, that which we live, speak, enact, and perform. At the same time, our lives are to be more than a theatrical rendition of a script. Scripture's full work is to transform us personally and communally, to establish and then to deepen our relationship to the God who speaks through it. As Richard Hays says, "The value of our exegesis and hermeneutics will be tested by their capacity to produce persons and communities whose character is commensurate with Jesus Christ and thereby pleasing to God" (1996: 7).

Literary Genre and Types of Appeals to Scripture

One of the most important considerations in the appropriation of Scripture is the *genre* of the text under consideration: application depends largely on *the nature* of Scripture's utterances. If the text in question is already in the form of an imperative, the application (assuming that the evaluative task has shown the command to be generally pertinent to God's people) is usually self-evident. When we read in Ephesians 4:28, "Let the one who steals steal no longer" (cf. NIV), it does not take an advanced degree in ethics to figure out how one should apply the text. In a similar vein, many texts naturally commend themselves to straightforward liturgical application. We apply the Psalms by reciting them in suitable personal and communal settings. We apply hymns by singing them, doxologies by exultantly declaring them, prayers by praying them.

But the matter is not always so simple. A considerable portion of the Bible is in story form. How does one apply a story? Richard Hays observes that appeals to Scripture take different forms (Hays, 1996: 209). As I have already noted, *commands and prohibitions* may have a straightforward application. Other texts express broader notions of moral values or character qualities, which provide *principles* to govern our decision-making processes. Principles are usually applied by analogy rather than directly. We consider the biblical situation and the way in which God's Word addressed it. Then we look for a similar modern situation that may be different in many respects from the ancient one but has some fundamental correspondence. Finally, we imagine how the *principle*, rather than the *particulars*, of the ancient situation might carry over to our modern circumstances, and we contemplate how God's Word would speak to us in an analogous fashion.

As an illustration, Paul's directives against eating meat that was left over from pagan sacrifices (1 Cor. 8) have no direct application to modern Western Christians, whose meat comes from butchers rather than temples. But for Paul a principle is at stake: sometimes Christians of mature faith engage in ethically neutral behavior that Christians of less mature faith find objectionable. This may lead the latter group to violate their consciences and so suffer harm. Paul insists that the welfare of others is more important than the full expression of one's personal liberty. This *principle* may very well apply to some modern Christians whose fellow believers find certain habits or pastimes objectionable, say, consuming alcohol, celebrating Halloween, or reading Harry Potter novels. (This principle of Paul's precludes neither the need for sound teaching on what constitutes Christian maturity nor the fact that some behavior that young Christians find offensive is *not* ethically neutral.)

Hays also speaks of *paradigms* as "stories or summary accounts of characters who model exemplary conduct (or negative paradigms: characters who model reprehensible conduct)" (1996: 209). Parables often function in this manner. Clearly the good Samaritan, who pitied the wounded traveler and tended to his needs, is put forward as a positive example of mercy and love toward one's neighbor (Luke 10:30–37). In contrast, the elder son in the parable of the prodigal son (Luke 15:11–32) is a model of ingratitude and a lack of compassion. Historical narratives often have an instructive function too. On the one hand, it is a safe bet that Jesus's behavior is generally worthy of imitation. Scribes and Pharisees, on the other hand, are often portrayed as one-dimensional characters whose values and assumptions are to be rejected. Jesus's disciples present a more complex picture: a negative portrait in Mark's Gospel, a somewhat more positive one in the other Gospels. Narrative texts thus offer a very rich resource for both theological and ethical reflection and appropriation, but interpreters must take care to discern what is implied by the conduct of characters in a story, as well as the analogous ways that their conduct is to be imitated or avoided in our contemporary settings (see Green, 2007b: 164–70).

Finally, the broadest type of appeal is to *the symbolic world* of Scripture: Scripture's vision of the character of God, the human dilemma, the dynamics of redemption, and the call of discipleship. This use of Scripture is less oriented toward identifying specific conduct to be imitated or avoided and more concerned about a vision of how Christian disciples and their communities should order themselves in anticipation of God's kingdom. This type of appeal must not become a kind of abstraction that avoids concrete enactment. Indeed, the symbolic world of Scripture is a gestalt that may transcend the concrete and specific, but is certainly *no less* than the sum of those actions, values, and commitments. "Significant applications will not occur in vague realms of 'spirituality' or 'holiness' that have nothing to do with life as it is lived" (D. Thompson, 1994: 89). Stephen Fowl aptly describes this ultimate goal: "Christian interpretation of scripture is not primarily an exercise in deploying theories of meaning to solve textual puzzles. Rather, Christian interpretation of scripture is primarily an activity of Christian communities in which they seek to generate and embody their interpretations of scripture so that they may fulfill their ends of worshipping and living faithfully before the triune God" (Fowl, 1998: 161). The *entirety* of Scripture contributes to its symbolic world, but some texts, because of their evocative nature, may be especially rich resources: parables, hymns, prayers, visions, and so forth.

Faith, Practice, Ministry, and Imagination

It remains to consider specific questions that may help elicit the ways in which Scripture can inform and transform interpreters and their communities. It may be helpful to think in terms of four categories: faith, practice, ministry, and imagination. The first two—faith and practice—are a handy way to sum up Christian discipleship in terms of its theological content (faith) and its ethical performance (practice). The questions in list 1 on page 110 are potentially useful for the category of "faith." (In chapter 2 these questions were the crowning step of the exegesis of individual texts. Here they may be employed more broadly once the community has gathered the texts relevant to a particular issue, evaluated them, and sought their contemporary significance.) The general thrust of these questions is thus: what affirmations about God, Jesus, the Holy Spirit, humankind, creation, sin, salvation, righteousness, and so forth emerge from the texts in question?

The category of "practice" moves us toward consideration of conduct, character, virtues, vices, and so forth that the text commends or condemns. An essential reminder here is that the full appropriation of Scripture, in both theology and ethics, must be inclusive of personal, communal, and global dimensions. Christian discipleship ought to be concerned about matters of personal piety, but if it stops there or is disproportionately focused there, it is truncated discipleship. When we read Scripture, we must consider personal habits, behaviors, and commitments that may need to be changed; yet we must also consider the structures of society, the policies and practices at the local, state, national, and international levels that may hinder or promote the fulfillment of God's will and the establishment of God's reign. Finally, as advances in transportation, communication, geopolitics, and environmentalism have made us more aware of being a global community, Christian reflection on Scripture cannot neglect the global dimensions of discipleship. The body of Christ is a worldwide web, and the interpretation and embodiment of Scripture in one part will affect the lives of Jesus's followers in other parts.

The Christian life must not be dichotomized into personal versus social spheres, as if the two were mutually exclusive. There is both a time to enter your prayer closet and a time to enter the public arena. Personal piety, prayer, and Bible study should energize and inform social action. To recall the example with which this book started, we must be committed to a biblically informed faith both in matters of family values and in issues of peace and justice.

So one might pose questions of the following sort:

- How does the text inform all life before God? In the personal sphere? In communal matters? In the public sphere? On an international level?
- Does it offer instruction for personal practices of one's piety: prayer, fasting, charity, worship, devotion, study, service to others, and so on?
- Does the text offer perspectives in such areas as healing, racial reconciliation, economic justice, societal reform, war and military policies, sexuality, structures of marriage and family, care for the environment, the sanctity of life, the quality of life, the remediation and elimination of violence, care for the vulnerable, and so on?

I have included "ministry" as a category because of the specific tasks in Christian communities that are performed by leaders, both ordained and lay, that are deeply rooted in Scripture. These tasks could be folded into the category of "practice" depending on how one defines the latter, but I want to highlight activities such as preaching, teaching, administration, and pastoral care as especially needful of biblical shaping. Preaching, for example, was rooted in Scripture even before the Christian movement, in the Jewish synagogal practice of offering an exposition on the reading of the Law and the Prophets (Acts 13:15). Even before the creation of the earliest Christian lectionaries and certainly ever since, the link between Scripture and patterns of worship and preaching has been strong (Metzger and Ehrman, 2005: 46–47; K. Aland and B. Aland, 1987: 160–66). Likewise, the teaching office of the church, whether the topic is sexuality, the environment, or economic justice, should be grounded in the narratives, prophetic oracles, wisdom, and apostolic instruction of both Old and New Testaments. Administrative practices and pastoral care are similarly to be informed by Scripture, both in theological content and in ethos and demeanor. The interrelationship of Scripture and all of these topics is deserving of far more attention than they can be given here. Suffice it to say that these public and pastoral tasks should be thoroughly imbued by Scripture's truth. For further discussion and bibliography, see Hayes and Holladay (2007: 199–203, 209–10) and the helpful collection of essays in Ballard and Holmes (2006).

Finally, I include "imagination" because the symbolic world or gestalt of which I have already spoken is inclusive of, but larger than, the theological doctrines that we affirm and the discrete practices in which we engage. Scripture should drive our imagination to envisage the world in all its complex structures as God desires it to be. What sort of Christian identity and ethos does Scripture envision? What sort of relationships between human beings does Scripture warrant? What kind of relationship between human beings and God? Between human beings and the creation? What structures of community? In short, what sort of world does Scripture imagine?

In a provocative article, Luke Timothy Johnson advises: "If Scripture is ever again to be a living source for theology, those who practice theology must become less preoccupied with the world that produced Scripture and learn again how to live in the world Scripture produces" (1998: 165). If that admonition seems to devalue historical study, it is only because Johnson is seeking to correct an imbalance. The world that produced Scripture is obviously important, but Scripture itself invites us to reenvision our world as God wills it to be and to cooperate with God in its redemption. Scripture as a whole envisions a world in which the Lord's Prayer is fulfilled: a world in which God's name is hallowed, God's kingdom comes, and God's will is done.

Historical criticism presents both promise and peril. On the one hand, rigorous historical study is absolutely necessary to be able to understand the particularity of God's past revelation, so as better to envision its realization in the present. On the other hand, historical criticism's emphasis on the cultural and linguistic gulf between our world and the ancient world runs the risk of alienating us from Scripture. So how do we obtain the promise while avoiding the peril? We do it by interpreting Scripture in confessional communities as both a spiritual and a rational exercise. We do it by reflecting theologically on the text in a way that transcends, without denying, the cultural and linguistic differences. We do it by hearing the multiple voices of the canon and by drawing into our circle the witness of the church through the ages and around the globe. We do it by always engaging the written word in the context of devotion to the incarnate Word.

So will we ever get it right? Won't our efforts to interpret the Word always be partial, tentative, and halting? It is neither arrogance nor folly to desire to interpret the Bible faithfully, truly, and confidently, but the full realization of such interpretation is an ultimate goal, a *telos*. Yale theologian Hans Frei rightly observes that "the notion of a right interpretation of the Bible is itself not meaningless, but it is eschatological" (1992: 56). Or as Orthodox scholar Theodore Stylianopoulos says, "The total hermeneutical process, just as life itself, remains open-ended until the coming of the Lord" (1997: 236). Until Jesus comes, then, we need to persevere, engaging the Word with our most earnest efforts, the very best training and tools, the highest possible degree of self-awareness, and the fullest measure of commitment to the God who is revealed therein.

Parker Palmer says that "to teach is to create a space in which obedience to truth is practiced" (1983: 69). Perhaps the ultimate goal of biblical interpretation is to create a space in which obedience to *divine* truth can be practiced, truly practiced in our inner lives, communal lives, and global lives, all of which together are understood as life *coram Dei* (in God's presence). Practicing the truth of Scripture will entail confession and repentance, denial of self, daily discipleship, courageous witness, acts of compassion, advocacy for justice, and the highest of all applications, worship.

For Further Reading

The most important continuation of this chapter is not written on the pages of scholarly texts but in the lives of Christian communities (2 Cor. 3:3). Nevertheless, further guidance can be found in the following resources: Ballard and Holmes (2006), W. Brown (2002), Burridge (2007), Cosgrove (2002), Hayes and Holladay (2007: 199–203, 209–10), Hays (1996), L. Johnson (1996), and Wink (1973, 1989).

Appendix 1

Sample Exegesis Paper

"Jesus on Probation"
Luke 4:1–13

Introduction

Because of the scarcity of material about Jesus's early life, we tend to forget that being the Messiah was his second career. He had presumably worked in the family business of carpentry since his early teen years, and no doubt he was proficient in this trade. But a growing awareness since his childhood, the ministry of John the Baptist, and a heavenly revelation at his baptism would propel him in a dramatically new direction. Before beginning a second career, a person often undergoes training of some sort. There may even be a period of testing and trial to ascertain one's fitness for a task. Some cultures mark such transitions with a rite of passage in which the person is exposed to danger.[1] In vocational contexts, this trial period, whether a matter of weeks or months, is often called probation. Jesus's wilderness trial is a kind of probationary period.

After narrating the birth of Jesus and one incident from his childhood in chapters 1–2, Luke summarizes his youth and young adult years in one verse (2:52), and then leaps to the mature Jesus, age 30, at his baptism (3:21–23). That baptism serves to announce Jesus's divine sonship and endowment with the Holy Spirit. He now seems ready to embark on his ministry, but Luke describes a period of testing first. Jesus must demonstrate the nature of his sonship and ministry. His

---

1. Isaak, 2006: 1212.

169

mettle must be tested, not so as to meet some standard of messianic machismo, but to reveal his uncompromising dependence on and devotion to the God of Israel.

Literary Context of Luke 4:1–13

In Luke 3:1–2 the evangelist sets the events of his Gospel on the stage of the world. Beginning with the Roman emperor and moving through a list of regional governors and religious leaders, Luke arrives at John, the son of Zechariah, whose conception, birth, and growth parallels that of Jesus in Luke 1–2. John's ministry implicitly fulfills the words of Isaiah 40:3–5: a ministry of preparation for the Lord's coming. Luke 3:7–20 describes John's preaching and the varied responses of the crowd. John disavows the rumor that he is the Messiah, and he speaks in anticipation of a coming one who will baptize with the Holy Spirit.

Luke briefly mentions John's imprisonment by Herod in (3:19–20), and the action moves on to the baptism of Jesus, at which event the Holy Spirit descends on him like a dove and a voice from heaven affirms his divine sonship and favored status (3:21–22). Chapter 3 concludes with the Lukan genealogy of Jesus, which moves back chronologically from Joseph all the way to Adam, the son of God. The genealogy thus confirms both the declaration at Jesus's baptism and the annunciation to Mary (1:31–35). The evangelist embarks on chapter 4 with the affirmation of Jesus's divine sonship and his reception of the Holy Spirit still fresh in our hearing.[2]

After Jesus's temptations, he returns to Galilee, still filled with the power of the Spirit (4:14; cf. 4:1), and inaugurates his teaching ministry, particularly through the event of his preaching in the synagogue in Nazareth. Again a text from Isaiah serves as the Scriptural anticipation of contemporary events (4:14–30; cf. 3:4–6). The ministry of John has thus prepared "the way of the Lord" (3:4), but the temptations of Jesus also seem to be a necessary anteced-ent of his ministry, demonstrating and shaping the nature of Jesus's Sonship.

Literary Structure of Luke 4:1–13

These verses obviously cohere around the event of Jesus's temptation or testing by the devil.[3] The devil enters the stage in the opening verses, and his depar-ture serves as the conclusion of the pericope (4:13). The internal structure of the passage is likewise unambiguous. There is an introduction followed by a series of three discrete temptations.

2. The order of events—baptism, temptation, ministry—is clearly significant (Seesemann, 1968: 34; Green, 1997: 191).

3. Bovon (2002: 139) notes the clear introduction and definite conclusion: "The boundaries in the text are distinct."

The introduction (vv. 1–2a) describes Jesus's spiritual state ("full of the Holy Spirit," "led by the Spirit") and spatial location ("returned from the Jordan," "in the wilderness"). Then verse 2a describes the duration ("forty days") and agent of the testing ("the devil"). This introduction sets the stage, introduces the cast of characters, and prepares the reader for the temptations proper.

The first temptation is tersely narrated (vv. 2b–4) and has a simple structure.

1. The setting: Jesus's abstention from food and resultant hunger
2. The devil's address: a conditional clause followed by a command
3. Jesus's citation of Scripture introduced with the formula "It is written"

The second temptation spans four verses (5–8). The central element differs slightly.

1. The setting: a transcendent or visionary state rather than a place
2. The devil's address: a conditional offer prefaced by a promise and a claim
3. Jesus's citation of Scripture, introduced with the formula "It is written"

The third temptation also spans four verses (9–12) and has a similar structure, but in the central element the devil notably adds his own appeal to the Old Testament.

1. The setting: a specific city (Jerusalem) and building (the temple)
2. The devil's address: a condition followed by a command and a scriptural warrant
3. Jesus's citation of Scripture with a slightly different introductory formula

The pericope concludes with verse 13. It draws the episode to a close by declaring the testing complete and narrating the departure of the tempter.[4]

Commentary

The threefold temptation narrative is found in Matthew 4:1–11 as well as in Luke 4:1–13.[5] In both accounts the combination of the wilderness, a forty-day period, and fasting indicates an extended period of isolation and deprivation, but the aim is not simply ascetic. Jesus is fresh from his baptism, and Luke

---

4. Garrett (1989: 41–42) notes that the basic pattern of testing and faithful endurance, followed by the departure of Satan, is reflected in the *Testament of Job* 27.2–6 and Shepherd of Hermas, *Mandate* 12.5.2.

5. This fact would assign the pericope to the collection of traditions known as Q. Unlike most of Q, however, the present passage is narrative rather than sayings material.

says that he is "full" of the Holy Spirit. Moreover, he is led by the Spirit in the wilderness.[6] The connection of the Spirit to the temptation is not quite as explicit in Luke as in Matthew. In Matthew the Spirit leads Jesus into the desert *in order to be tempted* by the devil (Matt. 4:1). In Luke the temptation by the devil is a concurrent action, but likely the *implicit* purpose of the Spirit's leading.[7] In any event, the testing of Jesus is purposeful in the sense that it serves both a spiritual and a literary function. It prepares and empowers Jesus for what lies ahead in the Nazareth episode (4:14–30). He proves himself ready and able via the Spirit's empowering presence.

Some commentators reflect on the genre and origin of this narrative.[8] Did the historical Jesus actually retreat into the wilderness and encounter a personified Satan and engage him in dialogue? If so, did Jesus relate the substance of this experience to the disciples at some later point such that it entered the Christian tradition and eventually found a place in the Gospels of Matthew and Luke? Some would answer both questions in the affirmative. One scholar even suggested, "If the devil used Aramaic, then we have Christ's own translation of it or that of the Evangelist."[9] On the other hand, several features of the story suggest its transcendent and visionary nature.[10] The scene clearly lies beyond the limits of ordinary experience.

The account of Jesus's temptations would probably evoke memories of similar stories in the Old Testament.[11] Moses was on Mount Sinai for a period of forty days without food and drink when he received the Ten Commandments from God (Exod. 34:28; cf. Deut. 9:9–11). The prophet Elijah journeyed in the wilderness for forty days without food (1 Kings 19:4–8). But the most significant parallel would be Israel's wandering in the wilderness for forty years (Deut. 8:2; Ps. 95:8–10).[12] Even given the terseness of the description,

6. Many manuscripts read "into the desert" in Luke 4:1 rather than "in the desert." It may be a slight stylistic improvement to have a preposition of direction with a verb of leading, but more likely it is a scribal harmonization with both Mark 1:12 and Matt. 4:1. Luke's preposition suggests that the Spirit's leading was "durative—not just directional. . . . Luke's account relates that the Spirit was leading Jesus every day he was in the wilderness" (Comfort, 2008: 177). This would fit with Luke's use of the imperfect tense: "he was being led." See the comment by Cyril of Alexandria (1983: 86) and Just (2003: 73).

7. Wallace, 1996: 636n6.

8. E.g., Fitzmyer, 1981: 509–10.

9. Robertson, 1934: 1009.

10. E.g., direct dialogue with a supernatural being, miraculous transport to various sites, envisioning the kingdoms of the world in an instant, the sudden departure of the devil, and the lack of human witnesses. All of this suggests that the literary genre of this pericope is myth, in the sense of "symbolic narrative."

11. Johnson (1991: 76) discusses Old Testament parallels as well as connections that Hellenistic readers would perceive.

12. Green, 1997: 192–93. Less obvious are comparisons between Christ's temptation and Adam's temptation. Various early church writers developed this connection (Just, 2003: 73–74, 76; Cyril of Alexandria, 1983: 88). See also Jeremias, 1964: 141; and Fitzmyer, 1981: 512.

there are sobering echoes in Luke 4:1–2b that suggest this episode will be both momentous and defining in the career of Jesus.

In broad terms, *peirazō* may denote two different actions.[13] It may mean, "to examine the nature or character of something by testing, to try, to put to the test." Alternately, it may have a more sinister aim: "to entice to improper behavior, to tempt." Given the designation of an agent ("the devil")[14] in our passage and the nature of the devil's actions in the three mini-episodes, we are likely dealing with an instance of the second meaning. In each case, the devil wishes to lure Jesus into wrongful conduct. It is possible, however, that the same act is viewed differently by the other agent in the scene: the Holy Spirit. Despite the devil's pernicious intent, from the Holy Spirit's perspective, the sojourn in the wilderness has the function of testing Jesus's resolve to rely on and serve God alone. While the devil is clearly the adversary, the Holy Spirit is present in the scene as a guiding, empowering, and preserving force.[15]

The First Temptation (4:2b–4)

The first temptation begins with a terse description of Jesus's activity during the forty-day period, or more properly, his *non*activity, and the resultant physical state. Fasting in ancient Israel was practiced for various reasons: as an expression of mourning (2 Sam. 1:12; Neh. 1:4), repentance (1 Sam. 7:6; Ezra 9:5–6; Jon. 3:5), or religious devotion (Jdt. 4:13). Fasting could also be preparatory for the reception of visions and revelations or a means of calling upon God before war or in a national crisis (Exod. 34:28; 2 Macc. 13:12). It has been suggested that Jesus's fast may reflect "elements of preparing both for revelations and for 'war' with Satan."[16] Tertullian notes that when one fasts for God, "Heaven fights for you" and "divine defense will be granted."[17] At the end of the forty days, Luke says with painful understatement: "He was hungry."

In the devil's first challenge, he assumes for the sake of argument the truth conveyed in the baptismal scene of Luke 3:21–23. He does not, therefore, question the *fact* of Jesus's divine sonship but rather its *nature*.[18] The temptation is not that Jesus will doubt that he is God's Son but that he might misconstrue and so misuse that relationship. Specifically, the devil tempts Jesus to exploit his divine powers for personal advantage by satisfying his hunger. It is less likely that the temptation to create bread out of stone refers to Jesus's

13. Danker, 2000: 792–93. See also Spicq, 1994: 3.84–85; and Nolland, 1989: 178–79.
14. A few manuscripts read "Satan" instead of "the devil," a harmonization with Mark 1:13.
15. This is scarcely the first appearance of the Spirit in Luke; see 1:15, 35, 41, 67; 2:25–27; 3:16, 22.
16. Smith-Christopher, 2000: 456.
17. Tertullian, *On Fasting* 7; in Tertullian, 1956: 4.106.
18. Wallace, 1996: 450–51; Robertson, 1934: 1009; Green, 1997: 194; Bovon, 2002: 143.

performing spectacular miracles and thereby ingratiating himself with the multitudes. The setting pertains to Jesus's individual and immediate need, not the broader needs of the poor. In addition, both "stone" and "bread" are singular, suggesting the limited scope of the miracle that the devil demands.[19] It is primarily about the rumbling of Jesus's stomach, not the rumbling of the Judean peasantry. If the provision of bread to the masses lies in the background, one should note that Jesus later uses his power for the benefit of others rather than himself (cf. Luke 9:12–17).[20]

Jesus rejects the devil's command, but he does so without denying the goodness of food or his need for it. Neither does he exert his own direct authority. Instead, he appeals to the authority of Scripture (Deut. 8:3) and the inadequacy of bread *alone* to sustain the full life that God gives.[21] The passage in Deuteronomy addresses the temptation of the Israelites to be arrogant and self-sufficient (8:1–20). It recalls Israel's forty-year sojourn in the wilderness, an event to which Luke 4:1–4 has many parallels and is surely meant to recall. God sustained Israel in its discontent and disobedience; surely God will sustain Jesus, the faithful and obedient Son, in his distress. The alternative that is rejected is the exploitation of power for personal convenience and comfort, when one is called to trust God to supply what is needed for life. Luke's story does not quote the remainder of Deuteronomy 8:3, which clarifies that one lives by "every word that comes from the mouth of the Lord,"[22] but anyone familiar with the verse and the episode to which it refers would know that the alternative to hoarding bread is relying on God's promise.

The Second Temptation (4:5–8)

The second temptation in Luke clearly involves a visionary experience.[23] The devil transports Jesus to a height and shows him "all the kingdoms of the world in an instant." The "world" here is not the *kosmos*, referring to the creation or universe, but rather the *oikoumenē*, the inhabited world of human beings.[24] The connection with "kingdoms" makes sense. The whole phrase refers to the social and political order, not so much the handiwork of God as the handiwork of humankind. It is the glory and

19. Green, 1997: 193.
20. Danker, 1988: 101.
21. The quotation in Luke 4:4 follows Deut. 8:3 LXX.
22. Some manuscripts add these words to the end of Luke 4:4, but Metzger notes that the shorter text has good external support, and the longer text is surely an assimilation to Matt. 4:4 or Deut. 8:3 LXX. See Metzger, 1994: 113; Comfort, 2008: 177.
23. Luke's second temptation is third in Matthew's account (4:8–10). A few Latin manuscripts transpose Luke 4:5–8 and 4:9–12 to achieve the Matthean order. See Metzger, 1994: 114: Comfort, 2008: 178.
24. Danker, 2000: 699; Garrett, 1989: 40.

the authority of this world's kingdoms that the devil claims to be able to give. He "promises the Messiah *royal* glory—that attaching to domination, magnificence, splendor."[25]

Verse 6 raises an important theological question: does the devil really have the power to bestow worldly authority on whomever he wishes? Is this an instance in which narrative critics might appeal to "point of view" and argue that the devil's claim is not true because he is an unreliable character? Surely the devil as a character is not to be trusted, but in this instance the extravagant claim made by the devil may be true. The devil has the power to thwart the reception of God's word and the salvation of its hearers (Luke 8:12). Satan is able to inflict physical ailments and entice persons to do evil (Luke 13:16; 22:3; Acts 5:3; 10:38). Of particular significance is Luke 22:31, in which Jesus remarks that Satan has asked "to sift [the disciples] like wheat." The remainder of the Gospel suggests that his wish is granted.[26]

Other New Testament texts corroborate this idea. The devil's claim to worldly authority is clearly reflected in 1 John 5:19: "The whole world lies under the power of the evil one." The Gospel of John often calls the devil "the ruler of this world" (John 12:31; 14:30; 16:11). The Pauline tradition views Satan as "the god of this world" or "the ruler of the power of the air" (2 Cor. 4:4; Eph. 2:2; cf. Col. 1:13). Apocalyptic ideology in particular understands Satan as the preeminent authority in this fallen world. In Revelation 13:2–8 the dragon gives his power, throne, and great authority to the beast from the sea, who then exercises authority over all the inhabitants of the earth except for the saints. So what at first appears to be the devil's exaggerated claim actually reflects thinking common among early Christians.[27] This fallen world is in rebellion against God and is under Satan's authority. (It might also be noted that Jesus does not challenge the truth of the devil's claim.)[28]

It is clear, however, that the devil's authority is neither unlimited nor inherent. It is limited to the fallen order of human habitation, not the entirety of creation, and it has been granted to him, as the passive verb "it has been given over" indicates. So who has granted power to the devil? Sometimes grammarians call the use of the passive voice to express superhuman actions the "divine passive." That might be the usage here, or the agent of the "giving over" may be suppressed for rhetorical effect.[29] Whatever power the devil has, it must have been granted to him by God (cf. Job 1:12; 2:6), but since these

25. Spicq, 1994: 1:367, with added emphasis.

26. Luke obviously uses "Satan" and "the devil" interchangeably (Nolland, 1989: 177). For a concise discussion of the names and characteristics of the devil, see Watson, 1992: 183–84; and Bovon, 2002: 141–42.

27. Green, 1997: 194; see also Watson, 1992: 183; and Garrett, 1989: 38; 1998: 47.

28. Other texts of the New Testament, however, offer a more positive view of earthly authorities (as in Rom. 13:1–7; 1 Tim. 2:1–2; 1 Pet. 2:13–14).

29. Wallace, 1996: 437; see also Fitzmyer, 1981: 516.

words come from the devil's mouth, he is scarcely going to credit God as the source of his power.

The devil displays the realms over which he has authority and then, in a sort of Hail Mary pass, offers it all to Jesus in exchange for his absolute allegiance. The scene may be surreal and otherworldly, but the temptation that it represents is thoroughly concrete, political, and this-worldly. Jesus's religious authority, personal charisma, and miraculous talents put enormous social and political power within his reach (Luke 4:22, 36; 19:37–40; cf. John 6:15).[30] If he would be willing to cast aside his divine calling and commit himself to a diabolical agenda, he could aggrandize himself beyond measure. Instead, he cites Scripture again (Deut. 6:13; cf. 10:20).[31]

Deuteronomy 6 is the Torah's commentary on the first of the ten commandments, listed in Deuteronomy 5:6–21. Moses recalls the Abrahamic covenant and the exodus from Egypt as warrants for Israel to maintain their supreme devotion to God and to no one else (6:10–15). The text prohibits the worship of any other gods at the risk of offending Israel's God, who has repeatedly acted in their behalf (6:14–15). Blessing accompanies those who are faithful to the covenant; judgment awaits those who serve any other god. Jesus understands that offering allegiance to the devil for any reason or any reward would be the ultimate violation of the first commandment and the supreme affront to God.

The Third Temptation (4:9–12)

The final temptation also involves Jesus's being transported to a lofty place, not to survey the world's kingdoms but with a view to a perilous challenge. The mention of Jerusalem and the temple puts before the reader the city and the institution that will play a prominent role in the outcome of the story. In this Gospel more than any other, Jesus is resolutely journeying to Jerusalem (Luke 9:51), and the entire story concludes in the temple (24:53). At the pinnacle or summit of the temple, the devil employs his final stratagem.[32]

The premise once again is Jesus's divine sonship. If Jesus is God's Son, he ought to be able to hurl himself from this apex and rely on the protection of

30. For a nonpolitical interpretation of this temptation, see Twelftree, 1992: 824; but cf. 826.

31. The text of Luke 4:8 follows Codex A of the LXX in reading "you will worship" rather than "you will fear."

32. Luke's third temptation is second in Matthew's account. If we assume that Matthew's order is more primitive (Twelftree, 1992: 823; Fitzmyer, 1981: 507–8; Bovon, 2002: 139), there could be various reasons for Luke's transposition: (1) The image of Jesus casting himself down from a height could prepare for Luke 4:29; (2) the devil's use of Scripture seems most appropriate in the third exchange now that he has observed Jesus's mode of response; (3) Luke 4:12 is a fitting and perhaps ironic ending to the threefold testing of "the Lord"; or (4) a climactic test in Jerusalem at the temple could foreshadow the passion. The last of these is most plausible. On the other hand, the temptation to worship the devil, Matthew's third test, could be seen as the natural climax of the sequence.

Providence.[33] The devil has learned something from the first two temptations: Jesus appeals to Scripture's authority and insists on living in accord with it. So the devil launches a preemptive attack. He employs the formula that Jesus has used ("it is written") and cites Psalm 91:11–12 (90:11–12 LXX). The text follows the Septuagint verbatim with one significant omission. Psalm 91:11 concludes with the phrase "in all your ways." By omitting these words (as well as ignoring the broader context of the verses), the devil conceals the fact that the psalm refers to divine protection from the risks inherent in daily life. The literary context also makes it quite clear that this protection is promised to those who abide in God and make God their refuge (91:1–2, 9). The devil has twisted a promise of general providence into a promise of immunity from harm in self-inflicted peril.[34]

Rather than directly challenge the devil's exegesis of the psalm, Jesus returns to Deuteronomy and cites a warning against testing the Lord (Deut. 6:16).[35] In its original context the verse alludes to an instance of testing recounted in Exodus 17:2–7. In that instance the testing involves a demand for proof of God's providential presence. In a similar manner the devil now tempts Jesus to force the hand of God in the third temptation. Yet for Jesus to hurl himself from the temple would not demonstrate trust but rather manipulation, and God will not be manipulated so as to become codependent in human folly. Moreover, the providence of God often saves *through* suffering and death rather than *from* them.[36]

The (Temporary) End of the Temptations (4:13)

The series thus comes to a suitable conclusion with Jesus's citation of a prohibition against testing "the Lord." For what has the devil been doing but just that? Yes, Jesus should not hurl himself from the pinnacle of the temple, but neither should the devil continue hurling impious enticements at the Son of God. So having finished every test, the devil withdraws for a time. This suggests the obvious: Jesus is not done with Satan.[37] He will return as an instigator of the passion, at which time the venality of Judas Iscariot presents the devil with "an opportune time" (Luke 22:3).[38]

33. Nolland (1989: 183) aptly observes: "By the Devil's logic there should be no martyrs."

34. The devil's dubious use of Scripture was noted by Origen and Ephrem the Syrian (Just, 2003: 76) and by Cyril of Alexandria (1983: 90–91). Garrett notes that Ps. 91 seems to have been interpreted in Jesus's day as "a promise of protection from demonic powers" (1989: 56, 139n71). If so, then "Satan's use of this particular psalm to dare Jesus is wickedly ironic" (Garrett, 1998: 58n18).

35. The citation formula used by Jesus differs this time: "it has been said" rather than "it is written." Two manuscripts change it to the latter in order to make the formula consistent with previous verses. See Comfort, 2008: 178.

36. Bovon, 2002: 145; Green, 1997: 195.

37. Twelftree, 1992: 826.

38. Augustine envisioned the devil as a serpent in the wilderness but said that he would return at Christ's passion "in the form of the roaring lion" (Just, 2003: 77).

Conclusion

Jesus meets the adversary in the wilderness, equipped only with the Spirit, and survives a threefold test of his person and mission. Will he privilege the gratification of immediate need over reliance on God? Will he forsake exclusive allegiance to Israel's God in order to acquire boundless political power? Will he act recklessly and presumptuously, assuming that God can be manipulated to his own advantage? In each case, Jesus rejects the devil's offer and appeals to Torah as providing the instruction, limitations, and wisdom by which his person and mission will be defined.

It was noted earlier that certain features of the temptation story suggest its visionary quality. It would be a mistake to infer from this, however, that the substance of the temptations was unreal or even that the general circumstances of the account were sheer fiction. It is quite plausible that Jesus withdrew for a time of solitude and reflection before his public ministry, and more important, it is theologically essential that he experienced temptation (Heb. 2:17–18; 4:15). It is part and parcel of the incarnation. In Christ, God accepted the vulnerability of the human condition and experienced hunger, weakness, and deprivation without resorting to a miraculous remedy. Jesus showed that God's way is not to rely on coercive, kingly force but to privilege truth over power. He showed that it is not God's character to exploit and manipulate but to act with wisdom and trust. When Jesus suffered, whether in the wilderness or on the cross, it was not due to powerlessness but in the obedience of faith.[39]

As Judith Lieu has argued, the temptations of Jesus were not a sham, a bit of theater played out with no real possibility of sin or failure on Jesus's part.[40] On the contrary, the encounter with the devil in the wilderness was a genuine struggle in which Jesus faced the seductive power of sin and had the option of succumbing to it. Jesus's experience of the wrenching torment of acute hunger shatters any notion of a docetic Christology. His rejection of worldly authority and domination shows his awareness of the social and political realities of his day and dispels any image of him as a *purely* spiritual figure. His refusal to coerce God's hand to perform a spectacle demonstrates his commitment to the mission of his Father (cf. Luke 2:49).

So the temptation narrative is deeply christological, but the story has a paraenetic function too.[41]

That is, it has relevance for Jesus's followers, because Jesus is not only the Son of God but also the model of a godly life.[42] The story provides both encouragement and an example. Disciples of Jesus must follow him in the

39. Bovon, 2002: 145.
40. Lieu, 2005: 88.
41. Lieu, 2005: 91.
42. Not all interpreters see an analogy between Jesus's temptations and ours. Calvin rejected the comparison, fearing an emphasis on meritorious human deeds (Bovon, 2002: 146).

path of self-denial, reliance on God and exclusive devotion to God, and trusting reverence toward God—all of this as over against reliance on spectacle, coercion, and power.[43] If we do this, we will demonstrate the preparedness for our mission that Jesus evinced when he was "on probation."

Bibliography

Bovon, François. 2002. *Luke 1: A Commentary on the Gospel of Luke 1:1–9:50.* Translated by Christine M. Thomas. Minneapolis: Fortress.

Comfort, Philip W. 2008. *New Testament Text and Translation Commentary.* Carol Stream, IL: Tyndale House.

Cyril of Alexandria. 1983. *Commentary on the Gospel of Saint Luke.* Translated by R. Payne Smith. Reprint, Astoria, NY: Studion Publishers. Original, Oxford: Oxford University Press, 1859.

Danker, Frederick W. 1988. *Jesus and the New Age: A Commentary on St. Luke's Gospel.* Rev. and exp. ed. Philadelphia: Fortress.

———, ed. 2000. *A Greek-English Lexicon of the New Testament and Other Early Christian Literature.* 3rd ed. Based on a German original by Walter Bauer and on previous English editions by W. F. Arndt, F. W. Gingrich, and F. W. Danker. Chicago: University of Chicago Press. (BDAG)

Fitzmyer, Joseph A. 1981. *The Gospel according to Luke I–IX.* Garden City, NY: Doubleday.

Garrett, Susan R. 1989. *The Demise of the Devil: Magic and the Demonic in Luke's Writings.* Minneapolis: Fortress.

———. 1998. *The Temptations of Jesus in Mark's Gospel.* Grand Rapids: Eerdmans.

Green, Joel B. 1997. *The Gospel of Luke.* New International Commentary on the New Testament. Grand Rapids: Eerdmans.

Isaak, Paul John. 2006. "Luke." Pages 1203–50 in *Africa Bible Commentary.* Edited by Tokunboh Adeyemo. Grand Rapids: Zondervan.

Jeremias, Joachim. 1964. "*Adam.*" Pages 141–43 in vol. 1 of *Theological Dictionary of the New Testament.* Edited by Gerhard Kittel. Translated by G. W. Bromiley. Grand Rapids: Eerdmans.

Johnson, Luke Timothy. 1991. *The Gospel of Luke.* Sacra pagina. Collegeville, MN: Liturgical Press.

Just, Arthur A., Jr. 2003. *Luke.* Ancient Christian Commentary on Scripture: New Testament 3. Edited by Thomas C. Oden. Downers Grove, IL: InterVarsity.

43. Johnson, 1991: 77.

Lieu, Judith. 2005. "Reading Jesus in the Wilderness." Pages 88–100 in *Wilderness: Essays in Honour of Frances Young.* Edited by R. S. Sugirtharajah. New York: Continuum.

Metzger, Bruce M. 1994. *A Textual Commentary on the Greek New Testament.* 2nd ed. Stuttgart: Deutsche Bibelgesellschaft.

Nolland, John. 1989. *Luke 1:1–9:20.* Word Biblical Commentary 35A. Dallas: Word.

Robertson, A. T. 1934. *A Grammar of the Greek New Testament in the Light of Historical Research.* 4th ed. Nashville: Broadman.

Seesemann, Heinrich. 1968. *"Peira."* Pages 23–36 in vol. 6 of *Theological Dictionary of the New Testament.* Edited by Gerhard Friedrich. Translated by G. W. Bromiley. Grand Rapids: Eerdmans.

Smith-Christopher, Daniel L. 2000. "Fasting." Page 456 in *Eerdmans Dictionary of the Bible.* Edited by David Noel Freedman. Grand Rapids: Eerdmans.

Spicq, Ceslas. 1994. *Theological Lexicon of the New Testament.* Translated and edited by James D. Ernest. 3 vols. Peabody, MA: Hendrickson.

Tertullian. 1956. "On Fasting." Page 106 in vol. 4 of *The Ante-Nicene Fathers.* Edited by Alexander Roberts and James Donaldson. Reprint, Grand Rapids: Eerdmans. Original, 1885–87.

Twelftree, Graham H. 1992. "Temptation of Jesus." Pages 821–27 in *Dictionary of Jesus and the Gospels.* Edited by Joel B. Green, Scot McKnight, and I. Howard Marshall. Downers Grove, IL: InterVarsity.

Wallace, Daniel B. 1996. *Greek Grammar Beyond the Basics.* Grand Rapids: Zondervan.

Watson, Duane F. 1992. "Devil." Pages 183–84 in vol. 2 of *The Anchor Bible Dictionary.* Edited by David Noel Freedman. New York: Doubleday.

Appendix 2

Sample Exegetical Brief

Hebrews 1:1–4

Context and Structure

Context: As the opening words to Hebrews, these verses serve as the preface to the entire work. Thus there is no preceding context. Hebrews 1:1–4 introduces language and themes that are important in subsequent chapters: the God who speaks (cf. 12:25), the comparison of Jesus to other means of divine revelation, such as the prophets, the title "Son" for Jesus (cf. 1:2, 5, 8; 2:6, 10; 3:6; 4:14; 5:5, 8; 6:6; 7:28; 10:29), priestly imagery ("purification for sins": see esp. chaps. 7–10), and "sitting at the right hand of God" (cf. 1:13; 8:1; 10:12; 12:2). As for the following context, Hebrews 1:1–4 prepares for and connects well to 1:5–14. The word "angels" in 1:4 is a catchword that introduces the major theme and means of comparison in 1:5–2:18.

Structure: These verses, with an elaborate series of clauses, are a single sentence in Greek. The main verb is "[God] spoke" (*elalēsen*; v. 2). Everything else hangs on this grammatically. All of verse 1 is a participial clause describing God's past speech. After the main clause in 2a, the Greek has a series of three relative clauses: "whom he appointed" (v. 2b), "through whom he made" (v. 2c), and "who . . . sat down at the right hand" (v. 3). The third relative clause is quite elaborate, having four subordinate participial clauses attached to the verb "sat down." Those clauses are "being the radiance" (v. 3a), "bearing all things" (v. 3b), "having made purification" (v. 3c), and "having become as much superior" (v. 4). The sentence is one of the most syntactically ornate in the New Testament.

Exegetical Notes

In many and various ways: The artistry of the passage is seen in the opening alliterative Greek words, which contain five initial "p" sounds. Indeed, three of the first four words begin with the syllable "pol/pal." The author thus demonstrates not only theological depth but also a significant rhetorical skill.

In these last days: This phrase not only contrasts with "long ago" but also reveals the author's eschatological perspective. This view is assumed elsewhere in the epistle (10:36–37) and seems to have been the widespread belief of early Christianity (Matt. 24:32–35; Mark 13:28–31; 1 Thess. 4:13–18).

Heir of all things: As the Son, Jesus naturally inherits all things. But the language of "heir" and "inheritance" occurs elsewhere in Hebrews. Noah is called "an heir of righteousness" (11:7). Abraham looked forward to a place of inheritance (11:8). All believers inherit salvation (1:14) and the promises of God (6:12; cf. 9:15). Esau, on the other hand, forfeited his chance to inherit the blessing (12:17).

Through whom he also created the worlds: The idea that Jesus was God's agent in creation is found elsewhere in the New Testament (John 1:3; 1 Cor. 8:6; Col. 1:16; Rev. 3:14) and has precedents in Old Testament theology, particularly the personified notion of divine Wisdom (Prov. 8; Wis. 7:22).

He is the reflection of God's glory: The Greek word *apaugasma* occurs only here in the New Testament. It has both an active sense of "radiance, effulgence" and a passive sense of "reflection" (Danker, 2000: 99). This may be an echo of Wisdom of Solomon 7:26: "For she [Wisdom] is a reflection of eternal light."

The exact imprint of God's very being: The Greek word *charaktēr* can refer to an impression on a coin, a representation, or reproduction. It denotes the visible aspect or appearance. "Very being" is the Greek word *hypostasis*. It refers to "the essential or basic structure/nature of an entity, substantial nature, essence, actual being, reality" (Danker, 2000: 1040). Thus Jesus was the visible aspect of God's invisible, essential nature. This is similar to the Pauline idea of Christ as the image of God (2 Cor. 4:4; Col. 1:15).

Sustains all things by his powerful word: The Son is seen as not only involved in creation but also in the maintenance of the created order. This too is early Christian thought (Col. 1:17) that is an echo of Old Testament wisdom theology (Wis. 7:27).

When he had made purification for sins: This is the only hint in the preface of what will be the major theme of the epistle: the priestly function of Christ. The Greek *katharismon* refers to a "cleansing from inward pollution" (Danker, 2000: 489).

He sat down at the right hand: This reference to the exaltation of Christ alludes to Psalm 110:1. This is a key verse for the author of Hebrews. The session of Jesus at God's right hand is mentioned five times in the epistle (1:3, 13; 8:1; 10:12; 12:2). Psalm 110 is frequently quoted or alluded to by other New

Testament writers and seems to have been used by Jesus himself (Matt. 22:44; Mark 12:36; Luke 22:69; Acts 2:34; Rom. 8:34; Eph. 1:20; Col. 3:1). The right hand of God is clearly the place where early Christians understood the risen and exalted Christ to be. It was a sign of divine favor and status.

Having become as much superior to angels: The word "superior" (Greek: *kreittōn*) is a favorite word for this author. Of its nineteen New Testament uses, thirteen are in Hebrews. Among the various things described as "superior, greater" in Hebrews are hope (7:19); the covenant (7:22; 8:6); sacrifices (9:23); possession (10:34); and resurrection (11:35).

The name he has inherited: Presumably the name referred to here is "Son." This quasititle is the only name by which Jesus has been designated so far in Hebrews (v. 2), and it is the name featured prominently in the verses that follow (vv. 5, 8) as God's way of addressing Jesus.

Theological Comments

God's revelation: It should not be overlooked that the preface *affirms* God's revelation through the prophets. The contrast is *not* one of revelation (Jesus) versus nonrevelation (the Hebrew prophets), but of two types of revelation. The contrast involves three elements: (1) Time: "in the past" versus "in these last days." (2) Means or manner: plural prophets versus a single Son, or varied revelations versus unified revelation. (3) Those addressed: "our ancestors" versus "us." But note that the very same verb is used to refer to God's revelation through the prophets and through the Son (*laleō*).

Christology: The most prominent ideas in the preface have to do with the status, functions, and character of Christ. The revelation through Jesus is especially to be heeded because of his rank as God's Son. "In the Greco-Roman world, one's honor or standing depended largely on one's parentage" (deSilva, 2000b: 85). As God's Son, Jesus is worthy of the honor that is due God. Jesus's sonship also establishes him as the heir of all things (cf. Ps. 2:8).

Jesus also functions as God's agent in creation. He is thus both protological (preexistent) and eschatological (the means of God's communication in these last days). Christ also inherits what he created. Additional functions include sustaining creation and providing purification for sins. In the latter role, Jesus's priestly or mediatorial function is evident. As the Son who is seated at God's right hand, Jesus is uniquely positioned to be a broker of God's favor. In appropriating the royal Psalm (110:1), the author implies that Jesus is an anointed king in the tradition of David.

Angelology: Although angels are only mentioned in the last verse of the preface and are treated in much greater detail in what follows, it is already evident that this author regards God's Son as having a status superior to angels. This superior status is evident in the very designation "Son." The author is not necessarily engaging in a polemic against first-century angel worship (deSilva, 2000b: 92–94), but this passage still might have a useful function in our day against any excessive preoccupation with angels.

Ideas to Profess, Practice, and Proclaim

This text obviously focuses on the means of God's communication with humankind. We believe in a God who speaks, not a God who is incommunicado, silent, or uncaring. The preface of Hebrews (as well as the writing as a whole) emphasizes both continuity and progression or development in God's communication. It is the *same* God who speaks and the *same* verbal means of communication, whether prophetic or filial. (We are thus reminded that God is able to communicate verbal truth, not just signs or emotions.) But the agent of God's communication has changed to a higher order. Without denigrating the prophets, the author exalts Jesus as the newest, fullest, most authoritative messenger for God. We should embrace Jesus's message as the momentous and obligatory communication that it is: God's Word through God's Son.

APPENDIX 3

Pictograph of Philippians

PHILIPPIANS — A JOYFUL THANK-YOU

| PAUL'S RELATIONSHIP WITH THEM 1:3-11 | PAUL'S PERSONAL CIRCUMSTANCES 1:12-26 | EXHORTATIONS AND EXAMPLES 1:27-2:30 | RIGHTEOUS IN THE LAW OR IN CHRIST 3:1-4:1 | EXHORTATIONS—UNITY, JOY, VIRTUE 4:2-9 | THANKS FOR GIFT, THANKS TO GOD 4:10-20 |

PRAYER FOR...

PRECIOUS PARTNERS

— YOU —

GOSPEL IN PRISON

IMPURE PREACHERS

DELIVERANCE OR DEATH

CHRIST - THE PRIME EXAMPLE

TIMOTHY AND EPAPHRODITUS— PASSING EXAMPLES

TRASH HEAP

CERTIFIED RELIGIOUS ZEALOT

NO CONFIDENCE IN THE FLESH

PRESSING TOWARD PERFECTION

EARTHLY AND HEAVENLY ALLEGIANCE

SPECIFIC EXHORTATION EUODIA & SYNTYCHE

JOY

PEACE

PRAYER

THINGS TO THINK & DO

GENERAL EXHORTATIONS

CONTENT IN ALL CIRCUMSTANCES

PAUL'S NEED SUPPLIED

APPENDIX 4

Pictograph of 2 Corinthians

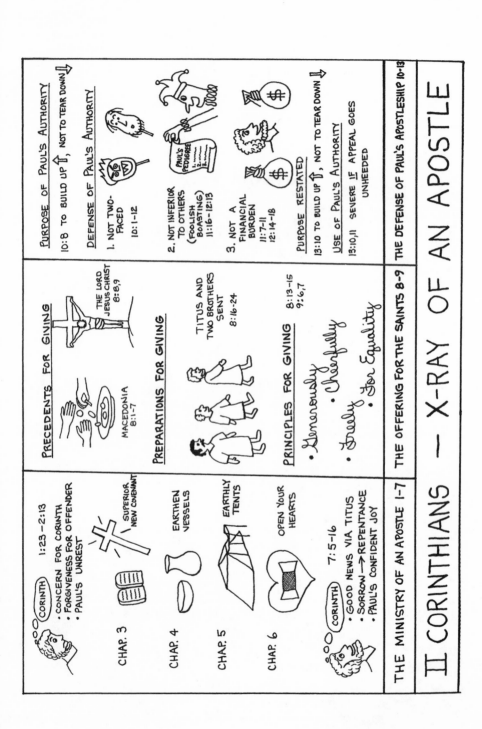

PURPOSE OF PAUL'S AUTHORITY

10:8 TO BUILD UP ⇑, NOT TO TEAR DOWN ⇓

DEFENSE OF PAUL'S AUTHORITY

1. NOT TWO-
FACED
10:1-12

2. NOT INFERIOR
TO OTHERS
(FOOLISH
BOASTING)
11:16-12:13

PAUL'S PEDIGREE
1.
2.
3.

3. NOT A
FINANCIAL
BURDEN
11:7-11
12:14-18

PURPOSE RESTATED

13:10 TO BUILD UP ⇑, NOT TO TEAR DOWN ⇓

USE OF PAUL'S AUTHORITY

13:10,11 SEVERE IF APPEAL GOES
UNHEEDED

PRECEDENTS FOR GIVING

THE LORD
JESUS CHRIST
8:8,9

MACEDONIA
8:1-7

PREPARATIONS FOR GIVING

TITUS AND
TWO BROTHERS
SENT
8:16-24

PRINCIPLES FOR GIVING   8:13-15
9:6,7

• Generously
• Cheerfully
• Freely
• For Equality

CORINTH   1:23 – 2:13
• CONCERN FOR CORINTH
• FORGIVENESS FOR OFFENDER
• PAUL'S UNREST

SUPERIOR,
NEW COVENANT

CHAP. 3

EARTHEN
VESSELS

CHAP. 4

EARTHLY
TENTS

CHAP. 5

OPEN YOUR
HEARTS

CHAP. 6

CORINTH   7:5-16
• GOOD NEWS VIA TITUS
• SORROW → REPENTANCE
• PAUL'S CONFIDENT JOY

| THE MINISTRY OF AN APOSTLE 1-7 | THE OFFERING FOR THE SAINTS 8-9 | THE DEFENSE OF PAUL'S APOSTLESHIP 10-13 |

II CORINTHIANS — X-RAY OF AN APOSTLE

Appendix 5

Chart of the Gospel of Mark

The Gospel according to Mark

	1—John the Baptist opens; Jesus launches ministry	2—Paralytic walks; Pharisees balk	3—Jesus's disciples and Jesus's family	4—Seedy parables, stormy weather	5—Demon possession, death, and disease	6—Mission, murder, and manna	7—Purity debate, gentile woman, deaf man	8—Jesus cures blindness . . . in Peter too!
Chapter Titles								
Structure	Prologue (1:1–15); Jesus recruits, exorcises, heals (1:16–45)	Five controversy narratives (2:1–3:6)	Transition (3:7–12) — Jesus teaches and performs miraculous deeds (3:13–6:6a)			Mission in Galilee and beyond despite disciples' blindness (6:6b–8:21)		
Geography	In the wilderness (1:4); Galilee (1:14); Capernaum (1:21)	Capernaum (2:1); beside the sea (2:13)	At the sea (3:7); on a mountain (3:13); home (3:19)	Beside the sea (4:1); across the sea (4:35)	Country of Gerasenes (5:1); crosses the sea again (5:21)	In his hometown (6:1); among the villages (6:6); a deserted place (6:32); Bethsaida (6:45)	Gennesaret (6:35); Tyre (7:24); by Sidon (7:31); to the Sea of Galilee, to the Decapolis	Dalmanutha (8:10); crosses to the other side (8:13); Bethsaida (8:22); Caesarea Philippi (8:27)
Christology	Christ (1:1); Son of God (1:1); Lord (1:3); "you are my Son" (1:11); holy one of God (1:25)	Son of Man (2:10, 28); Lord (2:28)	Son of God (3:11)		Son of the most high God (5:7); Lord (5:19)			Christ (8:29); Son of Man (8:31); Son of Man (8:38)
Disciples: + and -	They leave their nets and follow (1:16–20); they assist Jesus's healing ministry (1:29–34); they seek him (1:37)	Levi leaves tax booth and follows Jesus (2:13–14)	Disciples prepare a boat for Jesus (3:9); Jesus appoints the Twelve (3:13–19); Jesus's family = disciples (3:31–35)	They do not understand the parable (4:13); they lack faith during the storm (4:40–41)		Clueless as to how to feed 5,000 (6:37); they do not understand about the loaves (6:51–52)	They don't understand Jesus's teaching about defilement (7:17–18)	Doubt about feeding 4,000 (8:4); they do not see, hear, or understand (8:17–21)
"Messianic Secret"	Does not permit demons to speak (1:34); "say nothing to anyone" (1:43–44)		Orders demons not to make him known (3:11–12)		*"Go home and tell what the Lord has done" (5:19); orders onlookers that no one should know about the raising of the little girl (5:43)		Orders no one to tell about healing (7:36)	Sternly orders no one to tell about him (8:30)
Miracles of Jesus	Unclean spirit cast out (1:21–28); heals Peter's mother-in-law et al. (1:29–34); leper is cleansed (1:40–45)	Heals a paralytic (2:1–12)	Heals a man's hand (3:1–6)	Stills a storm (4:35–41)	Heals the Gerasene demoniac (5:1–20); heals a woman's flow of blood, raises a girl to life (5:21–43)	Feeds the 5,000 (6:30–44); walks on the sea (6:45–52); heals many (6:53–56)	Heals Syrophoenician woman's daughter (7:24–30); heals a deaf man with a speech impediment (7:31–37)	Feeds the 4,000 (8:1–10); heals blind man at Bethsaida (8:22–26); foretells death and resurrection (8:31)
Fear and Wonder	Others are astonished by his teaching (1:22); "they were all amazed" (1:27)	"They were all amazed" (2:12)	"He has lost his mind" (3:21)	"They were filled with great awe" (4:41)	"They were afraid" (5:15); "everyone was amazed" (5:20); fear and trembling (5:33); overcome with amazement (5:42)	"Many were astounded" (6:2); Jesus is amazed (6:6); Herod is perplexed (6:20); terrified and astounded (6:50–51)	"They were astounded beyond measure" (7:37)	

9—Trans-figured Jesus predicts again	10—Jesus teaches, pre-dicts a third time, and heals	11—Ho-sanna to the temple cleanser	12—Leaders interrogate Jesus	13—Watch for destruc-tion and persecution	14—Anointed Jesus tried by council	15—Pilate has Jesus crucified	16—Women at empty tomb
Passion predictions, obtuse disciples need further instruction (8:22–10:52)		Ministry in Jerusalem: last days for Jesus, last days for the temple? (11:1–13:37)			Passion of the Christ: Jesus sups and prays, is tried and crucified (14:1–15:47)		Epilogue: resurrection announced (16:1–8)
Upon a high mountain (9:2); down from the mountain (9:9); Galilee (9:30); Capernaum (9:33)	Judea beyond the Jordan (10:1); going up to Jerusalem (10:32); Jericho (10:46)	Bethphage and Bethany (11:1); Enters Jeru-salem, returns to Bethany (11:11); back to Jeru-salem (11:15)	In Jerusalem; in the temple (12:35)	From the temple (13:1); Mount of Olives (13:3)	Bethany (14:3); into the city (14:13); Mount of Olives (14:26); Gethsemane (14:32); courtyard (14:59)	To Pilate (15:1); palace court-yard (15:16); Golgotha (15:22); in the tomb (15:46)	At the tomb (16:2)
Rabbi (9:5); "this is my Son" (9:7); Son of Man (9:9, 12, 31); Christ (9:41)	Son of Man (10:33, 45); Son of David (10:47–48)	Lord (11:3); rabbi (11:21)		Son of Man (13:26)	Son of Man (14:21, 41, 62); Rabbi (14:45); Christ (14:61); Son of the Blessed One (14:61)	King of the Jews (15:2, 9, 12, 18, 26); Christ (15:32); God's Son (15:39)	
Peter confesses Jesus as the Messiah (8:29); Peter rebukes Jesus and gets rebuked by him (8:32–33)	Peter doesn't know what to say (9:5–6); they are unable to exorcise (9:18, 28); argument about greatness (9:33–34)	Disciples deter children (10:13); they are perplexed at Jesus's teaching (10:24); request of James and John (10:35–41)	Disciples fetch a colt (11:1–7)		Judas agrees to betray Jesus (14:10–11); disciples prepare upper room (14:12–16); denial foretold (14:26–31); sleeping (14:37)	Violent resistance (14:47); all flee (14:50); Peter's three denials (14:66–72); women at cross and tomb (15:40–41)	Women come to anoint Jesus's body (16:1); women flee in fear and silence (16:8)
Tells disciples not to tell about what they saw at the Transfigu-ration until the Son of Man is risen from the dead (9:9); none are to know (9:30)							
Casts unclean spirit out of boy (9:14–29); foretells death and resurrection again (9:30–32)	Foretells death and resurrection a third time (10:32–34); heals blind Bartimaeus (10:46–52)	Curses fig tree (11:12–14; 20–24)					"He has been raised and he is not here" (16:6)
"They were terrified" (9:6); "they were over-come with awe" (9:15); "they were afraid to ask" (9:32)	"They were perplexed" (10:24); "they were greatly astounded" (10:26); amazed and afraid (10:32)	Crowd is spell-bound (11:18); disciples are afraid of the crowd (11:32)	They fear the crowd (12:12); they are "ut-terly amazed" (12:17)		Jesus is distressed and agitated (14:33)	Pilate is amazed (15:5); Pilate wonders if Jesus was already dead (15:44)	The women are alarmed (16:5); "do not be alarmed" (16:6); terror and amazement, "they were afraid" (16:8)

APPENDIX 6

Nestle-Aland²⁷ and UBS⁴ Comparison Chart

Similarities

The NA²⁷ and UBS⁴ share the same Greek text. The differences between these editions have to do chiefly with the textual apparatus. The editors for both texts were Barbara Aland, Kurt Aland, Johannes Karavidopoulos, Carlo M. Martini, and Bruce M. Metzger. The Greek text is eclectic: the editors did not base their decisions on a single manuscript or text type but rather considered both external evidence (all manuscripts) and internal evidence (authorial and scribal tendencies) in determining the original readings.

Differences

NA²⁷	UBS⁴
1. Originally designed for scholars.	1. Originally designed for translators.
2. No section headings.	2. Section headings in English.
3. Apparatus includes a large number of textual variants.	3. Apparatus includes *only selected* variants deemed significant.
4. Apparatus gives the most important witnesses for each variant, but only selected information on translations and patristic quotations.	4. Apparatus gives an extensive list of witnesses including many references to translations and patristic quotations.
5. The reading printed in the text appears *last* in the apparatus.	5. The reading printed in the text appears *first* in the apparatus.

NA[27]	UBS[4]
6. Uses a system of symbols to put more information into a small space.	6. Does *not* use a system of symbols. Variants are printed in full.
7. Textual issues are separated from one another by a solid vertical line; variant readings for each issue are separated from one another by a broken vertical line.	7. Each textual issue has its own footnote; variant readings within a footnote are separated by a double diagonal line.
8. No ratings are assigned to textual decisions.	8. A rating {A, B, C, or D} is assigned to each textual decision.
9. Stately blue cover.	9. Noble burgundy cover.

APPENDIX 7

In the Laboratory with Agassiz

BY A FORMER PUPIL (SAMUEL H. SCUDDER)
Every Saturday 16 (April 4, 1874): 369–70

It was more than fifteen years ago that I entered the laboratory of Professor Agassiz and told him I had enrolled my name in the scientific school as a student of natural history. He asked me a few questions about my object in coming, my antecedents generally, the mode in which I afterwards proposed to use the knowledge I might acquire, and finally, whether I wished to study any special branch. To the latter I replied that while I wished to be well grounded in all departments of zoology, I purposed to devote myself specially to insects.

"When do you wish to begin?" he asked.

"Now," I replied.

This seemed to please him, and with an energetic "Very well," he reached from a shelf a huge jar of specimens in yellow alcohol.

"Take this fish," said he, "and look at it; we call it a Haemulon [pronounced Hem-YU-lon]; by and by I will ask what you have seen."

With that he left me, but in a moment returned with explicit instructions as to the care of the object entrusted to me.

"No man is fit to be a naturalist," said he, "who does not know how to take care of specimens."

I was to keep the fish before me in a tin tray, and occasionally moisten the surface with alcohol from the jar, always taking care to replace the stopper tightly. Those were not the days of ground-glass stoppers and elegantly shaped exhibition jars; all the old students will recall the huge, neckless glass bottles with their leaky, wax-besmeared corks half eaten by insects and begrimed with cellar dust. Entomology was a cleaner science than ichthyology, but the example of the professor, who had unhesitatingly plunged [his hand] to the bottom of the jar to produce the fish, was infectious; and though this alcohol had "a very ancient and fishlike smell," I really dared not show any aversion within these sacred precincts and treated the alcohol as though it were pure water. Still I was conscious of a passing feeling of disappointment, for gazing at a fish did not commend itself to an ardent entomologist. My friends at home, too, were annoyed, when they discovered that no amount of eau de cologne would drown the perfume which haunted me like a shadow.

In ten minutes I had seen all that could be seen in that fish, and started in search of the professor, who had, however, left the museum; and when I returned, after lingering over some of the odd animals stored in the upper apartment, my specimen was dry all over. I dashed the fluid over the fish as if to resuscitate it from a fainting-fit, and looked with anxiety for a return of the normal, sloppy appearance. This little excitement over, nothing was to be done but return to a steadfast gaze at my mute companion. Half an hour passed, an hour, another hour; the fish began to look loathsome. I turned it over and around; looked it in the face—ghastly; from behind, beneath, above, sideways, at a three-quarters' view—just as ghastly. I was in despair; at an early hour I concluded that lunch was necessary; so, with infinite relief, the fish was carefully replaced in the jar, and for an hour I was free.

On my return, I learned that Professor Agassiz had been at the museum, but had gone and would not return for several hours. My fellow students were too busy to be disturbed by continued conversation. Slowly I drew forth that hideous fish, and with a feeling of desperation again looked at it. I might not use a magnifying glass; instruments of all kinds were interdicted. My two hands, my two eyes, and the fish; it seemed a most limited field. I pushed my finger down its throat to feel how sharp its teeth were. I began to count the scales in the different rows until I was convinced that that was nonsense. At last a happy thought struck me—I would draw the fish; and now with surprise I began to discover new features in the creature. Just then the professor returned.

"That is right," said he; "a pencil is one of the best of eyes. I am glad to notice, too, that you keep your specimen wet and your bottle corked."

With these encouraging words he added, "Well, what was it like?"

He listened attentively to my brief rehearsal of the structure of parts whose names were still unknown to me: the fringed gill-arches and movable operculum; the pores of the head, fleshy lips, and lidless eyes; the lateral line, the spinous fin, and forked tail; the compressed and arched body. When I had finished, he waited as if expecting more, and then, with an air of disappointment, "You have not looked very carefully; why," he continued, more earnestly, "you haven't seen one of the most conspicuous features of the animal, which is as plainly before your eyes as the fish itself; look again, look again!" and he left me to my misery.

I was piqued; I was mortified. Still more of that wretched fish! But now I set myself to my task with a will, and discovered one new thing after another, until I saw how just the professor's criticism had been. The afternoon passed quickly, and toward its close, the professor inquired, "Do you see it yet?"

"No," I replied, "I am certain I do not, but I see how little I saw before."

"That is next best," said he earnestly, "but I won't hear you now; put away your fish and go home; perhaps you will be ready with a better answer in the morning. I will examine you before you look at the fish."

This was disconcerting; not only must I think of my fish all night, studying, without the object before me, what this unknown but most visible feature might be; but also, without reviewing my new discoveries, I must give an exact account of them the next day. I had a bad memory; so I walked home by Charles River in a distracted state, with my two perplexities.

The cordial greeting from the professor the next morning was reassuring; here was a man who seemed to be quite as anxious as I that I should see for myself what he saw.

"Do you perhaps mean," I asked, "that the fish has symmetrical sides with paired organs?"

His thoroughly pleased, "Of course, of course!" repaid the wakeful hours of the previous night. After he had discoursed most happily and enthusiastically—as he always did—upon the importance of this point, I ventured to ask what I should do next.

"Oh, look at your fish!" he said, and left me again to my own devices. In a little more than an hour he returned and heard my new catalogue.

"That is good, that is good!" he repeated, "but that is not all; go on." And so, for three long days, he placed that fish before my eyes, forbidding me to look at anything else, or to use any artificial aid. "Look, look, look," was his repeated injunction.

This was the best entomological lesson I ever had—a lesson whose influence has extended to the details of every subsequent study; a legacy the professor has left to me, as he has left it to many others, of inestimable value, which we could not buy, with which we cannot part.

A year afterwards, some of us were amusing ourselves with chalking outlandish beasts upon the museum blackboard. We drew prancing star-fishes; frogs in mortal combat; hydra-headed worms; stately craw-fishes, standing on their tails, bearing aloft umbrellas; and grotesque fishes, with gaping mouths and staring eyes. The professor came in shortly after and was amused as any at our experiments. He looked at the fishes.

"Haemulons, every one of them," he said. "Mr. [Scudder] drew them."

True; and to this day, if I attempt a fish, I can draw nothing but Haemulons. The fourth day, a second fish of the same group was placed beside the first, and I was bidden to point out the resemblances and differences between the two; another and another followed, until the entire family lay before me, and a whole legion of jars covered the table and surrounding shelves; the odor had become a pleasant perfume; and even now, the sight of an old, six-inch, worm-eaten cork brings fragrant memories!

The whole group of Haemulons was thus brought in review; and whether engaged upon the dissection of the internal organs, the preparation and examination of the bony framework, or the description of the various parts, Agassiz's training in the method of observing facts and their orderly arrangement was ever accompanied by the urgent exhortation not to be content with them.

"Facts are stupid things," he would say, "until brought into connection with some general law."

At the end of eight months, it was almost with reluctance that I left these friends and turned to insects; but what I had gained by this outside experience has been of greater value than years of later investigation in my favorite groups.

Bibliography

Achtemeier, Paul J. 1980. *The Inspiration of Scripture: Problems and Proposals.* Philadelphia: Westminster.

———. 2008. *Jesus and the Miracle Tradition.* Eugene, OR: Cascade.

Achtemeier, Paul J., Joel B. Green, and Marianne Meye Thompson. 2001. *Introducing the New Testament: Its Literature and Theology.* Grand Rapids: Eerdmans.

Adam, A. K. M., Stephen E. Fowl, Kevin J. Vanhoozer, and Francis Watson. 2006. *Reading Scripture with the Church: Toward a Hermeneutic for Theological Interpretation.* Grand Rapids: Baker Academic.

Adams, Marilyn McCord. 1996. "Hurricane Spirit, Toppling Taboos." Pages 129–41 in *Our Selves, Our Souls and Bodies: Sexuality and the Household of God.* Edited by Charles Hefling. Cambridge, MA: Cowley.

Adeyemo, Tokunboh, ed. 2006. *Africa Bible Commentary.* Grand Rapids: Zondervan.

Adler, Mortimer J., and Charles Van Doren. 1972. *How to Read a Book.* Revised and updated edition. New York: Simon & Schuster.

Akin, Jimmy. 2004. "The Original Languages." *This Rock* 15 (July–August): 31–33.

Aland, Barbara, et al. 1993. *The Greek New Testament.* 4th, rev. ed. New York: United Bible Societies.

———. 2000. *Novum Testamentum Graece.* 27th ed., corr. Stuttgart: Deutsche Bibelgesellschaft.

Aland, Kurt, ed. 1985. *Synopsis Quattuor Evangeliorum.* 13th ed. Stuttgart: Deutsche Bibelgesellschaft.

Aland, Kurt, and Barbara Aland. 1987. *The Text of the New Testament: An Introduction to the Critical Editions and to the Theory and Practice of Modern Textual Criticism*. Grand Rapids: Eerdmans.

Allison, Dale C. 2000. *The Intertextual Jesus: Scripture in Q*. Harrisburg, PA: Trinity Press International.

Atkinson, Nigel T. 1997. *Richard Hooker and the Authority of Scripture, Tradition, and Reason*. Carlisle, Cumbria: Paternoster.

Attridge, Harold W. 1989. *The Epistle to the Hebrews*. Hermeneia. Philadelphia: Fortress.

Augustine. 1996. *De Doctrina Christiana*. Edited and translated by R. P. H. Green. Oxford Early Christian Studies. Oxford: Clarendon.

Aune, David E. 1983. *Prophecy in Early Christianity and the Ancient Mediterranean World*. Grand Rapids: Eerdmans.

———. 1987. *The New Testament in Its Literary Environment*. Philadelphia: Westminster.

Bacote, Vincent, et al., eds. 2004. *Evangelicals and Scripture: Tradition, Authority, and Hermeneutics*. Downers Grove, IL: InterVarsity.

Bailey, Derrick. 1955. *Homosexuality in the Western Christian Tradition*. London: Longmans, Green, & Co.

Bailey, James L., and Lyle D. Vander Broek. 1992. *Literary Forms in the New Testament: A Handbook*. Louisville: Westminster John Knox.

Bailey, Randall C., ed. 2003. *Yet with a Steady Beat: Contemporary U.S. Afrocentric Biblical Interpretation*. Atlanta: Society of Biblical Literature.

Bailey, Randall C., Tat-siong Benny Liew, and Fernando F. Segovia, eds. 2009. *They Were All Together in One Place: Toward Minority Biblical Criticism*. Atlanta: Society of Biblical Literature.

Bainton, Roland H. 1950. *Here I Stand: A Life of Martin Luther*. Nashville: Abingdon.

Baird, William. 1992. *History of New Testament Research*. Vol. 1, *From Deism to Tübingen*. Minneapolis: Fortress.

Ballard, Paul, and Stephen R. Holmes, eds. 2006. *The Bible in Pastoral Practice: Readings in the Place and Function of Scripture in the Church*. Grand Rapids: Eerdmans.

Balz, Horst, and Gerhard Schneider, eds. 1990–93. *Exegetical Dictionary of the New Testament*. 3 vols. Grand Rapids: Eerdmans.

Barclay, John M. G. 1996. *Jews in the Mediterranean Diaspora: From Alexander to Trajan (323 BCE–117 CE)*. Berkeley: University of California Press.

Barr, James. 1961. *The Semantics of Biblical Language*. Oxford: Oxford University Press.

———. 1980. *The Scope and Authority of the Bible*. Philadelphia: Westminster.

Barrett, C. K. 1995. *The New Testament Background: Selected Documents.* Rev. and exp. ed. San Francisco: HarperSanFrancisco.

Bartchy, S. Scott. 1997. "Narrative Criticism." Pages 787–92 in *Dictionary of the Later New Testament and Its Developments.* Edited by Ralph P. Martin and Peter H. Davids. Downers Grove, IL: InterVarsity.

Bartholomew, Craig, et al., eds. 2000. *Renewing Biblical Interpretation.* Scripture and Hermeneutics 4. Grand Rapids: Zondervan.

Barton, John, and John Muddiman, eds. 2001. *The Oxford Bible Commentary.* Oxford: Oxford University Press.

Bauckham, Richard. 1988. "Tradition in Relation to Scripture and Reason." Pages 117–45 in *Scripture, Tradition, and Reason: A Study in the Criteria of Christian Doctrine.* Edited by Richard Bauckham and Benjamin Drewery. Edinburgh: T&T Clark.

————. 2002. *God and the Crisis of Freedom: Biblical and Contemporary Perspectives.* Louisville: Westminster John Knox.

Bauckham, Richard, and Benjamin Drewery, eds. 1988. *Scripture, Tradition and Reason: A Study in the Criteria of Christian Doctrine.* Edinburgh: T&T Clark.

Bauer, David. 2003. *An Annotated Guide to Biblical Resources for Ministry.* Peabody, MA: Hendrickson.

Beale, G. K., ed. 1995. *The Right Doctrine from the Wrong Texts? Essays on the Use of the Old Testament in the New.* Grand Rapids: Baker Academic.

Beale, G. K., and D. A. Carson, eds. 2007. *Commentary on the New Testament Use of the Old Testament.* Grand Rapids: Baker Academic.

Beard, Mary, John North, and Simon Price. 1998. *Religions of Rome.* Vol. 1, *A History.* Vol. 2, *A Sourcebook.* Cambridge: Cambridge University Press.

Beardsley, Monroe C. 1968. "Textual Meaning and Authorial Meaning." *Genre* 1:169–81.

Bell, Albert A. 1998. *Exploring the New Testament World: An Illustrated Guide to the World of Jesus and the First Christians.* Nashville: Nelson.

Berding, Kenneth, and Jonathan Lunde, eds. 2008. *Three Views on the New Testament Use of the Old Testament.* Grand Rapids: Zondervan.

Bird, Phyliss A. 1994. "The Authority of the Bible." Pages 33–64 in vol. 1 of *The New Interpreter's Bible.* Edited by Leander E. Keck. Nashville: Abingdon.

Blackburn, Barry L. 1992. "Miracles and Miracle Stories." Pages 549–60 in *Dictionary of Jesus and the Gospels.* Edited by Joel B. Green, Scot McKnight, and I. Howard Marshall. Downers Grove, IL: InterVarsity.

Blass, F., and A. Debrunner. 1961. *A Greek Grammar of the New Testament and Other Early Christian Literature.* Translated and edited by Robert W. Funk. Chicago: University of Chicago Press.

Blomberg, Craig L. 1987. *The Historical Reliability of the Gospels*. Downers Grove, IL: InterVarsity.

———. 1992. "Form Criticism." Pages 243–50 in *Dictionary of Jesus and the Gospels*. Edited by Joel B. Green, Scot McKnight, and I. Howard Marshall. Downers Grove, IL: InterVarsity.

Blount, Brian K. 1995. *Cultural Interpretation: Reorienting New Testament Criticism*. Minneapolis: Fortress.

Blount, Brian K., et al., eds. 2007. *True to Our Native Land: An African American New Testament Commentary*. Minneapolis: Fortress.

Boa, Kenneth D., and Robert M. Bowman. 2006. *Faith Has Its Reasons: Integrative Approaches to Defending the Christian Faith*. 2nd ed. Waynesboro, GA: Paternoster.

Bockmuehl, Markus. 2006. *Seeing the Word: Refocusing New Testament Study*. Grand Rapids: Baker Academic.

Bockmuehl, Markus, and Alan J. Torrance, eds. 2008. *Scripture's Doctrine and Theology's Bible: How the New Testament Shapes Christian Dogmatics*. Grand Rapids: Baker Academic.

Booth, Wayne C. 1979. *Critical Understanding: The Powers and Limits of Pluralism*. Chicago: University of Chicago Press.

———. 1988. *The Company We Keep: An Ethics of Fiction*. Berkeley: University of California Press.

Booty, John. 1982. *What Makes Us Episcopalians?* Wilton, CT: Morehouse Barlow.

Borg, Marcus J., and N. T. Wright. 1999. *The Meaning of Jesus: Two Visions*. San Francisco: HarperSanFrancisco.

Boring, M. Eugene, Klaus Berger, and Carsten Colpe, eds. 1995. *Hellenistic Commentary to the New Testament*. Nashville: Abingdon.

Boring, M. Eugene, and Fred B. Craddock. 2004. *The People's New Testament Commentary*. Louisville: Westminster John Knox.

Borsch, Frederick Houk, ed. 1984. *Anglicanism and the Bible*. Wilton, CT: Morehouse Barlow.

Bovon, François. 2002. *Luke 1: A Commentary on the Gospel of Luke 1:1–9:50*. Translated by Christine M. Thomas. Minneapolis: Fortress.

Braaten, Carl E. 1981. "Can We Still Hold the Principle of 'Sola Scriptura'?" *Dialog* 20 (Summer): 189–94.

Braaten, Carl E., and Robert W. Jenson, eds. 1995. *Reclaiming the Bible for the Church*. Grand Rapids: Eerdmans.

Braxton, Brad Ronnell. 2002. *No Longer Slaves: Galatians and African American Experience*. Collegeville, MN: Liturgical Press.

Bromiley, Geoffrey W., ed. 1979–88. *The International Standard Bible Encyclopedia*. Rev. ed. 4 vols. Grand Rapids: Eerdmans.

Brooks, J. A., and C. L. Winbury. 1979. *Syntax of New Testament Greek.* Washington, DC: University Press of America.

Brown, Colin, ed. 1975–85. *New International Dictionary of New Testament Theology.* 3 vols. plus an index vol. Grand Rapids: Zondervan.

———. 1990. *Christianity and Western Thought: A History of Philosophers, Ideas and Movements.* Downers Grove, IL: InterVarsity.

Brown, Raymond E. 1970. *The Gospel according to John XIII–XXI.* New York: Doubleday.

———. 1981. *The Critical Meaning of the Bible.* New York: Paulist Press.

———. 1993. *The Birth of the Messiah: A Commentary on the Infancy Narratives in the Gospels of Matthew and Luke.* Updated ed. New York: Doubleday.

———. 1994. *The Death of the Messiah.* 2 vols. New York: Doubleday.

Brown, Raymond E., Joseph A. Fitzmyer, and Roland E. Murphy, eds. 1990. *The New Jerome Biblical Commentary.* Englewood Cliffs, NJ: Prentice Hall.

Brown, William P., ed. 2002. *Character and Scripture: Moral Formation, Community, and Biblical Interpretation.* Grand Rapids: Eerdmans.

Bruce, F. F. 1969. *New Testament History.* Garden City, NY: Doubleday.

———. 1988. "Scripture in Relation to Tradition and Reason." Pages 35–64 in *Scripture, Tradition, and Reason: A Study in the Criteria of Christian Doctrine.* Edited by Richard Bauckham and Benjamin Drewery. Edinburgh: T&T Clark.

———. 1990. *The Acts of the Apostles: Greek Text with Introduction and Commentary.* 3rd ed. Grand Rapids: Eerdmans.

Bultmann, Rudolf. 1963. *The History of the Synoptic Tradition.* Rev. ed. Oxford: Basil Blackwell.

———. 1971. *The Gospel of John: A Commentary.* Philadelphia: Westminster.

———. 1984. "Is Exegesis without Presuppositions Possible?" Pages 145–53 in *New Testament Theology and Other Basic Writings.* Edited and translated by Schubert M. Ogden. Philadelphia: Fortress.

Burgess, John P. 1998. *Why Scripture Matters: Reading the Bible in a Time of Church Conflict.* Louisville: Westminster John Knox.

Burkert, Walter. 1985. *Greek Religion.* Cambridge, MA: Harvard University Press.

Burridge, Richard A. 1990. "Gospel." Pages 266–68 in *A Dictionary of Biblical Interpretation.* Edited by R. J. Coggins and J. L. Houlden. London: SCM; Philadelphia: Trinity Press International.

———. 2004. *What Are the Gospels? A Comparison with Graeco-Roman Biography.* 2nd ed. Grand Rapids: Eerdmans.

————. 2007. *Imitating Jesus: An Inclusive Approach to New Testament Ethics.* Grand Rapids: Eerdmans.

Burton, Ernest DeWitt. 1900. *Syntax of the Moods and Tenses in New Testament Greek.* Chicago: University of Chicago Press. Reprint, Grand Rapids: Kregel, 1976.

Cadbury, Henry J. 1958. *The Making of Luke-Acts.* London: SPCK.

Caird, G. B. 1980. *The Language and Imagery of the Bible.* Philadelphia: Westminster.

————. 1994. *New Testament Theology.* Completed and edited by L. D. Hurst. Oxford: Clarendon.

Campbell, Ted A. 1991. "Scripture as an Authority in Relation to Other Authorities: A Wesleyan Evangelical Perspective." *Quarterly Review* 11, no. 3 (Fall): 33–40.

Carson, D. A. 2008. *New Testament Commentary Survey.* Grand Rapids: Baker Academic.

Charles, J. Daryl. 1997. "Noncanonical Writings, Citations in the General Epistles." Pages 814–20 in *Dictionary of the Later New Testament and Its Developments.* Edited by Ralph P. Martin and Peter H. Davids. Downers Grove, IL: InterVarsity.

————. 2002. "Passionately Seeking the Truth: Unpunctual Protestant Reflections on *Fides et Ratio.*" *Pro Ecclesia* 11, no. 2 (Spring):133–45.

Charlesworth, James H., ed. 1983–85. *The Old Testament Pseudepigrapha.* 2 vols. Garden City, NY: Doubleday.

Charry, Ellen T. 1993. "Is Christianity Good for Us?" Pages 169–93 in *Reclaiming Faith: Essays on Orthodoxy in the Episcopal Church and the Baltimore Declaration.* Edited by E. Radner and G. Sumner. Grand Rapids: Eerdmans.

Chesterton, Gilbert K. 1959. *Orthodoxy.* Garden City, NY: Doubleday.

Chilcote, Paul Wesley. 2005. "Rethinking the Wesleyan Quadrilateral." *Good News Magazine* (January–February): 22–23.

Childs, Brevard S. 1995. "On Reclaiming the Bible for Christian Theology." Pages 1–17 in *Reclaiming the Bible for the Church.* Edited by Carl E. Braaten and Robert W. Jenson. Grand Rapids: Eerdmans.

Christopher, Joseph P., and Charles E. Spence, eds. 1943. *The Raccolta: Prayers and Devotions Enriched with Indulgences.* 3rd ed. New York: Benziger.

Clark, Kelly James, Richard Lints, and James K. A. Smith. 2004. *101 Key Terms in Philosophy and Their Importance for Theology.* Louisville: Westminster John Knox.

Coggins, R. J., and J. L. Houlden. 1990. *A Dictionary of Biblical Interpretation.* London: SCM; Philadelphia: Trinity Press International.

Collins, John J. 1979. "Introduction: Towards the Morphology of a Genre." Pages 1–20 in *Apocalypse: The Morphology of a Genre*. Semeia 14. Edited by John J. Collins. Atlanta: Society of Biblical Literature.

———. 2000. *Between Athens and Jerusalem: Jewish Identity in the Hellenistic Diaspora*. 2nd ed. Grand Rapids: Eerdmans.

Collins, John J., and Daniel Harlow, eds. 2010. *The Eerdmans Dictionary of Early Judaism*. Grand Rapids: Eerdmans.

Colson, Charles, and Richard John Neuhaus, eds. 2002. *Your Word Is Truth: A Project of Evangelicals and Catholics Together*. Grand Rapids: Eerdmans.

Comfort, Philip W. 2008. *New Testament Text and Translation Commentary*. Carol Stream, IL: Tyndale House.

Congar, Yves M.-J. 1964. *The Meaning of Tradition*. New York: Hawthorn.

———. 1967. *Tradition and Traditions: An Historical and a Theological Essay*. New York: Macmillan.

Cosgrove, Charles H. 2002. *Appealing to Scripture in Moral Debate: Five Hermeneutical Rules*. Grand Rapids: Eerdmans.

———, ed. 2004. *The Meanings We Choose: Hermeneutical Ethics, Indeterminacy, and the Conflict of Interpretations*. London: T&T Clark.

Cousins, Ewert, ed. 1978. *Bonaventure*. Classics of Western Spirituality. New York: Paulist Press.

Croatto, J. Severino. 1987. *Biblical Hermeneutics: Toward a Theory of Reading as the Production of Meaning*. Maryknoll, NY: Orbis.

Cross, F. L., and E. A. Livingstone, eds. 1997. *The Oxford Dictionary of the Christian Church*. 3rd ed. New York: Oxford University Press.

Croy, N. Clayton. 1998. *Endurance in Suffering: Hebrews 12:1–13 in Its Rhetorical, Religious, and Philosophical Context*. Society for New Testament Studies Monograph Series 98. Cambridge: Cambridge University Press.

———. 2001. "A Case Study in Translators' Bias: Could a Woman Have Been an Apostle—Even 'Prominent among the Apostles'?" *Priscilla Papers* 15 (Spring): 9.

———. 2003. *The Mutilation of Mark's Gospel*. Nashville: Abingdon.

———. 2007. "By Faith Sarah . . . (Heb. 11:11)." *Priscilla Papers* 21 (Winter): 9.

Dana, H. E., and Julius R. Mantey. 1927. *A Manual Grammar of the Greek New Testament*. Toronto: Macmillan.

Danby, Herbert. 1933. *The Mishnah: Translated from the Hebrew with Introduction and Brief Explanatory Notes*. New York: Oxford University Press.

D'Angelo, Mary Rose. 1998. "Hebrews." Pages 455–59 in *Women's Bible Commentary*. Exp. ed. Edited by Carol A. Newsom and Sharon H. Ringe. Louisville: Westminster John Knox.

Danker, Frederick W., ed. 2000. *A Greek-English Lexicon of the New Testament and Other Early Christian Literature*. 3rd ed. Based on a German lexicon edited by Walter Bauer and on previous English editions by W. F. Arndt, F. W. Gingrich, and F. W. Danker. Chicago: University of Chicago Press.

————. 2003. *Multipurpose Tools for Bible Study*. Rev. and exp. ed., with CD-ROM. Minneapolis: Fortress.

Davis, Ellen F., and Richard B. Hays, eds. 2003. *The Art of Reading Scripture*. Grand Rapids: Eerdmans.

Davis, Stephen T. 2006. "What Do We Mean When We Say, 'The Bible Is True'?" Pages 86–103 in *But Is It All True? The Bible and the Question of Truth*. Edited by Alan G. Padgett and Patrick R. Keifert. Grand Rapids: Eerdmans.

Deissmann, G. Adolf. 1901. *Bible Studies*. Edinburgh: T&T Clark.

————. 1927. *Light from the Ancient East*. 4th ed. London: Hodder & Stoughton.

deSilva, David A. 2000a. *Honor, Patronage, Kinship and Purity: Unlocking New Testament Culture*. Downers Grove, IL: InterVarsity.

————. 2000b. *Perseverance in Gratitude: A Socio-Rhetorical Commentary on the Epistle "to the Hebrews."* Grand Rapids: Eerdmans.

————. 2004. *An Introduction to the New Testament: Contexts, Methods, and Ministry Formation*. Downers Grove, IL: InterVarsity.

Dibelius, Martin. 1935. *From Tradition to Gospel*. New York: Charles Scriber's Sons.

————. 2004. *The Book of Acts: Form, Style, and Theology*. Edited by K. C. Hanson. Minneapolis: Fortress.

Dimant, Devorah. 1992. "Pesharim, Qumran." Pages 244–51 in vol. 5 of *The Anchor Bible Dictionary*. Edited by David Noel Freedman. New York: Doubleday.

Dodd, C. H. 1936. *The Parables of the Kingdom*. London: Nisbet.

Donaldson, T. L. 1983. "Parallels: Use, Misuse, and Limitations." *Evangelical Quarterly* 55:193–210.

Douglas, J. D., and Merrill C. Tenney, eds. 1999. *New International Bible Dictionary*. Rev. ed. Grand Rapids: Zondervan.

Dowling, William C. 1983. "Intentionless Meaning." *Critical Inquiry* 9 (June): 784–89.

Dunn, James D. G. 1988a. *The Living Word*. Philadelphia: Fortress.

————. 1988b. *Romans 9–16*. Word Biblical Commentary 38B. Dallas: Word.

————. 2003a. "Criteria for a Wise Reading of a Biblical Text." Pages 38–52 in *Reading Texts, Seeking Wisdom*. Edited by David F. Ford and Graham Stanton. Grand Rapids: Eerdmans.

————. 2003b. *Jesus Remembered*. Vol. 1 of *Christianity in the Making*. Grand Rapids: Eerdmans.

Eagleton, Terry. 1983. *Literary Theory: An Introduction.* Minneapolis: University of Minnesota Press.

Eichele, George, et al., the Bible and Culture Collective. 1995. *The Postmodern Bible.* New Haven: Yale University Press.

Elliott, John H. 1981. *A Home for the Homeless: A Sociological Exegesis of 1 Peter, Its Situation, and Strategy.* Philadelphia: Fortress.

————. 1993. *What Is Social-Science Criticism?* Minneapolis: Fortress.

Ellison, Marvin M., and Sylvia Thorson-Smith, eds. 2003. *Body and Soul: Rethinking Sexuality as Justice-Love.* Cleveland: Pilgrim.

Epp, Eldon J. 1997. "Textual Criticism in the Exegesis of the New Testament, with an Excursus on Canon." Pages 45–97 in *A Handbook to the Exegesis of the New Testament.* Edited by Stanley E. Porter. Boston: Brill.

————. 2005. *Junia: The First Woman Apostle.* Minneapolis: Fortress.

Ericksen, Robert P. 1985. *Theologians under Hitler: Gerhard Kittel, Paul Althaus, and Emanuel Hirsch.* London; New Haven: Yale University Press.

Esler, Philip. 1995. *Modeling Early Christianity: Social-Scientific Studies of the New Testament in Its Context.* New York: Routledge.

————, ed. 2000. *The Early Christian World.* 2 vols. London and New York: Routledge.

Evans, Craig A., ed. 2004. *From Prophecy to Testament: The Function of the Old Testament in the New.* Peabody, MA: Hendrickson.

————. 2005. *Ancient Texts for New Testament Studies: A Guide to the Background Literature.* Peabody, MA: Hendrickson.

Evans, Craig A., and Stanley E. Porter, eds. 2000. *Dictionary of New Testament Background.* Downers Grove, IL: InterVarsity.

Fackre, Gabriel. 1987. *The Christian Story: A Pastoral Systematics.* Vol. 2, *Authority: Scripture in the Church for the World.* Grand Rapids: Eerdmans.

Fee, Gordon D. 1993. *New Testament Exegesis: A Handbook for Students and Pastors.* Rev. ed. Louisville: Westminster John Knox.

————. 2000. *Listening to the Spirit in the Text.* Grand Rapids: Eerdmans.

Felder, Cain Hope, ed. 1991. *Stony the Road We Trod: African American Biblical Interpretation.* Minneapolis: Fortress.

Ferguson, Everett, ed. 1998. *Encyclopedia of Early Christianity.* 2nd ed. New York: Garland.

————. 2003. *Backgrounds of Early Christianity.* 3rd ed. Grand Rapids: Eerdmans.

Filson, F. V. 1982. "Gospels, Synoptic." Pages 532–36 in vol. 2 of *The International Standard Bible Encyclopedia.* Edited by Geoffrey W. Bromiley. Rev. ed. Grand Rapids: Eerdmans.

Fish, Stanley. 1980. *Is There a Text in This Class? The Authority of Interpretive Communities.* Cambridge, MA: Harvard University Press.

Fitzgerald, J. T. 1988. *Cracks in an Earthen Vessel: An Examination of the Catalogue of Hardships in the Corinthian Correspondence.* Atlanta: Scholars Press.

Fowl, Stephen E., ed. 1997. *The Theological Interpretation of Scripture: Classic and Contemporary Readings.* Cambridge, MA: Blackwell.

———. 1998. *Engaging Scripture: A Model for Theological Interpretation.* Malden, MA: Blackwell.

———. 2000. "The Role of Authorial Intention in the Theological Interpretation of Scripture." Pages 71–87 in *Between Two Horizons: Spanning New Testament Studies and Systematic Theology.* Edited by Joel B. Green and Max Turner. Grand Rapids: Eerdmans.

France, R. T. 1999. "From Romans to the Real World: Biblical Principles and Cultural Change in Relation to Homosexuality and the Ministry of Women." Pages 234–53 in *Romans and the People of God: Essays in Honor of Gordon D. Fee on the Occasion of His Sixty-fifth Birthday.* Edited by Sven K. Soderlund and N. T. Wright. Grand Rapids: Eerdmans.

———. 2002. *The Gospel of Mark: A Commentary on the Greek Text.* Grand Rapids: Eerdmans.

France, R. T., et al., eds. 1994. *New Bible Commentary: 21st Century Edition.* Downers Grove, IL: InterVarsity.

Francis, Fred O., and J. Paul Sampley. 1992. *Pauline Parallels.* 2nd ed. Minneapolis: Fortress.

Freedman, David Noel., ed. 1992. *The Anchor Bible Dictionary.* 6 vols. New York: Doubleday.

———. 2000. *Eerdmans Dictionary of the Bible.* Grand Rapids: Eerdmans.

Frei, Hans W. 1974. *The Eclipse of Biblical Narrative: A Study in Eighteenth and Nineteenth Century Hermeneutics.* New Haven: Yale University Press.

———. 1992. *Types of Christian Theology.* Edited by George Hunsinger and William C. Placher. New Haven: Yale University Press.

Frye, Northrop. 1962. *Fearful Symmetry: A Study of William Blake.* Boston: Beacon.

Gagarin, Michael, ed. 2010. *The Oxford Encyclopedia of Ancient Greece and Rome.* 7 vols. New York: Oxford University Press.

Gagnon, Robert A. J. 2001. *The Bible and Homosexual Practice: Texts and Hermeneutics.* Nashville: Abingdon.

Gallagher, Michael Paul. 1988. *Help My Unbelief.* Chicago: Loyola University Press.

Gebler, Karl von. 1879. *Galileo Galilei and the Roman Curia*. Translated by Jane Sturge. London: C. K. Paul. Reprint, Merrick, NY: Richwood Publishing, 1977.

Gildas, M. 1913. "Bernard of Clairvaux." Pages 498–501 in vol. 2 of *The Catholic Encyclopedia*. Edited by Charles G. Herbermann. New York: The Encyclopedia Press.

Gillingham, Susan. 2002. *The Image, the Depths, and the Surface: Multivalent Approaches to Biblical Study*. Sheffield: Sheffield Academic Press.

Glynn, John. 2007. *Commentary and Reference Survey: A Comprehensive Guide to Biblical and Theological Resources*. Grand Rapids: Kregel.

Goldingay, John. 1994. *Models of Scripture*. Grand Rapids: Eerdmans.

———. 1995. *Models of the Interpretation of Scripture*. Grand Rapids: Eerdmans.

González, Catherine Gunsalus. 1999. *How United Methodists Study Scripture*. Nashville: Abingdon.

González, Justo L. 1996. *Santa Biblia: The Bible through Hispanic Eyes*. Nashville: Abingdon.

Gorman, Michael J. 2001. *Elements of Biblical Exegesis: A Basic Guide for Students and Ministers*. Peabody, MA: Hendrickson.

Gottwald, Norman K. 1995. "Framing Biblical Interpretation at New York Theological Seminary: A Student Self-Inventory on Biblical Hermeneutics." Pages 251–61 in *Reading from this Place*. Vol. 1, *Social Location and Biblical Interpretation in the United States*. Edited by Fernando F. Segovia and Mary Ann Tolbert. Minneapolis: Fortress.

Green, Joel B., ed. 1995. *Hearing the New Testament: Strategies for Interpretation*. Grand Rapids: Eerdmans.

———. Review of François Bovon, *Luke 1: A Commentary on the Gospel of Luke 1:1–9:50*. *Review of Biblical Literature* (http://www.bookreviews.org).

———. 2005a. "Commentary." Pages 123–27 in *Dictionary for Theological Interpretation of the Bible*. Edited by Kevin J. Vanhoozer. Grand Rapids: Baker Academic.

———. 2005b. "Dictionaries and Encyclopedias." Pages 175–77 in *Dictionary for Theological Interpretation of the Bible*. Edited by Kevin J. Vanhoozer. Grand Rapids: Baker Academic.

———. 2007a. "Introducing the *Journal of Theological Interpretation*." *Journal of Theological Interpretation* 1, no. 1: i–ii.

———. 2007b. *Seized by Truth: Reading the Bible as Scripture*. Nashville: Abingdon.

Green, Joel B., and Max Turner, eds. 2000. *Between Two Horizons: Spanning New Testament Studies and Systematic Theology*. Grand Rapids: Eerdmans.

Green, Joel B., Scot McKnight, and I. Howard Marshall, eds. 1992. *Dictionary of Jesus and the Gospels*. Downers Grove, IL: InterVarsity.

Greene-McCreight, Kathryn. 2005. "Rule of Faith." Pages 703–4 in *Dictionary for Theological Interpretation of the Bible*. Edited by Kevin J. Vanhoozer. Grand Rapids: Baker Academic.

Greenslade, S. L., ed. 1956. *Early Latin Theology: Selections from Tertullian, Cyprian, Ambrose, and Jerome*. Library of Christian Classics 5. Philadelphia: Westminster.

Grobel, K. 1962. "Gospels." Page 449 in *The Interpreter's Dictionary of the Bible*. Vol. 2. Edited by George Arthur Buttrick. Nashville: Abingdon.

Gunn, David M. 1993. "Narrative Criticism." Pages 171–95 in *To Each Its Own Meaning: An Introduction to Biblical Criticisms and Their Application*. Edited by Steven L. McKenzie and Stephen R. Haynes. Louisville: Westminster John Knox.

Gunter, W. Stephen, et al. 1997. *Wesley and the Quadrilateral: Renewing the Conversation*. Nashville: Abingdon.

Guthrie, George H. 2007. "Hebrews." Pages 919–95 in *Commentary on the New Testament Use of the Old Testament*. Edited by G. K. Beale and D. A. Carson. Grand Rapids: Baker Academic.

Hagen, Kenneth, ed. 1994. *The Quadrilog: Tradition and the Future of Ecumenism; Essays in Honor of George H. Tavard*. Collegeville, MN: Liturgical Press.

Hahn, Scott. 2003. *Scripture Matters: Essays on Reading the Bible from the Heart of the Church*. Steubenville, OH: Emmaus Road Publishing.

Hall, David R. 1990. *The Seven Pillories of Wisdom*. Macon, GA: Mercer.

Hanson, Paul D. 1989. "Biblical Authority Reconsidered." *Horizons in Biblical Theology* 11:57–79.

———. 1992. "Biblical Authority Today." *Dialog* 31:176–80.

Hatch, Edwin, and Henry A. Redpath, eds. 1998. *A Concordance to the Septuagint and the Other Greek Versions of the Old Testament*. 2nd ed. Grand Rapids: Baker Academic.

Hauerwas, Stanley. 1974. "Love's Not All You Need." Pages 111–26 in *Vision and Virtue: Essays in Christian Ethical Reflection*. Notre Dame, IN: Fides Publishers.

Hawthorne, Gerald F., Ralph P. Martin, and D. G. Reid, eds. 1993. *Dictionary of Paul and His Letters*. Downers Grove, IL: InterVarsity.

Hayes, John H., ed. 1999. *Dictionary of Biblical Interpretation*. Nashville: Abingdon.

Hayes, John H., and Carl R. Holladay. 1987. *Biblical Exegesis: A Beginner's Handbook*. Rev. ed. Atlanta: John Knox.

———. 2007. *Biblical Exegesis: A Beginner's Handbook*. 3rd ed. Louisville: Westminster John Knox.

Hays, Richard B. 1989. *Echoes of Scripture in the Letters of Paul*. New Haven and London: Yale University Press.

———. 1996. *The Moral Vision of the New Testament: A Contemporary Introduction to New Testament Ethics*. San Francisco: HarperSanFrancisco.

———. 1997. "Salvation by Trust? Reading the Bible Faithfully." *Christian Century* 114 (February 26): 218–23.

Helyer, Larry R. 2002. *Exploring Jewish Literature of the Second Temple Period: A Guide for New Testament Students*. Downers Grove, IL: InterVarsity.

Hemer, Colin J. 1990. *The Book of Acts in the Setting of Hellenistic History*. Winona Lake, IN: Eisenbrauns.

———. 2001. *The Letters to the Seven Churches of Asia in Their Local Setting*. Grand Rapids: Eerdmans.

Hengel, Martin. 1974. *Judaism and Hellenism: Studies in Their Encounter in Palestine During the Early Hellenistic Period*. 2 vols. Philadelphia: Fortress.

Hinlicky, Paul R. 1999. "The Lutheran Dilemma." *Pro Ecclesia* 8, no. 4:391–422.

Hirsch, E. D. 1967. *Validity in Interpretation*. New Haven: Yale University Press.

Hodgson, R. 1983. "Paul the Apostle and First-Century Tribulation Lists." *Zeitschrift für die neutestamentliche Wissenschaft und die Kunde der älteren Kirche* 74:59–80.

Hooker, Richard. 1977. *Of the Laws of Ecclesiastical Polity*. Book 5 in vol. 2. Edited by W. Speed Hill. Folger Library Edition. Cambridge, MA: Belknap Press of Harvard University Press.

Hornblower, Simon, and Anthony Spawforth, eds. 1996. *The Oxford Classical Dictionary*. 3rd ed. New York: Oxford University Press.

Horsley, G. H. R., ed. 1981–89. *New Documents Illustrating Early Christianity*. Vols. 1–5. North Ryde, N.S.W., Australia: Ancient History Documentary Research Centre, Macquarie University.

Horsley, Richard. 1994. "Jesus, Itinerant Cynic or Israelite Prophet?" Pages 68–97 in *Images of Jesus Today*. Edited by James H. Charlesworth and Walter P. Weaver. Valley Forge, PA: Trinity Press International.

Horst, Pieter Willem van der. 1992a. "Corpus Hellenisticum Novi Testamenti." Pages 1157–61 in vol. 1 of *The Anchor Bible Dictionary*. Edited by David Noel Freedman. New York: Doubleday.

———. 1992b. "Did Sarah Have a Seminal Emission?" *Bible Review* (February): 35–39.

Huffman, D. S. 1992. "Genealogy." Pages 253–59 in *Dictionary of Jesus and the Gospels*. Edited by Joel B. Green, Scot McKnight, and I. Howard Marshall. Downers Grove, IL: InterVarsity.

Hultgren, Arland J. 2000. *The Parables of Jesus: A Commentary*. Grand Rapids: Eerdmans.

Hultsch, F., ed. 1876–78. *Pappi Alexandrini Collectionis: Quae supersunt.* 3 vols. Berlin: Weidmann.

Ingraffia, Brian D. 1995. *Postmodern Theory and Biblical Theology: Vanquishing God's Shadow.* Cambridge: Cambridge University Press.

Instone-Brewer, David. 2004–. *Traditions of the Rabbis from the Era of the New Testament.* Vols. 1–. Grand Rapids: Eerdmans.

Iseminger, Gary, ed. 1992. *Intention and Interpretation.* Philadelphia: Temple University Press.

Iser, Wolfgang. 1978. *The Act of Reading: A Theory of Aesthetic Response.* Baltimore and London: Johns Hopkins University Press.

Jasper, David. 2004. *A Short Introduction to Hermeneutics.* Louisville: Westminster John Knox.

Jeffers, James S. 1999. *The Greco-Roman World of the New Testament Era: Exploring the Background of Early Christianity.* Downers Grove, IL: InterVarsity.

Jeremias, Joachim. 1963. *The Parables of Jesus.* 2nd ed. New York: Charles Scribner's Sons.

Jodock, D. 1989. *The Church's Bible: Its Contemporary Authority.* Minneapolis: Fortress.

John Paul II, Pope. 1998. *Fides et Ratio: Encyclical Letter on the Relationship between Faith and Reason.* Boston: Pauline Books & Media.

Johnson, Luke Timothy. 1989. "The New Testament's Anti-Jewish Slander and the Conventions of Ancient Polemic." *Journal of Biblical Literature* 108:419–41.

———. 1995. *The Letter of James: A New Translation with Introduction and Commentary.* New York: Doubleday.

———. 1996. *Scripture and Discernment: Decision Making in the Church.* Nashville: Abingdon.

———. 1998. "Imagining the World Scripture Imagines." *Modern Theology* 14, no. 2 (April): 165–80.

———. 1999. *The Writings of the New Testament: An Interpretation.* Rev. ed., with CD-ROM. Minneapolis: Fortress.

Johnson, Marshall D. 1998. *The Purpose of the Biblical Genealogies.* 2nd ed. Cambridge: Cambridge University Press.

———. 2002. *Making Sense of the Bible: Literary Type as an Approach to Understanding.* Grand Rapids: Eerdmans.

Johnston, Robert K., ed. 1985. *The Use of the Bible in Theology: Evangelical Options.* Atlanta: John Knox.

Juhl, P. D. 1980. *Interpretation: An Essay in the Philosophy of Literary Criticism.* Princeton: Princeton University Press.

———. 1983. "Stanley Fish's Interpretive Communities and the Status of Critical Interpretations." *Comparative Criticism* 5:47–58.

Kannengiesser, Charles. 2006. *Handbook of Patristic Exegesis: The Bible in Ancient Christianity*. Leiden: Brill.

Karris, R. J. 1996. *A Symphony of New Testament Hymns*. Collegeville, MN: Liturgical Press.

Keble, John, ed. 1888. *The Works of That Learned and Judicious Divine Mr. Richard Hooker*. Revised by R. W. Church and F. Paget. Vol. 2. 7th ed. New York: Burt Franklin.

Keck, Leander E., ed. 1994. *Genesis to Leviticus*. Vol. 1 of *The New Interpreter's Bible*. Nashville: Abingdon.

Kee, Howard C. 1983. *Miracle in the Early Christian World*. New Haven: Yale University Press.

Kelly, J. N. D. 1972. *Early Christian Creeds*. 3rd ed. New York: Longman.

Kelsey, David H. 1975. *Uses of Scripture in Recent Theology*. Philadelphia: Fortress.

Kennedy, George. 1984. *New Testament Interpretation through Rhetorical Criticism*. Chapel Hill: University of North Carolina Press.

Kermode, Frank. 1979. *The Genesis of Secrecy: On the Interpretation of Narrative*. Cambridge, MA: Harvard University Press.

Kimball, Roger. 1998. *Tenured Radicals: How Politics Has Corrupted Our Higher Education*. Rev. ed. Chicago: Ivan R. Dee.

Kittel, Gerhard, and Gerhard Friedrich, eds. 1985. *Theological Dictionary of the New Testament: Abridged in One Volume*. Grand Rapids: Eerdmans.

———. 1964–76. *Theological Dictionary of the New Testament*. Translated by G. W. Bromiley. 10 vols. Grand Rapids: Eerdmans.

Klauck, Hans-Josef. 2003. *The Religious Context of Early Christianity: A Guide to Graeco-Roman Religions*. Minneapolis: Fortress.

———. 2006. *Ancient Letters and the New Testament: A Guide to Context and Exegesis*. Waco: Baylor University Press.

Knapp, Steven, and Walter Benn Michaels. 1982. "Against Theory." *Critical Inquiry* 8 (Summer): 723–42.

Koester, Craig R. 2001. *Hebrews: A New Translation with Introduction and Commentary*. Anchor Bible 36. New York: Doubleday.

Kohlenberger, John R., III and Edward W. Goodrick. 1999. *The NIV Exhaustive Concordance*. 2nd ed. Grand Rapids: Zondervan.

Kohlenberger, John R., III, Edward W. Goodrick, and James A. Swanson. 1995. *The Exhaustive Concordance to the Greek New Testament*. Grand Rapids: Zondervan.

————. 1997. *The Greek-English Concordance to the New Testament*. Grand Rapids: Zondervan.

Kohlenberger, John R., III and Richard E. Whitaker. 2000. *The Analytical Concordance to the New Revised Standard Version of the New Testament*. Grand Rapids: Eerdmans; New York: Oxford University Press.

Koop, Karl, and Mary H. Schertz, eds. 2000. *Without Spot or Wrinkle: Reflecting Theologically on the Nature of the Church*. Elkhart, IN: Institute of Mennonite Studies.

Koptak, Paul E. 2005. "Intertextuality." Pages 332–34 in *Dictionary for Theological Interpretation of the Bible*. Edited by Kevin J. Vanhoozer. Grand Rapids: Baker Academic.

Kreeft, Peter. 1993. *Christianity for Modern Pagans: Pascal's Pensées*. Fort Collins, CO: Ignatius.

Kreeft, Peter, and Ronald K. Tacelli. 1994. *Handbook of Christian Apologetics*. Downers Grove, IL: InterVarsity.

Kroeger, Catherine Clark, and Mary J. Evans, eds. 2002. *The IVP Women's Bible Commentary*. Downers Grove, IL: InterVarsity.

Kruse, Colin G. 1993a. "Afflictions, Trials, Hardships." Pages 18–20 in *Dictionary of Paul and His Letters*. Edited by Gerald F. Hawthorne, Ralph P. Martin, and Daniel G. Reid. Downers Grove, IL: InterVarsity.

————. 1993b. "Virtues and Vices." Pages 962–63 in *Dictionary of Paul and His Letters*. Edited by Gerald F. Hawthorne, Ralph P. Martin, and Daniel G. Reid. Downers Grove, IL: InterVarsity.

Küng, Hans. 1980. "Toward a New Consensus in Catholic (and Ecumenical) Theology." Pages 1–17 in *Consensus in Theology? A Dialogue with Hans Küng and Edward Schillebeeckx*. Edited by Leonard Swidler. Philadelphia: Westminster.

Kurz, William S. 1990. *Farewell Addresses in the New Testament*. Collegeville, MN: Liturgical Press.

Lachs, Samuel Tobias. 1987. *A Rabbinic Commentary on the New Testament: The Gospels of Matthew, Mark, and Luke*. Hoboken, NJ: Ktav.

Lampe, Geoffrey W. H., ed. 1961. *A Patristic Greek Lexicon*. Oxford and New York: Clarendon.

Lancaster, Sarah Heaner. 2002. *Women and the Authority of Scripture: A Narrative Approach*. Harrisburg, PA: Trinity Press International.

Lane, A. N. S. 1975. "Scripture, Tradition, and Church: An Historical Survey." *Vox evangelica* 9:37–55.

————. 1994. "*Sola Scriptura*? Making Sense of a Post-Reformation Slogan." Pages 297–327 in *A Pathway into the Holy Scripture*. Edited by P. E. Satterthwaite and D. F. Wright. Grand Rapids: Eerdmans.

Langford, Thomas A., ed. 1991. *Doctrine and Theology in the United Methodist Church*. Nashville: Abingdon.

Larson, Gary. 1982. *The Far Side*. Kansas City, MO: Andrews & McMeel.

Lash, Nicholas. 1986. *Theology on the Way to Emmaus*. London: SCM Press.

Levison, John R., and Priscilla Pope-Levison. 2004. *Return to Babel: Global Perspectives on the Bible*. Louisville: Westminster John Knox.

Lewis, Hunter, ed. *The Words of Jesus*. 1998. Mount Jackson, VA: Axios.

Lichtenberg, Georg Christoph. 2000. *The Waste Books*. Translated with an introduction and notes by R. J. Hollingdale. New York: New York Review Books.

Liddell, Henry G., and Robert Scott. 1940. *A Greek-English Lexicon*. 9th ed. Revised and augmented by Henry S. Jones. With a 1968 supplement. Oxford: Oxford University Press.

Lightfoot, John. 1979. *A Commentary on the New Testament from the Talmud and Hebraica: Matthew–1 Corinthians*. 4 vols. Grand Rapids: Baker Academic. Reprint of a seventeenth-century work.

Llewelyn, S. R., ed. 1992–2002. *New Documents Illustrating Early Christianity*. Vols. 6–9. Grand Rapids: Eerdmans.

Lohse, Bernhard. 1986. *Martin Luther: An Introduction to His Life and Work*. Philadelphia: Fortress.

Louw, J. P. 1982. *Semantics of New Testament Greek*. Atlanta: Scholars Press.

Louw, J. P., and Eugene A. Nida, eds. 1988. *Greek-English Lexicon of the New Testament Based on Semantic Domains*. 2 vols. New York: United Bible Societies.

Lust, J., E. Eynikel, and K. Hauspie, eds. 1992–96. *A Greek-English Lexicon of the Septuagint*. 2 vols. Stuttgart: Deutsche Bibelgesellschaft.

Luther, Martin. 1959. *Luther's Works*. Vol. 51, *Sermons*. Edited by Helmut T. Lehmann. Philadelphia: Fortress.

———. 1962. *Luther's Works*. Vol. 45, *The Christian in Society*. Edited by Walther I. Brandt. Philadelphia: Muhlenberg.

Luz, Ulrich. 1989. *Matthew 1–7: A Commentary*. Translated by Wilhelm C. Linss. Minneapolis: Augsburg Fortress.

Lyon, Robert W. 1982. "Evangelicals and Critical Historical Method." Pages 135–64 in *Interpreting God's Word for Today: An Inquiry into Hermeneutics from a Biblical Theological Perspective*. Edited by Wayne McCown and James Earl Massey. Anderson, IN: Warner.

Macey, David. 2000. *The Penguin Dictionary of Critical Theory*. New York: Penguin.

Malherbe, Abraham J. 1986. *Moral Exhortation: A Greco-Roman Sourcebook*. Philadelphia: Westminster.

Malina, Bruce J. 1996. *The Social World of Jesus and the Gospels*. New York: Routledge.

———. 2001. *The New Testament World: Insights from Cultural Anthropology*. 3rd ed. Louisville: Westminster John Knox.

Marshall, I. Howard. 2004. *Beyond the Bible: Moving from Scripture to Theology*. Grand Rapids: Baker Academic.

Marshall, I. Howard, et al., eds. 1996. *New Bible Dictionary*. 3rd ed. Downers Grove, IL: InterVarsity.

Martin, Dale B. 2006. *Sex and the Single Savior: Gender and Sexuality in Biblical Interpretation*. Louisville: Westminster John Knox.

———. 2008. *Pedagogy of the Bible: An Analysis and Proposal*. Louisville: Westminster John Knox.

Martin, Ralph P. 1993a. "Creed." Pages 190–92 in *Dictionary of Paul and His Letters*. Edited by Gerald F. Hawthorne, Ralph P. Martin, and Daniel G. Reid. Downers Grove, IL: InterVarsity.

———. 1993b. "Hymns, Hymn Fragments, Songs, Spiritual Songs." Pages 419–23 in *Dictionary of Paul and His Letters*. Edited by Gerald F. Hawthorne, Ralph P. Martin, and Daniel G. Reid. Downers Grove, IL: InterVarsity.

Martin, Ralph P., and Peter H. Davids, eds. 1997. *Dictionary of the Later New Testament and Its Developments*. Downers Grove, IL: InterVarsity.

Marty, Martin. 2004. *Martin Luther*. New York: Penguin.

Marxsen, Willi. 1993. *New Testament Foundations for Christian Ethics*. Minneapolis: Fortress.

Mathison, Keith A. 2001. *The Shape of Sola Scriptura*. Moscow, ID: Canon Press.

Mays, James L., et al., eds. 2000. *HarperCollins Bible Commentary*. Rev. ed. San Francisco: HarperSanFrancisco.

McGing, Brian, and Judith Mossman, eds. 2006. *The Limits of Ancient Biography*. Swansea: Classical Press of Wales.

McGrath, Alister E. 1999. *Reformation Thought: An Introduction*. 3rd ed. Oxford: Blackwell.

Meadors, Gary T., ed. 2009. *Four Views on Moving beyond the Bible to Theology*. Grand Rapids: Zondervan.

Meeks, Wayne A. 2004. "A Nazi New Testament Professor Reads His Bible: The Strange Case of Gerhard Kittel." Pages 513–44 in *The Idea of Biblical Interpretation: Essays in Honor of James L. Kugel*. Edited by Hindy Najman and Judith H. Newman. Leiden: Brill.

———. 2005. "Why Study the New Testament?" *New Testament Studies* 51:155–70.

Meier, John P. 1994. *A Marginal Jew*. Vol. 2, *Rethinking the Historical Jesus—Mentor, Message, and Miracles*. New York: Doubleday.

Metzger, Bruce M. 1994. *A Textual Commentary on the Greek New Testament*. 2nd ed. Stuttgart: Deutsche Bibelgesellschaft.

Metzger, Bruce M., and Bart D. Ehrman. 2005. *The Text of the New Testament: Its Transmission, Corruption, and Restoration*. 4th ed. New York: Oxford University Press.

Meyer, Ben F. 1989. *Critical Realism and the New Testament*. Allison Park, PA: Pickwick.

————. 1994. *Reality and Illusion in New Testament Scholarship: A Primer in Critical Realist Hermeneutics*. Collegeville, MN: Liturgical Press.

Moberly, R. W. L. 2000. *The Bible, Theology, and Faith: A Study of Abraham and Jesus*. Cambridge: Cambridge University Press.

Monroe, Ann. 2000. *The Word: Imagining the Gospel in Modern America*. Louisville: Westminster John Knox.

Montague, George T. 1997. *Understanding the Bible: A Basic Introduction to Biblical Interpretation*. New York: Paulist Press.

Moore, Stephen D. 1989. *Literary Criticism and the Gospels: The Theoretical Challenge*. New Haven and London: Yale University Press.

Morgan, Robert, with John Barton. 1988. *Biblical Interpretation*. Oxford: Oxford University Press.

Morris, Thomas V., ed. 1994. *God and the Philosophers: The Reconciliation of Faith and Reason*. New York: Oxford University Press.

Moule, C. F. D. 1959. *An Idiom Book of New Testament Greek*. 2nd ed. Cambridge: Cambridge University Press.

Moulton, James Hope, et al. 1908–76. *A Grammar of New Testament Greek*. Edinburgh: T&T Clark. Vol. 1, *Prolegomena*, 1908. Vol. 2, *Accidence and Word Formation*, by W. F. Howard, 1929. Vol. 3, *Syntax*, by Nigel Turner, 1963. Vol. 4, *Style*, by Nigel Turner, 1976.

Moulton, James Hope, and George Milligan. 1930. *The Vocabulary of the Greek Testament Illustrated from the Papyri and Other Non-literary Sources*. Grand Rapids: Eerdmans.

Moulton, W. F., and A. S. Geden. 1978. *A Concordance to the Greek Testament*. Revised by H. K. Moulton. 5th ed. Edinburgh: T&T Clark.

Muraoka, T. 2009. *A Greek-English Lexicon of the Septuagint*. 3rd ed. Leuven: Peeters.

Neuhaus, Richard John, ed. 1989. *Biblical Interpretation in Crisis: The Ratzinger Conference on Bible and Church*. Grand Rapids: Eerdmans.

Newbigin, Lesslie. 1996. *Truth and Authority in Modernity*. Valley Forge, PA: Trinity Press International.

Newsom, Carol A., and Sharon H. Ringe, eds. 1998. *The Women's Bible Commentary*. Exp. ed. Louisville: Westminster John Knox.

Nichols, Aidan. 1991. *The Shape of Catholic Theology: An Introduction to Its Sources, Principles, and History*. Collegeville, MN: Liturgical Press.

Nickelsburg, George W. E. 2005. *Jewish Literature between the Bible and the Mishnah*. 2nd ed., with CD-ROM. Minneapolis: Fortress.

Nietzsche, Friedrich. 1967. *The Will to Power*. Translated and edited by Walter Kaufmann. New York: Random House.

Nock, Arthur Darby. 1972. *Essays on Religion and the Ancient World*. Edited by Zeph Stewart. Cambridge, MA: Harvard University Press.

O'Brien, Peter T. 1993. "Benediction, Blessing, Doxology, Thanksgiving." Pages 68–71 in *Dictionary of Paul and His Letters*. Edited by Gerald F. Hawthorne, Ralph P. Martin, and Daniel G. Reid. Downers Grove, IL: InterVarsity.

O'Collins, Gerald, and Daniel Kendall. 1997. *The Bible for Theology: Ten Principles for the Theological Use of Scripture*. New York: Paulist Press.

O'Day, Gail R. 1995. *The Gospel of John*. Vol. 9 of *The New Interpreter's Bible*. Nashville: Abingdon.

————. 1999. "Intertextuality." Pages 646–48 in *Dictionary of Biblical Interpretation*. Edited by John H. Hayes. Nashville: Abingdon.

O'Day, Gail R., and David L. Petersen, eds. 2009. *Theological Bible Commentary*. Louisville: Westminster John Knox.

Oden, Thomas C., and Leicester R. Longden. 1991. *The Wesleyan Theological Heritage: Essays of Albert C. Outler*. Grand Rapids: Zondervan.

Ogden, C. K., and I. A. Richards. 1989. *The Meaning of Meaning: A Study of the Influence of Language upon Thought and of the Science of Symbolism*. New York: Harcourt Brace Jovanovich. Reprint of the 1923 original.

O'Keefe, John J., and R. R. Reno. 2005. *Sanctified Vision: An Introduction to Early Christian Interpretation of the Bible*. Baltimore: Johns Hopkins University Press.

Ollenburger, Ben C. 2000. "*Sola Scriptura*/No Other Foundation and Other Authoritative Sources?" Pages 65–92 in *Without Spot or Wrinkle: Reflecting Theologically on the Nature of the Church*. Edited by Karl Koop and Mary H. Schertz. Elkhart, IN: Institute of Mennonite Studies.

Olson, Roger E. 2003. "The Tradition Temptation: Why We Should Still Give Scripture Pride of Place." *Christianity Today* (November): 52–55.

Osborne, Grant R. 1991. *The Hermeneutical Spiral: A Comprehensive Introduction to Biblical Interpretation*. Downers Grove, IL: InterVarsity.

Oswalt, John N. 1979. "The Old Testament and Homosexuality." Pages 15–77 in *What You Should Know about Homosexuality*. Edited by Charles W. Keysor. Grand Rapids: Zondervan.

Pailin, David A. 1988. "Reason in Relation to Scripture and Tradition." Pages 207–38 in *Scripture, Tradition, and Reason: A Study in the Criteria of*

Christian Doctrine. Edited by Richard Bauckham and Benjamin Drewery. Edinburgh: T&T Clark.

Palmer, Parker J. 1983. *To Know as We Are Known: A Spirituality of Education*. San Francisco: Harper & Row.

Patte, Daniel M. 1995. *Ethics of Biblical Interpretation: A Reevaluation*. Louisville: Westminster John Knox.

———, ed. 2006. *Global Bible Commentary*. Nashville: Abingdon.

Pearson, Brook W. R., and Stanley E. Porter. 1997. "The Genres of the New Testament." Pages 131–65 in *A Handbook to the Exegesis of the New Testament*. Edited by Stanley E. Porter. Boston: Brill.

Pius XII, Pope. 1943. *Divino Afflante Spiritu: Encyclical Letter on Promoting Biblical Studies*. Washington, DC: National Catholic Welfare Conference.

Porter, Stanley E., ed. 1997a. *A Handbook to the Exegesis of the New Testament*. Boston: Brill.

———. 1997b. "The Use of the Old Testament in the New Testament: A Brief Comment on Method and Terminology." Pages 79–96 in *Early Christian Interpretation of the Scriptures of Israel: Investigation and Proposals*. Edited by C. A. Evans and J. A. Sanders. Sheffield: Sheffield Academic Press.

———. 2006. *Hearing the Old Testament in the New Testament*. Grand Rapids: Eerdmans.

Porton, Gary G. 1992. "Midrash." Pages 818–22 in vol. 6 of *The Anchor Bible Dictionary*. Edited by David Noel Freedman. New York: Doubleday.

Powell, Mark Allan. 1990. *What Is Narrative Criticism?* Minneapolis: Fortress.

———. 1995. "Narrative Criticism." Pages 239–55 in *Hearing the New Testament: Strategies for Interpretation*. Edited by Joel B. Green. Grand Rapids: Eerdmans.

———. 1999. "Narrative Criticism." Pages 201–4 in *The Dictionary of Biblical Interpretation*. Edited by John H. Hayes. Nashville: Abingdon.

———. 2001. *Chasing the Eastern Star: Adventures in Biblical Reader-Response Criticism*. Louisville: Westminster John Knox.

———. 2004. "The Forgotten Famine: Personal Responsibility in Luke's Parable of 'the Prodigal Son.'" Pages 265–87 in *Literary Encounters with the Reign of God*. Edited by Sharon H. Ringe and H. C. Paul Kim. New York: T&T Clark International.

———, ed. 2010. *Harper Collins Bible Dictionary*. Rev., 3rd ed. San Francisco: HarperCollins.

Radner, Ephraim, and George R. Sumner, ed. 1997. *The Rule of Faith: Scripture, Canon, and Creed in a Critical Age*. Harrisburg, PA: Morehouse.

Ralph, Margaret Nutting. 2003. *And God Said What? An Introduction to Biblical Literary Forms*. Rev. ed. Mahwah, NJ: Paulist Press.

Ray, Stephen K. 1997. *Crossing the Tiber: Evangelical Protestants Discover the Historical Church*. San Francisco: Ignatius.

Reid, Daniel G. 1997. "Virtues and Vices." Pages 1190–94 in *Dictionary of the Later New Testament and Its Developments*. Edited by Ralph P. Martin and Peter H. Davids. Downers Grove, IL: InterVarsity.

Reinhartz, Adele. 1994. "The Gospel of John." Pages 561–600 in *Searching the Scriptures*. Vol. 2, *A Feminist Commentary*. Edited by Elisabeth Schüssler Fiorenza. New York: Crossroad.

Renehan, Robert. 1973. "Classical Greek Quotations in the New Testament." Pages 17–46 in *The Heritage of the Early Church: Essays in Honor of the Very Reverend Georges Vasilievich Florovsky*. Edited by David Neiman and Margaret Schatkin. Rome: Pont. Institutum Studiorum Orientalium.

Resseguie, James L. 2005. *Narrative Criticism of the New Testament: An Introduction*. Grand Rapids: Baker Academic.

Reynolds, L. D., and N. G. Wilson. 1974. *Scribes and Scholars: A Guide to the Transmission of Greek and Latin Literature*. 2nd ed. Oxford: Oxford University Press.

Ricoeur, Paul. 1970. *Freud and Philosophy: An Essay on Interpretation*. New Haven: Yale University Press.

———. 1991. *A Ricoeur Reader: Reflection and Imagination*. Edited by Mario J. Valdés. Toronto: University of Toronto Press.

Robbins, Vernon K. 1996a. *Exploring the Texture of Texts*. Valley Forge, PA: Trinity Press International.

———. 1996b. *The Tapestry of Early Christian Discourse: Rhetoric, Society, and Ideology*. London: Routledge & Kegan Paul.

Robertson, A. T. 1934. *A Grammar of the Greek New Testament in the Light of Historical Research*. 4th ed. Nashville: Broadman.

Robertson, A. T., and W. Hersey Davis. 1977. *A New Short Grammar of the Greek Testament*. 10th ed. Grand Rapids: Baker Academic.

Robertson, John C. 1979. "Hermeneutics of Suspicion versus Hermeneutics of Goodwill." *Studies in Religion / Sciences Religieuses* 8:365–77.

Robinson, Elaine A. 2003. "Our Formative Foursome: The Wesleyan Quadrilateral and Postmodern Discipleship." *Covenant Discipleship Quarterly* 18, no. 2 (Spring): 1–10.

Rogers, Jack B., ed. 1977. *Biblical Authority*. Waco: Word.

Rogers, Jack B., and Donald K. McKim. 1979. *The Authority and Inspiration of the Bible*. New York: Harper & Row.

Root, Michael. 1984. "Dying He Lives: Biblical Image, Biblical Narrative, and the Redemptive Jesus." *Semeia* 30:155–69.

Root, Michael, and James J. Buckley, eds. 2008. *Sharper Than a Two-Edged Sword: Preaching, Teaching, and Living the Bible*. Grand Rapids: Eerdmans.

Rosscup, Jim. 2006. *Commentaries for Biblical Expositors*. The Woodlands, TX: Kress Christian Publications.

Russell, Letty M., ed. 1985. *Feminist Interpretation of the Bible*. Philadelphia: Westminster.

Safrai, S., and M. Stern. 1974–76. *The Jewish People in the First Century: Historical Geography, Political History, Social, Cultural and Religious Life and Institutions*. 2 vols. Philadelphia: Fortress.

Sakenfeld, Katharine Doob, ed. 2006–10. *The New Interpreter's Dictionary of the Bible*. 5 vols. Nashville: Abingdon.

Sanders, Jack T. 1971. *The New Testament Christological Hymns: Their Historical Religious Background*. Cambridge: Cambridge University Press.

Sandmel, Samuel. 1962. "Parallelomania." *Journal of Biblical Literature* 81:1–13.

———. 1978. *Judaism and Christian Beginnings*. New York: Oxford University Press.

Sandnes, Karl Olav. 2005. "*Imitatio Homeri?* An Appraisal of Dennis R. MacDonald's 'Mimesis Criticism.'" *Journal of Biblical Literature* 124:715–32.

Schneiders, Sandra M. 1981. "From Exegesis to Hermeneutics: The Problem of the Contemporary Meaning of Scripture." *Horizons* 8:23–39.

———. 1991. *The Revelatory Text: Interpreting the New Testament as Sacred Scripture*. San Francisco: HarperSanFrancisco.

Schürer, Emil. 1973–87. *The History of the Jewish People in the Age of Jesus Christ*. Revised and edited by Geza Vermes, Fergus Millar, and Matthew Black. 3 vols. Edinburgh: T&T Clark.

Schüssler Fiorenza, Elisabeth. 1983. *In Memory of Her: A Feminist Theological Reconstruction of Christian Origins*. New York: Crossroad.

———. 1995. *Bread not Stone: The Challenge of Feminist Biblical Interpretation*. Boston: Beacon.

———, ed. 1997. *Searching the Scriptures: A Feminist Introduction*. New York: Crossroad.

Scudder, Samuel H. 1874. "In the Laboratory with Agassiz." *Every Saturday* 16 (April 4): 369–70.

Segovia, Fernando F. 1997. "The Significance of Social Location in Reading John's Story." Pages 212–21 in *Gospel Interpretation. Narrative-Critical and Social Scientific Approaches*. Edited by Jack Dean Kingsbury. Harrisburg, PA: Trinity Press International.

Segovia, Fernando F., and Mary Ann Tolbert, eds. 1995a. *Reading from This Place*. Vol. 1, *Social Location and Biblical Interpretation in the United States*. Minneapolis: Fortress.

————. 1995b. *Reading from This Place*. Vol. 2, *Social Location and Biblical Interpretation in Global Perspective*. Minneapolis: Fortress.

Segovia, Fernando F., and R. S. Sugirtharajah, eds. 2007. *A Postcolonial Commentary on the New Testament Writings*. London: T&T Clark.

Seitz, Christopher R. 1993. "Repugnance and the Three-Legged Stool: Modern Use of Scripture and the Baltimore Declaration." Pages 85–101 in *Reclaiming Faith: Essays on Orthodoxy in the Episcopal Church and the Baltimore Declaration*. Edited by E. Radner and G. Sumner. Grand Rapids: Eerdmans.

————. 2001. *Figured Out: Typology and Providence in Christian Scripture*. Louisville: Westminster John Knox.

Siker, Jeffrey S. 1997. *Scripture and Ethics: Twentieth-Century Portraits*. New York: Oxford University Press.

Smith, Wilbur M. 1979. "Bible Dictionaries and Encyclopedias." Pages 492–98 in vol. 1 of *The International Standard Bible Encyclopedia*. Edited by Geoffrey W. Bromiley. Rev. ed. Grand Rapids: Eerdmans.

Smyth, Herbert W. 1920. *Greek Grammar*. Cambridge, MA: Harvard University Press.

Snodgrass, Klyne R. 1992. "Parable." Pages 591–601 in *Dictionary of Jesus and the Gospels*. Edited by Joel B. Green, Scot McKnight, and I. Howard Marshall. Downers Grove, IL: InterVarsity.

————. 2008. *Stories with Intent: A Comprehensive Guide to the Parables of Jesus*. Grand Rapids: Eerdmans.

Soards, Marion L. 1994. *The Speeches in Acts: Their Content, Context, and Concerns*. Louisville: Westminster John Knox.

Sodano, A. R. 1970. *Porphyrii Quaestionum Homericarum Liber 1*. Naples: Giannini.

Spicq, Ceslas. 1994. *Theological Lexicon of the New Testament*. Translated and edited by James D. Ernest. 3 vols. Peabody, MA: Hendrickson.

Spinks, Christopher D. 2007. *The Bible and the Crisis of Meaning: Debates on the Theological Interpretation of Scripture*. Harrisburg, PA: T&T Clark.

————. 2009. "Theological Interpretation: Some Traits, a Key, and a List." *Catalyst* 35, no. 4 (April): 1–3.

Spong, John Shelby. 1992. *Born of a Woman: A Bishop Rethinks the Birth of Jesus*. San Francisco: HarperSanFrancisco.

Squitier, Karl A. 1990. *Thesaurus Linguae Graecae Canon of Greek Authors and Works*. 3rd ed. Oxford: Oxford University Press.

Stanton, Graham N. 1992. "Sermon on the Mount/Plain." Pages 735–44 in *Dictionary of Jesus and the Gospels*. Edited by Joel B. Green, Scot McKnight, and I. Howard Marshall. Downers Grove, IL: InterVarsity.

Steinmetz, David C. 1997. "The Superiority of Pre-Critical Exegesis." Pages 26–38 in *The Theological Interpretation of Scripture: Classic and Contemporary Readings*. Edited by Stephen E. Fowl. Cambridge, MA: Blackwell.

———. 2002. *Luther in Context*. 2nd ed. Grand Rapids: Baker Academic.

Stendahl, Krister. 1962. "Biblical Theology, Contemporary." Pages 418–32 in vol. 1 of *The Interpreter's Dictionary of the Bible*. Edited by G. A. Buttrick. 4 vols. Nashville: Abingdon.

Stenger, Werner. 1993. *Introduction to New Testament Exegesis*. Grand Rapids: Eerdmans.

Sternberg, Meir. 1992. "Between Poetics and Sexual Politics: From Reading to Counterreading." *Journal of Biblical Literature* 111:463–88.

Stirewalt, M. Luther, Jr. 2002. *Paul: The Letter Writer*. Grand Rapids: Eerdmans.

Stone, Michael E. 1984. *Jewish Writings of the Second Temple Period: Apocrypha, Pseudepigrapha, Qumran Sectarian Writings, Philo, Josephus*. Assen: Van Gorcum; Philadelphia: Fortress.

Stott, John. 1999. *Evangelical Truth: A Personal Plea for Unity, Integrity and Faithfulness*. Downers Grove, IL: InterVarsity.

Stowers, Stanley K. 1981. *The Diatribe and Paul's Letter to the Romans*. Chico, CA: Scholars Press.

———. 1986. *Letter Writing in the Greco-Roman World*. Philadelphia: Westminster.

———. 1990. "Epistle." Pages 197–98 in *A Dictionary of Biblical Interpretation*. Edited by R. J. Coggins and J. L. Houlden. London: SCM; Philadelphia: Trinity Press International.

Strack, Hermann L., and Paul Billerbeck. 1922–61. *Kommentar zum Neuen Testament aus Talmud und Midrasch*. 6 vols. in 7. Munich: Beck.

Stuhlmacher, Peter. 1977. *Historical Criticism and Theological Interpretation of Scripture*. Translated and with an Introduction by Roy A. Harrisville. Philadelphia: Fortress.

Stylianopoulos, Theodore G. 1997. *The New Testament: An Orthodox Perspective*. Vol. 1, *Scripture, Tradition, Hermeneutics*. Brookline, MA: Holy Cross Orthodox Press.

Swartley, Willard M. 1983. *Slavery, Sabbath, War, and Women: Case Issues in Biblical Interpretation*. Scottdale, PA: Herald Press.

———. 1997. "Intertextuality in Early Christian Literature." Pages 536–42 in *Dictionary of the Later New Testament and Its Developments*. Edited by Ralph P. Martin and Peter H. Davids. Downers Grove, IL: InterVarsity

Sykes, Stephen W. 1978. *The Integrity of Anglicanism*. New York: Seabury.

Tate, W. Randolph. 2006. *Interpreting the Bible: A Handbook of Terms and Methods*. Peabody, MA: Hendrickson.

Tenney, Merrill C., and Moisés Silva, eds. 2009. *The Zondervan Encyclopedia of the Bible.* Rev. ed. Grand Rapids: Zondervan.

Terrell, Patricia Elyse. 2009. *Paul's Parallels: An Echoes Synopsis.* New York: T&T Clark.

Tertullian. 1954. *Tertulliani Opera.* Part 1, *Opera Catholica, Adversus Marcionem.* Turnhout: Brepols.

Thesaurus Linguae Graecae. 1999. CD-ROM E. University of California, Irvine.

Thompson, David L. 1994. *Bible Study That Works.* Rev. ed. Nappanee, IN: Evangel Publishing House.

Thompson, John L. 2007. *Reading the Bible with the Dead: What You Can Learn from the History of Exegesis That You Can't Learn from Exegesis Alone.* Grand Rapids: Eerdmans.

Thompson, Marianne Meye. 2008. "The Trustworthy Witness of Scripture." *Theology, News and Notes* (Fuller Theological Seminary), Winter: 11–13, 24.

Thompson, Michael B. 1993. "Teaching/Paraenesis." Pages 922–23 in *Dictionary of Paul and His Letters.* Edited by Gerald F. Hawthorne, Ralph P. Martin, and Daniel G. Reid. Downers Grove, IL: InterVarsity.

Thorsen, Donald A. D. 1990. *The Wesleyan Quadrilateral: Scripture, Tradition, Reason, and Experience as a Model of Evangelical Theology.* Grand Rapids: Francis Asbury.

Throckmorton, Burton H., Jr., ed. 1992. *Gospel Parallels: A Comparison of the Synoptic Gospels.* 5th ed. Nashville: Nelson.

Torrance, James B. 1987. "Authority, Scripture and Tradition." *Evangelical Quarterly* 59, no. 3: 245–51.

Towner, Philip H. 1993. "Households and Household Codes." Pages 417–19 in *Dictionary of Paul and His Letters.* Edited by Gerald F. Hawthorne, Ralph P. Martin, and Daniel G. Reid. Downers Grove, IL: InterVarsity.

———. 1997. "Household Codes." Pages 513–20 in *Dictionary of the Later New Testament and Its Developments.* Edited by Ralph P. Martin and Peter H. Davids. Downers Grove, IL: InterVarsity.

Traina, Robert A. 1982. "Inductive Bible Study Reexamined in the Light of Contemporary Hermeneutics." Pages 53–109 in *Interpreting God's Word for Today: An Inquiry into Hermeneutics from a Biblical Theological Perspective.* Edited by Wayne McCown and James Earl Massey. Anderson, IN: Warner.

———. 2002. *Methodical Bible Study: A New Approach to Hermeneutics.* Reprint of the 1952 original. Grand Rapids: Zondervan.

Treier, Daniel J. 2005. "Theological Hermeneutics, Contemporary." Pages 787–93 in *Dictionary for Theological Interpretation of the Bible.* Edited by Kevin J. Vanhoozer. Grand Rapids: Baker Academic.

————. 2008. *Introducing Theological Interpretation of Scripture: Recovering a Christian Practice*. Grand Rapids: Baker Academic.

Turner, Nigel. 1963. *A Grammar of New Testament Greek*. Vol. 3, *Syntax*. Edinburgh: T&T Clark.

————. 1976. *A Grammar of New Testament Greek*. Vol. 4, *Style*. Edinburgh: T&T Clark.

Twelftree, Graham H. 1999. *Jesus the Miracle Worker: A Historical and Theological Study*. Downers Grove, IL: InterVarsity.

————. 2007. *In the Name of Jesus: Exorcism among Early Christians*. Grand Rapids: Brazos.

Underhill, Edward Bean. 1966. *Tracts on Liberty of Conscience and Persecution, 1614–1661*. New York: Burt Franklin.

Unger, Dominic J., ed. 1992. *St. Irenaeus of Lyons: Against the Heresies*. Ancient Christian Writers 55. New York: Paulist Press.

Vanhoozer, Kevin J. 1993. "Hyperactive Hermeneutics: Is the Bible Being Overinterpreted?" *Catalyst* (April): 3–4.

————. 1995. "The Reader in New Testament Interpretation." Pages 301–28 in *Hearing the New Testament: Strategies for Interpretation*, edited by Joel B. Green. Grand Rapids: Eerdmans.

————. 1998. *Is There a Meaning in This Text? The Bible, the Reader, and the Morality of Literary Knowledge*. Grand Rapids: Zondervan.

————. 2003. "Scripture and Tradition." Pages 149–69 in *The Cambridge Companion to Postmodern Theology*. Edited by Kevin J. Vanhoozer. Cambridge: Cambridge University Press.

————, ed. 2005. *Dictionary for Theological Interpretation of the Bible*. Grand Rapids: Baker Academic.

Verhey, Allen. 1984. *The Great Reversal: Ethics and the New Testament*. Grand Rapids: Eerdmans.

Wagner, Falk, and Robert F. Brown. 2005. "Reason." Pages 498–502 in *The Encyclopedia of Christianity*. Vol. 4. Edited by Erwin Fahlbusch et al. Grand Rapids: Eerdmans; Leiden: Brill.

Wall, Robert W. 2000. "Intertextuality, Biblical." Pages 541–51 in *Dictionary of New Testament Background*. Edited by Craig A. Evans and Stanley E. Porter. Downers Grove, IL: InterVarsity.

————. 2002. "Canonical Criticism." Pages 291–312 in *A Handbook to the Exegesis of the New Testament*. Edited by Stanley E. Porter. Boston: Brill.

Wallace, Daniel B. 1996. *Greek Grammar beyond the Basics*. Grand Rapids: Zondervan.

Wallace, Mark I. 2006. "The Rule of Love and the Testimony of the Spirit in Contemporary Biblical Hermeneutics." Pages 66–85 in *But Is It All True?*

The Bible and the Question of Truth. Edited by Alan G. Padgett and Patrick R. Keifert. Grand Rapids: Eerdmans.

Ward, Timothy. 2002. *Word and Supplement: Speech Acts, Biblical Texts, and the Sufficiency of Scripture.* New York: Oxford University Press.

Watson, Duane F. 1992. "Chreia/Aphorism." Pages 104–6 in *Dictionary of Jesus and the Gospels.* Edited by Joel B. Green, Scot McKnight, and I. Howard Marshall. Downers Grove, IL: InterVarsity.

———. 1993. "Diatribe." Pages 213–14 in *Dictionary of Paul and His Letters.* Edited by Gerald F. Hawthorne, Ralph P. Martin, and Daniel G. Reid. Downers Grove, IL: InterVarsity.

Watson, Francis. 1994. *Text, Church, and World: Biblical Interpretation in Theological Perspective.* Grand Rapids: Eerdmans.

———. 1997. *Text and Truth: Redefining Biblical Theology.* Grand Rapids: Eerdmans.

Webb, William J. 2001. *Slaves, Women, and Homosexuals: Exploring the Hermeneutics of Cultural Analysis.* Downers Grove, IL: InterVarsity.

Wenham, David, and Craig Blomberg, eds. 1986. *Gospel Perspectives 6: The Miracles of Jesus.* Sheffield: JSOT Press.

Wettstein, Johann Jakob. 1750–51. *Novum Testamentum Graecum.* Amsterdam: Dommerian.

Whidden, Woodrow W. 1997. "*Sola Scriptura*, Inerrantist Fundamentalism, and the Wesleyan Quadrilateral: Is 'No Creed but the Bible' a Workable Solution?" *Andrews University Seminary Studies* 35, no. 2 (Autumn): 211–26.

Wilder, Amos N. 1971. *Early Christian Rhetoric: The Language of the Gospel.* Cambridge, MA: Harvard University Press.

Wilken, Robert Louis. 2005. "Interpreting the New Testament." *Pro Ecclesia* 14, no. 1 (Winter): 15–45.

Wilkins, M. J. 1997. "Teaching, Paraenesis." Pages 1156–59 in *Dictionary of the Later New Testament and Its Developments.* Edited by Ralph P. Martin and Peter H. Davids. Downers Grove, IL: InterVarsity.

Williams, D. H. 1999. *Retrieving the Tradition and Renewing Evangelicalism: A Primer for Suspicious Protestants.* Grand Rapids: Eerdmans.

———. 2005. *Evangelicals and Tradition: The Formative Influence of the Early Church.* Grand Rapids: Baker Academic.

———, ed. 2006. *Tradition, Scripture, and Interpretation: A Sourcebook of the Ancient Church.* Grand Rapids: Baker Academic.

Wilson, Walter T. 2009. *Pauline Parallels: A Comprehensive Guide.* Louisville: Westminster John Knox.

Wimsatt, William K., and Monroe C. Beardsley. 1954. *The Verbal Icon: Studies in the Meaning of Poetry.* Lexington: University of Kentucky Press.

Wink, Walter. 1973. *The Bible in Human Transformation: Toward a New Paradigm for Biblical Study*. Philadelphia: Fortress.

———. 1989. *Transforming Bible Study*. 2nd, rev. and exp. ed. Nashville: Abingdon.

Work, Telford. 2002. *Living and Active: Scripture in the Economy of Salvation*. Grand Rapids: Eerdmans.

Wright, N. T. 1992a. *The New Testament and the People of God*. Minneapolis: Fortress.

———. 1992b. "What Is the Anglican Communion?" *Virginia Seminary Journal* 44:31–39.

———. 1992c. *Who Was Jesus?* Grand Rapids: Eerdmans.

———. 2005. *The Last Word: Beyond the Bible Wars to a New Understanding of the Authority of Scripture*. San Francisco: HarperSanFrancisco.

———. 2006. *Judas and the Gospel of Jesus: Have We Missed the Truth about Christianity?* Grand Rapids: Baker Academic.

Wu, Julie L., and Sharon Clark Pearson. 1997. "Hymns, Songs." Pages 520–27 in *Dictionary of the Later New Testament and Its Developments*. Edited by Ralph P. Martin and Peter H. Davids. Downers Grove, IL: InterVarsity.

Zerwick, Maximilian. 1963. *Biblical Greek Illustrated by Examples*. 4th ed. Adapted by Joseph Smith from the 4th Latin ed. Rome: Pontifical Biblical Institute Press.

Zerwick, Maximilian, and Mary Grosvenor. 1996. *A Grammatical Analysis of the Greek New Testament*. 5th, rev. ed. Rome: Pontifical Biblical Institute Press.

Subject Index

Author Index

233

Scripture Index